famous CRICKETING FAMILIES

from Graces and Headleys to Cairns' and Hadlees

famous CRICKETING FAMILIES

from Graces and Headleys to Cairns' and Hadlees

KERSI MEHER-HOMJI
Foreword by Richie Benaud

REED

Dedicated to Leila Pearl Crompton
Complete in her devotion to family and friends
and an inspiration to humanity

FAMOUS CRICKETING FAMILIES

First published in New Zealand in 2000 by Reed Books
A division of Reed Publishing (NZ) Ltd
39 Rawene Rd, Birkenhead, Auckland
www.reed.co.nz
Associated companies, branches and representatives throughout the world.

First published in Australia in 2000 by Kangaroo Press
An imprint of Simon & Schuster (Australia) Pty Limited
20 Barcoo Street, East Roseville NSW 2069

A Viacom Company
Sydney New York London Toronto Tokyo Singapore

© Kersi Meher-Homji 2000

ISBN 0 7900 0766 5

Cover photographs courtesy of ALLSPORT
Front cover, clockwise from top left: Chris Cairns, New Zealand vs England 1999
(*Adrian Murrell*); Martin Crowe, New Zealand vs England 1994
(*Adrian Murrell*); Dean Headley, England vs Australia 1998 (*Stu Forster*);
Hanif Mohammed, Pakistan v India 1962 (*Allsport/Hutton-Getty*);
Greg Chappell, Australia v England 1980 (*Adrian Murrell*)
Back cover: Shaun Pollock, South Africa vs England 1998 (*Laurence Griffiths*);
Imran Khan, Pakistan vs England 1992 (*Allsport*)

Cover design by Gayna Murphy, Greendot Design
Internal design by Jo Waite
Set in 10.3/13.7 Book Antiqua
Printed in China by Everbest Printing Co.

10 9 8 7 6 5 4 3 2 1

Contents

———— ● ————

Acknowledgments

———— ● ————

I AM GRATEFUL TO RICHIE Benaud, OBE, for readily agreeing to write a perceptive Foreword. My heartfelt thanks also to: Tricia Ritchings, for her word-processing skills, lightning-fast speed and dedication in sacrificing most of her lunch hours and a whole long weekend to help me finish the manuscript on time (Tricia hates cricket but likes the author!); Carl Harrison-Ford for editing the typescript and giving it a smoother finish; Ross Dundas for checking some of the statistics; Ronald Cardwell, Mark 'Snoop' Skarschewski (Allsport Australia), Frank Bohlsen (*World of Cricket* magazine), Rowley Morris, Ken Hill, John Benaud and Jack Pollard for lending me photographs; Bob Brenner (librarian, NSW Cricket Association Library), Colin Clowes, Stephen Gibbs and Robert Brooke for providing rare information; Brigitta Doyle, Jody Lee, David Rosenberg and others at Simon & Schuster, Australia; and my wife Villie for tolerating my 'magnificent obsession' of converting a tidy little study into a pigsty!

Some of the chapters in this book were previously published in my *Cricket's Great Families* (Garry Sparke, 1980), which has been out of print since 1983. The current publication is updated and revised, with many new chapters added. I acknowledge my gratitude to Garry Sparke and his associates.

The books and magazines consulted have been listed at the end of the book. However, four publications have been my constant companions: *Wisden Cricketers' Almanacks* (spanning three centuries), *Wisden Cricket Monthly* (from 1980 to now edited by David Frith and by Tim de Lisle), two volumes of *The Wisden Book of Test Cricket* and *The Wisden Book of Cricket Records* edited by Bill Frindall.

Every effort has been made to contact the owners of copyright.

Symbols and abbreviations used in this book

* = Not out
10 w/T = 10 wickets per Test
5w/i = five wickets per innings
Aus. = Australia
Avrge = average (batting or bowling)
Best = best bowling performance
Eng. = England
HS = highest score
Ind. = India
MCG = Melbourne Cricket Ground
NSW = New South Wales
NZ = New Zealand
Pak. = Pakistan
SAf. = South Africa
SA = South Australia
SCG = Sydney Cricket Ground
Tas. = Tasmania
Vic. = Victoria
WI = West Indies
Wkts = wickets
WSC = World Series Cricket
Zim. = Zimbabwe

Foreword

———— ● ————

ONE OF THE GREAT joys of cricket is that although it produces many boundaries, the game in fact has none. The key to it lies on the field of play, with all the brilliance and despair associated with success and failure, and the side issues with modern technology which brings the game into the living room and, at the same time, transports the viewer to the ground.

For someone brought up before reaching double figures on the printed word and the very large wireless in the corner of the room, modern technology is a wonderful thing as long as it doesn't become compulsory that we have to understand every aspect of it. The printed word, for me, still has fascination and I find time even in the new millennium to look back at Jack Fingleton's *Cricket Crisis* (1946), the Rev. James Pycroft's *The Cricket Field* (1873) and Clarrie Grimmett's *Grimmett on Getting Wickets* (1930). Computers may have become faster and faster and more informative day by day, but it still provides a great deal of pleasure to read something in a bound book rather than on a screen.

Variety has always been a wonderful part of the writing of the game of cricket and, even though the modern game is vastly different from the time when only Test matches were played between nations, there is always something new hitting the bookshelves. Kersi Meher-Homji did that 20 years ago with *Cricket's Greatest Families*, by no means the definitive list of families, but many of the more important ones. Kersi, with a versatile approach to the world of cricket rather than just one country, is ideally suited for the pleasurable task of gathering together information about families and, with his knowledge of the

game, he always adds a sympathetic touch to proceedings.

I played against some, but not most, of the families in this book. Ian Chappell started his first-class career in 1961–62, in a shortened game against Tasmania at the Adelaide Oval, but only a week earlier he had been 12th man on the same ground where South Australia gave New South Wales a real stoushing by 130 runs in front of the biggest Adelaide crowd since the end of World War II. Garry Sobers made 251 for South Australia.

I played alongside that outstanding all-rounder Ron Archer and against him and his brother Ken for Queensland. Both the Pollock brothers, Peter and Graeme, were in the 1963–64 South African side, Peter having been the young Grey College room attendant at Port Elizabeth in 1958 when a certain amount of short-pitched bowling from Neil Adcock and Peter Heine resulted in a bat flying from one end of the dressing-room to the other, and a flow of language a baby-faced college boy shouldn't have understood anyway.

I missed Merv but played against and with that great cricketer Neil Harvey and also his brother Ray; I missed the Waughs but have been captivated by their cricket over a long period and, over a much shorter time, by the skills and athleticism of the Lee brothers for New South Wales and in Australian matches.

The Mohammad dynasty was part of my playing life, not so the Khans and the Pataudis, but I have known them all and, like the others in this welcome book, they have enriched everyone's attitude to the game of cricket.

Richie Benaud
July 2000

CHAPTER 1

Kin
Is In

———●———

I T WAS A LOST book that sparked off my obsession on cricketing families. For my birthday in 1950, my eldest brother Behram (who had represented Bombay University as a wicket-keeper) presented me with Dudley Nourse's auto-biography, *Cricket in the Blood*. It opened new horizons for me; I was well and truly smitten.

It was the story of South Africa's great cricketer and captain Dudley Nourse and his equally famous father 'Dave' (real name Arthur) who was recognised as the Grand Old Man of South African cricket. I read and re-read the book until I had memorised pages of it, till 'Dave' and Dudley almost became part of my family. Then a terrible thing happened. Tragedy struck!

When my family moved from the tranquil village of Udvada (population 1000) to the overcrowded Bombay (now

Mumbai) my *Cricket in the Blood* got lost. I still remember the pang. To get over my loss, I started collecting press clippings on cricket families – anything involving fathers and sons, uncles and nephews, brothers and grandfathers, second cousins ... That was almost 50 years ago. If you find gaps in *Famous Cricketing Families*, the lacunae would have been greater had I not lost Nourse's book.

Cricket has probably produced more well-known families than any other sport. From 1877 when Test cricket started to the present time, the game has been dominated by notable families. From the 1870s to the turn of the century, there were the Walkers, Bannermans, Graces, Gregorys, Hearnes, Gunns, Fosters and Trotts. Then came the princely clan of Ranjitsinhji (Ranji) and Duleepsinhji (Duleep), the Tyldesley brothers, the aristocratic Pataudis, the Nourses,

Edriches, Benauds, Mohammads, Pollocks, Chappells, Hadlees, Amarnaths, Khans and the Crowes.

In the 1990s we watched the rise and rise of the Waugh twins and to a lesser extent the Flower and Lee brothers, as Chris Cairns, Shaun Pollock and Dean Headley carried on from where their illustrious fathers and grandfather had left off a few decades earlier.

Played 123 years ago, Test cricket is in its fifth generation. Amazingly, the first 100 years were well covered by a single family. William Cooper played his first Test for Australia in December 1881 and his great-grandson, the elegant batsman and superb fielder Paul Sheahan, played the last of his 31 Tests for Australia in January 1974.

English-born Dean Headley created history when he made his Test debut for England against Australia at Manchester in 1997. It was the first instance of three direct generations of Test cricketers. Dean's father Ron represented the West Indies in 1973 and his grandfather, the legendary George (nicknamed 'Black Bradman'), played for the West Indies from 1929 to 1954 with distinction.

Before this the only instance of three generations of Test-playing cricketers was an uncle–nephew line. The immortal Ranji passed on his magical batting skill to his equally famous nephew Duleep. Both played for England and hit scintillating centuries in their debuts against Australia in 1896 and 1930, respectively. Duleep's nephew, Indrajitsinhji, represented India as a wicket-keeper in the 1960s.

Australia's pride and joy, the Gregorys, also came close to three generations. Edward Gregory, his brother Dave (who was Australia's first Test captain), son Syd and nephew Jack dominated the Australian Test scene from 1877 to 1928.

Then there were the Hearne brothers, George, Alec and Frank, who played together in one Test in Cape Town in 1892, the first two for England and Frank for South Africa. A cousin, John Hearne, also represented England in that match. Frank's son, G.A.L., later played three Tests for South Africa.

In more recent times we have had the Mohammads of Pakistan, with four brothers – Wazir, Hanif, Mushtaq and Sadiq – playing Test cricket, as also did Hanif's son Shoaib, and the Chappells, Ian, Greg and Trevor, and their grand-father Victor Richardson who represented Australia with distinction.

The Waugh twins, Steve and Mark, have so far played 231 Tests between them (a record 85 times together as at October 2000) and guided Australia into the new millennium with superlative, if not consistent, performances.

The cricket world is small and fortunately there is a close camaraderie despite the occasional on-field sledging and accusations of bribery and match-fixing.

I did not realise just how small it was until I talked with Mushtaq Mohammad and Majid Khan, members of illustrious cricketing families. In 1972–73, when the Indo-Pakistan war was barely over, Mushtaq asked me: 'How is my good friend Bishan Bedi, my brother?' Also, Majid and I chatted about long-lost family connections. His father Jahangir Khan and my uncle Kharshed Meher-Homji were members of the Indian cricket team that toured England in 1936 and played together in the Manchester Test. But there is more! Our grand-uncles, Salamuddin Khan and Rustom Meher-Homji, toured England with the first All India team in 1911. We reminisced at the Sydney Cricket Ground in 1977, as Majid's cousin Imran Khan bowled Pakistan to an historic victory over Australia.

The conversation was the catalyst that spurred me to develop my research on cricket families and write a book which was published in 1980. However, the publisher in his wisdom left out important families: the Walkers, the Hearnes, the Gunns and my favourites, the Nourses ('My Kingdom for a Nourse') from the book. Also, in the 20 years since the first edition important families have sprung up – the Crowes of New Zealand, the prolific Waugh twins (who set new landmarks practically every month), the Flowers of Zimbabwe, the hard-hitting Cairnses from New Zealand and the pacey Lees from Wollongong, NSW.

An update (more like a revamp) was overdue and there is no time like the present as Mark Waugh coincided his 100th Test with the first Test of the new millennium on the Sydney Cricket Ground. Like twin brother Steve in January 1998, Mark made his century of Test appearances on the same ground exactly two years later. Also, the Australian limited-overs team for the Carlton and United Breweries series in the new century had a familial look when the Lee brothers, Shane and Brett, joined the Waugh twins. Chris Cairns continues breaking his father Lance's records and Shaun Pollock has overtaken dad, Peter, in the fast lane. Kin is in.

This book is not an encyclopaedia on cricketing families. It is a selection of the best known among them and some of my favourites.

CHAPTER 2

Open
Sesame

———●———

*It is interesting to glance through the first Test matches played
between various countries and note the family contributions.
In almost every case, brothers or their relations had combined
to make a significant impression on the game.*

IN THE INAUGURAL TEST match at
Melbourne in March 1877, the
Australian team included the Gregory
brothers, captain Dave (who won the
toss and the match) and Edward, and
Charles Bannerman who scored the first
run and the first Test century. Later on,
Charles' younger brother Alec
Bannerman played 28 Tests for Australia.
Also, England was captained by James
Lillywhite whose uncle William and
cousins Frederick, John and James snr
had earlier represented Sussex at first-
class level.

In the first-ever Test on English soil, at
The Oval in 1880, England fielded a trio
of brothers, all of whom were making
their Test debuts. They were Dr E.M., Dr
W.G. and G.F. Grace; the first two opened
the batting, adding 91 runs. W.G. went
on to score the first century for England
and was also associated in the first

century partnership in Test cricket. His
partner was A.P. Lucas, a member of
another prominent cricket family. In
this, his first and only Test, G.F. Grace
had the misfortune of recording the first
pair in Test cricket. He also took a
memorable catch, about 100 metres out
in deep, to dismiss the Australian six-
hitting giant George Bonnor. The
Australian batting was opened by Alec
Bannerman. Just as Charles had scored
the first run in Test cricket in Australia,
Alec scored the first run for Australia on
English soil.

When South Africa played her first
Test, against England at Port Elizabeth in
1888–89, Bernard (A.B.) Tancred opened
their batting and top-scored in both the
innings. In the second Test at Cape Town,
he carried his bat, the first such instance
in Test cricket. In South Africa's first Test
against Australia, at Johannesburg in

1902–03, brother Louis Tancred top-scored with 97.

In the initial Test played by the West Indies, against England at Lord's in 1928, England's Ernest Tyldesley, who was the younger brother of the more celebrated Johnny, scored a century. In the first Test played by the West Indies in Australia, at Adelaide in 1930–31, their captain, 'Jackie' (G.C.) Grant, whose younger brother Rolph Grant also led his country in 1939, scored 53 not out and 71 not out. Thus, he became the first man to score unbeaten half centuries in both innings of a Test match.

New Zealand played her first Test at Christchurch against England in 1929–30. The newcomers to Test status were captained by Tom Lowry, a brother-in-law of Percy (A.P.F.) Chapman, the former England captain. Lowry top-scored in the second innings with 40. England was captained by Harold Gilligan, the younger brother of another ex-England captain, Arthur Gilligan. Ranji's nephew Duleep top-scored in England's first innings, scoring 49 out of the total of 121.

In her first Test at Lord's in 1932, the Indian team also fielded a pair of brothers, Wazir and Nazir Ali, and was captained by C.K. Nayudu, whose brother C.S. Nayudu joined him in a Test side later. In the first Test on Indian soil, at Bombay against England in 1933–34, Lala Amarnath scored a century in his Test debut. Subsequently, his sons Surinder and Mohinder represented India. In the 1933–34 match brothers L. Ramji and L. Amar Singh shared the new ball with Mohammed Nissar.

In her first home Test, Pakistan included brothers Wazir and Hanif Mohammad against India at Dacca in 1954–55. The two had played for the first time in the Bombay Test of 1952, a game remembered mainly because Vinoo Mankad recorded his Test double of 1000 runs and 100 wickets in 23 Tests. This was then the quickest double achieved in Test cricket. In the 1960s and 1970s, Vinoo's son Ashok played 22 Tests for India. Against the West Indies in 1958 at Bridgetown, brothers Hanif (337) and Wazir added 121 runs for the fourth wicket in the second innings. Eric Atkinson, who had joined his elder brother Denis for the first time in a Test, dismissed Hanif in the first innings and both the Pakistani brothers in the second.

Sidath Wettimuny opened Sri Lanka's innings in her inaugural Test against England in February 1982 and Arjuna Ranatunga (then 18 and lean) became the first Sri Lankan to make a fifty. Sidath's elder brother Sunil had earlier played for Sri Lanka in unofficial Tests. In March 1983, Sidath and younger brother Mithra opened Sri Lanka's batting in their first Test against New Zealand, putting on 49 runs. Sidath contributed 69 not out and in the process became the first from Sri Lanka to carry the bat. Earlier, against Pakistan at Faisalabad in March 1982, he had become the first from his country to hit a century (157). Arjuna Ranatunga's elder brother Dammika in 1989–90 and younger brother Sanjeeva in the 1990s, also played Test matches.

In her inaugural Test against India at Harare in October 1992, Zimbabwe included the Flower brothers Grant (who opened the batting and scored 82 not out) and wicket-keeper Andy who made 59.

Thus, a member of an important cricket family scored the first run and the first century in both Australia and England, was first to be associated in a century partnership, first to carry his bat in a completed innings and first to score unbeaten fifties in each innings of a Test.

The family touch is not restricted to Test cricket. Relations had their place in the inaugural World Cup matches in 1975. Three pairs and a trio of brothers and six sons of well-known Test players were seen in action on English grounds from 7 to 21 June.

Australia was led by Ian and included Greg Chappell. Pakistan was represented by Mushtaq and Sadiq Mohammad and New Zealand by two sets of brothers, Hedley and Geoff Howarth, and Barry, Dayle and Richard Hadlee, sons of the former national captain Walter. All three Hadlee brothers played against England. India included Mohinder Amarnath and Anshuman Gaekwad, whose fathers, Lala Amarnath and Dattaji Gaekwad, had captained India in Test matches. The Pakistan team included Majid Khan, the son of Dr Jahangir Khan, and their skipper Asif Iqbal was the nephew of former Indian captain and ace off-spinner Ghulam Ahmed. There were at least two pairs of cousins: Clive Lloyd and Lance Gibbs, and Majid and Imran Khan.

Just as the Gregorys, Bannermans, Graces, Tancreds, Grants, Alis, Mohammads, Wettimunys and Flowers had said 'Open Sesame' to Test cricket, 16 blood relations ushered in the inaugural World Cup.

CHAPTER 3

The
Bannerman Brothers

———— ● ————

They were the pioneers of Test cricket. Elder brother Charles Bannerman, the first top-class Australian batsman, faced the first ball in a Test match, scored the first run and the first century. He scored 67.3 per cent of his side's total, which still remains the highest individual proportion in any Test innings. His younger brother, the pint-sized stonewaller Alec, scored the first run for Australia on English soil.

THE FIRST EVER TEST match started between England and Australia at 1 p.m. on 15 March 1877. A crowd of 3000 attended and, according to a press clipping, 'both youth and beauty were present'. Australia opened her innings with Charles Bannerman and Nat Thompson, both from New South Wales. Bannerman faced the first ball bowled in Test cricket, scored the first run, and went on to record the first Test century. At stumps he had made an unbeaten 126 out of Australia's score of 6 for 166. It was 'a grand and dominating innings'.

Soon after lunch on the following day, Charles' inspired innings ended when a fast ball from George Ulyett split his finger. He had made 165 of Australia's 245. His only first-class hundred, it included 18 fours and was a masterly

Charles Bannerman (right) with young Don Bradman in 1930. (*Jack Pollard Collection*)

effort which made history. Had it not been for his finger injury, Charles could have become the first batsman to carry his bat through a completed Test innings, perhaps hitting a double hundred on his, and Test cricket's, debut.

To Australia's 245, England replied with 196. In their second innings, Australia, with Bannerman dismissed for 4, collapsed and were 104 all out. But England, when her turn came, could muster only 108 and lost the match by 45 runs. Grateful Victorian spectators started a fund for Bannerman which brought in the sum of £83.

Alec Bannerman. Concentration was his forte. (© R.L. Cardwell)

Born in Kent, England, in 1851, Charles Bannerman was the first player for Australia to hit centuries in England (133 against Leicestershire in 1878), New Zealand and Canada. However, these matches were not given first-class status. Tall, brilliant in his stroke-play and a dazzling driver he was, according to famous Australian cricket historian A.G. 'Johnnie' Moyes, 'without doubt the first top-class Australian batsman'. William Caffyn, the well-known coach from Surrey, wrote: 'The best bat I ever saw, or coached, in Australia was undoubtedly Charles Bannerman'.

In the only Test at Melbourne in 1879, Charles was joined by his younger brother by eight years, the pint-sized stonewaller, Alec. 'Little Alec' was totally different from Charles, being ultra-defensive and virtually strokeless – an earlier-day Trevor Bailey. As Moyes summed up in *Australian Batsmen*: 'At times the crowd found him [Alec] as wearisome to the flesh as fleas in a warm bed'.

On the occasion of his Test debut in 1879, Alec almost 'did a Charles' by top-scoring with 73. Only 27 runs more and the Bannermans would have become the first and only pair of brothers to record a century each in their first Test appearance.

When 29, the popular Charles was forced to retire through ill health. Alec was more enduring – if a trifle less endearing to the spectators. Because of his fielding, Alec was selected to tour England in 1880 and in the Oval Test – the first Test played in England – he took Charles' place as Australia's opener and scored the first Test run for Australia on English soil.

Alec continued playing until 1893, making 1108 runs in 28 Tests, with 94 as his highest score. Alec's patience and J.J. Lyons' aggression enabled Australia to win the Sydney Test of 1892, despite trailing England by 163 runs on the first innings. The contrasting duo put on 174 runs, Lyons 134 and Alec 91, in seven and a half hours. The dour, gutsy Alec was at the crease on all three days and scored at the rate of 12 runs an hour. This earned 'Slasher' Alec the following tribute:

O Bannerman, O Bannerman,
We wish you'd change your
*   manner, man;*
We pay our humble tanner, man,
To see a bit of fun.
You're a beggar though to stick it,
But it ain't our sort of cricket;
They haven't hit your wicket,
Yet, you haven't got a run.

The reaction of the crowd or the press had not the slightest effect on Alec. To quote Moyes: 'Like Gallio of old, he cared for none of these things, concentrating entirely on the job in hand ... He could irritate, but never overawe, and two of him would have riled even a modern Job.'

In the Melbourne Test against England in 1891–92, Alec plodded for 435 minutes to score 45 and 41. For New South Wales against Victoria in 1890, he scored 45 not out in five and a half hours – at one stage taking 90 minutes for a run. Spectators rubbed their eyes in disbelief when once he did hit out. This happened in the Sydney Test of 1883 when he made a dashing 63. Trailing one match to two Australia had to win this

Test. Alec, having been missed behind the sticks, decided to attack and Australia won by four wickets to retain the Ashes.

Both Charles and Alec Bannerman took up coaching assignments on retirement, became umpires, and never lost their zest for the game they had so greatly enriched in their contrasting ways. Charles was present when Don Bradman hit 452 not out at Sydney against Queensland in 1929–30. Their meeting that day was treasured by both.

A stickler for proper etiquette, Alec was an intensely serious cricketer. One day a colleague was singing a popular song on the field till Alec could stand it no longer. He approached him and said, 'If you want to play cricket play it; if you want to sing, go and sing, but for Heaven's sake don't sing comic songs in the slips'. After he retired, Alec was often seen at the SCG, watching and coaching. He would meticulously study a new trainee in his charge, noting his attire and general appearance. If not pleased by what he saw, he would say, 'Son, if you are not a cricketer, you can at least look like one.'

	Tests	Runs	Avrge	HS	100s	50s	Wkts	Avrge	Best	5w/i	Catches
The Bannermans in Test Cricket											
Charles	3	239	59.75	165*	1	0	0	–	–	–	0
Alec	28	1108	23.08	94	0	8	4	40.75	3–111	0	21
Total	31	1347	25.90	165*	1	8	4	40.75	3–111	0	21

CHAPTER 4

The
Gregory Clan

———— ● ————

*Three generations of Gregorys produced four Test cricketers, including
two Australian captains. The Test scene was dominated by them for
52 years. They were one of the greatest families in cricket history.*

THE GREGORYS PRODUCED FOUR Test cricketers, including two all-time greats – Syd and Jack – and two Test captains. Four more played for New South Wales. With a break of 11 years, the Test scene was dominated by them for 52 years, from 1877 to 1928.

The Gregory story starts with Edward William Gregory, the father of Australia's first Test captain, Dave. He played in Sydney's Hyde Park in the 1820s, little imagining that his grandson, Jack, would be hitting headlines in three continents a century later. Of Edward's 13 children, seven were boys. Five of them played cricket for New South Wales. Twenty of his grandsons represented the State in various sports – cricket, sailing, athletics or football. The four sons who represented New South Wales in cricket were Edward jnr (Ned), Dave, Charlie and Arthur. Edward jnr and Dave played together for Australia in the first-ever Test, in 1877, in Melbourne.

Dave Gregory, Australia's first captain.
(© *R.L. Cardwell*)

Dave Gregory won the first toss in Test history and his team won. Dave was 188 centimetres tall, hefty and magnificently bearded. Women called him 'Handsome Dave'. He captained

Australia in two Test series against England, drawing the 1877 series 1-all and winning 1–0 in 1879. His highest Test score was 43 – top score in the second innings of the second Test – adding 88 for the opening wicket with Nat Thompson.

When the States formed the Australian Commonwealth, Dave was offered the post of federal Treasurer, together with a knighthood. He declined. Acceptance would have meant living in Melbourne and he could not bear to leave Turramurra – an elite suburb of Sydney.

Edward Gregory jnr, nicknamed 'Ned the Lionheart', was six years Dave's senior. He played only one Test and scored 11 runs in two innings. Ned will be remembered for the laying out of the area that became the SCG. It was also Ned who designed the SCG scoreboard. He had two cricket-playing sons, Syd and Charles.

Syd became the first son in Test history to follow his father's footsteps leading to Test fame. And, like his father, he scored a duck in his first Test innings. Incidentally, Syd's cousin Jack also scored nought in his Test baptism!

Charles, Syd's younger brother by eight years, was also talented. He became the first batsman to score a triple-century *in a day* in a first-class game, carving 383 for New South Wales against Queensland at Brisbane in 1906. He batted for 345 minutes and hit 55 fours. Unfortunately, Charles died from blood poisoning when 32.

Syd Gregory at 165 centimetres was among the shortest cricketers and was affectionately known as 'Little Tich'. He toured England eight times, the first time when he was 20. C.B. Fry, the well-known cricketer-scholar from England, called him 'the blackberry-eyed slip of accomplishment' and his immaculate batting technique inspired Australian writer A.G. Moyes to comment in 1954: 'There has possibly never been among Australian batsmen a better model for

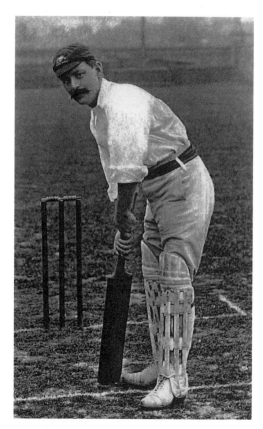

Syd Gregory toured England eight times.
(© R.L. Cardwell)

the young than Sydney Gregory. He was one of the most gifted players for his inches that the game has ever seen.'

Even today, Syd is considered by experts as among the best cover fielders of all time. Dr W.G. Grace once told him if he kept up his agile fielding, it should keep him in Test cricket for 20 years. The Master was right, for Syd kept on playing for 22 years. To quote Moyes, '[He] cut magnificently, loved to hook. Fast or slow bowling came alike to him ... he seemed to have walked straight out of the pages of the finest text book. No Australian of any generation was his superior in technique.'

Syd scored the first Test double-century on an Australian ground. It was in the bewilderingly fluctuating Sydney Test of 1894. Then 24, he scored 201 in 243 minutes of sheer rapture. Despite scoring 586 and leading England by 261 runs, Australia lost the Test by 10 runs.

Charles William Gregory in a studio portrait after his 383 in Brisbane. He was the first cricketer to score a triple century in a day.
(© R.L. Cardwell)

In the opinion of Ray Robinson, Sydney was 'one of the ablest and most courageous bad-wicket batsmen in a period before pitch covers made such challenges to the batsman rare'. In a match against Gloucestershire, Australia was 6 for 54 on an almost unplayable pitch before Syd made an undefeated 71. Later on, W.G. Grace's team was shot out for 17.

When Syd toured England for the seventh time, he was 39. In The Oval Test of 1909, he added 180 with Warren Bardsley for the first wicket – a record against England which stood for 55 years

before being broken by Bob Simpson and Bill Lawry in 1964. Those 180 runs came in 135 minutes. In 1911–12, when Sydney Barnes and Frank Foster were proving a handful for the Australian batsmen, 41-year-old Syd flayed them with a scintillating 186 not out. When six top players, Clem Hill, Victor Trumper, Warwick Armstrong, Vernon Ransford, 'Tibby' Cotter and Hanson Carter, declined to tour England in 1912 for the Triangular Test contest, Syd was made captain. Predictably, without the top players, he achieved little.

In 58 Tests, evergreen Syd Gregory scored 2282 runs – 2193 off English bowlers in 52 Tests. Till today, no player has played more Tests against England than Syd. 'There could never be another Syd,' eulogised Ray Robinson in *On Top Down Under*.

Syd's brother-in-law, Harry Donnan, played five Tests for Australia but had limited success. However, his cousin, Jack Gregory, was a superstar in his own right. Less classical than Syd, Jack was more versatile and eye-catching. He was acknowledged as the greatest all-rounder when he retired in 1928. To quote Robinson again: 'Like a fiery comet that flares into view every 70-odd years, a cricketer as spectacular as Jack Gregory is a rare sight for the world. Tests had been played more than 40 years before such an eye-catching all-rounder bounded on the scene. Soon he was the most feared express bowler before Larwood, a record-making slip catcher with fly-paper fingers and scorer of the fastest 100 in Test history.' 'Gelignite' Jack, according to Moyes, had 'little rhythm in his approach but abundant vigour and venom; all thunder and lightning like an electric storm'.

In fact, very little was known of Jack Gregory when the Australian Imperial Forces (AIF) selectors gave this lanky artilleryman – 'all arms and legs' – a chance after World War I. In a rare interview given to *The Cricketer*

(England) a few months before he died near Sydney in August 1973 at the age of 77, Jack modestly recalled to David Frith: 'Plum Warner gave me my chance. It was the name that did it. He found out I was Syd's cousin.'

Three accidents at this time helped Australian cricket enormously. When Jack injured his finger in the outfield, AIF skipper Herbie Collins brought him in to a slip position – a precious chance discovery because Jack subsequently became a wizard in that position. His acrobatic anticipation is still remembered by old-timers. Then when AIF's regular bowler Cyril Docker strained his back, a desperate captain gave Jack a bowl. His bowling action was clumsy but the speed he generated was phenomenal. One of his deliveries gashed keeper Ted Long's face. Another keeper had to be located in a hurry, and thus shy, little Bert Oldfield was pitchforked into the AIF XI. He went on to become one of the greatest stumpers of all time.

Jack captured 131 wickets and took 44 slip catches in 25 matches – thus becoming the only Australian to take over 100 wickets in his opening first-class season. In his first match at Melbourne, Jack bagged 7 for 22. He had a dramatic debut on the Sydney Cricket Ground. For AIF vs New South Wales, he scored 122 and 102 and took eight wickets in the match. In the Melbourne Test of 1921 he reached his hundred in 135 minutes and took 7 for 69.

His most destructive spell was taking three wickets without conceding a run in the 1921 Trent Bridge Test. With the stylish Ted McDonald, Jack Gregory formed the first double-edged pace attack. Like later partners in pace – Larwood and Voce, Lindwall and Miller, Trueman, Tyson and Statham, Hall and Griffith, Lillee and Thomson, Roberts and Holding – McDonald and Gregory were perfect foils for each other.

Against the grace and rhythm of

Jack Gregory was 'a fiery comet that flares into view every 70-odd years'– Ray Robinson.
(© R.L. Cardwell)

McDonald, Jack – 193 centimetres – looked awkward. He took 12 outsize steps of which the ninth was a kangaroo leap on the right foot. Jack's towering-inferno action, created by his hefty figure and fearsome expression, terrified the batsmen before he even bowled. The great Walter Hammond, when 18 years old, had a baptism of fire facing Gregory and later wrote: 'Jack Gregory had cultivated a fearsome stare and gave me the treatment. With knees trembling and hands shaking, I was relieved when he bowled me first ball.'

Jack bowled right-handed and batted

left-handed. He never bothered to put on a cap, gloves or a groin box. He played in 24 Tests against England and South Africa and totalled 1146 runs with two centuries. His batting average of 37 was better than Syd's of 24.5. Jack's electrifying century in 70 minutes in the Johannesburg Test of 1921–22 is, even today, the fastest Test hundred. His most consistent season was 1920–21 against England when he recorded 78, 77, 76 not out, and 93 in consecutive Test innings.

A cartilage operation on his right knee cramped his swashbuckling style and he seemed to be on the decline when touring England in 1926. But the following season he made his highest first-class score – 152 for New South Wales, having hit a century before lunch.

The first Test of 1928 against England proved historic, being the first Test played in Brisbane and the Test in which Don Bradman made his debut. Unfortunately, it was the last one for Jack Gregory. His knee gave out as he was bowling to Harold Larwood who, as a boy, had hero-worshipped Jack. 'I'm finished, boys,' was his much-quoted exclamation as he limped from the ground. This was the end not only of Jack's playing days, but of all the Gregorys. His tall son, John, was a pacey left-arm bowler for his college in Sydney but he did not play for his State.

Jack Gregory's record of 15 catches in a Test series still stands. Bill O'Reilly, who played against Hammond and saw other slip experts like Bob Simpson, Colin Cowdrey and the Chappells, ranked Jack Gregory as the greatest slip fielder he had seen. Scorer Bill Ferguson once said that Jack had arms like an octopus 'only they seemed twice as many and twice as long'.

The Gregorys in Test Cricket

	Tests	Runs	Avrge	HS	100s	50s	Wkts	Avrge	Best	5w/i	Catches
Edward jnr	1	11	5.50	11	0	0	–	–	–	–	1
Dave	3	60	20.00	43	0	0	0	–	–	–	0
Syd	58	2282	24.53	201	4	8	0	–	–	–	25
Jack	24	1146	36.96	119	2	7	85	31.15	7–69	4	37
Total	86	3499	27.12	201	6	15	85	31.65	7–69	4	63

CHAPTER 5

The
Grace Phenomenon

——— ● ———

*There was a time when cricket was grace and Graces were cricket. A story
of the legendary Grace brothers and their mother who always knew best.*

THE IMMORTAL GRACE FAMILY is possibly the best known and best remembered among sporting clans. And the best known among them was W.G. Grace, a legend in his lifetime and one of the most colourful characters in any field of sport. G.K. Chesterton once said that Pickwick was the true English fairy, and W.G., that bulky sprite, was a prodigious Puck in a truly mid-summer's day dream. W.G.'s elder brother, E.M. Grace, and younger brother, G.F. Grace, also contributed richly to cricket literature by their performances on and off the field. The Graces changed cricket into almost a national religion, with W.G. as the high priest.

Dr Henry Mills Grace, their father, was an obscure country doctor. He was a keen cricketer with limited ability and his wife, Martha, was a good-hearted and formidable woman. Her brother, Alfred Pocock, was a far better player than her husband. The doctor and his wife had five sons and all followed their father's profession, although the youngest, G.F., did not live to qualify. The father had a pitch laid in the grounds of his Bristol home in Gloucestershire. There the whole family practised before breakfast, joined by uncles, cousin, Martha Grace, her four daughters and their three retriever dogs, Don, Pronto and Noble.

Patrick Morrah gives a detailed description of the five brothers in his book, *The Golden Age of Cricket*: 'Henry, the eldest, was a good player by local standards and capable of holding his own in first-class company. The second brother, Alfred, played little cricket; his passion was hunting. It was the third brother, Edward Mills Grace, also known as "The Coroner", "The Little Doctor" or just "E.M.", who blazed the trail. E.M. revolutionised batting techniques. Before him, it was considered immoral if one did not play an off-side ball on the off-side. But E.M. was not in the least concerned with the "done" things. He was interested in runs, so he cultivated the pull shot – a stroke till then not mentioned in polite society.'

For the next few years, E.M. became the most discussed player in England. He scored fast and consistently and his best year was 1862. Against the Gentlemen of Kent, at Canterbury, he made 192, carrying his bat. He followed this by taking 15 wickets, including all 10 in the second innings; 5 for 77 and 10 for 69.

E.M., according to historians, was one of the finest fielders of all time. His specialty was standing close to the wicket or at point and snapping up ferocious hits just as the ball left the bat. He was small and wiry – a pocket dynamo, restless, pugnacious, bounding with energy. He chatted incessantly on the field, bubbled over with jokes and was as quick with his fists as with his tongue if anyone dared to disagree with him. In his later days, at Thornbury, it was said that no umpire within 20 miles dared to give him out lbw.

He had one fad, to take every possible run. Once, when batting with a cautious player, E.M. became exasperated by the fellow's slow running between the wickets and they had a violent argument in the middle. Subsequently, they refused to take runs for over an hour. The only runs came from boundary hits.

While playing the Australians at Bristol, a spectator refused to budge from his position in front of the sightscreen, so E.M. rushed to him, his eyes afire, lifted the intruder by his collar and the seat of his pants, and threw him outside the fence, blackening his eye in the process. When the irate offender later appeared in the dressing-room with two tough-looking mates, the short but equally short-tempered E.M. blackened his other eye. After that, free treatment was offered at his surgery.

E.M. was the first amateur to make an overseas trip when he toured Australia with George Parr's team in 1863. Unfortunately, he was a failure on Australian pitches. When he returned to England he found himself eclipsed by his younger brother by seven years, W.G. Wrote *Wisden*: 'But for the accident that his own brother proved greater than himself, E.M. Grace would have lived in cricket history as perhaps the most remarkable player the game has ever produced'. E.M. continued playing till he was 68. Often, after he had become the coroner for East Gloucestershire, he would delay inquests so that he could finish a game of cricket. He died in 1911, almost with his pads on. He collapsed while batting and was carried unconscious from the field, and died a few months later.

Magnificently bearded, massive, immovable, majestic, dignified; a gentlemanly tyrant with a kind heart underneath a rough exterior; a law unto himself; larger than life – Dr W.G. Grace was called all these, and more. It was said of him, as of Napoleon, and much later of Mohammad Ali, that 'he cast a doubt on all past glory, and rendered all future renown impossible'. Great Western trains would humbly wait for W.G. while he talked to a friend or drank to his health.

Born on 18 July 1848, William Gilbert Grace had the family strength of character. In cricket, his defence was sound and in later years it became rock-like. He practised daily from 5.00 a.m. and followed his coach's advice. In his prime, he had a superb athletic figure and it was only in later years that he developed the huge girth we all associate with him today. The great Ranjitsinhji commented in his *Jubilee Book of Cricket*: 'I hold W.G. to be not only the finest player born or unborn, but the maker of modern batting. He turned the old one-stringed instrument into a many-chorded lyre ... He made his execution equal to his invention ... W.G. discovered batting, he turned its many narrow straight channels into one great winding river ... The theory of modern batting is in all its essentials the result of W.G.'s thinking and working on the game.'

Failures were rare for W.G., but Australia's demon bowler Fred Spofforth often had the better of him. When Australia beat a strong MCC in one day, 27 May 1878, W.G. faced only four balls: a boundary and out, dropped and out. The 'Demon' got him both times. Recorded *Punch* magazine: 'Our Grace before dinner was very soon done, / And Grace after dinner did not get a run'. However, except for Spofforth, W.G. was severe on fast bowlers. According to cricket historians, W.G. killed professional pace bowling. For years they were afraid to bowl within his reach. Sir Neville Cardus wrote: 'Thus ironically W.G. was the cause of the first extensive development of spin.'

His cricket career extended from 1864, when he was 16, to 1908 when he reached 60. When a nomadic England XI was to be selected, Martha Grace wrote a letter to their captain recommending E.M., but informed him that she had another boy, W.G., growing up who could be even better than E.M. because his defence was sounder. This letter is preserved among the most cherished documents in the annals of cricket. When he was only 18, W.G. hit an unbeaten 224 for an England team against Surrey at The Oval, and from then on his supremacy was unchallenged. The bearded champion went on scoring centuries and setting new landmarks for the next 42 years.

At 47, and by then grossly overweight, W.G. astounded even his admirers by recording 1000 runs in the month of May. This feat has been achieved only twice since – by Wally Hammond in 1927 and Charlie Hallows, also of England, the following year. Grace achieved his 1000 runs in May in

W.G. Grace, the maker of modern batting.
(© R.L. Cardwell)

only 22 days, Hammond took 25 days and Hallows 27.

Not until the days of Bradman did a batsman show figures so far in advance of his contemporaries. In all, W.G. scored 54,896 runs – at an average 39.55 – and hit 126 centuries. These figures have been improved upon by other players since, but when one considers the condition of the pitches he played on, his achievements are staggering. Twenty-eight times W.G. completed 1000 runs in a season – a record equalled by Frank Woolley – and in 1871 he became the first to complete 2000 runs in a season. W.G.

was somewhat gratified to have recorded against his name all scores from 0 to 100.

He officially retired in 1908, but six years later agreed to play in a game to help raise money for a school cricket ground. On a shockingly uneven pitch, the 'Grand Old Man', then 66 years old, was badly bruised, and often, but still managed to score an unbeaten 69 (hitting one five and six fours).

An effective, fast-medium, round-arm bowler, he took 2876 wickets at 17.92. In addition, he was an excellent fielder at any position – though not as brilliant as E.M. at point.

Like Freddie Trueman, Dr W.G. Grace will always be remembered for his sense of humour. There are countless anecdotes – true or fabricated – which demonstrate his fun-loving, umpire-cheating character. When playing for Gloucestershire, in front of a large crowd, he was given out lbw to the first ball of the match. The doctor glared at the umpire and then proceeded to give his own instructions: 'Young man, these good people have come here to see me bat, not to see you umpire. Let's get on with the game without any of this nonsense.' He nevertheless had to leave the crease, but the point had been made and his dismissal killed public interest that day. It is indeed no wonder that for many years a notice appeared on county grounds: 'Admission threepence. If W.G. Grace is playing, Admission sixpence.'

The Gillette Book of Cricket and Football, edited by Gordon Ross, reports that during the lunch interval of W.G.'s last first-class match for the Gentlemen against Surrey, there was a snowfall, bringing its own silent, sad tribute to the great man. When he passed away on 23 October 1915, the news of his death took precedence over the reports of the World War. In a memorial speech, the Bishop of Hereford summed up: 'He was the best known of all Englishmen and the king of the English game least spoilt by vice.'

Added Neville Cardus in 1963, the year of *Wisden*'s centenary: 'Nobody before him, nobody following greatly in his train, has loomed to his stature, or so much stood for cricket, or done as richly for it'. Eulogised Michael Melford: 'The good he did for cricket was not "interred with his bones" – it lives'.

From the late 1860s, the youngest Grace – George Frederick – joined his brothers in their 'running concern'. Two years W.G.'s junior, and perhaps somewhat overwhelmed by E.M.'s and W.G.'s strengths, G.F. had a gentler personality. Patrick Morrah wrote: 'He was mild and sweet-tempered and a general favourite. He had most of W.G.'s qualities in smaller measure, and W.G. was the only cricketer in England who excelled him.' Described as 'a fine free-hitter with a perfect style', he was a useful bowler in the E.M.–W.G. mould, and a superb fielder. He toured Australia in 1871 under W.G. and in one country game at Ballarat – on a very hot day – England totalled 479 with W.G. scoring 126 and G.F. 112.

G.F. played in only one Test – the one in which the three brothers made their Test debuts: The Oval Test of September 1880. It was the first Test on English soil, but the Australian attack was depleted because of the absence of Spofforth. E.M. and W.G. opened for England and added 91 before E.M. was dismissed for 36. W.G. played gloriously on, scoring 152. But it was a sad day for G.F. who bagged a 'pair' on debut. He died the next month when only 30. He was due to qualify as a doctor the following year. However, G.F. will be remembered for an amazing catch he took in that Test. Australian giant six-hitter, George Bonnor, lifted a ball right in the sky ... or so it seemed. The hit was eventually caught by G.F. over 100 metres away – a sure six on any modern ground. As G.F. explained later: 'My heart stopped beating as I went on waiting'.

Australian player Sam Cosstick complained that 'at one stage there appeared to be a whole vast family of Graces'. But the Grace family was deeply loved and respected throughout England and Martha Grace, possibly aware of this, left behind for posterity a collection of her sons' clippings in scrapbooks which were *Wisden*-like in detail and accuracy. And *Wisden*, in turn, has retained Martha's, her husband's and sons' names in the *Births and Deaths of Cricketers* column.

Although an amateur, Dr W.G. Grace did not do too badly when it came to financial rewards from cricket. During his second visit to Australia in 1891 as captain of Lord Sheffield's team, all his expenses were paid, including a locum for his practice. He received in all £3000 – equivalent to almost £200,000 at current value. When he qualified in 1879, a national testimonial raised £1500. After his prolific season of 1895, 100th century and 1000 runs in May, three testimonial funds were launched for him and raised £9073. The London County paid him £600 per year and comfortable expenses. Not bad for an 'amateur'!

The great crowd-puller, however, was value for money. Due to his phenomenal performances and tactical acumen, Gloucestershire won the unofficial County Championship three times and once jointly. They have not won it since.

Today's generation may remember W.G. for his flowing beard and a big girth kept in check by a black belt. They may be amused by the countless anecdotes of umpire cheating. But W.G. Grace was larger than life and truly the first superstar of cricket. His towering presence, more than any single factor, transformed cricket into an unrivalled spectator sport of the summer – first in England and subsequently around the world.

The Graces in Test Cricket											
	Tests	Runs	Avrge	HS	100s	50s	Wkts	Avrge	Best	5w/i	Catches
E.M.	1	36	18.00	36	0	0	–	–	–	–	1
W.G.	22	1098	32.29	170	2	5	9	26.22	2–12	0	39
G.F.	1	0	0.00	0	0	0	–	–	–	–	2
Total	24	1134	29.84	170	2	5	9	26.22	2–12	0	42

CHAPTER 6

Walker
Times Seven

———— ● ————

Before the Graces established themselves as cricket immortals,
the mid-19th century produced seven Walker brothers who were behind
the formation of the Middlesex Cricket Club. All of them represented
their county; six played for the Gentlemen against the Players.
On two occasions, in 1860 and 1861, all seven played for the same club,
Southgate. Vyell Edward Walker, the 'beau ideal', was considered
the best all-rounder of his time. Russel Donnithorne Walker was
described as a genius who defied all rules. The youngest,
Isaac Donnithorne, would have captained England on the tour
of Australia in 1878–79 but for the serious illness of one of his brothers.

IT IS HARD TO explain why only one generation could produce a wealth of cricketing talent when there was practically no cricket in previous generations and none after. The Walkers of Southgate in Middlesex present such a challenge to those who believe in heredity. Neither their father nor grandfather played cricket at any level, although their uncle, Henry Walker, bowled left-handed at a fair pace and twice represented the Gentlemen of England against the Players.

As none of the brothers married, they could not pass on their cricketing ability.

However, all five of their sisters did marry and none of their progeny produced a cricketer of note.

The seven Walker brothers were John, Alfred, Frederick, Arthur Henry (A.H.), Vyell Edward (V.E. or 'Teddy'), Russel Donnithorne (R.D. or 'Russy') and Isaac Donnithorne (I.D. or 'Donny'). Their home was in Southgate and apart from John, all were born there. All – except the youngest, Isaac – suffered badly from gout during their playing days, especially Frederick. The second eldest, Alfred, was a slogger and a 'devil of a fast bowler'. However, consistency was not his game and he was the only brother who did not represent the Gentlemen against the Players.

The Walker brothers were the mainstays of the Middlesex County Club. At one time or another, they all represented their county. Strong brotherly affection bound them together and the eldest, John, appeared more like a father. They were all outstanding fielders, four of them – Fred, John, Vyell and Arthur – also kept wickets. The eldest five were educated at Stanmore in Middlesex, where their schoolmaster, Mr A. Woodmass ('Old Woody'), coached them in cricket. As described by W.A. Bettesworth in *The Walkers of Southgate*: 'Old Woody had a cricket wagon built on four wheels and was loaded with bats, balls and a tent. The boys carried it to the cricket ground – at times using a kite to lessen its weight.'

The youngest brothers, Russel and Isaac, went to a preparatory school at Bayford before they joined Arthur and Fred at Harrow. The eldest three, John, Alfred and Fred, represented Cambridge University at cricket, and Russel, Oxford. All the brothers failed in their first matches but made up for it in the second. They knew their cricket backwards and hence were good captains – especially Vyell. As well, they combined with instinct and insight. To quote Fred Gale in *Lillywhite* of 1880: 'The Walker combination when V.E. was bowling and fielding his own bowling at short mid-on and mid-off, with I.D. and R.D. like two terriers watching a rat hole in the field, was nearly if not quite as fatal as the three Graces ... There is no instance within the memory of living cricketers when the strategy of the game was better displayed when three Graces or three Walkers were on the outside.'

As the Walkers were financially well off, they were generous to friends in need of encouragement and money. According to Mr Arthur Wilson, a friend of the family: 'To know Teddy [V.E.] is one of

Vyell Walker, 'beau ideal'. (*Courtesy*, The Walkers of Southgate *by W.A. Bettesworth*)

the greatest privileges and pleasures, he was a king of cricket, he is a king among men; so genial, gentle and kind. And so were they all ... I never knew a family of such marked ability combining so much modesty as to their own performances.'

The eldest, John (1826–85), was the tallest of the family at 188 centimetres, broad and as conspicuous on the field as W.G. Grace later became. A good batsman, John was unsurpassed in fielding in any position. At times he kept wickets. He rarely bowled, employing lobs or slow, round-arm deliveries. A man of few words, he had organising ability. He was 38 when he first met W.G. and gave him a few words of encouragement. Known for his generous patronage, John encouraged cricket by spending large sums of money on remaking the Southgate cricket ground. He invited young talent to play for his team, which

Frederick Walker, a ferocious hooker. (*Courtesy, The Walkers of Southgate by W.A. Bettesworth*)

Surrey Club and was also the vice-president of Middlesex from its formation in 1864 till his death. As Bettesworth wrote in *The Walkers of Southgate*: 'Like all his brothers, Mr John played cricket because he loved the game without a thought about what would be said about his average in future days'.

Alfred (1827–70) is, unfortunately, remembered as the only Walker brother who did not represent the Gentlemen against the Players. Strong and well built – 183 centimetres tall and weighing 89 kilograms – he was a hefty hitter. Had he been more circumspect in his defence he would have played more frequently at Lord's. Instead, most of his matches were for Southgate and Clapton Clubs.

A colourful character, he appeared in some matches in red trousers which once stopped a train. He was on his way to a match and the train driver mistook his raised leg as a danger signal! Alfred was a slogger, lofty drives and hooks being the features of his batting. An exceedingly fast and accurate underarm bowler who generated a 'devil of a pace', he had a windmill action and could also bowl leg breaks. Like his brothers, he was a brilliant fielder. The umpire risked bodily harm if he did not stand three metres behind stumps when Alfred was bowling. Once an umpire ignored keeping clear of his swinging arms and got a heavy blow in the stomach. This upset the considerate Alfred more than it did the crouching adjudicator.

In matches for Clapton Club against strong opponents like Surrey, Alfred was often unplayable. In July 1850, Surrey was dismissed for 73 as Alfred claimed five wickets. In the second innings elder brother John took seven wickets and Clapton won by an innings. In the return match the same year, Surrey included five professionals and yet lost by 10 wickets. It was virtually Alfred vs Surrey as he hammered 42 out of Clapton's first

was in itself an honour. Good fielding was an essential criterion for inclusion. A martinet on the field, he did not tolerate any 'tomfoolery'.

He played with a straight bat and his best innings was 98 for the Gentlemen against the Players in 1862, when he was 36. In those days there were no boundary hits and John had to run for each of his shots. For the MCC against Sussex in 1850 he scored 83 out of the team total of 268. He hit the ball out of the grounds twice.

For Old Cantabs against New Cantabs in 1856, the former lost 9 for 67 before John (53) and the Hon. F. Ponsonby added 51 for the last wicket. John shone as a bowler for Southgate vs Ealing Dean in 1857 when he took 7 for 33 in the second innings and his team won by an innings and 100 runs. Forced to retire from cricket due to ill health, his greatest achievement was setting up the Middlesex County Cricket Club. He was on the committee of the MCC and the

Arthur Walker, accident-prone. (*Courtesy*, The Walkers of Southgate *by W.A. Bettesworth*)

The fourth Walker brother, Arthur Henry (1833–78), was accident-prone. In 1850 he showed enormous promise but next year had a prolonged and serious illness. After a lay-off for a year he came back with a spirited 74 but still appeared weak. He was at his best in 1860, before dislocating his kneecap. In 1862 he broke his thigh in a football match. His treatment involved wearing high boots, which signalled the end of his cricket career in major games.

For the Gentlemen of England against the Gentlemen of Kent in 1857, Arthur scored 90 runs and took 5 for 30 and 3 for 21. The match between Village and Herts XI on 4 July 1856 was dominated by three Walker brothers. Fred scored 68 of his team's total of 135, stumped two in the first innings and accepted two catches. Arthur took eight wickets in the match and Vyell the remaining 12. Like Alfred, Arthur died young, when 45.

Vyell Edward (1837–1906), 'Teddy' to his friends, was the greatest among the Walkers. According to *Lillywhite's Guide to Cricketers* of 1859, he was 'undoubtedly the best all-round cricketer in the world'. Bettesworth confirms this assessment: 'No other cricketer stood out so prominently above other men of his day with the exception of Dr W.G. Grace'. As a batsman he was the most graceful among the brothers, although not as consistent as Isaac. Essentially an on-side player, Vyell's defence was sound although he could hit out when necessary. Starting as a slow round-arm medium-pacer, he turned to fast underarm and later to lobs which made him famous. Vyell was also an amazing fielder – especially to his own bowling. So incredible was his anticipation and agility that once he caught and bowled a bewildered batsman behind the wicket-keeper!

He became the first bowler to take 10 wickets in an innings of a first-class

innings of 84. He also captured 15 wickets in the match. A kind-hearted man, he looked after Fred Lillywhite when he was ill and in financial strife. Alfred died young, four days before his 43rd birthday.

But for ill health plaguing his career and forcing him to retire before he was 30, Frederick Walker (1829–89) would have achieved much more than he did. He suffered badly from rheumatic gout. The shortest in the family at 170 centimetres, he kept wickets for Cambridge University from 1849 to 1852. For the university against MCC he took six second-innings wickets after top-scoring with 37. His best performance was on 20 July 1857, against Surrey Club and Ground, whose attack was as strong as Surrey's. Opening the innings, he scored 170 in three and a half hours. He was a ferocious hooker and his cutting was magnificent.

match twice, for Rest of England vs Surrey (10 for 74) in 1859 and for Middlesex vs Lancashire (10 for 104) in 1865. The others to achieve this 'dual distinction' were W.G. Grace, 'Tich' Freeman, Hedley Verity and Jim Laker – Englishmen all. Vyell took all 10 wickets in an innings for the third time for the Gentlemen of Middlesex vs the Gentlemen of Kent at Maidstone in 1864, but this match is not given first-class status.

Vyell first played for the Gentlemen against the Players in 1856 when only 19. The Hon. R.H. Lyttelton described him in *Giants of the Game* as a 'fine driving bat ... a leading lob bowler of his time and one of the best fields anywhere'. Vyell's most memorable match was for Rest of England against Surrey at The Oval in 1859. He scored 20 not out and 108 and took 10 for 74 and 4 for 14. Lyttelton called it 'the greatest cricketing feat on record', especially as Surrey was then the leading county in cricket.

That season, he reached his peak. After the above match against Surrey, he recorded the following feats in successive matches: 71 runs, 5 for 37 and 3 for 52 for Middlesex vs Kent at Canterbury; 88 runs, 3 for 80 and 6 for 48 for J. Walker's XVI vs UEE at Southgate; 7 and 69 runs, 5 for 92 and 4 for 69 for Gents of South vs Gents of North at Liverpool; and 2 and 69 not out, 8 for 76 and 2 for 64 for England XI vs XX Gents of Sussex at Brighton.

In 1860 Vyell was accidentally shot in the eye and for two years his cricket suffered. He later contributed brilliantly to Middlesex's stunning wins over Surrey by scoring 79 runs at Islington and then 74 not out in the return match at The Oval in 1866. Apart from his batting and bowling skills, he could have been selected in a team for his captaincy and fielding. Contemporary cricketers and critics rated him 'first among firsts as a captain'.

Vyell Walker was both popular and authoritative – a rare combination – and there was no panic when he captained. When a fielder grassed a catch, he adopted a sympathetic attitude. 'He never worried a man', to quote his biographer Bettesworth, yet got the best out of him. Under Vyell, young talent flourished. He was made President of the MCC in 1891. Earlier, along with Isaac, he was on the selection panel when the 1882 England team was picked against Australia for The Oval Test, the match which started the Ashes legend. His all-round brilliance prompted a contributor to *Cricket Today* – an early 20th-century publication – to write: 'Of fine physique and gifted with naturally generous impulses, it is questionable whether any one individual has done more to promote the growth of the game than Mr V.E. Walker'.

Russel Donnithorne (1842–1922), or 'Russy', was the longest-living among the Walker brothers and was a strong character. He had his own style and was described as a genius who defied all rules. As W.A. Bettesworth put it: 'No batsman was ever like him before, none has been like him since, there never will be one like him'. He went to bat padless and gloveless, yet it was the bowlers who feared him. According to Arthur Haygarth, a knowledgeable cricket critic of the 19th century: 'He has a style peculiar to himself, resembling perhaps no other cricketer, past or present and which must be seen but cannot be described'.

Many of Russy's big scores were made at Lord's, where the pitches favoured bowlers. His stance was ungainly but effective. His round-arm bowling had 'something' that baffled even top-grade batsmen. It seemed easy – too easy – until he got them out. Even the great W.G. fell to him time after time. Quick off the pitch, wristy and accurate,

Russel bowled with great success in all three games for Southgate against United England XI.

For XVI of Southgate against a strong England XI in 1861, Southgate with six Walker brothers won by 15 wickets. United England XI scored 93 (Russel 6 for 62) and 50 (Russel 8 for 23); Southgate XVI 133 (John 27, Arthur 17, Russel 16) and 11 for no loss.

In the return match the following season, Russel was the bowling hero again, bagging 6 for 43 and 4 for 43 as Southgate triumphed by an innings. The next year, it was once again an innings win over the United England XI, mainly due to Russel's hauls of 4 for 51 and 3 for 33, and Vyell taking 12 for 104 in the match.

As a fielder, Russel had the instinct to be in the right position at the right time and made difficult catches look easy. His exclusion from a Gentlemen vs Players match in 1869 caused a furore. He proved the selectors in error when he scored 152 for Free Foresters against the Gentlemen of North at Beeston the following year.

At Trent Bridge in 1866, Russel starred in Middlesex's innings win over Nottinghamshire. The home team had bowlers of the calibre of J.C. Shaw and George Wooton, but Middlesex totalled 221, Russel scoring 90 and Vyell 58. Notts then collapsed for 88 and 66 to the bowling of Tom Hearne, who took 12 wickets while Russel claimed the remaining eight.

Russel was also a billiards and chess player and, like Vyell and Isaac, a splendid rackets player. Russel represented Oxford at rackets in varsity matches. He toured Australia in 1878 but was past his best and played only two minor matches.

Isaac Donnithorne Walker (1844–98), 'Donny', was the baby of the family. He started off as a brilliant but inconsistent player and displayed great potential, but failed repeatedly in his earlier matches. Subsequently, he showed constant improvement and developed into a reliable batsman. Indeed his batting record was the best among the brothers. Of the 10 centuries by the Walkers in major matches, Isaac hit seven, Russel two and Vyell one. Isaac's 179 for the Gentlemen of South against the Gentlemen of North was the highest score among the brothers in any grade of cricket.

In minor matches, the Walkers hit 32 hundreds of which Isaac contributed 20, Russel nine, Vyell two and Fred one. When he retired in 1884, Isaac had scored 11,655 runs in first-class cricket at an average of 25.30. His best season was 1870, when he scored 820 runs at 37.6. He was originally selected to captain England's squad to Australia in 1878–79 but the serious illness of brother Arthur forced him to pull out. Lord Harris led the team instead.

Isaac played with a straight bat, had quick footwork and was strong on the off side. Cricket writers of his time wondered where he learnt his famous shot which flew over cover point's head. It was spectacular and breathtaking. He was also an awkward spinner. He captained Middlesex and the Gentlemen with success, although he lacked the cool charisma of Vyell.

For MCC against Nottinghamshire in 1870, Isaac put on 127 runs for the opening wicket with W.G. Grace before the team was dismissed for 183. In the second innings he scored 63. For Gentlemen of South vs Gentlemen of North the same year, he made his highest score of 179 and added 288 runs for the fourth wicket with G.F. Grace.

In 1883 three members of famous families, Alfred Lyttelton, C.T. Studd and Isaac Walker, batted splendidly for Middlesex. When scoring 145, his last century, for Middlesex vs Gloucestershire

Alfred Walker, a colourful character. (*Courtesy,* The Walkers of Southgate *by W.A. Bettesworth*)

at Clifton, he added 324 runs for the second wicket with Alfred Lyttelton who scored an equally brilliant 181.

The summer of 1884 was the last one for Isaac on the cricket field. He was 40 then and still fit enough to score 83 vs Cambridge, 40 not out vs Yorkshire, 47 not out vs Surrey; 54 and 31 vs Kent, a brilliant 80 vs Notts and 50 and 27 vs Gloucestershire in his – and the Walker brothers' – last major match. He believed in physical fitness and walked four hours every day during his active career. He was the founder of the Scarborough Cricket Festival in 1869. After his playing days, he coached at Harrow. The 51-year-old visited Australia in 1895–96 on an unofficial friendly tour of three matches. He died two years later.

On two occasions, all seven brothers played together in one match. For Southgate XVI vs United England in 1860, they lost by 22 runs. But for Southgate XI against Enfield XVII the next year, also on Southgate ground, the home team won by nine wickets. Six of the brothers played in the same match for Southgate 11 times.

Except for one game in 1862, at least one of the Walkers represented the Gentlemen vs Players from 1852 to 1872. Once, in 1857 at The Oval, four of them – John, Frederick, Arthur and Vyell – played together. In a further eight games, three Walkers played in tandem.

Apart from their playing abilities, the Walkers were crowd pullers. When John arranged a match between a Southgate team and a strong United All England XI on 23–25 August 1858, over 10,000 spectators turned up and the Great Northern Railways had to organise a special train service. The Southgate XVI included John, Fred, Alfred, Arthur and Vyell Walker, with Tom Hearne, whereas the opponents had big names including F. Bell, W. Caffyn, John Lillywhite, J. McCormick and John Wisden. To the spectators' delight, the Southgate XVI won by 59 runs. Vyell Walker was the major contributor to this win by scoring 37 and 31 run out – the only batsman to top 30 runs in the match – and taking 3 for 8 and 2 for 8.

The Walker reign in cricket spanned almost non-stop from 1846 to 1884. Their house was called Arnos Grove and an underground station was named after it.

CHAPTER 7

Triumphs
and Tragedies of Trotts

—— ● ——

*At the turn of the century, the popular Australian captain, Harry Trott,
and his dynamic younger brother, Albert, were more than useful
all-rounders. They were the endearing characters of the field. But their
cricket careers were tinged with tragedy.*

ONE OF THE FIRST things a sportswriter learns is to avoid sentiment and present facts as directly as possible. However, even the most hard-boiled scribe will find it impossible to keep emotion out when featuring the Trott brothers – especially the younger and more ebullient Albert.

For Albert Trott was not only an adventurous all-rounder and a crowd-pleaser but, according to the experts of his time, also in the genius category. Perhaps he was an erratic genius, but his performances were staggering although incredibly unrewarding. After averaging 102.5 runs with the bat in three Tests for Australia, and taking eight wickets in a Test innings, he was unceremoniously dropped. Disillusioned, Albert migrated to Middlesex, where he achieved miracles and near-miracles. He performed the then unique – and even

now, very rare – double of 1000 runs and 200 wickets in a season ... and he did it twice in succession. He played two Tests for England against South Africa and, despite taking 17 wickets at 11.64, he was never picked again.

Albert took many memorable slip catches for Middlesex and MCC and made colossal hits, becoming the only player to hit the ball over the Lord's pavilion. However, he ruined his own benefit match by bowling too well – taking four wickets in four balls, and later a hat-trick in the same innings. As the match ended early, Albert Trott suffered financially. Health and financial problems eventually proved too much for this endearing character, and he ended it all when only 41.

The elder brother, George Henry (Harry) Steven Trott, had a more rewarding cricket career, although his end was also sad. Born in Collingwood, an inner suburb of Melbourne, on 5 August 1866, Harry was the third of eight children. He became a postman but was later to make his mark as 'one of cricket's most admired captains', to quote Ray Robinson in *On Top Down Under*.

When 20, Harry scored 200 for South Melbourne against St Kilda. In his first State game, for Victoria against South Australia, he had the temerity to hit the great George Giffen over the heads of onlookers at the Adelaide Oval. He rapidly developed into one of Victoria's most attractive batsmen, driving and late-cutting with perfection. He made his Test debut when 21 and scored a duck. But, soon after, he hit a polished 172 for the Australian XI of 1888 against New South Wales. He toured England four times: in 1888, 1890, 1893, and as captain in 1896.

In all, he played 24 Tests, captaining Australia eight times, winning five Tests and losing three. On each of his four tours to England he scored well over 1000 runs. Six of his 10 centuries were hit on English soil. On the 1893 tour he shone as a slow leg-break bowler, capturing 60 wickets at 19.8. His best match on that tour was at Leicester where he hammered 100 runs in 130 minutes and bagged 11 wickets.

When 28, Harry captained Victoria against England, sent them in after winning the toss, and won the game. His 8 for 63 in 1895 is still the best for Victoria against England. His finest display of batsmanship was at Lord's in June 1896. In this Test, Tom Richardson shot out Australia for 53 and the Australian second innings seemed to be following the dismal first when Harry Trott and Syd Gregory got together. On a difficult pitch, they put on 221 runs at almost 80 runs an hour. They hit the immortal Richardson as if he were an ordinary bowler. And although Australia lost the

Test, every Australian was proud of Harry's 143 – his highest Test score.

More than his personal contributions, he inspired his team-mates to give of their best. When Frank Iredale was passing through a bad patch, Harry gave him a tonic to drink. This took care of Iredale's nerves to such an extent that he scored 108 in the Old Trafford Test. Later, Harry let out the secret that the mysterious tonic was good old brandy and soda.

Harry's peak performances were followed by physical and mental setbacks. In 1897–98 he led Australia to a thumping 4–1 victory over England – winning the last four Tests in a row. His series of misfortunes started after he suffered sunstroke in 1898 and lost the sight of one eye. He was then only 32.

An undiagnosed ailment left Harry with psychological fears that unhinged his reason, and after a prolonged stay in a mental hospital he moved to Bendigo. His love of cricket made him fight back to strength and sanity and in 1904 he staged a comeback as Victoria's captain against MCC. Four years later, he took 5 for 116 against England. He was 41 and it was his last big match. However, he continued playing first-grade cricket and headed South Melbourne's batting and bowling averages when 44. Apart from his batting and bowling, he was a magnificent point fielder, so much so that the position was named 'strong point' when Harry policed it.

Harry Trott will be remembered for his intuitive captaincy and deep understanding of players under him. This is what some of his colleagues thought of him. Clem Hill: 'As a captain, Harry Trott was in a class by himself – the best I have played under'. (Incidentally, Hill had played under such captains as Joe Darling, Hugh Trumble and Monty Noble.) George Giffen: 'Let his side be under the whip and you see him at his best ... And no matter how he may stonewall, he never loses his elegance of style ... His genial nature – I doubt whether anyone ever knew him to have a downright quarrel with any other player – helped him to gain ascendancy over his men, without which no captain can secure the best from his team.'

His team-mates called him 'Trotty' or 'Joe' and they resolved never to let him down. Wrote *Wisden*: 'Blessed with a humour that nothing could ruffle, he was always master both of himself and his team, whatever the position of the game'.

Harry Trott had a high opinion of his seven-years-younger brother, Albert. On one occasion he told George Giffen: 'Keep your eyes on the youngster. He'll be a good one.' It was not just brotherly love, for Albert Edwin Trott, born on 6 February 1873, was a natural cricketer. Like Harry, Albert was a big lumbering man, with enormous hands, a droopy moustache, a love of beer, and a smile for everybody.

Also like Harry, Albert was only 21 when he made his Test debut – against England in the 1894–95 series. But, unlike Harry, who had made a blob in his Test bow, Albert put in a brilliant all-round performance. This was the third Test in the series at Adelaide. Against an attack comprising all-time greats Richardson, Bill Lockwood, Bill Brockwell, Bobby Peel and Johnny Briggs, Albert went in at No. 10 and scored 38 not out and 72 not out. In the same Test Harry had opened the innings and scored 48 and 0.

This was the first of three Tests the Trott brothers were to play together. The younger Albert had already written his name in the record books, where it still remains after over 100 years. In the second innings he took 8 for 43 as Australia won by 382 runs. He became the first bowler to take eight wickets in an innings on debut. In the following Test in Sydney, Albert stroked an unbeaten 85 out of the team total of 284. Thus, he had scored 195 runs in his first

Harry Trott, a tragic figure. (*Jack Pollard Collection*)

two Tests without once getting out. In the final Test at Melbourne, although he failed, he still finished with a century batting average in the series.

By some strange mental aberrations which have never been explained, the Australian selectors dropped their find of the previous season from the team to tour England under Harry Trott in 1896. A.G. Moyes wrote in *Australian Batsmen*: '[Albert] might have been among the immortals had the Australian selectors shown more vision'.

Australia's loss was Middlesex's acquisition, for Albert, feeling justifiably bitter, left Australia for England. For Middlesex and MCC, Albert had his moments of glory. According to Patrick Morrah in *The Golden Age of Cricket*: 'Albert developed in England as one of the world's best bowlers. He had a swerve though it was less pronounced than George Hirst's, and his devastating yorker was perhaps the fastest ball ever bowled by a bowler not normally characterised as fast.'

Albert was chosen to represent England against South Africa in both Tests of a two-Test series in 1898–99. In the first Test at Johannesburg, he had match figures of 9 for 110. South Africa, needing only 132 runs to win, were skittled out for 99 – thanks to Albert Trott's 5 for 49. In the second Test, at Cape Town, he took eight wickets in the match, his 4 for 19 in the second innings, along with Schofield Haigh's 6 for 11, being major factors behind England's easy win. Albert had taken 17 wickets at an economical average of 11.64. Inexplicably, Albert, the ace performer, was not picked for a Test again. He was then only 26 years of age.

'Press on, regardless' must have been his motto, for he continued in the game, making spectacular hits, bowling with rare penetration and fielding like an acrobat. In 1899, Albert scored over 1000 runs (1175) and took over 200 wickets (239) in the one season – a feat no one had approached before him. The next season, Albert performed the double again, 1337 runs and 211 wickets. Only three cricketers have emulated Albert Trott's rare double: George Hirst in 1906, Alex Kennedy in 1922, and Maurice Tate in 1923, 1924 and 1925.

Albert's best batting display was seen at Lord's in 1899 when he hammered 164 runs against Yorkshire. After a slow start, he warmed up sufficiently to belt 137 runs out of 181 in 90 minutes of magnificent hitting. Included were 27 fours, many of which would now have been considered sixes. (In those days, even hits over the fence were called fours.)

In one burst of furious attacking, Albert smacked 33 runs in six minutes. This hurricane hitting was watched by the poet Francis Thompson, who wrote a verse to immortalise it:

The many-girded ground is shaking
With rolling claps and clamour, as soar

Fours after fours and even four!
West-end tent or pavilion rail,
He lashes them home with a thresher's
*   flail.*

This was the season in which Albert hit that huge shot over the Lord's pavilion. While playing for MCC and Ground against the Australians of 1899 on 31 July he dispatched a ball to the seats on the top balcony of the pavilion. That mighty effort, however, was just an entree to the main course. The historic hit followed a few minutes later. Monty Noble bowled a half-volley to Albert who lifted the ball right over the top of the pavilion, hitting a chimney and landing in a garden behind. No one – before or since – has succeeded in clearing the Lord's pavilion.

Albert, who used a three-pound bat – six ounces heavier than Bill Ponsford's 'Big Bertha' – made many spectacular hits, to the great delight of the spectators. On another occasion he slammed a ball clean out of the Trent Bridge ground and the ball damaged the spokes of a hansom cab passing the ground at the time. Unfortunately, once he had become a six symbol he ceased being a reliable batsman. He was obsessed with the idea of lofting the ball out of every ground on which he played and his batting suffered.

However, Albert still remained a bowler to be feared. Against Somerset at Taunton in 1900 he took all 10 wickets in the first innings for 42 runs. In the next match, against Gloucestershire at Clifton, he captured 5 for 41 and 8 (all bowled) for 47. Again for Middlesex, versus Sussex at Lord's in 1901, he took 15 for 187, claiming the wickets of all 11 opponents in the game.

And, as mentioned earlier, in 1907 'Alberto' ruined his own benefit match (versus Somerset) by bowling too brilliantly and taking 7 for 20 in one innings – including a top hat-trick (four wickets in consecutive balls) and a hat-trick. Unfortunately, the match ended too soon and was consequently a financial flop.

After this match, Albert began to go downhill. He gave up playing cricket in 1910, when 37, and took up umpiring. In his first-class career, he took 1674 wickets at an average of 21.09. He captured eight wickets in an innings nine times – once all 10. Subsequently, he suffered from dropsy, and his nerves were shot to pieces. The man who had given countless hours of joy to spectators was unable to sleep. For a while he was kept in hospital, but he insisted on returning home and, in 1914, he shot himself. He was only 41 and had mistakenly believed that he had incurable cancer.

Harry Trott died three years later. One of his great-grandsons is Stuart Trott, who at one time looked promising cricketing material. When only 15, Stuart scored an unbeaten century for Frankston Colts. But better financial rewards made him give up cricket for Australian Rules football, in which he became a star for St Kilda.

The cricket world is changing rapidly now, but the Trott brothers will continue to be remembered – Harry, who was everybody's friend and inspiration, and Albert, the ill-fated, wayward and endearing genius.

The third brother, Fred Trott, came to England in the early 1900s. He did not play first-class cricket but was on Lord's staff and represented Middlesex XI. He then went to Scotland as a professional for Peebles Cricket Club. He died young in Glasgow in March 1921.

The Trotts in Test Cricket

	For	Tests	Runs	Avrge	HS	100s	50s	Wkts	Avrge	Best	5w/i	Catches
G.H.S. (Harry)	Aus.	24	921	21.92	143	1	4	29	35.13	4–71	0	21
A.E. (Albert)	Aus. & Eng.	5	228	38.00	85*	0	2	26	15.00	8–43	2	4
Total		29	1149	23.94	143	1	6	55	25.62	8–43	2	25

CHAPTER 8

The
Giffens Were Different

— ● —

*George Giffen is considered one of Australia's best all-rounders.
Described as 'Australia's W.G. Grace', he is among the few cricketers
with a grandstand named after him. He was the first Australian to take
10 wickets in a first-class innings and the first cricketer to achieve the
Test double of 1000 runs and 100 wickets. He fought for the inclusion
of his younger and less talented brother, Walter, in Test cricket.*

GEORGE GIFFEN AND MERV Hughes had many similarities. Coming from different eras, they were heavily moustached and possessed enormous fists. Both completed 1000 runs and 100 wickets in Tests, took five wickets in a Test innings seven times and 10 wickets in a Test once, had similar bowling averages (27 for George, 28 for Merv) and accepted almost the same number of catches (24 for George, 23 for Merv). Both were crowd-pleasers and enjoyed a drink. There the similarities end.

While Merv huffed and puffed as he bowled, especially towards the end of his career, George was like a well-oiled machine without a squeak, even at 50. 'Nothing on two legs could undo him for stamina, not even an Olympic runner from Kenya,' wrote Ray Robinson in *On Top Down Under*. 'He was strong as a scrub bull, worked like a horse and developed thirst like a camel.'

The third son of a carpenter, George was born on 27 March 1859. He worked in a post office in South Australia as a letter sorter, and on cricket fields in Australia and England he sorted out opposing batsmen's weaknesses. His rise to fame was quick and remained steady over many years. He was selected at 17 to represent South Australia against England and for many years he was Mr South Australia personified; batting, bowling and fielding like a man possessed. He made his Test debut at 22 and continued playing until 1896 when he was 37, losing neither his enthusiasm nor his penetration.

He toured England in 1882, 1884, 1886, 1893 and 1896, after refusing to tour in 1888 and 1890. He also visited the USA, Canada and New Zealand. On the tour of 1893 he was accompanied by his younger brother, Walter, who was similar in build to George (180 centimetres tall and 85 kilograms) but less talented. It is believed that George once refused to tour England because Walter was not included, although he denied this charge. However, he did fight for the inclusion of Syd Gregory on an earlier tour to England.

George was a gifted all-rounder, a reliable batsman, a crafty off-spinner and a safe fielder anywhere. His feats in first-class cricket for his State and country were staggering. Among Australians he alone scored 10,000 runs and took 100 wickets in first-class matches. He captured 16 wickets in a match an incredible five times and five wickets in an innings an astonishing 48 times. At 24, he bagged all 10 wickets for 66 runs for an Australian XI against The Rest in Sydney in 1883–84. It remained a unique feat in first-class cricket in Australia for 59 years until Tim Wall (also of South Australia) took 10 for 36 against New South Wales in Sydney in 1932–33.

George puzzled batsmen by hiding his arms during his eight-step run-up. He mixed up his off-spin with cutters by varying his pace and flighted the ball cleverly. He remains the only cricketer to make a double-century and take 16 wickets in a match. For South Australia against Victoria at Adelaide in 1891–92, he scored 271 and took 9 for 96 and 7 for 70. This made the English cricket historian Harry Altham comment that it was 'surely the greatest all-round performance in recorded cricket history of any class'. Altham insisted that George was Australia's greatest all-rounder of his time although many critics preferred 'Monty' Noble, who came on the scene a decade later.

In January 1891, George scored 237 runs and captured 12 wickets (5 for 89 and 7 for 103) for South Australia against Victoria at Melbourne. Victoria must have been his favourite opponents as, in 1885–86 at Adelaide, he grabbed 17 for 201, the first Australian to take 17

George Giffen, 'nothing on two legs could undo him for stamina, not even an Olympic runner from Kenya'. – Ray Robinson (© *R.L. Cardwell*)

wickets in a match. After him, only two Australians have emulated this feat: 17 for 50 by Charles Turner in 1888 and 17 for 54 by Bill Howell in 1902–03.

During his 1884 tour of England, he became the first player to score a century and take a hat-trick in the same match. This was for the Australians against Lancashire at Manchester. (W.G. Grace had achieved such a feat for MCC vs Kent at Canterbury in 1874 but it was a 12-a-side fixture and hence non-first-class). No other Australian has performed this double. However, 12 of his 16 centuries were scored in Australia, of which four were double hundreds – all for South Australia. His 203 vs G.F. Vernon's England XI at the Adelaide

Oval in December 1888 was the first double-century against a touring team in Australia.

George was a dominant figure during his tours to England. He headed both the batting and bowling aggregates in 1886, amassing 1424 runs at 26.86 and taking 154 wickets at 17.36. He achieved the 1000 runs, 100 wickets double twice more on subsequent visits to England, in 1893 and 1896. Warwick Armstrong remains the only other Australian to achieve this double three times, during tours to England in 1905, 1909 and 1921.

All of George's 31 Tests were played against England and he scored 1238 runs at 23.35 and captured 103 wickets at 27.09, becoming the first individual to reach the Test double of 1000 runs and 100 wickets. Seven times he took five wickets in a Test innings, with 7 for 117 and 7 for 128 his best returns.

In the Sydney Test of 1891–92, he bagged 4 for 88 and 6 for 72, helping bundle out England for 157 when they needed 230 to win. He made his only Test hundred, 161, in Sydney in 1894–95, during which innings he added 171 runs with Frank Iredale and 139 with Syd Gregory. He considered this innings as his best. This was also his best series as he scored most runs (474 at 52.77) and took most wickets (34 at 24.11). George led Australia in the last four Tests, winning two and losing two. He was never asked to captain Australia again as 'he bowled himself too much', according to Sir Pelham Warner. Jack Pollard added, tongue-in-cheek, 'A change of bowling only meant changing ends for George!'

George Giffen retired at 42 but was recalled for a South Australia vs Victoria match. He had lost none of his skills as he scored 178 runs for once out and captured 15 wickets. His career statistics spanning 26 years (1877 to 1903) were outstanding: 11,758 runs at 29.54 and 1023 wickets at 21.29 apiece. In one 12-year period, he took five-eighths of the wickets and scored one-third of the runs for South Australia.

'While Giffen was wheeling along 46,355 balls for his wickets, his moustache was the only thing that drooped,' wrote Robinson in *On Top Down Under*. George was blunt but warm-hearted and respected cricket's enduring virtues. He was so popular that once, after a match, spectators donated 400 sovereigns – a tidy sun then. He coached after retirement from his post office job, and bowled immaculately even at 61. In a 'hit one stump while bowling' competition at Belair National Park in South Australia he struck the solitary stump nine times out of nine – coming straight from the pub. The next best score was two hits.

When he died in 1927, aged 66, Australian greats Joe Darling and Clem Hill eulogised him for his willing hours in matches and at net practice and for his coaching. In the Members Stand in Adelaide named after George Giffen hangs his portrait by May Grigg, a noted South Australian painter. A plaque outside recognises his lifelong service to cricket.

George's younger brother, Walter Frank Giffen (1863–1949), was a defensive batsman and a good outfielder with a powerful throw. His promising career was upset when he lost the tops of two fingers on his left hand in an accident at the Brompton Gasworks, Adelaide, in 1886, when he was 22. In a first-class career lasting from 1882 to 1902, he made 1178 runs at 15.92. In 13 Sheffield Shield matches for South Australia he averaged only 11.77 with the bat, his highest score being 89. His Test figures were even more mediocre, 11 runs at 1.83 and a catch in three Tests played in Australia (1886–87 and 1891–92). He was lucky to be picked to tour England in 1893, thanks to big brother George's prompting. Although a prolific scorer in Adelaide club cricket, he found English conditions hard to master and totalled 245 runs at 15.31, highest score 62.

Walter's son, Challand Giffen, played district cricket with Sturt and Port Elizabeth. He was a police sergeant and played for South Australia Country against Wally Hammond's English XI at Port Pirie in 1946. His top score was 159

for Morphet Vale in the Southern Cricket Association. Challand's son, Robert Giffen, was a promising schoolboy cricketer but had a tragic end. Wounded while piloting his helicopter over Vietnam, he died on his 23rd birthday in 1971.

That marked the end of the Giffen era, but still the name of George Giffen lives on. A story circulated in the early 1900s that Adelaide parents taught their children to say 'God bless Mummy and Daddy and George Giffen'.

The Giffens in Test Cricket											
	Tests	Runs	Avrge	HS	100s	50s	Wkts	Avrge	Best	5w/i	Catches
George	31	1238	23.35	161	1	6	103	27.09	7–117	7	24
Walter	3	11	1.83	3	0	0	–	–	–	–	1
Total	34	1249	21.17	161	1	6	103	27.09	7–117	7	25

CHAPTER 9

The
Tyldesley Tribe

——— ● ———

Six Tyldesleys formed the core of Lancashire cricket from 1895 to 1936.
They belonged to two unrelated families. The celebrated brothers, Johnny
(J.T.) and Ernest Tyldesley of Worsley, were magnificent batsmen who
played 45 Tests between them. In first-class cricket they amassed 76,771
runs, hitting 188 centuries, seven of them in Tests. Then there were four
Tyldesley brothers from Westhoughton, William, James, Harry and
Richard, who were the contemporaries of J.T. and Ernest. The youngest
brother Richard played in seven Tests as a spinner.

SEVERAL ENGLISH COUNTIES PRODUCED champion families who shaped their destinies. Gloucestershire had their Graces, Worcestershire their Fosters, Middlesex their Walkers and Hearnes, and Nottinghamshire their Gunns. Lancashire got their lift in the championship table mainly through two unrelated families of Tyldesleys. From 1895 to 1936, John Tyldesley and his younger brother by 15 years, Ernest, contributed largely to Lancashire winning the County Championship seven times. They were assisted by spinner Cecil Parkin, Australian fast bowler Ted McDonald and four Tyldesley brothers from a different stock.

With Ernest Tyldesley shining with the bat at No. 3 and unrelated Richard Tyldesley bluffing batsmen out with top-spinners-in-leg-break-clothing, Lancashire won four championships out of five from 1926 to 1930. They had a hat-trick of wins from 1926 to 1928.

Neville Cardus ranked John Thomas Tyldesley as one of the three greatest professional batsmen in the game's history. Even now, over 70 years after his death, J.T.T. is remembered with reverence in Lancashire. As a boy, he played for Rose Green which in a way was a Tyldesley club where both J.T.T. and Ernest learned their cricket. Johnny was England's most dashing professional batsman and was superb on turning wickets. In the first decade of the 20th century, no England team was complete without him batting at No. 3.

He flourished in the days of amateur batsmen and was the only professional who could be compared with F.S. Jackson, Archie MacLaren, Ranji and C.B. Fry.

His first appearance at Old Trafford, in July 1895, stamped Johnny as a batsman of class. In the second innings against Gloucestershire he made an unbeaten 33 on a wet wicket, which drew favourable comments from W.G. Grace. Gilbert Jessop later reported that the young batsman sent one or two past W.G. at point with sufficient speed to make the Grand Old Man sit up and take notice. In his next match, at Birmingham, Johnny played a brilliant innings of 152 not out which helped Lancashire wallop Warwickshire by an innings.

The shrewd C.B. Fry later ranked Johnny as a rival to Jack Hobbs in point of skill – especially on a sticky rain-spoilt wicket. The great stylist Archie MacLaren maintained that he had seen Johnny play an innings that Victor Trumper could not have bettered. As A.G. Moyes wrote: 'What further evidence do we need? A man who could merit comparison with Trumper and Hobbs was something above average.'

In 1901, Johnny topped 3000 runs in a season – a feat not achieved before 1899. (Ranji was the first to reach the milestone in 1900. Then Bob Abel, C.B. Fry and J.T.T. did likewise the next year.)

Johnny had earlier made his Test debut against South Africa at Johannesburg in 1898–99. He scored a century in the next Test at Cape Town. This was the famous topsy-turvy Test in which England was dismissed for 92 in the first innings and still won by 210 runs. After Johnny's 112 nullified the Springbok lead, the home team collapsed for 35 in the final innings. His second century (138) was in the Edgbaston Test against Australia in 1902. The value of this innings can be judged by the fact that Australia, with Victor Trumper,

Clem Hill, Syd Gregory, Joe Darling, Monty Noble and Warwick Armstrong, crashed for 36.

The following season, and on a treacherous Melbourne pitch, Johnny top-scored in both innings, scoring 97 and 62 (out of England's total of 103). Australia's answer came from Victor Trumper, who contributed 74 and 35 out of Australia's totals of 122 and 111 as Wilfred Rhodes ran amok taking 15 for 124.

In the 1905 series against Australia, Johnny scored 0 and 100 on a difficult Headingley wicket. According to A.A. Thomson in *Cricketers of my Times*: 'J.T.T. showed how impossible bowling could be rendered possible after his 100 stumped against Australia at Headingley'. In the final Test at The Oval, he hit another magical hundred – an undefeated 112. In 1906, his benefit brought him a more than tidy £3111.

A genuine Lancastrian, Johnny differed from other Lancashire professionals who were, pretty much by definition, dour and stolid. Like the imported Lancastrian professionals of the 1970s, Clive Lloyd and Farokh Engineer, he was a slayer of bowling. His batting 'was polished, enterprising and attractive', to quote Patrick Morrah from *The Golden Age of Cricket*.

Of medium height, Johnny stood up on his toes to play his strokes. He could cut and drive magnificently, his speciality being to hit the ball on the rise – a legacy of his wet-wicket experience of northern England. Wrote Sir Pelham Warner in *The Book of Cricket*: 'J.T.T. played square cut better than anybody else. He brought his bat down with an action which may be described as "throwing the bat at the ball without letting go of the handle".'

Fry explained that Johnny's backplay was as sure as that of Arthur Shrewsbury, who was regarded as a master of back-foot play. As a brilliant slayer of all types of bowling, Neville Cardus believed Johnny was equalled only by Don Bradman and Charlie Macartney. J.T.T. hit 13 double-centuries, including 272 in 1919 when he was almost 46 years old. He was a modest man too. During his playing days he wrote match reports for the *Daily Mail*. One of his reports went like this: 'On a perfect Worcester wicket, Mr MacLaren was at his best, Mr Spooner scored all round the wicket in fine style. I also managed to get a few.' Then, turning to the scorecard we read: 'MacLaren 86, Spooner 46 and Johnny Tyldesley 186 not out!'

In Lancashire, Johnny is still regarded as one of the greatest batsmen in cricket history. And they have placed George Ernest Tyldesley – Johnny's younger brother – on an equally high pedestal. A master on any kind of wicket, Ernest made batting look easy. A.A. Thomson wrote: 'Like his elder brother J.T., he [Ernest] played every ball on its merits and usually considered its merits to be low. There was a big gap between their ages and style but little to choose their intrinsic merits, for each stood among the highest of his period. J.T. attacked the bowling more fiercely and Ernest calmly composed his innings in classic style.'

Cardus ranked Ernest as 'one of the most accomplished batsmen ever to play for Lancashire'. He added in the *Guardian*: 'Johnny always kept a more than brotherly eye on Ernest but turned the other way when he saw the youngster cross-bat ... Ernest seldom began an innings without one or two anxious or tentative thrusts. Once he had "seen" the ball he could be as brilliant and as punitive as he was defensively sound.'

To follow in the footsteps of a 'genius' brother is always difficult and Ernest had to survive disheartening comparisons. However, the youngster never lost faith in his ability and at the end of their distinguished careers, Ernest had scored

a few more runs than Johnny: 38,874 runs in first-class cricket by Ernest at 45.46 against Johnny's 37,897 at 40.60. Their career records had many other similarities. Both topped 1000 runs in a season 19 times. Johnny exceeded 3000 runs once in 1901, 2000 runs in four seasons. Ernest amassed 3000 runs once in 1928 and 2000 runs in five seasons. Between them, they scored separate centuries in a match on five occasions, J.T. three times.

Once they hit centuries in the same innings, Johnny 210 and Ernest 110. This was the Lancashire vs Surrey game in 1913, remembered for Surrey's Tom Hayward getting his 100th century – the second batsman to do so after W.G. Grace. Ernest became the eighth player to reach his century of centuries in 1934. Johnny hit 86 centuries.

Ernest's most successful season was in 1928, scoring 3024 runs at 79.57. In 1926, he had scored four centuries in successive innings and seven centuries in consecutive matches. Despite his phenomenal achievements in county matches, Ernest was never an automatic choice for England. His era coincided with Frank Woolley's and then Wally Hammond's – each of whom was irreplaceable at No. 3. After scoring 78 not out and 39 against Australia in two Tests in 1921, Ernest was a stranger to the Test scene for five years apart from a solitary appearance against South Africa in 1924.

After scoring 81 against Australia in the Old Trafford Test in 1926, he was once again dropped. His most successful Test series was in South Africa in 1927–28, scoring 520 runs and topping the England averages at 65. All the runs were scored on matting wickets against a competent attack. His scores were 122 (adding 230 runs for the second wicket with Herbert Sutcliffe) at Johannesburg, 0 and 87 at Cape Town, 78 and 62 not out at Durban, 42 and 8 at Johannesburg, and 100 and 21 at Durban.

Ernest played against the West Indies at Lord's in 1928. This was the inaugural Test for the visitors and to Ernest went the honour of scoring the first hundred (122) against a Windies attack. Selected to tour Australia in 1928–29, he played only one Test – at Melbourne – and scored 31 and 21. This was his final Test. 'He received much less than his due from the selectors,' commented John Arlott.

Two years later Johnny died, aged 57. Ernest lived to be 73 years. The question will always be asked: 'Who was the greater?' A.A. Thomson evaluates: 'J.T. would say that Ernest was a better batsman than himself which Ernest would deny without heat, but with firm conviction. Ernest was right, but only just, for the only thing that separated them was that narrow, almost invisible line between the great and the very, very good ... Happy England, Happy Lancashire, to have two such bretheren.'

The Tyldesleys in Test Cricket

	Tests	Runs	HS	Avrge	100s	50s	Catches
Johnny T.	31	1661	138	30.75	4	9	16
G. Ernest	14	990	122	55.00	3	6	2
Total	45	2651	138	36.82	7	15	18

In First-class Cricket

	Span	Runs	HS	Avrge	100s	Runs in a season		
						3000	2000	1000
Johnny T.	1895–1923	37,897	295*	40.60	86	1	4	14
G. Ernest	1909–1936	38,874	256*	45.46	102	1	5	13
Total	1895–1936	76,771	295*	42.96	188	2	9	27

Now to the second Tyldesley family to adorn Lancashire cricket, although not to the same extent as Johnny and Ernest.

J.D. Tyldesley snr was a Westhoughton club professional who taught his four sons how to play cricket.

The eldest son, William Knowles, was a left-handed batsman who represented Lancashire. His career was cruelly cut short as he was killed in 1918 during World War I while a lieutenant in the North Lancashire Regiment. He was only 30. Second brother, James Darbyshire, was tried out as a fast bowler in 1910 but did not become a regular team member until 1913. At that time Lancashire had two pairs of Tyldesley brothers: Johnny and Ernest; William and James.

James was an all-rounder, better recognised as a quick bowler. He performed two hat-tricks for Lancashire, both at Manchester, vs Derbyshire in 1920 and vs Worcestershire in 1922. In the latter match, he had, at one stage, figures of 5 wickets for 9 runs.

His most satisfying match was against Yorkshire at Sheffield in 1914, when he carried his bat for 62 runs and took eight wickets. All his three centuries were for Lancashire at Old Trafford: 101 not out vs Warwickshire in 1912, 112 vs Surrey in 1921 and 112 not out vs Leicestershire in 1922. Sadly, he died the next year when only 33. In September 1923 a match was played between Lancashire and the Bolton League for his family's benefit.

The third brother, Harry, was on the

Lancashire ground staff for many years. He toured Australia and New Zealand under Archie MacLaren in 1922–23. He took 5 for 100 vs South Australia and 5 for 19 in a match in New Zealand. Yet he was not regularly picked for his county and played for several League clubs. He also died young, when 42.

Richard Knowles was the youngest, and the most talented, of the brothers. He was a spinner who used much guile and psychology to grab his wickets. A man of unusual bulk and medium height, Richard looked older than his age. Constant net practice when a boy perfected his length. With experience, he mastered spin and varied pace. He flighted the ball and used top-spinners to gain lbw decisions. His skill as a spinner increased, as did his waistline until he was a heavyweight among county bowlers.

He made his first-class debut in 1919, hit his maiden century in 1922, and established himself the next year when he took 106 wickets at 15.40. That season he was selected to play for the Rest vs England in a Test trial but was not given sufficient overs to prove his skill. In 1924 he played four Tests for England against South Africa. In his Test debut at Lord's he took 3 for 52 and 3 for 50, his best figures in a Test.

In fact, 1924 was a season to remember for Richard. Playing for Lancashire against the touring South Africans he took 7 for 28 and 5 for 50. Against Warwickshire he captured 10 for 103 in the match. He also dismissed five Leicestershire batsmen in five maiden overs – three were clean-bowled. Then against Northamptonshire he took 7 for 6 at Aigburth. With Cecil Parkin, another spinner of note, Richard shot out Yorkshire for 33, his figures being 6 for 18. He was picked to tour Australia in 1924–25 under Arthur Gilligan but the wickets down under did not suit his type of bowling. He played in only one Test and failed.

In 1926, Richard harassed Northants batsmen once again, taking 8 for 15 at Kettering. At Derby in 1929, he took four wickets in four balls, dismissing two batsmen with the last two balls of one innings and two more with his first two deliveries in the second innings.

From 1922 to 1931, Richard took 100 wickets a season. In 1930 he captured 121 at 14.73 and Lancashire became champions for the fourth time in five seasons. After taking 116 wickets at 16 in 1931 he had a disagreement with the Lancashire committee. They could not accede to his request to be paid a fixed salary of £400 a year, whether he played or not, and his association with the county ceased.

His Test career had come to an end a year earlier. He played two Tests in the series against Australia, his last being at Leeds. He troubled Don Bradman in the Trent Bridge Test of 1930. In all he played seven Tests, three vs Australia and four vs South Africa, and took 19 wickets at 32.57.

Richard's benefit match in 1930, when Surrey visited Old Trafford, earned him £2027. However, he could not play in his own benefit as it clashed with the Trent Bridge Test. In all first-class cricket he took 1509 wickets at 17.21 runs apiece and scored 6424 runs, averaging 15.04, with 105 at Old Trafford vs Nottinghamshire in 1922 at his best. He took 328 catches – mostly at short-leg. For Lancashire he took 1449 wickets, a number then exceeded only by John Briggs and Arthur Mold.

A.A. Thomson wrote: 'Richard was one of the true Lancashire characters. Just as [E.A.] McDonald's speed stood for a kind of ruthless destructiveness, so were Richard's methods full of guile. He was like the Pickwickian Fat Boy in two senses; firstly because he was in fact a fat boy of vast rotundity and because he loved to make the batsmen's flesh creep.' Richard would trick the batsmen into

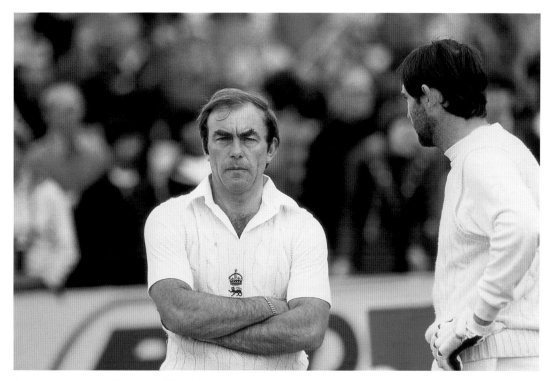

John Edrich, the working bee of English cricket. (*Allsport / Adrian Murrell*)

The voice of cricket and supreme all-rounder – Richie Benaud.
(*Allsport/Adrian Murrell*)

Down but not out, Mohinder Amarnath, the tireless Trojan.
(*Allsport / Adrian Murrell*)

The Chappell trio–Ian, Greg and Trevor. (*World of Cricket*)

Oh what a feeling! Another wicket for Shaun Pollock. (*Allsport/Adrian Murrell*)

Steve Waugh, an astute leader and a straight talker.
(*Ken Hill*)

When Steve Waugh joined Mark in the 1997 Manchester Test, Ben and Adam Hollioake were bowling. All four brothers in this Test were born in Australia. (*Rowley Morris*)

Opposite: Imran Khan lifts the 1992 World Cup at the MCG. (*Allsport*)

thinking that his ball was full of wickedness, venom and peril and may explode in his face. This made the batsmen feel 'as though they were sick of palsy'. According to experts of his time, Richard bowled 'bogus' leg-breaks which did not turn an inch! On a responsive pitch, they did and he was then a menace.

Richard formed a successful spin combination for Lancashire with C.H. Parkin. Both died within three months of each other in 1943. Richard was then 46 years old.

Richard Tyldesley in Test Cricket

Tests	Runs	Avrge	HS	100s	50s	Wkts	Avrge	Best	5w/i	Catches
7	47	7.83	29	0	0	19	32.57	3–50	0	1

CHAPTER 10

The
Hearne Heritage

———— ● ————

Three generations of the Hearne family produced 13 first-class cricketers,
including six Test players. Three brothers and a cousin played
in a single Test in 1891–92. J.T. and J.W. Hearne are recognised
as among the all-time greats of the game.

THE CAPE TOWN TEST of March 1892 between England and South Africa is unique in the annals of Test cricket. Two brothers and a second cousin made their debuts for England – and a third brother represented South Africa. They were George Gibbons (G.G.), Alec and J.T. 'Jack' Hearne for England, and Frank Hearne (the brother of George and Alec) for South Africa. Two years earlier, Frank had represented England against South Africa.

In the Cape Town Test, brothers Frank and Alec opened the batting for their respective countries. Frank top-scored in both innings, with 24 out of 97 and 23 out of 83, and took 2 for 40. For Alec and George, it was a forgettable match. They scored only nine runs between them in what was to be their last Test. But cousin J.W. ('Young Jack') Hearne was more

successful, with 40, his highest Test score. He also added 71 runs with H. Wood, a series record for England for the ninth wicket which still stands. England won by an innings. In his first of 12 Tests, J.T. took 1 for 12. He was recognised as one of the most accurate medium-pacers, with an eye-catching style.

The Hearnes popped in and out of England sides from 1888, when Frank Hearne played his first Test, to 1926 when his second cousin J.W. Hearne played his last. Frank's son, G.A.L. Hearne, also represented South Africa in the 1920s. Like the Graces, Gunns and Edriches of England, the Gregorys, Waughs and Chappells of Australia and the Mohammads of Pakistan, the Hearnes became an institution of family cricket.

Although the three Grace brothers in

1880, and the three Mohammads in 1969, did play together in a Test, the three Hearne brothers had an edge through the presence of a first cousin in that Cape Town Test. And, in quantity of first-class players – 13 including six Test cricketers – the Hearnes reign supreme. Their high quality came through J.T. and J.W. Hearne, among the all-time greats of cricket.

When brothers Thomas (snr) and Joseph Hearne decided to have families in the 1820s, they did not realise the difficult job they would be handing down to a cricket writer 180 years later. The three grandsons of Thomas (snr) played Test cricket, as did a great-grandson. Joseph's grandson, J.T. of Middlesex, became one of the most liked (except by opposing batsmen) cricketers. His graceful run-up and deadly accuracy as a medium-pacer fascinated and delighted critics and spectators from 1888 to 1923.

J.T.'s brothers, Herbert and Walter, represented Kent. Their cousin, J.W. Hearne, was 'one of the classic all-rounders' according to H.S. Altham and E.W. Swanton. Known as 'Young Jack' to distinguish him from J.T., J.W. scored 37,252 runs and took 1839 wickets in first-class cricket despite poor health. He played 24 Tests, scoring a polished century before he was 21.

Thomas (snr), himself a useful county cricketer, had two sons – Thomas, nicknamed 'Old Tom', and George. Both played first-class cricket. Old Tom was considered to be among the best all-rounders of the day and was a backbone of Middlesex for 10 years. He toured Australia in 1861–62. When 40, he averaged 35 with the bat and 13 with the ball. At that age, he scored an unbeaten 120 at Lord's, and 47 and 41 at The Oval to gain selection for Players against Gentlemen. Against Nottinghamshire at Islington, he threw the ball with such

power that he slew a flying pigeon. That pigeon was exhibited in the Jubilee Crystal Palace in 1897.

He was made head of ground staff in 1872, and was affectionately called 'Field Marshal of the Professionals'. A stickler for discipline, he measured the widths of bats of the incoming batsmen, to check that no one was cheating. Cricket today could do with a few Old Toms.

There is a story that Old Tom was watching a Middlesex game in which his nephew J.T. was bowling. J.T. was not well known then, and his medium-pacers looked friendly. Someone asked him whether J.T. was related to him and he replied, 'No, definitely no relation'. Later in the day, J.T. became unplayable and Old Tom was seen walking around the spectators saying, 'Did you see that relative of mine bowl? I just remembered, he's a close cousin!'

Denzil Batchelor, the well-known cricket writer, told this story in his *Book of Cricket* (1952), but adapted it to the better-known Hearnes, J.T. and J.W. I have this on the authority of the respected English cricket statistician and historian, Robert Brooke.

Old Tom had two cricket-playing sons, Thomas Arthur, a useful cricketer who did not play any first-class matches, and George Francis, who played for a number of years as an all-rounder, including one first-class match, against Nottinghamshire in 1876. In that match, George scored a duck and did not bowl. He served the MCC as a pavilion clerk at Lord's for almost 50 years.

G.F. Hearne's son, Thomas John, was a left-arm bowler. His one moment of glory was when he represented Middlesex against the visiting Philadelphians in 1908. He was included in the team as a late substitute for his celebrated cousin, J.T. However, he arrived late and did not bat or bowl. He never got another chance.

Old Tom's brother, George, was a

right-hand bat. He was associated with the cricketing clan of Walkers and played for Middlesex between 1861 and 1868. George had three sons who played in the Cape Town Test of 1892. They represented Kent with distinction, the middle brother, Frank, subsequently migrated to South Africa.

George Gibbons (G.G.), the eldest brother, was a left-arm batsman and, early in his career, an impressive left-arm medium-pacer. He scored 6475 runs for Kent, with three centuries, and took 503 wickets at 16.80. His initials, 'G.G', caused a barracker to comment: 'Do the Gee-gee initials have any relationship to the white horse of Kent emblazoned on the players' caps?'

Frank Hearne played two Tests for England against South Africa, and four for South Africa against his motherland. Short (165 centimetres), he was a batsman with sound defence and fine off-side strokes. He was a right-hand round-arm bowler and a brilliant cover point. He played for Kent from 1879 to 1889 and scored 3426 runs and took 41 wickets. His highest score was 144 for Kent against Yorkshire in 1887.

After touring South Africa with Major R.G. Wharton's team in 1888–89, he decided to settle there. In 1894 he was a member of the first South African team to visit England, and the following year he played three Tests for his adopted country. His finest performances were in England before he migrated. According to *Wisden* (1950), his best batting was his 111 for South of England against the Australians in 1886. That same season, Frank (142) and brother G.G. (126) added 226 for the second wicket, for Kent against Middlesex at Gravesend.

The three brothers figured in Kent's great victory over the Australians at Canterbury in 1884 – the only county to defeat the tourists that season. Opening the batting in the second innings, Frank made the second-highest score of 45. The youngest brother, Alec, took 5 for 36 and 2 for 30.

Frank maintained his interest in cricket throughout his life and watched the Cape Town Test against England in 1949, a few months before his death at 90.

Alec was a reliable batsman and an intelligent leg-spinner. Later on, he became an off-spinner because of a strained elbow. According to *Wisden* (1953), 'Alec was one of the best cricketers who never played for England [against Australia]'. Besides his 7 for 66 in the match against the 1884 Australians, he again contributed to a victory by Kent over the 1893 Australians by taking eight wickets. That season, he averaged 38 with the bat against the Australians, his highest score being 120 for the South of England at The Oval. He also took 17 wickets at an average of 18.

In 1899, Alec hit another century (168) for W.G. Grace's XI against the Australians at the Crystal Palace. He was a constant thorn in the Yorkshire flesh, once taking 13 wickets in a match. For 23 years he was a skilful run-getter for Kent, scoring 16,346 runs at 21.65 and taking 1160 wickets at 19 in all first-class matches.

Among his big scores was 162 not out against Nottinghamshire in 1899 when he added 351 with J.R. Mason for the third wicket – a Kent record which stood for 35 years. Alec also hit 155 against Gloucestershire in 1895, 154 not out against Worcestershire in 1906 and an unbeaten 152 against Essex in 1901.

His remarkable bowling figures included 5 for 15 against Hampshire; 4 for 0 against Somerset; 5 for 13 against Warwickshire; 8 for 36 against Middlesex at Lord's; and 4 for 10 and 8 for 15 against Gloucestershire in separate matches. Twice he performed the hat-trick – for the MCC against Yorkshire at Lord's in 1888 and for Kent against Gloucestershire at Clifton in 1900. 'Like all the other Hearnes, Alec was quiet of speech and manner, modest and an excellent judge of cricket,' wrote *Wisden*.

Frank took his son George Alfred Lawrence (G.A.L.) Hearne to South Africa at an early age. A good batsman, change bowler and an occasional wicket-keeper, G.A.L. represented Western Province and toured England with the 1924 South African team. He played three Tests for the Springboks, but without success. In his second Test, at Cape Town in 1923, he opened the batting and bagged a pair. This was the memorable thrill-a-minute Test which England won by one wicket. He died in November 1978, aged 90. He had retained his interest in cricket until the last.

Now to the Joseph Hearne side of the family. Joseph's son William was a useful cricketer for Buckinghamshire. William's three sons played first-class cricket; Herbert and Walter for Kent, and the famous J.T. for Middlesex and England.

Herbert is best remembered as a fast round-arm bowler who took 57 wickets for Kent at 24.84. Tall (183 centimetres) and strongly built, he was badly injured and retired when only 24. He became a coach and a carpenter but died when 44, a rare occurrence for the long-living Hearnes.

Walter's promising career was cut short by a knee injury. In 60 matches for Kent he took nearly 300 wickets. But for his injury, Walter would have played as long for Kent as J.T. did for Middlesex. Like J.T., he was a medium-pacer who could spin, and was accurate in line and length. Walter's best match was against Lancashire in 1893 when he took 15 for 119. In the next season he performed the hat-trick against them. He was at his peak in 1894 as he took 116 wickets at 13.34. In three successive matches in July he bagged 13 for 61 against Gloucestershire, 12 for 72 against Nottinghamshire and 13 for 98

against Surrey. However, the next season Walter's knee gave way so badly that he could not play. Finally, he broke down in 1896, in the match against Yorkshire at Leeds. He became the scorer for Kent, a position he held until he died in 1925, aged 61.

The fame of the Hearnes was established, however, by their two immortal Johns – 'Old Jack' (J.T.) and 'Young Jack' (J.W.).

John Thomas (J.T.) Hearne was one of the greatest medium-pacers the game has known. His aggregate of 3061 wickets in first-class cricket has been exceeded only by Wilfred Rhodes, Tich Freeman and Charlie Parker. He claimed four hat-tricks and took five wickets in an innings 255 times, but saved his best for Australia. In the Leeds Test of 1899 he performed the greatest ever hat-trick. In successive balls, he dismissed world-renowned batsmen Clem Hill, Syd Gregory and Monty Noble – all for ducks. He had also dismissed Gregory for a duck in the first innings.

J.T.'s most successful season was in 1896 when he took 257 wickets at 14.28. Against Harry Trott's Australians that season he collected 56 wickets. At Lord's, the Australians were dismissed for 18 against MCC, J.T. taking 4 for 4 and A.D. Pougher 5 for 0. In the second innings, J.T. took all nine wickets to fall – George Giffen did not bat – for 73, as the Australians scored 183 and lost by an innings. His match figures were 61.3 overs, 31 maidens, 13 wickets for 77 runs. He was equally devastating when playing for South of England, his figures: 17–13–8–6. In The Oval Test that season he took 6 for 41 and 4 for 19 and claimed 15 wickets in the series at 14.1.

The circumstances under which J.T. became a regular Middlesex player were dramatic. As he was coaching schoolboys in June 1890, he received a telegram asking him to play for Middlesex that very day. He dashed to the station and found from a newspaper that Middlesex was playing at Nottinghamshire. 'When I arrived at Lord's just before lunch-time, I saw 99 for none on the board. Not until reaching the dressing-room did I learn that my side was batting,' J.T. recalled. If Nottinghamshire had been batting, he would have been left out.

When he got a chance to bowl, he created a tremendous impression. The great Arthur Shrewsbury of Notts and England told him: 'If you bowl like that, you will get someone else out tomorrow'. He did, taking 6 for 62. Next season at Lord's he took 14 Yorkshire wickets for less than five runs apiece. In 14 matches he captured 118 wickets at an average of 10, topping the first-class bowling averages. As previously mentioned, J.T. made his Test debut in the Cape Town Test of 1891–92, along with his cousins, Alec and G.G. Hearne. On that tour, he took 63 wickets at less than seven runs a wicket.

J.T. toured Australia in 1897–98 and in the first Test at Sydney took 5 for 42 and 4 for 99. This was the only Test England won in the series. In the Melbourne Test he again worried the best of Australian batsmen, capturing 6 for 98. He continued playing until 1923 and took 6 for 64 against Scotland when 56. In a long and outstanding career, J.T. took 3061 wickets at 17.75. He captured 100 wickets in a season 15 times, including 200 wickets three times. He also scored 7137 runs at 11.04 and took 421 catches.

He will be remembered for his bowling. He had a graceful run-up, a swinging rhythmical action, superb length and a quick break-back. Like Hugh Trumble of Australia, he believed in change of pace. On crumbling pitches, he was unplayable. Here are some of the tributes he earned. *Wisden* (1945): 'It would be difficult to recall a bowler with a more beautiful delivery, made as his

left hand pointed down the pitch'. The editor of *Lillywhite* (1898): 'J.T. Hearne stands out as incomparably the best bowler of the year'. Sir Pelham Warner: 'J.T. may be taken as the beau-ideal of a medium-paced right-arm bowler'. Patsy Hendren in *Wisden*(1938): 'I cannot fail to mention J.T. Hearne, my great hero on and off the field. He was a very dear man and an outstanding example to young cricketers. I have never seen a bowler with prettier action.'

It is a mystery why J.T. was selected in only 12 Tests. More baffling is why he was picked only once after the Leeds Test of 1899 in which he dismissed the combined genius of Hill, Syd Gregory and Noble in the shortest possible time – three balls. After retirement, J.T. coached at Oxford University and endeared himself to the students. He also coached in India for the Maharajah of Patiala. In 1920 he was elected a member of the Middlesex County Club, then a rare honour for a professional.

In 1909, J.T. was joined by his cousin John William (J.W.) in the Middlesex team. To differentiate them, the newcomer was called 'Young Jack'. Before he retired from the first-class scene in 1936, Young Jack was known as one of England's best all-rounders. His cool temperament, impeccable style, sound defence and artistry in placing the ball brought him most of his 37,252 runs for Middlesex and England at an average of almost 41. A safe and attractive cutter, he was a master of on-side strokes. Of his 96 centuries, 11 were double hundreds and his highest score was 285 not out. He scored 1000 runs in an English season 19 times, including over 2000 runs four times.

J.W. was also a skilful leg-break and googly bowler, using the shortest of run-ups. Not consistently effective as a googly bowler, he was difficult to play when at his best. He took 1839 wickets at

24.42, held 349 catches, and completed the double of 1000 runs and 100 wickets five times. His best seasons were 1913 and 1914. In 1913, he scored 2036 runs and took 124 wickets. The following season, he made 2116 runs and took 123 wickets but his progress was interrupted by World War I.

His name is usually associated with that of the great Patsy Hendren. The best of friends, they devastated Hampshire's attack twice, putting on 325 runs at Lord's in 1919 and improving upon it in 1923 with 375 runs. Although Hendren is the better known, J.W. Hearne had his supporters. Wrote H.S. Altham and E.W. Swanton in *History of Cricket*: 'In grace of execution, Hendren's homely figure could not quite match the elegance of [J.W.] Hearne'. Patrick Morrah opined in *The Golden Age of Cricket*: 'J.W. appeared the better cricketer [than Hendren] ... '

Young Jack is remembered as one of the neatest cricketers who ever appeared on the field. He was not a fast scorer but his batting was the essence of tidiness. His action in his slow spin bowling was as easy and elegant as could be imagined. In appearance he was cool and cultured, in his dress, immaculate.

In 1910, J.W. took seven wickets for two runs in 5.1 overs against Essex at Lord's. In 1911, he scored an unbeaten, faultless 234 runs against Somerset, and against Essex he took 6 for 17 including a hat-trick. Watching his style and temperament, Pelham Warner pressed for his inclusion in England's team to Australia in 1911–12 and J.W. did not let his mentor down. After scoring 76 and 43 in his Test debut at Sydney, he made a polished 114 in the second Test in Melbourne, adding 127 runs with Wilfred Rhodes for the second wicket. Against Tasmania, he put on 264 runs with Frank Woolley.

In all, he played 24 Tests, scoring 806 runs at 26 and taking 30 wickets at 48.73. But, apart from his first two Tests, he did not live up to his reputation in the Test arena. In the Sydney Test of 1920–21 he scored 14 and 57. His best bowling in a Test was against South Africa at Johannesburg in 1914 when he took 5 for 49.

Ill health, rather than opposing players, prevented J.W. from reaching greater heights. He reached his peak in 1914. Against Essex, J.W. (106 not out) added 229 runs with Frank Tarrant (250 not out) as Middlesex reached 1 for 464 after being sent in to bat. To rub in the Essex captain's folly, J.W. took 7 for 54 and 7 for 92. A fortnight later, Tarrant (198) and J.W. (204) were together again, adding 380 for the second wicket. To keep up the good work, J.W. hit an unbeaten 191 against Surrey.

In his benefit match in 1925, J.W. scored 117 despite poor health. Against Yorkshire that year, Middlesex was in trouble being 420 in arrears. However, he led a rescue action, scoring 91 in three and a half hours. Then, against Nottinghamshire, he scored 51 and took 10 wickets in the match.

Against the West Indian tourists of 1928, J.W. showed that he could attack. Whereas his team-mates crawled against the pace of Learie Constantine, J.W. and Nigel Haig added 153 runs in two hours. However, this match was the beginning of the end for J.W. Hearne. He was badly injured while catching Constantine and was out for the season. Middlesex felt his absence. In eight matches that season, he had scored 682 runs (avrge 76) and taken 24 wickets.

According to Altham and Swanton: '[J.W.] Hearne goes down in history as one of the classic all-rounders. One may well pause to consider what more he might have achieved but for the perpetual and wearing struggle against illness.' In 1949, the MCC honoured the well-liked J.W. with life membership.

The Hearnes are known as much for their longevity as for their popularity and cricketing proficiency and the Hearne XIs were always a hard side to beat. 'I cannot speak too highly of every one of them,' was Lord Hawke's tribute to the magnificent cricketing clan.

The Hearne Family Tree

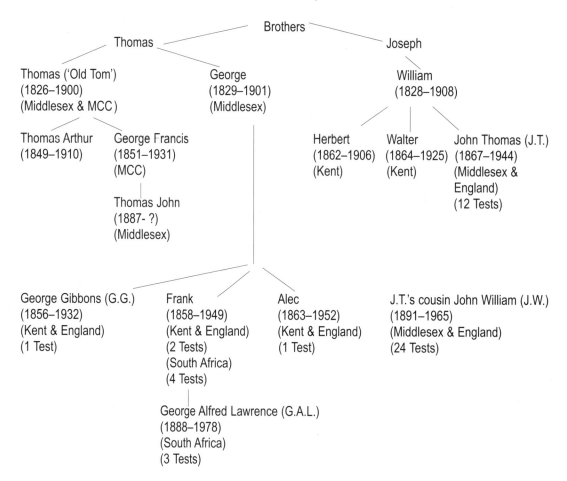

The Hearnes in Test Cricket

	Tests	Runs	Avrge	HS	100s	50s	Wkts	Avrge	Best	5w/i	Catches
George Gibbons (Eng.)	1	0	0	0	0	0	0	–	–	–	0
Frank (Eng. & SAf.)	6	168	16.80	30	0	0	2	20.00	2–40	0	3
Alec (Eng.)	1	9	9.00	9	0	0	0	–	–	–	1
John T. (Eng.)	12	126	9.00	40	0	0	49	22.08	6–41	4	4
George A.L. (SAf.)	3	59	11.80	28	0	0	0	–	–	–	3
John W. (Eng.)	24	806	26.00	114	1	2	30	48.73	5–49	1	13
Total	47	1168	18.84	114	1	2	81	31.90	6–41	5	24

CHAPTER 11

The Princely Clan
of Ranji and Duleep

———●———

If the word genius can be used in cricket, it applies to Ranji
and Duleep. They converted cricket into an art form,
introducing graceful strokes to the game.

IN AUGUST 1896, A slim, dark, elegant batsman hit two separate centuries *on the same day* – 100 and 125 not out – for Sussex against the champion county, Yorkshire. The author of this unique feat was Prince Ranjitsinhji, later to become H.H. the Jam Sahib of Nawanagar but affectionately remembered in the cricket world as Ranji.

Ranji is as much a cricket immortal as are Dr W.G. Grace, Victor Trumper, Sir Donald Bradman and Sir Jack Hobbs. He revolutionised batting with a style all his own and made it look easy. He broke many batting records but, more importantly, he charmed spectators with what many called his 'oriental magic'. As India did not play Test cricket until 1932, Ranji played all his Tests for England and he made his Test debut against Australia memorable by hitting a century. He passed on all he knew to his nephew, the talented Prince Duleepsinhji – known in the cricket world as Duleep and by his friends at Cambridge and Sussex as 'Tulip' and 'Mr Smith'.

Duleep also played Test cricket for England, and like Uncle Ranji he hit a magnificent century in his first Test against Australia. Had he not suffered from tuberculosis, which cut short his cricket career at the age of 27 when in peak form, Duleep would no doubt have been recognised as among the all-time great players. His nephew, Indrajitsinhji, kept wickets for India in the 1960s and toured Australia in 1967–68. His performances were ordinary compared to those of his illustrious ancestors, but in October 1964 he contributed as a batsman to India's two-wicket win over Australia in a Test in Bombay.

The great Ranji was born on 10 September 1872 in a village near

Jamnagar in western India. He learned the rudiments of cricket in India, but perfected his game at Cambridge University. In his first two years he failed to make the Cambridge side but practised very hard at the nets, where he sought out the most hostile bowlers. Later, as encouragement for them, he balanced sovereigns on the bails.

Gradually, young Ranji perfected the art of deflecting balls off the middle stump. The purists were horrified but he made the bowlers look silly by twisting his body, flicking his wrists at the moment of impact, and steering the ball to the leg side. This was the birth of a new stroke – the leg glide. He also inspired the expression 'flicking fours off the eyebrows' by standing his ground against bumpers and hooking them.

Ranji's debuts – both in county and Test cricket – were spectacular. In his first match for Sussex, against MCC at Lord's in 1895, he scored 77 not out and 150, 'playing an innings which beggars description' according to a press clipping. When Australia toured England the following year Ranji was kept out of the first Test as he was not English-born. The Lancashire selectors, however, insisted on picking him for the second Test at Old Trafford, with the consent of the sporting Australian team. And what a debut it was!

Ranji made 62 in England's first-innings total of 231, in reply to Australia's 412. Following on, England lost W.G. Grace, Andrew Stoddart, Robert Abel and Stanley Jackson while still 72 runs in arrears. Ranji, 41 not out overnight, played with dazzling brilliance to become the first player in Test history to score a century before lunch – on the third and final day of the Test. While none of his colleagues made more than 41, Ranji took the total to 305 and remained unbeaten with 154 in 190 minutes.

The victorious Australians were full

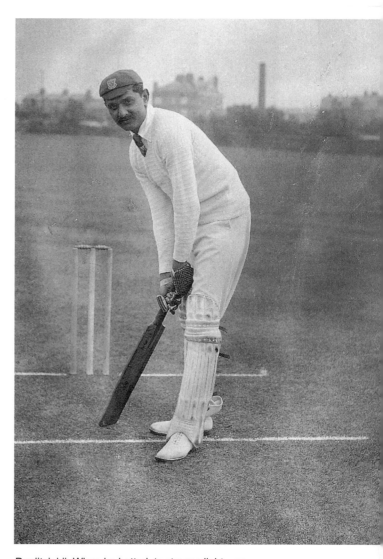

Ranjitsinhji. When he batted, 'a strange light was seen for the first time on English fields' – Neville Cardus (© *R.L. Cardwell*)

of praise for him. The veteran all-rounder, George Giffen, said: 'The Prince's 154 was absolutely the finest innings I have seen ... I have never seen anything to equal it. But then, Ranji is the batting wonder of the age.' The great Clem Hill was moved to exclaim: 'He is more than a batsman – he is nothing less than a juggler'. Soon after this juggling act, Ranji hit separate hundreds against Yorkshire on 22 August. Having scored 165 against Lancashire in the previous match, he had now scored three successive hundreds in four days against the two strongest counties of the day.

In the traditional Gentlemen vs Players match at Lord's shortly afterwards, Ranji belted 47 runs in 10 minutes off 12 balls, hitting 11 fours and one three, and was out lbw off the 13th ball. Honouring him as one of the Five Cricketers of the Year 1896, *Wisden* wrote: 'If the word genius can be employed in connection to cricket, it surely applies to the young Indian's batting'.

In 1897, Ranji scored the first of his 14 double-centuries in first-class cricket, 260 vs MCC at Lord's. When picked for the 1897–98 tour of Australia, the Aussies were so delighted they passed a special law in the Senate to excuse him from paying £1000 to enter the country. He opened the tour with 189 at Adelaide against South Australia, but his immense popularity was given a setback when he mentioned that speedster Ernest Jones was chucking the ball.

Before the first Test in Sydney, Ranji was ill with severe tonsillitis and asked to be dropped. Scribes maliciously suggested that he was scared of Jones and this made the normally placid, good-humoured Indian so wild he decided to defy medical advice and play. Going in at No. 7, he batted magnificently for 215 minutes to score 175 – and he was especially severe on Jones. Once again, he became the idol of Australians. They visited 'Ranji' bars, struck 'Ranji' matches, ate 'Ranji' sandwiches, and used 'Ranji' bats, chairs, ... even hair-restorers.

He regarded as his finest innings a dour 93 not out in the Trent Bridge Test of 1899 against Australia, in which he helped England to a draw against all odds.

Generous and modest, Ranji made friends as easily as runs. His fielding was razor-sharp, but not more so than his sense of humour. In a match against Yorkshire, a batsman drove a ball fiercely into the deep. Skipper F.S. Jackson shouted to Ranji: 'Run after it. What are you standing there for?' In reply, Ranji produced the ball from his pocket. He had caught and pocketed it faster than the eye could follow. His batting records were so impressive that *Punch* magazine nicknamed him 'Run-get-sinhji'.

Ranji played 500 innings to score 24,692 runs, averaging 56.37 and hitting 72 hundreds. His highest score was 285 not out vs Somerset in 1901 after fishing the whole of the previous night and not sleeping a wink. He was also the first batsman to score 3000 runs in a season. That was in 1899, and he repeated this feat in 1900. However, statistics alone do not reveal the entire story. They do not tell us that he suffered from asthma which left him awake most nights. They do not tell that he scored at a dizzy rate of 55 runs an hour, nor do they tell of his disbelief in amassing runs merely to break or create a record.

Ranji played his last innings in England in 1920, 13 years before he died. By that time he had lost an eye in a hunting accident, but never revealed the identity of the person responsible. He scored only 16 runs in that final innings, but provided for the generation a rare, thrilling moment, for they could tell their grandchildren: 'I saw Ranji bat – the Ranji of supple wrists, silk shirt, and genial ways'.

Ranjitsinhji died on 2 April 1933, aged 60. To perpetuate his memory, the Ranji Trophy for the National Championship of India was inaugurated the following year. Neville Cardus was inspired to write of him: 'When Ranji batted, a strange light was seen for the first time on English fields ... When Ranji passed out of cricket, a wonder and a glory departed forever. It is not in nature that there should be another Ranji. We who had the good luck to see Ranji, let us be grateful. Did he really happen? Or was he perhaps a dream all dreamed on some mid-summer's night, long ago?'

Ranji's nephew – the tall, stately Prince Duleepsinhji – was not far behind his uncle in grace, style, timing and run-making ability. A.G. Moyes, the perceptive Australian writer and commentator, wrote: 'One of the most accomplished batsmen and most perfect gentlemen I have known is Duleepsinhji who packed into a few short years a superlative record of achievement ... Duleepsinhji was an artist.'

He was modest by nature – and a perfectionist. Nothing but the best would do for him, and his ideal was Uncle Ranji. For Duleep, when Uncle spoke, let all others hold their peace. The year 1930 belonged as much to Duleep as to Don Bradman. That year, Duleep, 25, scored two centuries in a match twice – 116 and 102 not out for Sussex vs Middlesex, and 125 and 103 not out for Gentleman vs Players. Then he scored 333 runs in one day (one six, 34 fours), against Northamptonshire at Hove. He crowned that season with an innings to remember against Australia in the Lord's Test. This was his first Test against Australia and, like Uncle Ranji, he hit an incandescent century.

By 1932, it was all over. Tuberculosis, which had dogged his career, finally brought down the curtains when he was only 27, at the peak of his form, on the verge of leading Sussex to a rare Championship win, and already selected to tour Australia with Jardine's team. Duleep played in only 12 Tests. He hit three centuries and five fifties and averaged 58.53.

When tuberculosis forced his retirement, Duleep had played three fewer Tests than Ranji – but had scored more runs and at a higher average. But aggregates and averages appear out of place with Ranji and Duleep. Even today, Duleep's is a legendary name – especially in Sussex. Known as 'India's Frank Woolley', Duleep was a brilliant stroke-player, a touch artist with wiry wrists and swift footwork. As a slip fielder, he was as agile as Wally Hammond.

According to some critics, Duleep was the best amateur cricketer in England between the two World Wars. He could have reached the heights of Hammond and Len Hutton had illness not so tragically cut short his career.

Under Ranji's supervision, Duleep received the best cricket education. First, lessons at Cheltenham, where he scored a century for Lord's school, and then coaching by W.A. Woolfe and the South African great, Aubrey Faulkner.

After scoring 254 against Middlesex in 1927, Duleep, then only 22, was moved to Edinburgh Hospital the same night and subsequently had to spend a year in a sanatorium in Switzerland before he recovered. He came back to cricket and gained international recognition. After making his Test debut against South Africa in 1929 – perhaps the first non-white to play against the Springboks – he hit a century against New Zealand in 1929–30.

Duleep's proudest moment was at Lord's in 1930, in his first Test appearance against Australia. Batting at No. 4, after Hobbs, Sutcliffe and Hammond, he scored a majestic, thunder-stealing 173 in less than five hours before he threw away his wicket. When he returned to the pavilion amid deafening applause he was scolded by Ranji for playing that one careless shot!

The bowler who had suffered most was the great leg-spinner, Clarrie Grimmett.

In his shortened first-class career of eight years, he made 15,485 runs in 333 innings with a highest score of 333, averaged 50 runs an innings, and hit 50 hundreds. He topped 1000 runs in seven seasons, scoring over 2500 runs in 1929, 1930 and 1931.

After his enforced retirement, Duleep stayed in the game as an astute administrator in Indian cricket and acted as a cricket expert during Test match radio commentaries until 1958. He was appointed India's High Commissioner for

Australia – an office he held with grace and dignity. In 1947–48, Duleep toured Australia with the Indian cricket team as a press correspondent, impressing the Australians with his wit, knowledge and charm. However, his helpful hints to the Indian captain, Lala Amarnath, were not appreciated and he felt like an outsider among his own countrymen. Duleep died in December 1959, aged 54. To honour his name, the Duleep Trophy between the five zones of India was instituted in 1961–62.

Duleep's cousin, Prince Ranvirsinhji, toured Australia with the Indians in 1947–48 but was not selected in any of the Tests. And his nephew, Indrajitsinhji, kept wickets for India – three times against Australia in 1964–65 and once against New Zealand in 1969.

It is difficult to step into illustrious shoes such as those of Indrajit's uncle and grand-uncle. The modest Indrajit had no pretensions to greatness. He was a capable but not brilliant wicket-keeper and an average batsman just above the tail-enders class, although he opened India's innings in two Tests. His Ranji Trophy record was adequate: 2124 runs at 27.58 with 124 as his highest score, and 102 dismissals (67 caught and 35

stumped). He is among the three Indian wicket-keepers to have taken nine victims in a Ranji Trophy match (for Saurashtra vs Maharashtra in 1965).

Indrajit toured Australia and New Zealand under Nawab of Pataudi jnr in 1967–68 as a reserve wicket-keeper, but with Farokh Engineer in form he was not selected in any of the Tests.

In four Tests in India, he took six catches and effected three stumpings, but his big moment in Test cricket came as a batsman. In the Bombay Test of October 1964, against Australia under Bob Simpson, India needed 254 runs to win. With the score on 8 for 224, in came Indrajit, injured on the jaw and heavily doped with painkillers, but ready for the battle. Chandu Borde was in scintillating form, but he needed someone to hold one end up. And Indrajit did just that. He remained unbeaten and had scored three runs when Borde made the winning hit. But for Indrajit's support, India could have lost this cliffhanger of a Test.

Ranji, who had chided Duleep for throwing away his wicket after that glorious 173 at Lord's, would have been proud of Indrajit's undefeated and gutsy innings of three not out.

Ranjitsinhji and Duleepsinhji in Test Cricket										
	Tests	Runs	Avrge	HS	100s	50s	Wkts	Avrge	Catches	Stumpings
K.S. Ranjitsinhji (England)	15	989	44.95	175	2	6	1	39.00	13	–
K.S. Duleepsinhji (England)	12	995	58.53	173	3	5	0	–	10	–
K.S. Indrajitsinhji (India)	4	51	8.50	23	0	0	0	–	6	3
Total	31	2035	45.22	175	5	11	1	46.00	29	3

CHAPTER 12

The Gunns
of Nottingham

———— ● ————

William Gunn, his nephews John and George and the latter's son George jnr, were to Nottinghamshire cricket what Robin Hood and Little John were to Sherwood Forest. Three generations of Gunns played for Nottingham from 1880 to 1939. Three members of the family represented England – all making their Test debut at Sydney – and for George it was a debut to remember. The Gunns provide the only instance of both father and son scoring a century in the same innings of a first-class match.

THE GUNNS OF NOTTINGHAM have by now become a part of cricket history. Between them, the four accumulated 95,559 runs in first-class cricket, including 161 first-class hundreds. However, it is George Gunn (1879–1958) whose name crops up most frequently during cricket discussions, for there seldom was a cricketer more contrary, more baffling, or more endearing than good old George.

He was a supreme individualist, a batting genius with an impish streak. When in the mood, he could murder any bowling by jumping down the pitch to drive the fastest or the curviest of bowlers with wristy ease. However, he often preferred to push and prod even a mediocre attack. To quote Sir Neville Cardus: 'He would suddenly change mood and gear, and indulge in stone-walling, obviously at his own whim'.

Many stories have been told of this unique cricketer. Bert Oldfield remembered how George, in the 1920s, punished the dreaded Australian fast bowler Jack Gregory, cheekily converting Gregory's good-length express in-swingers into half volleys by dancing down the pitch. When he had scored 130-odd runs at a breakneck speed, he asked the umpire the time. On being told it was 1.05, he said: 'Goom, it's my loonch-time. I'm going to get oot now.' And he did just that, adding as he went, 'Eee, it's too hot in here, laads.'

Against Yorkshire, he scored 132 runs in about six hours, prompting his opponents to taunt: 'Has lost thy strokes, George?' He merely grunted: 'Next innings I'll show you some'. Sure enough, in the second innings he plundered 109 not out in 85 minutes out of Notts' score of 3 for 129, before rain stopped play. 'I decided to play swashbuckle, just to show them,' he explained.

Not only did he defend grimly without any reason, he also often swashbuckled without logic. In a match in 1928, when Notts needed 157 to win in ample time, he belted the attack to score 100 in 90 minutes and the match came to an abrupt, anti-climactic end. Apparently a spectator had annoyed him, 'so I went and took it out of Kent bowlin'', he told Cardus. The following season, he batted for 5 hours and 20 minutes to score 58. Although he was certainly contrary, it did seem, nevertheless, that paradoxical things happened to him. For instance, when in Australia for health reasons he was invited to play in a Test ... and scored a century on debut.

The scorer of two Test hundreds – both on the Sydney Cricket Ground – George was picked to play Test cricket in England only once, although he played county cricket for 30 years from 1902 to 1932 with enormous success. Perhaps his irreverent streak did not appeal to officialdom. It is generally believed that George was invited to tour South Africa in 1909–10, but missed out on the tour because he put the letter of invitation in his pocket and forgot to open it until after the team had sailed.

His habit of playing over-defensively despite possessing brilliant strokes could have been a legacy from his famous uncle, William Gunn. The names of William Gunn and Arthur Shrewsbury are closely linked. They constituted one of the great opening partnerships which were heartbreaking to bowlers. William was tall (190 centimetres) and well built. With his great reach and strong wrists, he could play attractively and gracefully

whenever he chose but he frequently played a painfully slow game.

'Why should such a reach and such a wrist be given to a man who makes so little use of them?' wondered the Hon. R.H. Lyttelton. It is possible that as Notts was weak in batting he and Shrewsbury had to defend to avoid defeat. But when they played for Players vs Gentlemen, they showed their natural attacking game.

Famous as a batsman and an out-field with a powerful return, William was ranked by Lyttelton as one of the three best among contemporary players in England. Unfortunately, he was not always in good health. He first played for Notts in 1880, when 22, and although he did not achieve much 'it was evident from the outset that a batsman of more than ordinary promise had been discovered', to quote *Wisden*.

The season of 1889 was an outstanding one for William. *Wisden* wrote: 'No batsman of the same height has ever played a more elegant and perfect form. Certainly we know no professional at the present day whom it is a greater pleasure to watch ... It is the general opinion of practical cricketers that in the long field and at third man he has never had a superior.'

William was a member of the Alfred Shaw and Shrewsbury team to Australia in 1886–87 and, on the tour, averaged about 20. He made an unimpressive Test debut at Sydney, scoring 0 and 4. On the whole, it was a disappointing tour for him, and his moment of glory came in an unimportant friendly match between Smokers and Non-Smokers, played at East Melbourne. English and Australian cricketers played together on both sides, and the Non-Smokers amassed 803, of which William contributed 150.

William's best innings were against Sussex. In 1890, with Shrewsbury, he added 398 runs at Trent Bridge, and in

1895 he played a great innings of 219. Against the touring Australians in 1888, William scored a majestic 228 in 570 minutes for Notts, playing with confidence the deadly duo of Charlie Turner and John Ferris who were then in their prime. On this occasion the pitch was not an easy one, for the Aussies were dismissed for 156 and 107. However, William's most celebrated innings was against Surrey, at Trent Bridge, when he tamed the great Tom Richardson who was at his peak as a fast bowler.

In Test cricket, William never really established himself. From 1886 to 1893 he was a big disappointment. Only in the 1893 series against Australia, when he was 35, did he come to terms with himself. Batting at No. 3, he added 152 runs for the second wicket with Shrewsbury. In the third Test of the series, at Old Trafford, William scored his only Test century – 102 not out, out of a total of 243. The next highest scorer was W.G. Grace with 40. On 18 July 1898 – W.G. Grace's 50th birthday – William scored 139 out of Players' total of 335 against Gentlemen.

In 1896, a crisis arose in English cricket in the form of a strike by five leading players over the issue of professional cricketers' pay. It came just before the Oval Test against Australia and the players involved were William Gunn, George Lohmann, Bobby Abel, Tom Richardson and Tom Hayward. They demanded a Test-match fee of 20 shillings for the final Test instead of the existing fee of 10 shillings. Others withdrew before the Test, but Lohmann and William stood their ground. William played only one more Test, against Australia in 1899, on his home ground at Trent Bridge.

For several years he was one of the most brilliant forwards in the country at Association football, but he gave it up to concentrate on cricket. He subsequently became a partner in a cricket outfitter's business in Nottinghamshire and died at the age of 63.

William's highest score of 273, against Derbyshire, remained a record for Notts until eclipsed by his nephew, John Gunn, who scored 294 against Leicestershire. This record existed for only a short time as the Notts skipper, A.O. Jones, hit 296 against Gloucestershire two months later.

From 1902 to 1904 the three Gunns – William, and his nephews John and George – played for Notts. William played his last Test in 1899, John his first in 1901–02. John Richmond Gunn was different from both his uncle and his younger brother, being a left-handed all-rounder who did not develop overnight, but by 1903 he had reached his peak in batting, bowling and fielding. Observed *Wisden* in 1904: 'During the past summer, John Gunn as an all-round cricketer had no superior in England, except George Hirst'.

That season he scored 1665 runs in first-class matches, averaging 42, and took 118 wickets at an average of 19. He was to perform the double of 1000 runs and 100 wickets in a season four times. It was also in 1903 that he scored 294 vs Leicestershire, breaking his uncle's record. As a bowler, he took 28 wickets in two games: 14 vs Surrey at The Oval, and 14 vs Essex at Leyton. As a batsman, he started by being stodgy and orthodox, but later in his career became more attacking. When young, he was a medium-pacer but subsequently became a slow bowler. Always accurate, John sent down very few bad balls.

As an all-rounder, he belongs to the exclusive club of players who have scored over 20,000 runs and taken over 1000 wickets, his tally being 24,557 runs and 1242 wickets. As a fielder, he was among the best cover points in England and, according to one of his contemporaries, 'no one except Jessop had a more deadly throw to the wicket'. John toured Australia with Archie MacLaren's team in 1901–02 and played in all five Tests. He made his Test debut – as per the family tradition – on the SCG. Apart from the Adelaide Test in which he captured 5 for 76 and 3 for 38, he was a failure in the series.

In 1913, John and his younger brother, George, were Notts' leading players. Although John scored 1397 at 46.56, he was overshadowed by George. The brothers continued playing first-class cricket until well past 50 years in age.

George Gunn was one of the immortals of the game. Shortish but well built, he batted as if facing fast bowlers on treacherous pitches were one of the joys of life. According to Patrick Morrah in *The Golden Age of Cricket*: '… not even Hobbs could make bowling look so simple on difficult wickets'. By 1906, he looked a certain Test cap, but a lung haemorrhage interrupted his progress. A winter in New Zealand helped him to recover and he played a big role in Notts' winning the County Championship. He was excluded from the team to tour Australia in 1907–08, so he could have further rest, but then came the turning point of his career. Skipper A.O. Jones was hospitalised and George took his place as a player in the first Test at Sydney.

And what a sensational debut it turned out to be. He top-scored in both innings, scoring 119 (in 150 minutes, hitting 20 fours) and 74. As England had been able to reach only 273 in the first innings, George's contribution is further appreciated. England lost by two wickets and followed with a one-wicket win in the next. George scored another century in the final Test at Sydney, so the man who was not originally picked for the team topped the tour averages.

When England toured Australia in 1911–12, he averaged 42 in the Tests, scoring four fifties. Against South Australia, he scored 106 in three hours. Subsequent to his twin failure in one Test in England, he was never picked to play another Test on English soil. However, after being kept in cold storage for 17 years, George was picked to tour the West Indies in 1929–30. He was then 51. In his farewell Test at Kingston – in the marathon Test lasting eight days and then ending in a draw – he opened the batting and scored 85 and 47. In the first innings he added 173 runs for the first wicket with Andy Sandham. Against Jamaica, also at Kingston, George Gunn and Sandham added 322 for the opening wicket.

A year earlier, George had celebrated his 50th birthday by scoring 164 unbeaten runs against Worcestershire. In all, he hit centuries in both innings of a match three times, the last time against Warwickshire when he was 48. With W.W. Whysall of Notts, he was associated in 40 century partnerships, of which the best was 252 against Kent at Trent Bridge in 1924. In a career spanning 30 seasons, George totalled 35,208 runs at 35.96, hit 62 hundreds and scored 1000 runs in a season 20 times. In Australia he made 1577 runs, averaging 52.

George was an excellent slip fielder, and in this position took most of his 438 catches. In 1931 he shared a unique partnership. Against Warwickshire, he and his son, George jnr, each scored a century in the same innings. George, then 53, hit 183, whereas George jnr made an unbeaten 100 – his first century.

George Vernon Gunn (jnr) played for Notts from 1928 to 1939, scoring 10,337 runs and capturing 281 wickets. His best season as an all-rounder was 1934, when he scored 922 runs and his slow leg breaks dismissed 77 batsmen. Against Hampshire in 1934 he took 10 for 120 in the match. In each of his last five seasons he topped 1000 runs, his best being 1765 (average 44) in 1937. His highest score was 184 against Leicestershire. After retiring from cricket he became a coach but he died in a car accident in 1957 at the age of 52. His father died the following year, aged 79. The Gunns hit 161 first-class centuries and exceeded 1000 runs in a season 48 times, dominating the county scene from 1880 to 1939. Surprisingly, they represented England only 32 times. Their talent, as batsmen and fielders, and personalities deserved better.

Their first-class span ranged from 1880 when William played his initial match to 1950 when George jnr played his last. They scored 95,742 runs between them (William 25,457, John 24,740, George 35,208, George jnr 10,337) at a combined average of 33.61. They hit 161 centuries and completed 1000 runs in a season 48 times. John also took 1245 wickets and achieved the double of 1000 runs and 100 wickets in a season four times.

The three generations of Gunns provided not only good cricket but also fun and entertainment for eight decades.

The Gunns at the SCG

William, John and George Gunn all made their Test debut on the Sydney Cricket Ground. George scored a century on his debut, and both his Test centuries were hit on the SCG. His scores in the Sydney Tests were: 119 and 74, 122 not out and 0, 4 and 62, 52 and 61. Thus, he totalled 494 runs at 70.57, hitting two centuries and four fifties. In his first three Test innings at the SCG he was associated in century stands: 117 for the fourth wicket, 113 also for the fourth wicket, and 134 for the second wicket. In his second Test, also at the SCG in 1897, William Gunn not only played but umpired as well for some time.

	Tests	Runs	Avrge	HS	100s	50s	Wkts	Avrge	Best	5w/i	Catches
William	11	392	21.77	102*	1	1	–	–	–	–	5
John	6	85	10.62	24	0	0	18	21.50	5–76	1	3
George	15	1120	40.00	122*	2	7	0	–	–	–	15
Total	32	1597	29.57	122*	3	8	18	21.94	5–76	1	23

The Gunns in Test Cricket

CHAPTER 13

Fostershire

———— ● ————

There was a time when Worcestershire was known as 'Fostershire'.
And little wonder. Seven Foster brothers represented it in county cricket
championships. Two of their sons also played first-class cricket –
one for Worcestershire.

In December 1903, a nervous Englishman made his Test debut on the Sydney Cricket Ground. It was the first Test of the 1903–04 series and Australia had scored 285. England were three down for 73 when a tall, slender, diffident debutant went in to bat. He started unimpressively and was dropped at 51, but gradually he gained confidence and then, assuming command, went on to score 287. It was the highest Test score up to that time and remained so until 1930. More importantly, his individual score was two runs more than that of the 11 Australian batsmen – who included Victor Trumper, Monty Noble, Reg Duff, Syd Gregory, Warwick Armstrong and Clem Hill.

In seven hours of scintillating batting the newcomer had hit 38 fours and added 192 runs for the fifth wicket with Len Braund, 115 for the ninth with Albert Relf and 130 runs in 66 minutes for the last wicket with Wilfred Rhodes. He became the first batsman to share in three century partnerships in the same Test innings.

The author of this incredible real-life drama was R.E. 'Tip' Foster – one of the seven Foster brothers who put Worcestershire on the cricket map. Worcestershire was granted first-class status in 1899 and for almost three decades (1899–1934), it was served by the Foster brothers: Harry (H.K.), Wilfred (W.L.), the Test captain Reginald Erskine (R.E.), Basil (B.S.), Geoffrey (G.N.), Maurice (M.K.) and Johnny (N.J.A.).

All were Malvernians and, to quote John Arlott, were equipped 'with the steely wrists of racket players, and several of them were accomplished at more than one sport'. R.E. Foster was the only one to play Test cricket, but his other brothers were talented enough to represent Worcestershire at one time or another.

They were the sons of the Rev. H. Foster who had captained Winchester College XI at cricket in the 1860s. The three eldest brothers, H.K., W.L. and R.E., were introduced to cricket and coached by their mother as soon as they could hold a bat. H.K. Foster captained Worcestershire for two seasons and *Wisden*, when naming him Cricketer of the Year in 1911, described him as 'one of the masters of style'.

On 8 and 9 August 1892, H.K. and W.L. – both still in their teens – were responsible for Worcestershire's stunning win over MCC. H.K. later helped in the formation of the Minor County competition in 1895. When he eventually retired he had scored 17,154 runs, including 29 centuries, and had exceeded 1000 runs in a season eight times. His son, C.K. Foster, later played for Worcestershire.

The names of W.L. and R.E. Foster will be linked together forever because of their combined feat in 1899 which stood unequalled for 75 years. In a county match against Hampshire in July of that year Major W.L. Foster, who opened, scored 142 and 172 not out while 'Tip' Foster, batting at No. 4, made 134 and 101 not out. Incidentally, H.K. also played in that match, scoring 16 and 10 at No. 3.

Eventually, their record was equalled by the Chappell brothers 75 years later, in the Wellington Test against New Zealand in March 1974. Without doubt, the most outstanding of the seven brothers was R.E. Foster. Noel Stone wrote in *Wisden* (1963): 'R.E., the supreme craftsman of the brothers, gave cricket connoisseurs displays to warm their hearts and he was the schoolboys' hero'. He was also a brilliant slip fielder.

R.E. also played for England as a centre-forward in soccer and represented Oxford University at cricket, soccer,

A supreme craftsman, R.E. Foster scored 287 runs in his Test debut. (*Courtesy, Mr H.K. Foster*)

rackets and golf. According to John Arlott in *Rothman's Jubilee History of Cricket 1890–1965*: 'As a cricketer R.E. watched the ball well and had a correct defence, but he caught the eye as an upstanding and commanding stroke-player, reflecting the off-side bias of his day, but secure against leg stump attack and an effortless long hitter'.

For R.E., 1900 was a particularly memorable year. Captaining Oxford University, he hit the then highest individual score of 171 and the same year scored an unbeaten 102 and 136 for Gentlemen vs. Players – the first batsman to do so. He played in eight Tests, five against Australia in Australia in 1903–04, and, under his captaincy, England won the three-Test home series against South Africa in 1907, 1-0 .

But his sublime moment came during his Test debut in the Sydney Test of

December 1903 and his 287 is still the highest score by a visiting player in a Test in Australia. It was surpassed as the highest Test score anywhere when Andy Sandham of England amassed 325 in the Caribbean in 1929–30.

R.E. was also the only batsman to score a double-century on his Test debut until West Indian Lawrence Rowe scored a double-hundred and a hundred in his first Test – 214 and 100 not out against New Zealand in the Kingston Test of 1971–72. R.E.'s 287 is still a record for the highest score by any player on his Test debut. His 130-run last-wicket partnership with Rhodes remained unbeaten for 69 years. In the Auckland Test of 1973, New Zealanders Brian Hastings and Richard Collinge added 151 runs for the 10th wicket against Pakistan.

In his second Test, at Melbourne in January 1904, R.E. Foster scored 49, adding 99 runs in an unbroken stand with Johnny Tyldesley before illness forced him to retire. In the series, Foster easily topped the English batting average, scoring 486 runs at 60.75.

R.E. is remembered as much for his distinctive, loose-limbed style as for his quick scoring. In 1901 at Derby he scored a century against Derbyshire in 60 minutes, a Worcestershire record. Then against Gloucestershire at Worcestershire in 1907, he hit a century before lunch on the opening day. He went on to score 144. Once, he hit W.G. Grace for four consecutive sixes.

In *The Cricket Statistician* (England) is mentioned R.E. Foster's most staggering batting performance. When playing for H.W. de Zoeste's XI against Witham at Witham on 19 June 1909, Witham declared at 4 for 343. Zoeste's XI were set an 'impossible' task of scoring 344 runs in 95 minutes to win. They lost four for 60 in 20 minutes when R.E. took over. He scored 206 not out in 75 minutes and his team won by five wickets.

On another occasion he scored 246 not out in four and a half hours against Kent, and that too in his first appearance of the season. Three times in two years, 1900–01, he scored two separate centuries in a match. Against a Middlesex XI that included the best bowling in England, Wilfred Rhodes, Albert Trott and Walter Mead, he scored 136 out of 195 in 105 minutes, belting 24 fours.

According to Patrick Morrah, 'He remains one of the most brilliant amateur batsmen of all time. Again and again he showed the capacity for coming into a team without practice and playing at the top of his form. His batting was as sparkling as it was consistent. As an off-side hitter he has seldom been equalled; in H.S. Altham's view he had no rival as a cutter except Ranjitsinhji.'

But R.E. did not last long. Cricket-lovers were shocked and saddened at his death from diabetes at age 36 in 1914. He had scored 602 runs at 46.30 in eight Tests.

Business kept G.N. Foster in London and away from cricket, but whenever he had the opportunity he showed his prowess. In 1913, against Middlesex at Lord's, he scored 132 and added 254 runs with Frank Chester, later to become a well-known umpire. Subsequently, G.N. qualified to play for Kent and his son, P.G. Foster, also played for the county. B.S. Foster played for Worcestershire and later for Middlesex.

The career of the sixth brother, M.K. Foster, was interrupted by war. In his first full season in 1914 he had topped 1000 runs and made his career-best score of 158. In all, he scored 8281 runs with 12 centuries and captained Worcestershire for three seasons.

The youngest of the Fosters, N.J.A., died on 9 December 1977, aged 87. After representing Worcestershire, he settled in Malaysia and returned to England in 1961. He figured in a memorable match for Malaya against Australia which included Test players Charlie Macartney, Bill Woodfull, Warren Bardsley, Tommy

Andrews and Samuel Everett. N.J.A. led Malaya to an incredible 39-run victory over Australia on 6 June 1927 at Kuala Lumpur. A writer observed: 'No one except the actual spectators believed the news. It was against the order of nature. It was as if Queen Victoria was amused, as if Hitler had become a Jew ... '

N.J.A. won the toss and 'kept a grip on the game with the tightness and craft of W.G. Grace'. Malaya was all out for 108, N.J.A. Foster top-scoring with 30. Then the mighty Australians were skittled out for 85. Dr Hennessey, a 50-year-old spinner, took 7 for 42. In the second innings, Malaya scored 158 and Australia, needing 182 to win, were all out for 142, Woodfull scoring 37.

According to an old report: 'Macartney, with the sportsmanship of good cricketers, rushed down the pavilion steps and was the first to congratulate Foster and his team ... Foster was inundated with telegrams and probably had to engage a special shorthand typist to cope with them!'

The run flow of the Fosters did not dry up with the retirement or passing away of the brothers. Two of their sons continued playing county cricket: C.K., the son of H.K., for Worcestershire, and G.N.'s son P.G. for Kent.

Their elegant batsmanship and team spirit made such an impact upon the public that Worcestershire was affection-ately named 'Fostershire'.

R.E. Foster in Test Cricket						
Tests	Runs	Avrge	HS	100s	50s	Catches
8	602	46.30	287	1	1	13

CHAPTER 14

Fate
and the Tates

———— ● ————

*Fate treated Fred Tate badly in his only Test appearance, but his son,
the immortal Maurice, made it up to him in a big way.*

IN THE FOURTH TEST between England and Australia at Old Trafford in July 1902, Victor Trumper scored a majestic century before lunch. Bill Lockwood, the English fast bowler, took 11 wickets in the match for 76 runs – at one stage capturing 8 for 13. Yet the man most remembered in this thrilling Test which resulted in a three-run win for Australia is neither Trumper nor Lockwood, but an outstanding failure – Fred Tate.

Off-spinner Tate, 35, was then having a successful season with Sussex but his inclusion in the Old Trafford Test at the expense of Syd Barnes, George Hirst and wet-wicket expert Schofield Haigh raised many eyebrows. No wonder the modest, rotund Tate trembled when he heard of his selection. It proved a nightmare debut (and farewell) for him. Apart from his poor batting, 'he could not field anywhere except at slip'

according to C.B. Fry. In this epic Test of fluctuating fortunes, Australia collapsed from 1 for 173 to 299 all out and England recovered from 5 for 44 to 262. Then Lockwood struck and Australia lost three wickets for 10 when left-handed Joe Darling joined Syd Gregory.

English bowler Len Braund wanted a safe deep fielder to have the daring Darling caught at square leg. He asked for Lionel Palairet, but since this was for one ball only, he got the slip specialist Tate. Sure enough, Darling fell into the trap. His high shot came down to just where Tate was waiting. Tate moved to his right and then to the left – and dropped the catch. No Englishman has quite forgiven him for it, even after almost 100 years.

Darling made hay with a dynamic 37 out of Australia's 86 all out. Still, England needed only 124 to win.

However, because of some freak catches by Clem Hill and Gregory, and some irresponsible batting, England were 9 for 116. In came Fred Tate – choked with advice and a barrage of *don'ts*. In a trance, he edged Saunders for a four, but a few balls later was bowled off a really good ball and England had lost the Test by three runs, and also the Ashes. Paradoxically, this Test is remembered as 'Tate's Test'. Poor Fred was full of remorse. On his way home he told Braund: 'I've got a little kid at home who'll make it up for me'. This has become one of cricket's most touching episodes and, as it turned out, a bang-on prediction.

The Old Trafford Test of 1902 certainly was Fred's first and last Test, but the seven-year-old Maurice Tate grew up to become one of the immortals of the game: the finest of his type to grace the cricket fields – a happy player who infected team-mates and spectators with his bouncing enthusiasm and toothy smile.

The 1902 Test disaster did not stop Fred from enriching Sussex County cricket. He made his county debut in 1887 as a 19-year-old and the next year took five wickets for one run against Kent – clean-bowling all five. He seemed to reserve his best efforts for battles against Kent: 6 for 23 in 1893 and 11 wickets in the match in 1895. This was a special year for Fred. That year Ranji joined Sussex and Fred's first child – a son, Maurice – was born. To quote Gerald Brodribb from his biography of Tate: 'For the next few years [1895 onwards], the Sussex bowling really meant Tate – a situation that was to recur some 25 years later'.

In 1899 Fred took 121 wickets and the following year 141. His best effort was 14 wickets in a match – vs Kent (who else)! C.B. Fry considered him to be 'one of the two or three best medium-pace bowlers in England ... He has a beautifully elastic action, and a wonderful natural spin.' In 1901 he reached his highest score of 84 – a contribution which helped to save Sussex from defeat. Even after his horror Test debut, he showed no loss of form for Sussex, taking 8 for 28 vs Hampshire, and he had his revenge against the Australians when, in the last match of the season, for South of England, he dismissed Darling, Saunders, Trumper, Gregory, Duff and Armstrong. His season's total was 180 wickets, surpassed only by Wilfred Rhodes (213).

As a batsman, Fred had his moments. Once he partnered Ranji to add 160 for the ninth wicket in 70 minutes – Fred contributing an unbeaten 61. After 1903 he faded out from playing cricket but continued coaching and, to his dying day, at the age of 75 in 1943, he enthralled the customers of his inn in Derbyshire by narrating the moving saga of the 'Tate Test' – leaving many eyes moist.

Fred had 10 children – three sons and seven daughters. Cecil Tate, 13 years Maurice's junior, played four games for Derbyshire in 1928 as a medium-pace left-arm bowler. He then represented Warwickshire six times.

Unlike Fred, Maurice's Test debut was positively sensational. Against South Africa at Edgbaston on 16 June 1924, Maurice opened the bowling with his Sussex and England captain, Arthur Gilligan, and took a wicket with his first delivery in Test cricket. He took 4 for 12, Gilligan 6 for 7, and the Springboks were routed for an all-time low of 30. In that series, Maurice took 27 wickets. A few months later, in Australia, he had his most successful Test series, capturing 38 wickets at 23. They were precious scalps – the cream of Australian batsmen – and his triumph came despite dropped catches, near misses and a painful toe.

But to return to the beginning. Maurice was keen on cricket, but he showed little early ability and was not good enough to represent his school. One of his masters advised him: 'We know your father is a great cricketer, but you'll never be one. You stick to football!' However, Maurice could not be convinced. After all, to quote him: 'My baby milk was diluted with cricket. I was weaned on it and it was served after every meal'.

Was he guided by his father? 'I want to put it on record that I was never coached in bowling. It came to me naturally and must have been inherited from my father,' he recalled.

Maurice left school at 14 to become an apprentice fitter with a gas company. The following year, on a request from Sussex County Club, Fred took his son to Hove for a fortnight's trial. The committee members were unimpressed by the clumsy, awkward boy with long legs, enormous feet and prominent teeth. But, to his surprise and delight, he was engaged in the Sussex nursery. In his first season, his off-breaks earned him 55 wickets. He made his debut for Sussex in 1912, aged 17. At the end of the 1913 season he played for Haywards Heath and scored 84. The opposition included 46-year-old Fred Tate who scored 65 not out and hit the winning run.

World War I interrupted Maurice's cricket career and he enlisted in the army. By the end of the war he had filled out and become a lumbering giant. He had lost his shyness and awkwardness and had become a happy extrovert who enjoyed his cricket. Cricket resumed in 1919, and Maurice scored his first century on 30 July – 108 in 110 minutes vs Lancashire at Old Trafford. He also completed 1000 runs during the season – a habit he kept up for 11 years in a row. Against Oxford University in 1920, he showed his all-round ability, scoring 90 and 35 and taking 5 for 48 and 6 for 42.

Until 1922, Maurice was an off-spinner with a bowling action so similar to his father's that, according to Arthur Gilligan, 'it was almost uncanny to watch them'. Maurice was then considered more of a batsman. He scored 151 and 47 not out vs Notts, 142 in 114 minutes vs Hampshire, and 203 vs Northamptonshire in 180 minutes – adding 385 runs with Ted Bowley. After this hitting spree, Maurice was nicknamed 'Boundary Tate'.

In 1922 he was reborn as a fast-medium bowler who could move the ball both ways. His transformation from a rather harmless off-spinner to a pacey terror was one of cricket's happy chance discoveries and had a great impact on Test cricket tactics. There are several versions of Maurice's metamorphosis and they are detailed in Gerald Brodribb's extremely readable book, *Maurice Tate*.

One version is that Maurice was exasperated at being hit all over the place by Philip Mead and, in desperation, he bowled a faster ball which beat a stunned Mead, taking his leg stump.

In his autobiography, Maurice described this as a fluke, but Brodribb is not convinced. According to him, other batsmen, including his captain, Gilligan, had been surprised by Maurice's faster balls before the encounter with Mead. Whatever the genesis, Maurice's abandonment of the spin for the cut was a stroke of luck for Sussex, England and cricket. In a matter of weeks, he became England's premier bowler and remained so for 10 years until Douglas Jardine introduced bodyline in 1932.

Even at his swiftest, Maurice was not genuinely fast. But after pitching, the ball maintained incredible pace. Soon after his transformation he played for England vs The Rest and wrecked the opposition, who crashed from 5 for 202 to 205 all out – Maurice taking the last 5 wickets in 10 balls without conceding a run. And he produced all this fire with a run-up of barely eight paces.

After he took 8 for 18 vs Worcestershire in 1924, *Wisden* called him 'unplayable'.

His short run-up produced additional problems for the batsmen, for it did not give them time to relax. 'One ball had hardly gone when another was on its way like some relentless bowling machine,' was the way a county batsman saw Tate the Terror. To batsmen it was also terrifying to see his flailing arms and big hands coming at them like a monster spider. He gave the ball a whip with the swing of his body and a flip of the wrist, so that it gathered speed – or so it seemed – off the pitch. To those unaccustomed to his bowling, the ball sounded like a hissing snake.

The seasons 1923, 1924 and 1925 were memorable ones for Maurice Tate. He topped 200 wickets and scored 1000 runs for three years in a row – a record without parallel. Only two players had achieved this rare double before him – Albert Trott (twice) and Albert Kennedy (once). Since 1925 no one has done it even once. In 1924, he made his never-to-be-forgotten debut against South Africa at Edgbaston (4 for 12). Then, in Australia in 1924–25, he reached the peak of his power.

In England in 1924 he had one precious moment to remember. Playing against Yorkshire, he scored an unbeaten century and, during the innings, he received a telegram informing him of the birth of his first son, Maurice jnr. Oddly, a few minutes previously, Herbert Sutcliffe had also received a telegram about the birth of his daughter. Sutcliffe, too, celebrated the occasion with a century.

Everything went smoothly for Tate's overseas tour to Australia in 1924–25. Against a strong New South Wales team he captured 7 for 74 and among his victims were Charlie Macartney, Tommy Andrews and Alan Kippax – all for ducks. This was the first of his many 'mad moments' on the tour.

Even though Bill Ponsford scored a century in the first Test at Sydney, he was all at sea against Tate, and his captain, Herbert Collins, had to shield him. Tate had a marathon spell of 712 balls in this Test and captured 11 for 228. In the second Test at Melbourne he bowled 627 deliveries and by the time the third Test started in Adelaide his toenail had been pushed back into his flesh and he was in agony. Although he was the Australian batsmen's worst enemy, he was every Australian barracker's best friend. They loved him and they shared his pain. His big toe and big feet were headline news. Once a placard for an evening paper read: 'TATE'S NEW FOOT' – which was, fortunately, only a misprint for 'Tate's New Boot'.

In the final Test at Sydney, interest was centred around his record: 'Would he get past Mailey's 36 wickets in a series?' As a climax, he broke Mailey's stumps and record in one ball. Maurice's 38 wickets in a Test series was a record aggregate in Australia until 1978–79 when Rodney Hogg took 41 against England. Skipper Arthur Gilligan commented after the series: 'With ordinary luck, Tate would have taken 58 instead of 38 wickets' referring to the number of dropped catches and near misses which shaved the bails or stumps. Herbert Collins said, 'Tate was the best bowler seen in Australia for 25 years and was, in some respects, better than the great Barnes, as he sent down more unplayable balls'. And Bert Oldfield noted, 'Of all the bowlers I have faced, slow, fast or medium, I regard Tate as *the greatest*'.

Fast or medium-pace bowlers usually become stale after a tour of Australia, but not Maurice. He enjoyed his cricket and was as devastating as ever in county cricket for Sussex, taking 7 for 23 and 7 for 35, 8 for 100, 7 for 58 and 5 for 36 within a fortnight.

In the third Test at Leeds, against Australia, he dismissed left-handed opener, Warren Bardsley, off the first ball of the Test. In the same over, the great Macartney was dropped and went on to make a masterly hundred. Although Maurice took only 13 wickets in the series, he was still the most feared bowler from either side. In the final Test at The Oval he took 4 for 52 in 46 overs – an important factor in England regaining the Ashes.

In 1926–27, the MCC toured India. Maurice played in 28 matches, scored 1160 runs at 36, and took 116 wickets at 13.7, to become the first English player to perform the 'double' outside England. At Bombay, G.F. Earle and Maurice delighted 45,000 fans by adding 154 runs in 65 minutes. On the tour, Maurice wrote: 'I don't suppose I shall ever again have such a wonderful trip as I had through India'.

In the domestic season of 1927, Tate was at his best as an all-rounder, hitting three centuries in a row and also bowling effectively. He was among the first picked to tour Australia in 1928–29. Although he was unable to recapture the fire of the previous tour, he took 17 wickets and was the key figure in the attack, and in England retaining the Ashes 4–1.

He scored his only Test century against South Africa in 1929, at Lord's. For a change, his batting saved England when he added 129 with Maurice Leyland in 70 minutes. When the Australians toured England the following year, Don Bradman stole all the limelight. But when 'the little devil' was not playing in a match against Sussex, Maurice took 6 for 18 before lunch – his victims being Ponsford, McCabe, Jackson, Richardson, Fairfax and a'Beckett.

This was Maurice's final fling against the Aussies. Although he toured Australia for the third time in 1932–33, skipper Jardine had no room for him in his bodyline tactics. Larwood later commented: 'Tate was still good enough to play for England, but was too much of a gentleman to express his disappointment'.

Tate scored 1198 runs and took 155 wickets in 39 Tests. This included 83 Australian wickets in 20 Tests.

When he retired from first-class cricket in 1937 he had scored 21,717 runs at 25, with 23 centuries. He had also grabbed 2784 wickets at 18, taking five wickets in an innings 195 times and 10 wickets in a match 44 times. He performed the 'double' of 1000 runs and 100 wickets in eight consecutive seasons.

Just as his father had had a memorable batting partnership with Ranji, Maurice had a big stand with Ranji's nephew, Duleep. They put on 205 runs in 105 dazzling minutes – Tate 111 and Duleep 333 in one day.

Maurice's proudest moments came when he was asked to captain Sussex occasionally. It was a rare honour for a professional in those days and he proved a successful and popular leader. After his retirement, he took coaching assignments in Tonbridge School in Kent and it was here that he spotted the talent of Colin Cowdrey.

Tate's sons, Maurice jnr and Michael, tried their hands at becoming professional cricketers for Sussex and Kent but could not quite make it. One success Michael had with Kent was to clean-bowl Cowdrey at the nets.

Just three weeks before Maurice's sudden death of heart failure on 18 May 1956, he had umpired a match between Ian Johnson's Australians and the Duke of Norfolk's XI at Arundel Castle. He was then almost 61. A day to remember for the Tate family came on 17 May 1958, when the Maurice Tate Memorial Gates at the entrance of the county ground at Hove were opened by the Duke of Norfolk.

Maurice Tate is considered to be one of the four greatest medium-pacers in cricket history – Syd Barnes, Alec Bedser and Fazal Mahmood being the others.

Experts who saw both Tate and Bedser ranked Tate higher, although it may be fair to point out that Bedser did not get uncovered pitches whereas Tate did. But to balance this, the new lbw rules introduced after 1935 would have helped Tate to trap more victims. So accurate was he that his Sussex keeper said, 'You could keep wicket to Maurice sitting in an easy chair'.

When asked to select the best opening bowlers among his contemporaries, Bradman once said, 'Ted McDonald with the wind, Maurice Tate into it'.

More than for his accuracy, penetration and endurance, big Maurice Tate will be remembered for his big smile, big heart and big feet, and for his 'Tateisms' – his mangling of words such as 'stannima' for 'stamina' and saying the most trivial and obvious things with a sombre, secretive face. In a letter to Gerald Brodribb, Don Bradman said of Maurice: '... as an opponent he was marvellous, always jovial, and a joy to play against'.

To sum up, I quote John Arlott from *Rothman's Jubilee History of Cricket: 1890–1965*: 'A humorous character with a relish for life and a great enthusiasm for the game; Maurice Tate felt that his bowling made some amends for his father's error in the Old Trafford Test of 1902'.

The Tates in Test Cricket

	Tests	Runs	Avrge	HS	100s	50s	Wkts	Avrge	Best	5w/i	Catches
Fred	1	9	9.00	5*	0	0	2	25.50	2–7	0	2
Maurice	39	1198	25.48	100*	1	5	155	26.16	6–42	7	11
Total	40	1207	25.14	100*	1	5	157	26.15	6–42	7	13

CHAPTER 15

The
Gilligan Brothers

●

Both Arthur Gilligan and his younger brother, Harold,
captained Sussex and England – but they never played together
in a Test match. Their eldest brother, Frank Gilligan, captained
Oxford University and kept wicket for Essex.

TALL CATCHES ARE REMEMBERED as much as huge sixes or an unplayable ball that bamboozles a well-set batsman. Spectators discuss such events forever. One such instance was Arthur Gilligan's marvellous catch on the Sydney Cricket Ground which dismissed Australia's Jack Gregory in 1924. This was for MCC against New South Wales. To quote Bert Oldfield: 'Gilligan, running at full speed, threw himself parallel to the ground and held a magnificent catch and, falling to the ground, spun like a top'.

Besides being a specialist mid-off fielder, A.E.R. (Arthur) Gilligan was, at his peak, a genuine fast bowler, an adventurous lower-order batsman, one of the most popular and inspiring English captains, and a jovial personality.

In 1929, Arthur passed on the Sussex captaincy to A.H.H. (Harold) Gilligan – his younger brother by two years – who

went on to lead England in four Tests in New Zealand. His daughter, Virginia, married the great Peter May who captained England with distinction and scored 4537 runs at 46.77 in 66 Tests.

The three Gilligan brothers were together in the Dulwich XI in 1913, giving rise to a newspaper comment: 'The Gilligans of Dulwich seem destined to become as famous in sport as the Fords of Repton, the Lytteltons of Eton and the Fosters of Malvern'. The eldest was Frank, who captained Oxford University. In two university matches, Arthur Gilligan – playing for Cambridge University – and Frank, for Oxford, opposed each other. For many years Frank also kept wickets for Essex during the university holidays.

Arthur Gilligan, the most notable in the family, retired from first-class cricket in 1932 but kept himself in the game he loved by writing for London's *News Chronicle* and giving lectures. He was chairman of the Sussex County Cricket Club for a long time and became president of the MCC in 1967. He remained fit and active past the age of 80. A short time before his death on 5 September 1976 he was to be seen watching cricket at Lord's, Hove or Arundel.

After World War II, Arthur became a BBC commentator and visited Australia to cover the Anglo-Australian Test series for the ABC. Not surprisingly, Australians regard Arthur Gilligan as their very own as his famous radio partnership with Vic Richardson made him a household name.

Born on 23 December 1894, Arthur played for Dulwich Cricket XI, captaining it in 1913 and 1914. He was also a distinguished athlete. By 1913 he was playing cricket for Sussex Second XI but World War I delayed his blossoming until 1919. He obtained his Cambridge University Blue as a quick bowler and attracted attention when he took 6 for 52 against Oxford. In one spell of 57 balls, he trapped 5 victims for 16. For Cambridge against Sussex in 1919, Arthur batted at No. 11 and scored a century, adding 177 runs in 65 minutes with J.H. Naumann.

After playing three matches for Surrey, Arthur started with Sussex in 1920 and went on till 1932 – as captain from 1922 until 1929. His best years were from 1922 to 1924, capturing 135 wickets at 18.75 in 1922, 163 at 17.50 in 1923, and 103 at 19.36 in 1924. He performed the double of 1183 runs and 163 wickets in 1923.

Although picked to tour South Africa in 1922–23, Arthur played only two Tests and had moderate success. In the final Test at Durban, he made his highest Test score of 39 not out and took 3 for 35 and 3 for 78 as a fast bowler. The 1924 season was particularly successful for him. He was appointed England's captain against the touring Springboks and led his country to three wins in the first three Tests. In the first two Tests, England won by an innings and Arthur contributed significantly by taking 16 wickets for 214 runs.

The first Test at Birmingham was a match of milestones for the debutant skipper, Gilligan, and another debutant player Maurice Tate. The two quickies routed South Africa for 30 runs in 45 minutes. Gilligan took 5 for 83 in the second innings as South Africa totalled 390 but lost by an innings. His match figures were 11 for 90. In the next Test, at Lord's, he took 3 for 70 and 2 for 54. With his Sussex partner-in-pace, Maurice Tate, also in top form, it seemed that England's search for a pace pair was over. Both were honoured by *Wisden* as Cricketers of the Year.

Arthur Gilligan always believed that to beat Australia, a pair of fast bowlers was a must and England was already smacking her lips for the tour down under in the next season. To add to their optimism, the Gilligan–Tate combination kept destroying the best of county opposition for low scores. Two of the strongest batting sides – Surrey and Middlesex – were routed, for 53 and 42 runs, within a week. Against Surrey at The Oval, Arthur took 4 for 24 and Tate 6 for 22. Against Middlesex at Lord's, Arthur captured 8 for 25. 'Everything went right for us, and I seldom remember such wonderful catching and fielding as Sussex put up that day,' said Arthur after the Middlesex debacle.

Just then, something went wrong – very wrong – and England's hopes were dashed. While batting for Gentlemen vs Players at The Oval, Arthur received a heavy blow over the heart from medium-pacer Pearson of Worcestershire. Although he was soon dismissed, he insisted on batting in the second innings, against medical advice, when Gentlemen were asked to follow-on and the score read 7 for 207. He played a brilliant innings of 112 out of 165, in only 90 minutes. With Michael Falcon, he added 134 for the last wicket in a whirlwind 75 minutes. But that was the end of Arthur Gilligan, the fast bowler. After that, he could bowl only at medium pace and England's dream of a pace pair was shattered. The doctor who treated Arthur ordered him to rest and told him that he would never be able to bowl fast again. He later admitted: 'Being obstinate and pig-headed, I thought he was wrong, and as soon as I could play again I immediately started fast bowling.' However, in the next two Tests against South Africa he could take only one wicket. Of his batting in the second innings of that Gentlemen vs Players game, he wrote, 'That was probably the worst thing I ever did'.

England toured Australia under Arthur Gilligan in 1924–25. But with no support for Tate they lost the series 1–4. Gilligan, now a medium-pacer, could take only 10 wickets at 51.9. Nevertheless, he fielded brilliantly and his captaincy was an inspiration to his team. England lost the third Test by only 11 runs and won the fourth by an innings. It was England's first post-war victory and was applauded everywhere. On the series result, Jim Swanton wrote in *Sort of a Cricket Person*: 'If Gilligan, in his early 1924 form could have given due support to the magnificent Tate, the tables might well have been turned'.

His leadership contributed much to the tour success and he endeared himself to all the professionals by refusing any invitation which said 'amateurs only'. After the Australian tour of 1924–25, he did not play at Test level again but he was appointed a Test selector in 1926. The following season he captained an MCC team to India, Burma and Ceylon. The 1932 season was Arthur Gilligan's last in first-class cricket but he retained a keen interest in the game till his death.

Although better known for his fast bowling and acrobatic fielding (as a mid-off he had no rival), he was an attractive and useful tail-end batsman. All his 12 centuries in first-class cricket came against strong opposition and at an exhilarating rate of a run a minute.

A keen golfer as well, Arthur was president of the English Golf Union in 1959. R.L. Arrowsmith wrote in his obituary in *Wisden* (1977): 'As a captain he may not have been in the top rank of tacticians, but no one excelled him in getting the best out of his side and inspiring them in the field. From every point of view, he was a cricketer with whom England could do with now.' Johnnie Moyes wrote in his *A Century of Cricketers*: 'He had the spirit to win and his brilliant fielding inspired his colleagues. He could smile in defeat and in victory and that is remembered in Australia to this day.'

In 1929 Arthur passed on the Sussex captaincy to brother Harold, who was a good middle-order batsman as well as a brilliant fielder at cover. Arthur at mid-off, Harold at cover and Tate at extra cover, formed what was then known as the 'iron ring'. Besides being a picture of elegant efficiency at cover, Harold could hit hard. In Sussex cricket, some fabulous hitting by Tate and Harold is well remembered. In 1919 they put on 71 runs in 30 minutes for Sussex. In 1924 they added 61 runs in 25 minutes against Middlesex at Hove. And in 1929 the two again savaged a Middlesex attack to add 114 in 65 minutes at Lord's.

Born on 29 June 1896, Harold was appointed England's captain for the tour to New Zealand in 1929–30. Under him, England won by eight wickets at Christchurch. This was the inaugural Test for New Zealand. With the remaining three Tests drawn, England returned home winners. In these four Tests, Harold scored only 71 runs at 17.75, his highest score being 32. His individual performance was thus disappointing, but, like Arthur, he had won the first Test – and the series – as England's captain. For Harold, it was his last Test series too.

Harold holds an unusual record. In the 1923 English season he played 70 innings – the most ever, and likely to remain so with the reduction in number of first-class matches. That season he scored 1186 runs at an average of 17.70, the lowest average for a player scoring 1000 runs in a season.

The Gilligan brothers are remembered today not for huge scores or heaps of wickets and lofty averages, but because they exemplified the spirit of cricket. They loved the game above the prize.

	Tests	Runs	Avrge	HS	100s	50s	Wkts	Avrge	Best	5w/i	Catches
The Gilligans in Test Cricket											
A.E.R. (Arthur)	11	209	16.07	39*	0	0	36	29.05	6–7	2	3
A.H.H. (Harold)	4	71	17.75	32	0	0	–	–	–	–	0
Total	15	280	16.47	39*	0	0	36	29.05	6–7	2	3

CHAPTER 16

My
Kingdom for a Nourse

——— ● ———

The period from 1895 to 1953 was virtually a Nourse dynasty in
South African cricket. Dave played 45 Tests from 1902 to 1924
and his son, Dudley, 34 from 1935 to 1951. Holders of several
South African records, they became the first father–son combination in
Test history to top 2000 runs each. Dudley's batting in England
in 1935 reminded Sir Pelham Warner of Dave and he commented:
'A Nourse, a Nourse, my Kingdom for a Nourse'

THE FIRST VISIT OF the South African cricketers to Australia in 1910–11 is remembered for a novel occurrence. In the opening match of the tour against South Australia on 12 November, the tourists' No. 3 batsman, A.W. ('Dave') Nourse, hit an unbeaten 201. Within hours of this achievement he received a cable from home informing him of the birth of a son. The Governor-General of Australia, Lord Dudley, on hearing about Dave's dual joy, expressed a wish that the son be named after him. Dudley eventually grew up to become one of South Africa's all-time great batsmen.

Dave Nourse, the father, played 45 Tests in a row, spanning 20 years, and 40

years at first-class level. He was called the Grand Old Man of Springbok cricket. Dudley, brought up the hard way and without much coaching, broke most of his father's records. There were certainly some similarities in their Test careers. Both made three tours to England. In their first Test series against England – about 30 years apart – they helped South Africa emerge victorious. Both were durable, Dave retiring from the Test arena when 46, and Dudley when 41.

As players, they were as different as chalk from cheese. Dave was a left-arm all-rounder, an ultra-defensive batsman, while Dudley, a right-hander, was so attractive a stroke-player that even Denis

Compton could not outshine him in 1947.

Arthur William 'Dave' Nourse, the spinal column of South African cricket, kept on playing first-class cricket till he was 58. He was broad and powerfully built, with a gigantic pair of hands. Early in his career he was an opening bowler but with advancing age he became a spinner of merit. He was also a remarkable fielder in short slip. Dave toured England in 1907, 1912 and 1924 and built a reputation as a batsman of impregnable defence. The 1912 tour was his most successful as an all-rounder, his highest score on that tour being an unbeaten 213 against Hampshire. His career best was 304 not out for Natal vs Transvaal at Johannesburg in 1919–20.

In 45 Tests he made 2234 runs and took 41 wickets and 43 catches, his only century being against Warwick Armstrong's Australians in 1921. To Dave, however, his proudest moment was scoring 93 not out in the 1906–07 Test against England under Sir Pelham Warner. This was the nerve-wrecking Test which South Africa won by one wicket. It was his country's first win against England, and Dave contributed by scoring 18 not out and 93 not out as well as taking 2 for 7. On the Australian tour of 1910–11, Dave had an aggregate of 1473 at 59. In that Test series, his highest score was an undefeated 92.

Arthur Dudley Nourse inherited his father's skill, concentration and big-match temperament, but had in addition, to quote A.G. Moyes, 'a more polished and attractive style and a touch of genius for attack'. Stocky, broad-shouldered and with powerful blacksmith forearms, he was particularly strong off his back foot. When hooking, driving to the off, or cutting square, he struck the ball as if with a bludgeon.

It is natural to assume that Dudley was coached by his father, but actually he was self-taught. To quote from his autobiography, *Cricket in the Blood*: 'Strangely enough, he [father] never in any way – as far as I can remember – encouraged me in my games ... I saw little of my father in the impressionable years. He was often away from home and much of his time was taken up in travelling around with sporting teams.'

The father felt that Dudley must learn his cricket the hard way, as he himself had done. When 12, Dudley hit a century and was invited for coaching conducted by former Hampshire professional Alec Kennedy. At that time, soccer had a far greater fascination for young Dudley and cricket coaching seemed a bit of a drag. 'There seemed to be too many do's and don'ts for my liking,' he remembered and he became a drop-out after only two seasons. When Dudley was 14, he nearly became an Australian by adoption. The family bade farewell to Durban, ready to leave for Australia, when his mother was taken ill and the trip was abandoned. So Dudley Nourse remained in South Africa to become one of its most celebrated sporting heroes.

He was influenced by the stylish Herbie Taylor of South Africa and the great Wally Hammond. Natal and Springbok captain, Herbert Wade, also took a keen interest in Dudley and guided him at the beginning of his career. His most dramatic moment came in the 1931–32 season when Western Province met Natal in a Provincial game. Both teams possessed a Nourse. Western Province had Dave, then 54, and Natal's Dudley was 22.

As this was the first time Dudley had seen his father batting, he was naturally tense. To his relief, his father was out for 2 and Dudley was 'sorry and pleased in the same breath'. When Dudley's turn came to bat, Dave crouched at first slip – large hands ready to pounce on a filial edge. But nothing perturbed the determined junior who reached the first of his 41 hundreds – to the utter delight of his father who rushed to him saying, 'I hope there will be many more to follow this one'.

Three years later, in 1935, Dudley played Test matches in England. The tour was a memorable one for him. He started with a flourish, scoring 736 runs by May in matches preceding the Tests. In three successive innings he scored centuries – including 147 and 108 not out against Surrey. This prompted Sir Pelham Warner, who thought very highly of both the Nourses, to comment at a luncheon at Lord's: 'A Nourse, a Nourse, my Kingdom for a Nourse!'

In all, Dudley totalled 1861 runs on the tour, second only to Eric Rowan. However, in the Tests he was a failure. After hitting the first ball he received in Test cricket for a four, he ran into difficulties against Hedley Verity. Notwithstanding his failures, South Africa won the Test series in England for the first time.

Dudley played like a man possessed when Australia, under Vic Richardson, toured South Africa the following season. Express bowler E.L. McCormick and the celebrated spin trio of Bill O'Reilly, Clarrie Grimmett and Chuck Fleetwood-Smith posed no major problems for him. His 91 in the Durban Test was followed by a duck in the second at Johannesburg. In the second innings, however, he hit a magnificent 231, including 36 fours, in less than five hours. Thus, his first Test century was a double-century, and to have scored it against O'Reilly and Grimmett was even more of an achievement.

His undefeated innings in the following Test was just as valuable. On a bad wicket, South Africa was shot out for 102. Dudley, at No. 6, contributed a priceless unbeaten 44. Grimmett (5 for 32) paid him the ultimate tribute: 'I tried to add you to my list, but you were one too good for me. I am glad you came in later. Had you come in earlier, we might have had a more difficult task.' Dudley made

518 runs in the series, which gave him immense satisfaction.

In the domestic season of 1936–37, Dudley scored 260 not out, 135, 32 and 240 for Natal in four games, to average 222 as Natal won the Currie Cup. Two seasons later, in a home series against Hammond's Englishmen, Dudley hit two hundreds including an uncharacteristically slow 103 in the final timeless Test at Durban. In this frustrating match where time stood still – it lasted 10 days and was unfinished – Nourse took six hours over his century.

During World War II, Dudley was posted to Egypt. In between the fighting, he continued playing with other English, New Zealand and South African cricketers. In a match at Alexandria, he hit nine sixes in nine balls! But while in the Middle East, Dudley contracted pneumonia and was invalided home. During convalescence he put on a lot of weight and took a long time to regain his masterly footwork and crisp timing. He worked extremely hard to regain physical fitness and ended the season scoring 676 runs in the Currie Cup – over 100 runs more than the next player. He also led Natal to victory.

Then followed his most successful tour – to England in 1947. In Tests, Dudley made 621 runs, averaging 69. In the Nottingham Test he put on 319 runs with skipper Alan Melville. This was a Test record which was soon broken by Compton and Bill Edrich.

At Manchester, on a rank, bad wicket, Dudley Nourse hit a glorious 115. His second 50 came in only 35 heart-warming minutes and on a bowler's pitch he achieved the impossible – he forced the bowlers onto the defensive. 'This was batting rich in conception and superlative in operation,' wrote A.G. Moyes. According to *Wisden*, 'This was Nourse at his best'.

Wrote Dudley himself in *Cricket in the Blood*: 'I like to regard my second innings of 115 in that Manchester Test, as the best I have ever played. No innings I have ever played before, or any I have played since, gave me half the satisfaction than one at Manchester did that day.'

When England toured South Africa in 1948–49, he was appointed the captain. This made his seven-year-old, cricket-loving son Peter exclaim: 'Congratulations, Dad, but don't expect too much from me.' By a coincidence, England also had a new captain who was the son of a famous Test player – F.G. Mann, the son of F.T. Mann. And although England won the rubber 2–0 the home side could almost have won, so close was the series.

England won the first Test by two wickets, the winning run coming off the last ball of the Test, and that off a leg bye! The final Test, at Port Elizabeth, was just as thrilling. A sporting declaration by Nourse set England 172 to get in 95 minutes. England reached it – but with only minutes and three wickets to spare. Nourse once again exceeded 500 runs in the series, with centuries at Cape Town and Johannesburg.

When Lindsay Hassett led the successful Australian team to South Africa in 1949–50, Nourse topped the aggregate and averages among his countrymen. In the second Test at Cape Town he scored 65 and 114.

On his last tour to England in 1951, Dudley played a captain's innings of 208 in the first Test at Nottingham. It was a gallant knock, having batted with a broken thumb for nine hours. This heroic double-century was the inspiration behind his country's win, their first in 16 years. However, in the following four Tests, Nourse was sadly out of touch, and

scored only 93 runs. England were easy winners, 3–1.

This was the end of Dudley as a Test player, although he continued in first-class games until 1953. When he retired, his Currie Cup average of 65.85 was the best recorded in the competition to that time.

Dave Nourse was 70 when he saw Dudley score a century in a Currie Cup game, and was moved to say: 'What a pity, Dudley, you are not a left-hander. They would be able to compare us as batsman so much more easily. They tell me you are now in sight of some South African batting records. Well, go after them and improve on them and so keep the name flourishing. I like what I have seen and I feel proud that if anyone has to break my records it is likely to be you.'

Dave was then a sick man and those were almost the last words he ever spoke to Dudley. He died a few months later. As expected, Dudley surpassed most of Dave's records. First to go was his Test aggregate, then the number of centuries in the Currie Cup, followed by the number of runs in the Currie Cup and, finally, first-class hundreds – 41 against his father's 38. According to Dudley, to be the son of a well-known personality is not easy. 'It is no sinecure being the son of a famous sportsman. Somehow, even sub-consciously, one becomes aware of the hopes and aspirations of parents at a tender age: will the traditions be carried on? Is there cricket in the blood?'

Dudley died in August 1981. The two pillars of South African cricket, Dave and Dudley, had lived the biblical age of three score and ten.

The Nourses in Test Cricket											
	Tests	Runs	Avrge	HS	100s	50s	Wkts	Avrge	Best	5w/i	Catches
'Dave'	45	2234	29.78	111	1	15	41	37.87	4–25	–	43
Dudley	34	2960	53.81	231	9	14	0	–	–	–	12
Total	79	5194	39.95	231	10	29	41	38.10	4–25	–	55

CHAPTER 17

Three
Generations of Headleys

———— ● ————

They called him 'Atlas' because he carried the West Indies batting on his shoulders. George 'Atlas' Headley was among the all-time great batsmen and his sons, Ron and Lindy, were internationals in cricket and athletics. His grandson, Dean, occasionally opens the English attack. The Headleys provide the only instance of three direct generations to play Test cricket.

MENTION THE NAME GEORGE 'Atlas' Headley and you picture a big man with broad shoulders and swarthy blacksmith's arms. Actually, he was a short man, small in build. Don Bradman and Sachin Tendulkar are on the short side too, and so was Syd Gregory – but then, nobody called them 'Atlas'. However, take a look at Headley's scores in relation to team totals – especially in Tests – and you will understand the reason behind the nickname. He virtually carried the West Indies batting in the late 1920s and 1930s.

George Headley scored a double-century in his second international match; a century on his Test debut; a century in his first match at Lord's; a century in both innings in a Test on two occasions; a record 487-run stand for the sixth wicket; and 10 centuries in 22 Tests – that is a century every second Test!

What phenomenal consistency! And all for a weak side depending on him.

Born into a poor family in 1909 and cared for by his aunt, George Headley saw his first big match from the branches of a tree. When 13, in a 'catch-ball-bowl' game, George batted on the afternoons of a Monday, Tuesday, Wednesday and Thursday without getting out. To his disgust, no one turned up to bowl to him on the Friday! When 16, and still in short pants, George scored his first century in an important match. Even then, he batted at No. 3, his favourite position in his entire cricket career.

In 1927 he was inspired by watching English batsman Ernest Tyldesley's batting – especially on sticky wickets – and the next year was selected to represent Jamaica against the touring MCC side. George reacted to this news with his customary coolness. Even on his first-class debut he did not show any nervousness, his motto being 'a little prayer and a little luck'. But luck played a trick on the teenager. As he struck the first ball he received, the bat flew out of his hand and fell down the pitch. That was not the result of first-match jitters, it was caused by smooth, spikeless boots. He made 16 and 71. Curiously enough, 45 years later, in 1973, his son Ron's bat was also thrown out of his grasp by the fury of Mike Procter's pace.

Returning to George and 1928 ... He was given one more chance against Lord Tennyson's XI and he scored 211. Overnight, the 19-year-old had become a sensation and a poem was written about 'Headley G.' – the first of many. But despite the fact that he scored 409 runs at 81.8 that season, he missed selection to tour England for the West Indies' first Test series. He was considered too young. Eventually, he made his Test bow against England at Barbados on 11 January 1930 and scored 176 in the second innings. At 20 years and 226 days, he became the youngest player to hit a hundred on debut.

That was only the beginning of George Headley's run-orgy. A month later, in the third Test at British Guyana, he hit a century in each innings. With the series locked 1-all, the fourth and final Test was played to the finish. And what a marathon it turned out to be! England went on relentlessly to amass 849, Andy Sandham recording Test cricket's first triple-hundred. The West Indies replied with 286 – 563 runs behind – yet the England captain, the Hon. F.S.G. Calthorpe, did not enforce the follow-on. He batted on and set the West Indies an astronomical 835 runs to win.

Headley took up the challenge and told his skipper R.K. Nunes: 'I will not get out if you will stay with me'. They added 228 for the second wicket. When rain caused play to be abandoned, the West Indies were 5 for 408 and George's

George Headley, more than a 'Black Bradman'. (*Courtesy, Frank Bohlsen*, World of Cricket)

223 established a new Test record for the highest individual second-innings score. It was his fourth century in the four-Test series and he totalled 703 at an average of 88.

A few months later, the West Indians toured Australia. Headley failed in the first two Tests as wily leg-spinner Clarrie Grimmett troubled him. However, he broke through in the third Test at Brisbane, scoring a priceless unbeaten 102 out of the team total of 193. Incidentally, Bradman also failed in the first two Tests and scored a brilliant 223 in the third. In the final Test at Sydney, Headley scored another century. The West Indies won the Test but lost the series 1–3. Headley scored 1066 runs

Dean Headley, whose 6 for 60 was behind England's shock win over Australia in the 1998 Melbourne Test. (*Allsport / Stu Foster*)

down under and forged many friendships – especially with Stan McCabe.

Back in the Caribbean, George (344 not out – his career best) and Clarence Passailaigue (261 not out) added 487 against Lord Tennyson's XI. This is still a world record for the sixth wicket. George's unbeaten triple-century was followed by 84, 155 not out and 140 vs MCC – all within a month!

On his first appearance at Lord's during the tour of England in 1933 George scored a splendid 129 against MCC. He became the success of the tour, scoring well on good fast wickets, and also top-scored in some vital matches on wet wickets. According to his biographer, Noel White, 'His batting reached its zenith in the second Test at Old Trafford'. He hit a sparkling 169 and his lusty hits reminded one cricket writer of Frank Woolley. In Tests, he averaged 55.4. The next best West Indies batting average was only 23.8. On the tour, Headley totalled 2320 at 66. Only England's Wally Hammond had a slightly better average.

George Headley recalls being introduced to King George V by West Indies captain George ('Jackie') Grant, and the King wisecracking: 'Three Georges together!'

When England returned the visit to the Caribbean in 1934–35, Headley top-scored in at least one innings of every Test, climaxing with an unbeaten 270 in the final Test at Kingston, Jamaica. Thanks to his amazing consistency, the home team won a rubber for the first time ever.

Back to England in 1939 there was more glory for George. In the first Test at Lord's he scored a century in each innings – a feat without parallel at cricket's headquarters. He also became only the second batsman, after Herbert Sutcliffe, to hit a century in each innings twice in Test cricket. After this dual triumph at Lord's, C.B. Fry remarked: 'His middle name should be Atlas'. To celebrate his memorable batting at Lord's, Headley and two of his team-mates went to a Chinese restaurant. Soon after they came out, the restaurant was bombed!

George scored 1745 runs on the tour at 72.7, and Sir Pelham Warner said of him, '… he ranks in that very small class of stylists which includes Hobbs, Woolley, Kippax and Hammond. He is an extremely fine fielder.' Wrote R.C. Robertson-Glasgow: 'He delights in hooking, in delaying deflections to the leg, and in cutting square or late. In these arts he has no living superior … In Headley's art there is no noise. But it answers the test of greatness.'

At a farewell function, the immortal Sir Neville Cardus praised George Headley and referred to him as the 'Black Bradman', which was not well received by the West Indians. Denzil Batchelor noted, ''There are times when I think that the Don at his very best was fit to be called, ''the White Headley''.' And in the opinion of A.G. Moyes: '[Headley's] exceptional capacity for heavy scoring, led some to dub him ''the Black Bradman'', which was absurd. There were fleeting glimpses of similarity, especially on the leg-side, but that was all. Headley was gifted enough to stand on his own two feet. He was the substance not the shadow … He was without doubt one of the most accomplished batsmen seen between the two wars.' Cardus later called him 'the greatest living cricketer of my generation'.

After World War II Headley became a falling star. Against England in 1947–48 he was appointed captain but, after the first Test at Barbados, injury kept him out. He played in only two more Tests before he retired in 1954, aged 45. He was appointed coach of Jamaica in 1955, a post he held until 1966.

In recognition of his services to cricket, George Headley was granted full salary as a pension by the then Prime Minister of Jamaica. The Queen honoured him in 1955 with an MBE and in 1973 he was presented with the prestigious Norman Manley Award for Excellence in the Field of Sports. Fittingly enough, a road in Kingston has been named Headley Avenue, and a cricket and social club in New York City annually holds the George Headley Award Dinner to honour deserving individuals. George Headley died in 1983, mourned by many. It was like a State funeral.

George was very proud of his sons, Ron and Lindy, who shone in cricket and athletics, respectively. Left-handed Ron –

remembered for his consistent perform- ances for Worcestershire in county cricket until 1974 – learnt cricket in much the same way as his father. As a small boy, Ron played with other boys using a coconut branch bat, a string or tennis ball and an oil-drum. He represented his school before he left Jamaica at 11.

When George played League cricket for Dudley in England, the sons stayed in England and when Ron was 14 he represented Dudley Casuals along with his father. In 1955, Ron made the Dudley First XI, heading the batting averages, and was invited by Worcestershire for a trial. In 1958 he played for them as an amateur, but he soon took up cricket as a profession. In his first full season, in 1960, he scored over 1000 runs and was the only player from his county to top 2000 runs in 1961.

In 1964 he scored over 1500 runs and took 50 catches, thus contributing to Worcestershire's first-ever County Championship. They won the Championship three times in 11 years, and Ron was a member of all three winning sides. He toured Jamaica in 1965 with the Cavaliers and batted so well that the Jamaican selectors asked Worcestershire for permission to let Ron play for them against Australia. However, they were unsuccessful. In 1971, Worcestershire was lying third in the John Player Sunday League with only four matches left. As Norman Gifford had been injured, Ron was asked to take over as captain. Under his leadership, Worcestershire won all four matches, in the process defeating the champions, Lancashire, to win the title.

The same season, Ron Headley and P.J. Stimpson made first-wicket century partnerships on each of the four occasions they opened the innings together: 125 and 147 vs North- amptonshire at Worcester and 102 and 128 not out vs Warwickshire at Birmingham. The following year, Ron

(94) and New Zealander Glenn Turner (156) added 259 runs for the first wicket in Ron's benefit match. Despite the loss of the first day through rain, Ron received over £10,000 – a measure of his popularity.

In 1973, Ron realised his life's ambition to play Test cricket for the West Indies. Against England, he opened the innings in both Tests, but his highest score was only 42. However, his 1064 runs in 1974, with three centuries, contributed to Worcestershire's third County Championship.

Ron's brother, Lindy, gained interna- tional recognition in track athletics. The highlight of his career was representing Jamaica in the Tokyo Olympics of 1964. Lindy reached the semi-final in the 100 metres and was a member of the Jamaican 4 x 100-metres relay team which finished fourth. Lindy also represented Jamaica at the British Commonwealth Games in 1966.

The Headley dynasty chugs along nicely, well into the new millennium. George's grandson and Ron's son, Dean Warren Headley, opens the English attack on occasions. When he made his Test debut, on 3 July 1997, against Mark Taylor's Australians at Manchester, he became the first Test cricketer whose father and grandfather had also played Test matches, albeit for a different country. Also, unlike his father and grandfather, who were batsmen, Dean is a fast-medium bowler. He made a sensational debut for Middlesex in 1991, taking 5 for 46 and claiming the wicket of Ashley Metcalf with his first ball. Later he played for Kent.

Dean had been knocking on Test doors since 1996, when he equalled a world record for taking three hat-tricks in one season. These were for Kent against Derbyshire at Derby, against Worcestershire at Canterbury, and against Hampshire also at Canterbury (taking four wickets in four balls).

Despite a hip problem, he finished the season taking 51 wickets, his best return being 8 for 98 against Derbyshire at Derby. This earned him a well-deserved call-up to England's one-day squad against Pakistan.

England was desperate to find a replacement for Ian Botham. Quite a few were tried and Dean Headley got his chance in the Manchester Test against Australia in 1997. It was a promising debut and he made some heads turn – especially those of Australian openers Mark Taylor and Matthew Elliott – on his way to taking 4 for 72 and 4 for 104.

Handed the new ball, he went straight into action, striking Taylor on the head as he ducked into a bouncer in Dean's opening over. He pressed home the advantage in his third over, delivering a fiery ball which Taylor edged to slip. Soon he added Elliott and Michael Bevan to his victim list. He dismissed the above three batsmen in the second innings and added the scalp of match hero Steve Waugh (108 and 116) to his precious collection.

Dean's impressive debut would have turned memorable had Alec Stewart not dropped Paul Reiffel when he was 13 off his bowling. Reiffel went on to make 31 and added 70 precious runs with Steve Waugh. Commentators consider this partnership as the turning point in the series as Australia would have lost its seventh wicket with the score still under 200 and would possibly have lost the Test and the Ashes. In three Tests against Australia that summer Dean took 16 wickets at 27.75. Well, not exactly a Bothamesque performance, but it was promising.

His best haul so far was in Melbourne in December 1998, when he took 6 for 60 in the second innings and helped England win their only Test in the series. Set a modest win target of 175, Australia were cruising along at 2 for 103 when Dean Headley struck. Australia were shot out for 162 and England won the fascinating, seesawing Test by 12 runs. Man of the Match, Dean later said, 'I don't think I'm overly gifted. I'm the kind of bowler who has to work hard at Test level.'

In the next Test, in Sydney, he bowled intelligently to claim 4 for 62 and 4 for 40. He topped England's bowling averages for the tour, taking 19 wickets at 22.26 in three Tests. Since then he has been in and out of the English Test team, but the 30-year-old is still enthusiastic. He has not set the world on fire (60 wickets in 15 Tests at 27.85) as his grand-dad did, but has performed better than his father.

'Dad talks about cricket all the time,' he told Jonathan Agnew in *Wisden Cricket Monthly*. 'It drives me mad! That's where we differ because I need to switch off from the game but he just *loves* it. Goodness knows what he was like when he was playing! When I was living on my own, Dad found it hard to believe that I was playing professional cricket and doing all my washing. He just couldn't understand it, not because he was lazy when he played; just that he was so totally focussed on cricket.'

Was there any conflict for a cricketer with prominent West Indian connections playing for England? 'I know this has been an issue over the last few years but no one can possibly doubt my right or desire to play for England,' Dean told Agnew. 'Besides, I think if you are faced with a decision about who to play for and your heart really isn't in it you'll soon be found out.'

When he was picked for England in 1997, Dean received a fax from the West Indies Board of Cricket Control. It said, 'Well done and many congratulations. Your dad must be very proud.' And Dean is likewise very proud of his cricket heritage. 'I'll always be George's grandson. ... I'm extremely proud because as far as I know we are the only family to do this [three direct generations to play internationally] in any sport, but I'm going to an island [Jamaica] where George is a legend,' he said before touring the West Indies in early 1998.

Dean is amused when he is referred to as the 'third generation Headley'. Rather than considering this as a cross to bear, he deals with it with modesty and decorum. There can be no second George Headley, just as there can be no second Don Bradman.

How do the other great West Indian batsmen – Worrell, Walcott, Weekes, Sobers, Kanhai, Lloyd, Vivian Richards, Lara – compare with George Headley? Although it is not possible to compare class batsmen of different eras, veteran writer E.M. Wellings put Headley on the top of the tree. He wrote in *Wisden* (1963): 'His more recent rivals [3 Ws, Sobers, etc.] shone in strong teams. Headley scintillated in weak sides relying very largely on him.' Wellings, who saw the best innings by Bradman, Hutton, McCabe and Hobbs, rates Headley's two centuries in the Lord's Test of 1939 as the most outstanding batting performance.

The Headleys in Test Cricket

	Tests	Runs	Avrge	HS	100s	Wkts	Avrge	Best	5w/i	Catches
George	22	2190	60.83	270*	10	0	–	–	–	14
Ron	2	62	15.50	42	0	0	–	–	–	2
Dean	15	186	8.45	31	0	60	27.85	6–60	1	7
Total	39	2438	39.32	270*	10	60	31.68	6–60	1	23

CHAPTER 18

The
Pataudis

———●———

*Both captained India and both scored centuries on their Test debuts
against Australia. Both learnt their cricket in England – initially coached
by the great Frank Woolley – and both represented Oxford University
and an English county. Both won their Oxford Blue and scored a century
against Cambridge at Lord's as freshmen. They were named* Wisden's
Cricketers of the Year *in 1932 and 1968 respectively.*

BETWEEN THEM, THE NAWABS of Pataudi –
Iftikhar Ali Khan and his son, Mansur
Ali Khan – set many records in English,
Indian and Test cricket – enchanting
spectators with their contrasting magic
while batting or fielding. Both were
classical batsmen, but whereas Iftikhar
was all subtlety and grace, Mansur tended
to be more dynamic.

In the words of Rusi Modi, a former
Indian Test cricketer who played with
Iftikhar: 'Iftikhar was cast in the classic
mould of Len Hutton; Mansur is robust
and explosive like Garry Sobers'. Mansur
announced his retirement from Test cricket
in 1975. However, his exploits and
adventures – like his father's – will not be
forgotten.

The senior Nawab of Pataudi, Iftikhar,
was born of princely stock in Pataudi in
Punjab on 16 March 1910. His father-in-
law, the Nawab of Bhopal, was a leading

polo player, a keen yachtsman, a rifle shot
and a cricketer. He captained the University
of Aligarh, which recorded surprising wins
over strong opposition under his leadership. He became the President of the
Board of Cricket Control in 1936.

Most of Iftikhar's cricket was played in
England because India was not granted
Test status until 1932. After recording a
century in the traditional varsity match
against Cambridge in his first year in 1929,
he went on to record a brilliant and
unbeaten 238 against them at Lord's in
1931. That was his most glorious summer.
For Worcestershire and Oxford he amassed
1307 runs in 16 innings, averaging 93.36.

In the university match, A.T. Ratcliffe
of Cambridge recorded the first double-
century – eclipsing the 1904 record of 172
runs scored by J.F. Marsh. At the close of
play, Iftikhar told his friends that Ratcliffe's
record would not stand for 24 hours and,

true to his Muhammad Ali-like prediction, the next day Iftikhar scored a magnificent 238 not out in five hours. After 68 years, this record still stands. Iftikhar's greatest innings was his 165 for Gentlemen against Players at Lord's.

His 8750 runs in first-class cricket included three double-centuries for Worcestershire. Like two other well-known Indian cricketers, Ranji and Duleep, Iftikhar represented England in Tests. And he made his Test debut memorable by recording a century. This was against Australia in 1932–33 in the Sydney Test. But the law-unto-himself skipper, Douglas Jardine, dropped him after the second Test. During this – the bodyline – series, Jardine had instructed his close-in fielders never to flinch when a batsman hooked. When Jardine himself flinched visibly, Iftikhar jovially remarked: 'Skipper, you seem to have forgotten your own instructions!' Jardine was not amused and Iftikhar did not make the following Test.

When he was asked to lead India in England in 1946, Iftikhar was in semi-retirement. Many felt Vijay Merchant should have captained India as Iftikhar was past his best – and a 'foreigner' to other Indian cricketers. India lost the series 0–2, but Iftikhar performed adequately, scoring four hundreds on the tour. His best innings was 71 not out of the Indians' 132 on a sticky wicket at Gloucestershire. Commented Denzil Batchelor: 'Under him [Iftikhar] an Indian team, previously most difficult to blend, proved tractable and docile'.

Iftikhar did not believe in false modesty, and was well aware of his true merits as a cricketer, a first-class hockey player and a past master at billiards. He filled out the application form of his son, Mansur, for Winchester College in England with characteristic flourish. To the question 'other aptitudes' he wrote: 'My son'.

To Mansur, his father was a hero. The walls of his bedroom were adorned with pictures of Iftikhar at the crease. Mansur was nicknamed 'Tiger' as a child but it had nothing to do with his aggressive batting approach, fielding or field-placing. 'As an infant I had a tigerish propensity for crawling energetically on all fours,' he explains. When celebrating his 11th birthday he heard about his father's death from a heart attack whilst playing polo. Iftikhar was only 41.

On Iftikhar's wishes, Mansur was sent to England for education and cricket. Mansur appreciates the intensive coaching he received from George Cox jnr, the Sussex coach. In four years at Winchester College he totalled 2036 runs – the last 1068 coming in 18 innings. When only 16, he made his debut for Sussex. Wisden (1968) noted that Mansur's cricket appeared vigorous whereas his father's had been deft. Like his father, Mansur won his Oxford Blue and scored 131 (including one six and 18 fours) against Cambridge at Lord's in his first year. This was the first instance of a son emulating his father by reaching a century in the historic inter-varsity match. Playing against champion county Yorkshire, Mansur hit a century in each innings. In the next match, against Middlesex, he hit another ton but fell one short of his father's record for Oxford in which he had hit four centuries in a row. However, he reached heights his father could not.

Mansur captained both Oxford and Sussex, honours which had eluded the senior Pataudi. The junior's climb to the top was delayed when a car crash resulted in damage to his right eye in 1961 at the age of 20. At that stage he needed only 92 runs in four matches to better his father's record aggregate of 1307 runs in an Oxford season. Cricket was far from his mind when he returned to India.

The Indian selectors, not knowing the extent of his eye injury, asked him to captain the President's XI against Ted Dexter's MCC at Hyderabad. Mansur jumped at the chance, but batting created problems. When he used contact lenses he could see two balls six to seven inches apart. 'By picking the inner one I managed to score 35 by tea,' Mansur related in his autobiography, *Tiger's Tale.* 'Then I removed the contact lenses and, keeping the bad eye closed, completed the top score of 70.' After this, he was included in the Delhi Test. In the final Test at Madras – his third – he hit a splendid 103 which included two sixes and 16 fours. He added 104 in 95 minutes with skipper Nari Contractor. Mansur considers his century at Madras to be among three of his most important innings. It convinced him that he 'had the handicap licked'. And by this time he had learned the best way to bat. Pulling the peak of his cap over his right eye to eliminate the blurred double image, he scored 2793 runs at 34.91 in 46 Tests – hitting six centuries.

Mansur Pataudi became India's emergency captain in the Caribbean in 1962 when Contractor had a near-fatal injury. Mansur was a little over 21 then and thus became the youngest-ever Test captain. He retained the captaincy until the end of 1969 – an unprecedented feat in Indian cricket. He captained India in 40 Tests – 21 times in a row – and each performance was then an Indian record. In Test history, there are only two instances of both father and son captaining their country. Beside the Pataudis, F.T. and F.G. Mann captained England in their respective eras. Vic Richardson and grandsons Ian and Greg Chappell later captained Australia.

Mansur scored the first double-century by an Indian against England. However, he does not rank his unbeaten 203 at Delhi against England in 1963–64 as among his best. 'The first 90-odd runs were helpful, but the remainder had no bearing on the result,' he admits.

Besides his 103 against England in 1961–62, he considers his unbeaten 128 at

The gallant Pataudi jnr (right), with the author. (The Indian Down Under)

Madras in his first Test against Australia, his 75 and 85 against Australia on the green and bouncy Melbourne pitch in December 1967, and his 148 at Heading-ley six months earlier as his most memo-rable Test innings. His gallant century at Headingley came after India was forced to follow on 386 runs behind. In reply to England's monumental 4 for 550, India were crumbling at 7 for 92 before being revived by Mansur's gallant 64. In the second innings he hit a glorious 148.

Wisden made him Cricketer of the Year that year, 36 years after his father had been so honoured. Only the Parks, J.H. in 1938 and his son the wicket-keeper J.M. in 1968, were both similarly recognised by *Wisden.*

Mansur won the Australian writers' and spectators' hearts after his two masterly innings in the Melbourne Test of 1967–68. These twin knocks were all the more remarkable because he was recovering from a painful hamstring injury. His easy stroke-play reminded commentator Lindsay Hassett of the Bradman days. 'The Melbourne Test is special to me, 'Mansur recalled. 'The pitch was as green as the outfield and the score was 5 for 25 as I limped in and Garth McKenzie was on fire.'

In New Zealand, under Mansur in 1968, India won her first Test – and first series – overseas. About that time Mansur acquired the common touch, dropping his Nawab title. When New Zealand and Australia returned their visits to India, Pataudi showed moderate form. Subsequently he was replaced as captain and Ajit Wadekar led India to the West Indies and England in 1971. Mansur staged a comeback against England in India in 1972–73 and scored a match-winning 74 in the third Test. Wadekar's shock retirement in 1974 pitchforked Pataudi, 34, into India's captaincy against a strong West Indies team. His leadership was imaginative and forceful and India won two Tests. But his batting was in a shambles – only 94 runs at 13.4. Thus, his retirement did not come as a surprise.

Although often accused of being an aloof captain who had his favourites, Pataudi gave to Indian cricket both character and positiveness. He improved India's image abroad and the 'dull dogs' became the light brigade of the late 1960s.

Who was the greater cricketer – the father or the son? The answer would be unfair to either. Sir Donald Bradman, who saw them both, wrote in the preface of Rusi Modi's *Some Indian Cricketers*: 'Pataudi Senior was a fine player, but from observation I feel Pataudi Junior, taking into account his physical affliction, displayed even greater qualities, and the full flower of Mansur's prowess never quite blossomed'.

According to Rusi Modi, who played under Iftikhar's captaincy and watched Mansur mature: 'I consider Iftikhar a far better batsman than Mansur. On the other hand, Mansur was a better captain and the best fielder I have seen. Iftikhar was a correct and a stylish batsman. Once Faulkner, the well-known coach, said that Stan McCabe is not half the batsman Iftikhar Pataudi is. As to their personality, Iftikhar was an extrovert, Mansur an introvert. A gregarious character, Iftikhar was always immaculately dressed; he loved his Sulka ties and Savile Row suits. I wonder if Mansur has even worn a Sulka tie!'

Both Iftikhar and Mansur had a fine sense of humour. Iftikhar wrote in a friend's autograph book: 'Fast women and slow horses are no good for a sportsman'. When he read this several years later, Mansur wrote on the opposite page: 'I know nothing about horses, Dad'. Mansur married a movie star, the beautiful Sharmila Tagore, a grand-daughter of the poet, Rabindranath Tagore.

Another member of the Pataudi clan showed talent as a cricketer. He was Saad Bin Jung, Mansur's sister's son. He started brilliantly, scoring a splendid century for South Zone against the touring West Indies in 1978 when still a schoolboy. He had a pleasing style and timed the ball well, but his fielding let him down and his potential remained unfulfilled.

Mansur wrote in *Tiger's Tale*: 'My father's name and fame have followed me throughout life and following father's footsteps can sometimes be a drag. Since the accident ... I have had to compromise with my ambition to become a truly great batsman. I have concentrated instead on trying to make myself a useful one, and a better fielder than my father was.'

A prince, a Test captain and the husband of a glamorous actress, Mansur 'Tiger' Pataudi lived in the constant floodlight of publicity. Before he gave up the Nawab title, his home contained 150 rooms, employed well over 100 servants, seven or eight being his personal attendants. However, to be recognised as 'one of the best cover point and extra-cover fielders in the world' was far more satisfying.

Neil Harvey: a touch of class. 'Had Michaelangelo been a cricketer, he would have batted like
Neil Harvey' – Ray Robinson. (*Allsport / Adrian Murrell*)

Martin Crowe loses his bat during his Manchester Test century.
(*Allsport / Adrian Murrell*)

Mark Waugh in an adventurous mood. (*Rowley Morris*)

Mark Waugh in a relaxed mood in Sri Lanka in 1999.
(*Ken Hill*)

Twins galore! James Marshal (left) and identical twin brother Hamish with the Waugh twins Steve and Mark before the Northern Districts match against the Australians in Hamilton, NZ, in March 2000. (*Rowley Morris*)

Steve (left) and Mark Waugh as babies with dad Rodger and mum Bev. (*Bev Waugh*)

The Pataudis in Test Cricket

	Tests	Runs	Avrge	HS	100s	50s	Wkts	Avrge	Best	5w/i	Catches
Iftikhar (Eng. & Ind.)	6	199	19.90	102	1	0	–	–	–	–	0
Mansur (Ind.)	46	2793	34.91	203*	6	16	1	88.00	1–10	0	27
Total	52	2992	33.24	203*	7	16	1	88.00	1–10	0	27

CHAPTER 19

The
Winning Benauds

———— ● ————

*The success story of a schoolteacher and cricket coach who showed
his sons how to play winning cricket. Richie Benaud was one of the
greatest all-rounders in the history of the game and John was
a dynamic batsman and a no-nonsense personality.*

THE NAME BENAUD MEANS many things to many people. The first to spring to mind is Richie Benaud, who is more than just a Test cricketer. Although retired from active cricket since 1964, his is a household name in Australia and wherever cricket is played. Then there is John, his younger brother by 13 years, with batting as explosive as his viewpoints – a joy to watch but underrated by the selectors. And their father, Lou, an obscure country schoolteacher and a respected first-grade cricketer who was behind the success of Richie and John.

One of the few truly great all-rounders in the history of cricket is Richie Benaud – a crafty leg-spinner and googly expert who captured 248 wickets in Tests, an attacking lower-order batsman who hit the third-fastest Test century, a brilliant gully fielder with

amazing anticipation and reflexes, and a crowd-puller wherever he played. He was also a courageous and victorious leader of men who lost neither a series nor his cool. Now as a media personality, he is the voice of cricket.

The Benaud saga begins with Lou, who was of French origin. Named Louis Richard, he was born in Coraki on the Richmond River, NSW, in 1904. Thirteen years later, the family moved to Grafton and he spent four happy years at Grafton High School. Schoolmate Max Johnston showed him how to bowl leg-spin. In 1921, when he was 17, the family moved to Penrith. He studied at Parramatta High and soon was chosen in the Combined High School cricket team.

Selected for second grade for Penrith, teenager Lou tasted everlasting fame. For Penrith Waratah Club against St Mary's, he took all 20 wickets in the match: 10 for 30 in the first innings, including four wickets in four balls, and 10 for 35 in the second. This led to his being promoted to first-grade.

In Jugiong, near Yass in New South Wales, he established himself as a leg-spinner who could bat a bit with consistent performances; 7 for 55, 8 for 24, 8 for 37, 8 for 19, 6 for 1, 9 for 48, 116 retired and 5 for 24, 42 and 7 for 43, 113 retired and 3 for 22. These were outstanding figures by any standard and he would have gone higher but for his transfer from Parramatta High (where he was teaching) to One Tree Farm Provincial School, almost 1000 kilometres from Sydney. He tried his best to change this transfer but the Education Department refused his appeals. As A.G. 'Johnnie' Moyes wrote, '... had Lou been stationed in the city, had he been able to return to the city earlier in life, he might well have become the first of his name to play for his State'.

While he was in One Tree Farm, Lou played for the Combined Casino side against a Combined New South Wales team captained by the well-known Test cricketer Alan Kippax at Lismore. Lou took 3 for 65 and scored 39 not out and his team lost by a mere 12 runs. Impressed, Kippax invited Lou to the dressing-room, congratulated him and added that if he could come to Sydney he would arrange for him to play for a club. Unfortunately, the Education Department refused him leave to bowl on the SCG in front of the New South Wales selectors.

The best thing to happen to Lou was getting married to Rene Saville in 1929 – the union that resulted in two outstanding personalities. Education Department notwithstanding, Lou had a long association with the Cumberland Club. He became the fourth player to take over 300 wickets for the club, capturing 360 in 12 seasons. He continued playing until 1956 when he was 52.

Lou was also a spotter of talent. When in semi-retirement he was so excited to see the batting of a young boy in second grade that he raved to Richie that the boy would certainly play for Australia one day. That boy was Norman O'Neill. However, the first talent spotted by Lou was probably Richie's.

He encouraged his son to play single-handed cricket by bowling a tennis ball against a wall and hitting it on the rebound. More than the actual coaching, it was the atmosphere that captured the imagination of young Richie. In the words of Moyes: 'From the time he could toddle around, Richie lived in, and breathed, the cricket atmosphere'.

Born in 1930, Richie played his first competition match for Jugiong School, when six, scoring 11 runs. At eight, he played in the First XI of Burnside School near Parramatta, and later led the team to a competition win. With his own cricket clothes packed ready, in case a player should fail to turn up, Richie travelled around to see his father play for his district and clubs. Watching the great spinner Clarrie Grimmett bowl was an inspiration to Richie and, as he recalls in his book *Willow Patterns*, 'I think it was the avid watching of Grimmett more than any one thing that made me want to be a leg-spinner'.

Lou, thinking Richie's hands were not large enough, did not allow him to bowl leg-spinners until he was 17. Instead, emphasis had been kept on length and direction. Up to that time, Richie had been considered more of a batsman. When 16, he reached a rewarding stage. He was promoted to first-grade for Central Cumberland and his team-mates for the first game included his father. 'It was a great thrill to walk alongside him,' recalled Richie. In the next match he made a brilliant 98. However, the way to the top was not paved with roses. There was a cracked skull, a broken thumb, a crushed finger and a ball in the mouth.

But nothing could dent his determination to succeed. According to A.A. Thomson, 'he had courage in excelsis'.

The skull-cracking episode came when, as a teenager, he was batting for NSW Second XI. He tried to hook a ball, missed it, and was struck a shattering blow on the forehead above the right eye. Richie was out of cricket for a year, but the blow left no psychological scar – for years later he hooked tearaway terrors Wes Hall, Freddie Trueman and Frank Tyson with tremendous power.

In his Shield debut in 1948, when 18, he scored two and did not bowl. He had to wait until he was 21 to hit his first hundred, which included two sixes and 12 fours. With the series against the West Indies in 1951–52 already won, the Australian selectors blooded three youngsters, Richie being one of them. Once again, his debut was far from promising – scores of 3 and 19 in a low-scoring match, and the sole wicket of fellow-spinner Alf Valentine – a prize rabbit. Thank heavens no cameraman whispered, 'Can't bat, can't bowl!'

England in 1953 was not a successful tour for Richie but he had his moments. Against Yorkshire, at Bradford, he hit a scintillating 97 in two hours, with four sixes and 11 fours. He also took 7 for 46. His best was to come in the final match of the tour. At Scarborough, against Pearce's XI – a virtual England side – Australia were set 320 to win in 220 minutes. Benaud opened with Arthur Morris and took time to play himself in. When Len Hutton teasingly remarked, 'What's matter, laad, playing for average?' Richie's answer was 11 sixes – a world record at the time. 'This was hardly liberty, it was licence,' commented A.A. Thomson.

After reaching his first hundred in England, Richie drove Roy Tattersall for four successive sixes. Even the steady Alec Bedser and the crafty Johnny Wardle were belted over the fence. He scored 135 in 110 minutes and Australia went on to win in the last over.

During this tour fellow spinner Doug Ring passed on valuable tips to Richie – especially on how to bowl a top-spinner. Also on this tour, the great Bill O'Reilly suggested a few changes in his bowling method. 'It was very good advice and from that I steadily improved,' he acknowledges.

Earlier, Richie had improved his batting stance by seeking Keith Miller's advice and practising in front of a mirror. The young Benaud was learning fast and acquiring the century habit. In three successive matches against Queensland in the Sheffield Shield seasons of 1953–54 and 1954–55, he hit three tons. Against Western Australia, he scored 112 and 59 as an opener, and took seven wickets as well.

In the Kingston Test of 1955, he hit a dazzling 121 in 85 minutes, with two sixes and 15 fours, his century coming in 78 minutes. It was the third-fastest Test century – following Jack Gregory's century in 70 minutes in 1920–21 and G.L. Jessop's in 75 minutes in 1902. Benaud's onslaught prompted a Jamaican barracker to shout: 'Do it to England, maan, not to us'. Earlier in the series he had captured three wickets in four balls, and he headed the bowling averages, taking 18 wickets at 27 runs apiece.

In 1956, Richie's second tour of England started with a spectacular 160 (three sixes, 22 fours) against Worcestershire in the opening match. Then, in the Lord's Test, he put on a memorable performance, scoring a magnificent 97 off 113 balls in 144 minutes when 117 runs were added with Ken Mackay. Later, he took what is described by knowledgeable observers as 'the catch of the century' when he caught Colin Cowdrey in the gully. Thus, Richie had contributed sensationally to Australia's only win in the series.

Richie Benaud rates this Lord's Test as one of his most enjoyable games and, as for that Cowdrey catch, he modestly explains that instead of his catching the ball, actually the ball caught him, 'for good as it looked, I never saw the ball other than as a blur from the moment it left Colin's bat'.

The same year, Australia toured Pakistan and India. A day before the Madras Test, Benaud decided to shorten his run to save energy. Bowling with this shortened run-up he captured 7 for 72 – his best Test figures – as Australia won by an innings. Then followed his most successful tour – to South Africa, under Ian Craig in 1957–58. 'This experience,' wrote A.A. Thomson, 'formed the springboard from which he leaped to three successive victories over England. It could be said that on the veldt, he eventually found his feet.' On his South African performances, *Wisden* of 1959 noted: 'The outstanding personality was R. Benaud who, in bowling and batting, enjoyed a tour of unbroken success'. In Tests he scored 329 runs, including two centuries, and took 30 wickets. In all first-class games, he scored 817 runs with four hundreds, and took 106 wickets.

In fact, Benaud is the only bowler other than C.T.B. Turner of the 19th century to have taken 100 wickets in a season outside England. His performances in the five Tests included: 122; 4 for 95 and 5 for 49; 5 for 114; 100, 4 for 70 and 5 for 84; 43 and 5 for 82. Seldom had an all-rounder in the history of the game performed so consistently in one series. And Benaud did not reach the pinnacle of his form by waiting for inspiration.

As Bob Simpson – who took over as captain when Benaud retired – recalls: 'His practice session on that tour had to be seen to be believed. He laboured long after other players had left practice; a lonely figure bowling with a youngster to retrieve the balls aimed at a handkerchief placed on a good length spot. His legendary accuracy developed here.'

Ill health forced the premature retirement of Craig from Test captaincy and in the 1959–60 series against England Benaud was appointed captain. He lost the toss four times out of five, yet won the series 4–0. Benaud himself contributed handsomely to the success by taking 31 wickets in the series and by his dynamic leadership. Cricket pundits were baffled by Australia's easy wins over Peter May's highly fancied side, especially as Benaud was a rookie compared to the elegant May. Benaud had the whole team behind him. A born PR man, he had pre-Test match meetings where every player's viewpoint was considered and grievances settled.

The excellent team spirit that existed was very clear to the spectators. The fall of a wicket was followed by ecstatic scenes in the middle, with the players congratulating and hugging the bowler or fielder concerned. Thus, he could be called the father of modern cricket with all its extrovert expressionism. These emotional get-togethers tended to nauseate old-timers, but the players felt 10 feet tall and gave their all. Benaud retained the Ashes in England in 1961 (winning 2–1) and in Australia in 1962–63 (drawing 1-all).

Throughout the 1961 tour of England, Richie's right shoulder troubled him a great deal. At times it was so painful he could not shave himself, let alone bowl googlies. He had to miss the Lord's Test but played in the fourth Test at Manchester despite the fibrositis.

This was the Test which, in a few overs, Benaud converted from a certain defeat into a stirring victory. England were set 256 to win in 230 minutes and were galloping towards victory with the score 1 for 150 and Ted Dexter going great guns. It was then that Benaud produced his *pièce de résistance*. Because of his painful shoulder, he did not attempt excessive spin, but by going round the wicket and pitching in the rough of Trueman's footholds he imparted an awkward lift. In an incredible spell, he took four vital wickets for 13 runs: Dexter caught behind off a high snick; May, to his chagrin, bowled first ball; Brian Close caught after attempting a desperate shot; and the opener, Subba Row, bowled after batting sensibly for almost three hours. England lost nine wickets for 51 after being one for 150, and Benaud finished with 6 for 70. It was Richie's biggest triumph – a victory against all odds. Following this tour, Benaud was awarded an OBE by the Queen.

But even more than in this series, Benaud had gained immortality the previous season against Frank Worrell's West Indians – the series that revived an interest in cricket. The rubber included a tie, a draw made possible by the last pair batting for two hours and a win by two wickets in the series-deciding final Test. Although Worrell has been given the credit for this tantalising series, Benaud was equally responsible. Moyes considered Benaud to be a more brilliant skipper than Worrell. 'In applauding the West Indians for lighting the fires of cricket's rehabilitation,' he wrote, 'I give full marks to Benaud for providing all the fuel he could to keep it burning brightly, both then and in after years.'

'The fame of the series is Benaud's monument to cricket,' summed up Simpson.

In the first Test at Brisbane, resulting in the first of the two ties in Test history and considered 'the greatest Test of all time', Australia were set 233 to win at 45 runs an hour. They were 6 for 92 when Benaud joined Alan Davidson. Their 134-run stand for the seventh wicket tilted the match in Australia's favour. Then, within one run, both were dismissed, Davidson for 80 and Benaud for 52. In

the final over, with the score level, the last two batsmen were run out.

Richie Benaud was also engaged in another tie four years earlier – the first tie in Sheffield Shield history. That was between New South Wales and Victoria on the Melbourne Cricket Ground in December 1956. New South Wales were set 161 to win and made 160 – Benaud top-scoring with 63. It was also for New South Wales that Richie had his best bowling figures at first-class level. Against MCC under Dexter in 1962–63, he took 7 for 18 in the second innings as New South Wales won by an innings, with a day to spare.

Shoulder trouble forced Richie to retire when 33, and with plenty of cricket left in him, during the series against South Africa in 1963–64. By then, he had become the first player to score over 2000 runs and take over 200 wickets in Tests. As an all-rounder, Benaud ranks with the truly great ones, Garry Sobers of the West Indies, Ian Botham of England, Richard Hadlee of New Zealand, Imran Khan of Pakistan and India's Kapil Dev.

Benaud's biographer, Moyes, rated him 'the finest captain I have seen since Bradman'.

Bob Simpson considers Benaud the father figure of modern cricket: 'When he took over the Australian captaincy, he took cricket by the scruff of the neck and shook life back into it'. According to Charles Eliott, the noted English umpire, Richie was the best overseas captain.

Wrote Ray Robinson in *On Top Down Under*: 'His [Benaud's] achievements, put on the scale with his skippership successes, lead me to rank him first among captains I have known.'

Benaud's contribution to cricket went further than scoring runs and grabbing wickets. Pakistan cricket benefited from his advice when he suggested to the then president Ayub Khan that they do away with matting wickets. This was done and it led to an improvement in their cricket standard.

The Benaud family – Richie, John, father Lou and grandfather Richard. Inset: John Benaud.
(*Courtesy, the Benaud family album*)

As a media personality, he successfully argued the case for full Test status recognition of New Zealand by the Australian authorities. And in 1976, as manager of the International Wanderers, he toured South Africa and fought for multiracial cricket in that country. The report that South Africa would end segregation in sports pleased Richie so much that he referred to it as 'the best news I have heard in years'.

A professional journalist and TV commentator, Richie has written eight perceptive books on cricket. To me, his *Willow Patterns* is the most enjoyable. He was one of the key figures in the formation of World Series Cricket in 1977. Today, he is perhaps the most enduring face and voice in the world of cricket, his grey hair making him look distinguished. He is recognised as cricket's shrewdest television analyst,

delivering his insights with the dry humour and incisiveness which are his hallmark. Imitation is perhaps the best form of flattery and there are probably as many Richie Benaud impersonators as there are for Elvis Presley.

To quote fellow commentator Bill Lawry from a foreword in Mark Browning's *Richie Benaud*: *Cricketer, Captain, Guru*: 'There is no doubt that Richie Benaud has one of the most brilliant cricket brains in the world and on reflection, cricket has suffered from the fact that he has never taken an administration position in world cricket, apart from the fact that he had a part to play in the success of World Series Cricket, a dramatic period in the history of Australian cricket, a period which changed world cricket forever and fortunately, lifted the game into the modern era, both for players and spectators'.

John Benaud had 'a profile like a Red Indian's minus feathers' – Ray Robinson. (*K. M-H*)

One can sympathise with young and talented John Benaud trying to climb the ladder and make his mark in cricket when big brother Richie was already a successful Test captain and an internationally known figure. 'Ever since John could remember,' wrote David Lord in *World of Cricket*, 'he has been "Richie's young brother", often without a name.'

Unfavourable comparisons – often well meant – were hurtful to John, who was a powerful cricketer in his own right. Always, John Benaud had to fight for recognition, to gain his own identity. He was a dynamic batsman who thrilled the crowd, a leader of men, a dedicated fielder and a useful bowler. But according to some, 'he was passed over so that selectors could not be accused of picking him because his brother was the Test captain'. As John told Lord, 'I reckoned I was hitting the ball better than most of my age group by the time I was 20, yet to crack the NSW Colts' side was practically impossible'.

He eventually made a sound 40

against Queensland Colts, but failed in the next game and was dropped. It was frustrating for a person who was burning with a desire to succeed. He felt that he 'had always to fire, to stay'. He also stood up for his rights when made captain of New South Wales in 1969–70 during the absence of Brian Taber, who was touring overseas. Wearing ripple-sole shoes against official orders led to his getting the 'boot' – a most regrettable incident. But he still feels that the ripple-soles are more convenient, so why not wear them? Now many cricketers do.

In fact, John had sought permission to wear the comfortable ripple-sole shoes because of blisters on his feet. But it was refused and he was dropped from the team as punishment for disobeying their instructions. In protest, Richie resigned as NSW Cricket Association life member and Lou refused to watch a match at the SCG. 'It was a childish action by the Association, where delegates were weak enough to allow themselves to be dominated by one man,' Lou was quoted in Richie Benaud's book *On Reflection*.

The four innings that John remembers with pleasure are the ones that placed his team in a strong position when all appeared lost.

- When 16, and playing for Rangers in a local Parramatta church's competition, he batted for five hours to score 70.
- A century for New South Wales vs Victoria in a 2nd XI clash – 99 coming before lunch.
- New South Wales won a virtually lost game, when skipper, John, scored 129 – a defensive knock.
- 142 against Pakistan in the second Test at Melbourne, 1972–73, when Australia was in trouble. This was in his second, and second-last, Test.

According to Ray Robinson: 'The way John Benaud plays cricket, always

The Benaud family – Richie, John, mother Rene and John's wife Lindsay.
(*John Benaud*)

positive, sometimes unorthodox, rouses people's interest'.

John is slightly taller than Richie, has fair hair, blue eyes and 'a profile like a Red Indian's minus feathers'. He was selected to play in three Internationals against a World XI in 1971–72. And, despite scoring a gallant 99 in the final International at Adelaide, after Australia was 3 for 35, his name was missing from the Australian squad to tour England in 1972. As a point of interest, in the six innings John played against the World XI he fell to Pakistan's spinner, Intikhab Alam, five times.

The next season he was reappointed as the captain of New South Wales. In the opening match against Queensland he hammered 73 runs in 82 minutes – hitting four sixes. He certainly had to fire to stay, and this firing brought him back into the Australian Test team against Pakistan in 1972–73. In the first innings of the Melbourne Test, his old 'foe' Intikhab dismissed him for 13. The team for the next Test at Sydney was selected that day and John Benaud was dropped.

However, the following day he hit the selectors for a six by scoring a brilliant 142. When 94, he jumped out to Intikhab and hit a six to score his first and only Test century.

John remembers that Test with mixed feelings. On the evening of 1 January 1973 he was 11 not out when told about his omission from the Sydney Test. He candidly expresses his feelings on that night in his perceptive book, *Matter of Choice*: 'There's no doubt about it, getting dropped in the middle of a Test match, especially when you are not out, has a way of sharpening your focus ... What should a cricketer do? Expect his captain [Ian Chappell] to ring up the chairman and threaten to go on strike? Or, should the player confront the selectors himself and offer something in the way of abuse? Go out and get pissed, maybe? Call Lifeline?'

Instead, he scored a magnificent hundred, 93 of which came before lunch against a strong Pakistani attack. 'It was one of those perfect days ... our 233-run partnership [with Paul Sheahan] was a record that lived for a decade,' John recalls.

Subsequently he played one Test in the Caribbean and retired from first-class cricket when only 29. His potential and performances entitled him to more Test appearances. If only he had been granted half the opportunities given to Richie. John continued playing first-grade cricket for Penrith for a decade and was news editor of Sydney's *Sun* before it folded in the 1980s. He became an Australian selector from 1988 to 1993, and NSW selector in 1997–98. He writes provocative columns for Sydney's *Sun-Herald*. He is proud of his cricket heritage. 'I'm very grateful to my father [Lou] for all the time he put in with me as a youngster. He deserves to have sired two sons who played Test cricket for Australia.'

In a touching dedication to his parents in his latest book, *Anything but ... an Autobiography*, Richie wrote: 'It is said about life that one thing you cannot do is choose your parents, but I couldn't have been luckier in my years numbering almost three scores and ten. Lou and Rene were pioneers in the very best sense of the word, straightforward people, hard workers, honest, loving and dedicated to bringing up two sons and having an influence on youngsters who passed their way in classrooms or in everyday life.'

Lou passed away in 1994 but Rene is still active, tending to roses wearing a sunhat. It is always a thrill to receive a Christmas card with a thoughtful message from her every year.

The Benauds in Test Cricket											
	Tests	Runs	Avrge	HS	100s	50s	Wkts	Avrge	Best	5w/i	Catches
Richie	63	2201	24.45	122	3	9	248	27.03	7–72	16	65
John	3	223	44.60	142	1	0	2	6.00	2–12	0	0
Total	66	2424	25.52	142	4	9	250	26.86	7–72	16	65

CHAPTER 20

The
Enduring Edriches

———— ● ————

From 1934 to 1978, the name Edrich figured prominently in English first-class cricket. In the 1940s, four Edrich brothers, Eric, Bill, Geoffrey and Brian, played in the county championships for Lancashire, Middlesex, Kent and Glamorgan. A story of the bulldog breed Bill Edrich and his cousin John (who earned 116 Test caps between them in 39 years), and of their other relatives who regularly fielded strong Edrich XIs.

THE YEAR 1947 BELONGED to the 'Middlesex twins', Denis Compton and Bill Edrich. Their combined run-getting spree has never been approached until today. In style and technique, no 'twins' were less identical; Compton, a cavalier overflowing with charisma, a cricketing genius who could ad lib his strokes, and Edrich, equally well-equipped in stroke production though more down to earth – an efficient plumber who knew his taps.

But in the glorious summer of 1947 he matched his glamorous cricket twin stroke by stroke and run by run. Both broke Tom Hayward's record of 3518 runs in a season by scoring 3816 (Compton) and 3539 (Edrich). Compton's record aggregate still stands. They were associated in seven partnerships of over 200 runs that season, twice in Test matches against South Africa. Their third-wicket partnership of 370 against the Springboks is still a world record. In Tests they totalled 1305 runs between them – Compton 753 in five Tests and Edrich 552 in four. Edrich also took 16 wickets in the series.

The South African captain, Dudley Nourse, later commented: 'As individuals we liked and admired Edrich and Compton ... As a pair together at the wicket they strained our friendship to the limit. There was a wholesale massacre of our bowling on a grand size scale.' According to English writer Basil Easterbrook in *Wisden*: 'It was, although none knew it at the time, the last great pyrotechnic display before the game was overtaken by our egalitarian times'.

As a finale to that memorable season, Middlesex beat All England by nine wickets, Compton and Edrich making mincemeat of the powerful attack by scoring 246 and 180 respectively, before both were stumped by Godfrey Evans. It was intoxicating cricket.

Then followed the match between an Edrich XI and a Norfolk XI. It was in Norfolk that all cricket-playing Edriches were born and bred and learned their cricket. The Edrich XI was comprised of Bill's father, his three brothers – all first-class county players – three uncles and three nephews. John Edrich, a future Test player, was only 10 years old and was not included. Bill's grandfather, a demon fast bowler of his time, had died a short time before 'but I expect his spirit was looking on', sensed Bill. Bill scored 49 and his elder brother, Eric, the wicket-keeper, a hurricane hundred as the Edrich XI closed at 6 for 280. The opponents could total only 110, Bill's younger brother Brian taking 6 for 35.

Growing up in such a background, it is not surprising that John became one of the more reliable English batsmen of the 1960s and early 1970s. In his autobiography, *Runs in the Family*, published in 1969, John sheds further light on the amazing family. 'My grandfather, Harry Edrich of Manor Farm, Blofield – a village near Norfolk – spent his days farming, cricketing and raising 13 children. One of his sons became my father, Fred, and another, Bill snr, the father of Geoff (Lancashire), Brian (Kent and Glamorgan), Eric (Lancashire) and Bill (the famous W.J. of Middlesex and England).'

Bill snr (William Archer) was the eldest of Harry Edrich's 13 children, who were born between 1880 and 1907. He taught his four sons (Eric, Test player Bill, Geoff and Brian) and daughter Edna how to play cricket. His constant advice was: 'Play straight and keep over the ball when you play the cut'. They must have followed the advice for all four sons played first-class cricket. He died in 1979 at the age of 89.

His younger brother, Edwin, was a pace bowler who became the first in the family to play for Norfolk. But it was as a batsman that he shone in that match, scoring 15 and 71 not out in a low-scoring game and contributing to his team's victory.

Fred, born in 1905, was the ninth son and 12th child of Harry. He was a useful cricketer who encouraged his son, John Edrich, who retired in 1978 after scoring a century of centuries and making over 5000 runs in Test cricket. 'He [father] never converted my left-handed tendency,' remembers John. His sister Freda often joined in to play cricket.

Harry's youngest daughter (13th offspring), Alice Miriam, bowled accurately and hit hard. Nicknamed 'Cis', she captained the Norfolk ladies team. She often dismissed her five well-known nephews – including Bill and John – at the family nets.

Bill Edrich acknowledges that his success is due to the coaching he received from his father and his schoolmaster, Mr Fred Scott. It was Scott who laid a concrete wicket at the school to foster the obvious talents of Bill. Years later, the same Mr Scott predicted to John's mother that John would follow Bill into the England side.

In 1938, when John was an 11-month-old baby, Bill played his second first-class season. He scored over 2000 runs – including 1000 runs before May – and was picked in all four Tests against Australia. Bill started the season so prodigiously that from 30 April to 23 May he accumulated 981 runs – his scores being 104, 37, 115, 63, 20 not out, 182, 71, 31, 53 not out, 45, 15 and 245. He required only 19 runs in eight days to join the select band of five cricketers with 1000 runs before May, but just then his luck seemed to run out. He scored a duck against Worcester and nine in the first innings against the Australians. With rain affecting this game, Bill's chances seemed remote, but Don Bradman sportingly declared the innings 40 minutes before stumps, telling Edrich: 'See if you can get those 10, Bill.' Bill got 20 and found himself not only in the record books but also in the Test side.

Incidentally, 35 years passed before Glenn Turner of New Zealand reached his 1000 runs before May in 1973 and, just like Turner, Edrich found the strain of scoring 1000 runs by the end of May a psychological barrier to Test success.

In four Tests, Bill Edrich could make only 67 runs after playing six innings. But the selectors had seen enough of his potential and picked him for the tour of South Africa. Once again, Edrich failed dismally in Test matches, scoring only 4, 10, 0 and 6 in the first four Tests. Yet Wally Hammond persevered with him and, in the second innings of the timeless Test at Durban, Edrich justified his skipper's confidence by scoring a magnificent 219. This was the Test in which England was set 696 runs to win.

Edrich, with 88 runs in eight Tests, had lost all his confidence when Hammond told him: 'You can make runs, Bill, if you try. Don't be afraid to go for the ball if you can see it.' With these words ringing in his ears, Bill played the innings of his life. 'Justification came just in front of the bailiff,' wrote A.G. Moyes. Then came World War II and six crucial years of Bill's life were cricketless. He became a pilot in Bomber Command and won a DFC for a daring daylight attack. Test cricket resumed in 1946 but, because of his patchy form, he was not an automatic choice. About that time, he developed his tearaway fast-medium bowling.

It was his all-round ability and the luck of the Edriches – he scored 222 not out and took 7 for 69 in a match against Northants at the right moment – that won him a place in the English team to tour Australia in 1946–47. Batting at No. 3, he showed courage and skill to top-score for England in both innings (71 and 119) in the Sydney Test. As he revealed later in his autobiography, *Cricket Heritage*: 'My bat felt light in my hands and my feet light on the ground.' This light feeling must have chased him to Melbourne, where he hit 89. But his most satisfying moment of the tour was bowling Bradman in the Brisbane Test.

Then came 1947, the season of Edrich and Compton. To quote Moyes: 'They were a pair of joy-bringers who introduced a touch of the village green into their cricket'.

Edrich continued playing Test cricket until 1955 and first-class cricket until 1958 when he was 52. However, he could never even remotely recapture his 'class of '47'. In 39 Tests he averaged 40, while scoring 2440 runs with six centuries, captured 41 wickets and took 39 catches. He hit 86 first-class centuries.

Bill's brothers, Eric, Geoffrey and Brian, represented three counties from 1938 to 1958. The eldest one, Eric, played fairly regularly for Lancashire as a wicket-keeper. He touched his peak in 1948. Against the googlies of Warwickshire's Bill Hollies, he scored 106 not out in 155 minutes, showing, according to *Wisden*, 'cultured shots'. His late cuts were well executed and he was not afraid to loft the slow deliveries.

His best performance was in the Roses (Lancashire vs Yorkshire) match that year when he scored 121, his career best, adding 170 with Test opener Cyril Washbrook. On his personality, Denys Rowbotham wrote in *The Guardian*: '[Eric] Edrich is a merry, unselfconscious humorist; he loves every ball that is bowled to him and grins happily at every crack of his bat on it'. That season his great thrill was stumping Don Bradman.

Third brother, Geoff, was a consistent batsman for Lancashire. In 1950 he hit three centuries in four innings. Next season he scored seven hundreds, five of them in championship matches and one against the touring South Africans. 'I treasure that innings most of all, because

McCarthy (the Springbok quickie) pinged me when I was about 60,' Geoff recalled in Ralph Barker's *The Cricketing Family Edrich*. As he was receiving medical attention in the pavilion, three wickets fell in 20 minutes. Geoff came out to score a gallant 121. Team-mate Brian Statham later said: 'Geoff possessed the outstanding characteristic of all the Edrich family. He had guts and more guts.'

For the first and only time in his career, Geoff topped 2000 runs in a season in 1952. He was selected to tour India with a Commonwealth team in 1953–54, where he averaged 40 and hit two centuries. In 1954 he scored 134 against the touring Pakistanis.

Whenever Washbrook was not available, Geoff captained Lancashire. Of the 10 matches he captained, six were won outright and three on first innings while the other was abandoned due to rain. Under his leadership, Lancashire whipped Leicestershire without losing a wicket in either innings. Leicestershire made 108 and 122, Lancashire none for 166 declared and none for 65.

Geoff resembled Bill and once had cricket author Jim Swanton puzzled. Seeing prisoner-of-war Geoff bowling in the Singapore Island in 1942, he wondered, 'Goodness, I did not know the Japs had caught Bill Edrich.' Ben Barnett, the Australian wicket-keeper, observed that 'Geoff was a top-class player and his splendid batting gave a lot of pleasure to the many prisoners who watched these games.'

The youngest brother, Brian, played for Kent and Glamorgan. His most successful season was for Kent in 1949. Against Hampshire he took 7 for 41, his best figures in first-class cricket. Then followed his memorable match against Sussex. He scored 60 out of Kent's 237. When Kent was asked to follow on, Brian saved his county from an innings defeat by hitting magnificently to score 193

unbeaten runs on a wearing pitch. He added 161 runs in 70 minutes with Fred Ridgway for the ninth wicket. Sussex lost four wickets before winning with minutes to spare. Brian had taken three of the four wickets to complement his quickfire batting. This led to his being awarded the county cap for which he had waited for 10 years. Inspired, he took 7 for 68 in the next match against Gloucestershire.

Without doubt, Bill Edrich was the most celebrated among the brothers. When 16, he played his first big match for Norfolk against the touring Indians in 1932. Norfolk was in trouble against Indian fast bowler Mohammad Nissar, being 5 down for 20 when Bill came in. 'He was just a boy,' remembers his mother Edith, 'and the big dark Nissar was bowling. I almost fainted when I saw him walk out of the pavilion, he looked so small.'

His school was given a half-day holiday and they roared encouragement. Bill gritted his teeth and scored 20 out of his team's total of 49, the only player to get double figures as Nissar finished with 6 for 14. This was just the beginning. When Bill retired from Test cricket in 1954–55 and from county cricket in 1958 he was recognised as among the greats in the game.

Basil Easterbrook paid Bill Edrich this tribute: 'To see him come through the gate at Lord's and walk out to the middle was to see the personification of self-confidence and aggressiveness ... He walked with chest thrust out like the human fighting cock he was, but as light on his feet as a girl going to her first dancing class.'

Exit Bill Edrich from the first-class scene in 1958. And enter John Edrich, the left-hand opening batsman on the first-class circuit in 1959. John Edrich, the working bee of English cricket, had to struggle to get into a county XI, let alone a Test side. In order to avoid comparison with cousin Bill, John joined the junior staff of Surrey rather than Middlesex.

To quote John from his auto-biography, *Runs in the Family*: 'If I was going to make the grade in county cricket and eventually to international honours, I wanted to make it on my own ability. I did not want accusations that the Edrich name had opened doors on my behalf ... I have never once turned to Bill for advice in sorting out my cricketing problems. And there have been many.'

Despite this, the approach of the two Edriches – both of them short and stocky in appearance – was similar. Both were pugnacious fighters possessing a full range of strokes, but using them sparingly to gather more runs for England.

In 1955, John, then 18, headed the Surrey Second XI batting averages but was drafted for National Service for two years. He made up for this lost time in 1959 and in only his second game for Surrey's first XI he scored a century in each innings and went on to hit four centuries in his first seven innings before giving Freddie Trueman the treatment. When 'Fiery Fred' cracked John's shoulder with a nasty kicking ball, the agony inspired the junior to hit three sixes in two overs.

Undoubtedly, there have been better stroke-players than John Edrich in the 1960s and 1970s, but few more gallant players. Frank Tyson, Peter Pollock, Charlie Griffith and Dennis Lillee put him into hospital on various occasions, but the bulldog Englishman always came back and resumed his interrupted cricket career.

He made his Test debut against the West Indies in 1963 and then toured India without overtaxing the scorers. His magic moment came in 1964 when Bob Simpson's Australians toured England.

In his first Test against them at Lord's, he hit a century. 'This was a sublime moment,' he remembers. But so loaded was England with batsmen that Edrich was dropped in the final Test. Those were bad days for John.

His first marriage to an American tennis player was breaking up. After being dropped from the final Test against Australia, he was excluded from the England XVI to tour South Africa. He wanted to quit the game. Just then he met an Australian girl, Judy Cowan, whom he subsequently married – with Ken Barrington as best man. Judy was the best thing to happen to John. He gave up drinking completely and kept regular hours. 'She made all the difference,' he acknowledges.

John fought his way back to Test cricket in the Headingley Test against New Zealand. And what a comeback! He hit an unbeaten 310 with 52 fours and five sixes. It was a dazzling display of aggressive driving and spectacular hooking. No other batsman in Test cricket has hit over 200 runs in boundary hits in the course of an innings.

Against South Africa, John was struck by an express delivery from Peter Pollock. His temple became swollen so quickly that his partner Geoff Boycott commented: 'Looks like you've got half the ball in it!' Oddly, the same day, his cousin Bill was also hospitalised while fielding for Norfolk in a minor county match.

John considers his tour of Australia in 1966–67 as his happiest. In successive Tests in Melbourne and Sydney he hit 109 and 103. He believes he learned more about batting on the hard surfaces of Australia, the West Indies and South Africa than in England. He also carries happy memories of the Caribbean tour of 1968 when England beat the unofficial world champions. In the Kingston Test, notorious for the riot, he made 96 on a difficult pitch.

In the Bridgetown Test, Boycott and Edrich put on 172 for the first wicket, Edrich scoring a superb 146. This century opening partnership was the first for England in 19 Tests. With another opening stand of 55 by the same pair, England went on to score 215 runs in 165 minutes and won the Port-of-Spain Test. Then followed John's three most prolific seasons.

Against the Australians led by Bill Lawry in England in 1968, he totalled 554 runs in the series with 164 and four fifties in successive innings. He was also voted Player of the Series. In the summer of 1969, he scored 2238 runs at a time when no one else approached 2000. This included 747 runs against the touring West Indians, 545 of which were in Tests. Aged 33, Edrich was not expected to set the Australian spectators on fire when he toured in 1970–71. But by scoring 648 runs in the Test series – with centuries at Perth and Adelaide – he, with Boycott, provided the solid base for England to regain the Ashes.

Four successive seasons of high scoring at Test level at last brought John out of cousin Bill's shadow. When Australia toured England in 1972, John found Dennis Lillee's pace too hot to handle and it seemed it was the end of the road for the 35-year-old warhorse. But he bounced back with a gritty century against India and, in 1974–75, toured Australia for the third time – as vice-captain.

Once again, Lillee and Jeff Thomson posed problems for all the Englishmen and John was *hors de combat* twice. Although his highest score was 70, he played two sterling knocks of 50, and an unbeaten 33 in the Sydney Test. This was the Test in which he took over as captain from an out-of-form Mike Denness. In the second innings John was struck below the rib cage off the first ball he received from Lillee. He was rushed to hospital but came back to the crease and stayed there undefeated for two and a half hours – and very nearly drew the Test.

In 1975, when Ian Chappell's Australians toured England, John was written off by the press as a jaded old-timer, lacking his old zeal. The appropriate answer came in the form of a marathon 175 at Lord's, 62 in the Headingley Test and 96 on his home ground at The Oval. His 428 runs in the four-Test series topped the English aggregate and was only one run behind Ian Chappell's total.

In the first Test at Trent Bridge against a strong West Indies side in 1976, he became the 13th player to score over 5000 runs in Test cricket. On 12 July 1977 he completed a century of centuries, the 17th cricketer to achieve this. This was for Surrey against Derbyshire on his home ground, and it was his 945th innings. He became only the third left-hander – after Phil Mead and Frank Woolley – to reach the milestone of 100 first-class centuries.

When John Edrich wrote his autobiography in 1969, he had two unfulfilled ambitions. They were: to be a member of an England side which licked Australia in a series, and to help Surrey win the County Championship. Both these ambitions were realised within two years – England beating Australia, in Australia, 2–0 in 1970–71, and Surrey winning the County Championship in 1971. John retired from the first-class scene at the end of the 1978 season after accumulating 39,790 runs and recording 103 centuries. The performing flea of English cricket has earned his place among those who served the game with unshakeable determination.

Trevor Bailey neatly analysed the batsmanship of John Edrich in a special article in *The Cricketer International* of 1974. According to him, Edrich had two most productive or 'bread-and-butter' strokes: a firm punch off the legs which sent the ball in an arc between mid-wicket and fine leg, and a run-down through the gully off a cleverly angled bat. But there were occasions when John showed his range and power – the blistering cover drive off the front foot and a lofted on-drive into the crowd.

How do the Edriches view their cricket? Wrote John: 'I hate losing. So do all members of the Edrich cricket family. We have always been determined to succeed. Sometimes we have struggled – and struggled painfully.' In *Cricket Heritage* Bill Edrich pondered: 'In the Edrich family cricket is essential. You remember how the Doones in Blackmore's immortal book used to turn out of their valley any young Doone who did not fill a doorway touching top and sides? Well, we Edriches are like that about cricket!'

The Edriches in Test Cricket											
	Tests	**Runs**	**Avrge**	**HS**	**100s**	**50s**	**Wkts**	**Avrge**	**Best**	**5w/i**	**Catches**
Bill	39	2440	40.00	219	6	13	41	41.29	4–68	0	39
John	77	5138	43.54	310*	12	24	0	–	–	–	43
Total	116	7578	42.33	310*	18	37	41	41.85	4–68	0	82

CHAPTER 21

Dream Debutants
– *the Amarnaths*

———— ● ————

Lala Amarnath and son Surinder made sensational debuts,
becoming the only father and son to record centuries in their first Tests.
Younger son Mohinder was the tireless Trojan of Indian cricket.
A third brother, Rajinder, showed promise.

WITH THE FIRST INDIAN cricket team to visit Australia, in 1947–48, there were problems even before the tour started. The appointed captain, Vijay Merchant, was ruled medically unfit. His opening partner, the dashing Mushtaq Ali, No. 3 batsman Rusi Modi and all-rounder Fazal Mohammad were also unavailable. Thus, Lala Amarnath (real surname Bhardwaj), a dazzling stroke-player and a swing bowler, but with little experience in captaincy, was given an experimental side to lead. The team he opposed was probably the strongest side in the entire history of Test cricket. The same team, now known as the Invincibles and led by Don Bradman, was to slaughter England 4–0 in England the following year.

Under these circumstances, it was not surprising that India were mauled 0–4 in a five-Test series – especially with the weather on the side of the much stronger XI. Despite the one-sided Test series, four Indian players emerged with credit – Vijay Hazare, Vinoo Mankad, Dattu Phadkar and Lala Amarnath.

Amarnath's performances in State matches were so brilliant that, according to Arthur Mailey, people thronged to the Test grounds to see Amarnath bat, not Bradman. And although he was a complete failure in the Tests as a batsman, he accumulated 1162 runs on the tour – the highest ever by an Indian in Australia – at an average of 58, hitting five centuries and an unbeaten 94. He also captured 30 wickets on the tour including 13, more than any other Indian bowler, in the Tests.

Against South Australia in Adelaide, he hit 144 and 94 not out. Bradman set the Indians 287 to win in 180 minutes. They had lost 4 for 20 when Amarnath joined Mankad and added 175 incandescent runs in two hours as India fell 52 runs short of victory with five wickets in hand.

However, the match against Victoria provided Lala's supreme hour. India had lost three of her best batsmen without a run on the board – all to Bill Johnston – when Amarnath walked to the middle with his characteristic swagger. In a blazing display which held Melburnians spellbound with admiration, Lala ruthlessly attacked Johnston and then the spinning pair of Doug Ring and Ian Johnson. He remained unbeaten with 228 and it was one of the most memorable innings ever witnessed on the MCG. 'Like Shelley's *West Wind*, Amarnath was preserver as well as destroyer,' raved Indian writer Sujit Mukherjee in *The Romance of Indian Cricket*.

In the match preceding the first Test, Amarnath hit another sparkling century, an unbeaten 172 against Queensland. His failure in the Test series is explained by his deputy Hazare: 'Amarnath trusted his ability and eyes to such an extent that he allowed himself the luxury of hitting against the break in Australia. He could get away with it in State games, but in Tests, bowlers got the better of him.'

During the tour, Bradman and Amarnath disagreed on one issue. The Australian Cricket Board suggested covering the pitch, but Amarnath was against it. Bradman tried to convince the Indian skipper that covering the pitch would be advantageous to India as Australian players were more experienced on 'sticky' wickets. However, the strong-willed, almost dogmatic, Amarnath stuck to his viewpoint. Aware of the limitations of his side, Lala thought that the only chance India had of winning, was to bat on a dry wicket and – with luck – catch the Aussies on a sticky gluepot. Actually, things happened in quite the reverse fashion in three Tests out of five, but at Sydney, when the Australian bats

Amarnath brothers Mohinder (left) and Surinder. (*Bhagwat Singh*)

did encounter wet conditions, they could total only 107 and were 81 runs behind the tourists.

Bradman thought highly of Amarnath as a captain and a player. In *Farewell to Cricket* the Don wrote: 'I look back on the season with him [Amarnath] as my opposite number as one of my most pleasant cricket years ... In the batting line, Amarnath and Hazare were outstanding. They were fit to be classed with any company.'

When India toured Australia in the 1977–78 season, 30 years after that pioneering visit, the team included two Amarnaths – Surinder and Mohinder –

Mohinder (middle) discussing tactics with Surinder (right) and Yashpal Sharma. (*Rio Photos*)

the sons of Lala. The younger, Mohinder, was an all-rounder, a No. 3 batsman and a medium-pace bowler. Surinder was a bit of an enigma. A match-winner when in the mood, he sometimes lacked application during a crisis. A left-hander with a superb range of strokes, Surinder did not quite fulfil the promise he had shown as a teenage marvel.

Mohinder was unlike his father and Surinder. Reliability rather than brilliance was his watchword. And he was no stranger to Australian conditions. When the Indian Schoolboys toured Australia in 1967–68, Mohinder received good notices in the Australian press as he topped the tour bowling averages. One writer turned nostalgic, headlining his story, 'Echoes from the Past' – referring to Lala Amarnath's 1947–48 down-under visit.

The Amarnaths provided the second instance of a father and two sons playing in the Test arena – the Hadlees of New Zealand being the first. But the Amarnaths have one record all to themselves. Lala in 1933–34 and Surinder in 1975–76 scored centuries on their Test debuts, a unique occurrence.

Lala was 22 when he played his first Test at Bombay in December 1933. It was also the first Test on Indian soil. India,

facing a deficit of 219, lost both the openers cheaply. Out came Lala, oozing confidence after top-scoring with 39 in the first innings. He soon showed English speedsters 'Nobby' Clarke and Morris Nichols who the boss was. Drives, square cuts and hooks flowed from his bat and skipper Douglas Jardine did not know how to set a field for this raw, audacious newcomer. Lala hit 21 delightful fours in his truly magnificent 118 in 210 minutes and was showered with gifts. This was the first century by an Indian in Test cricket.

Although he played 23 more Tests, Lala could not score another century. However, in first-class cricket against strong opposition he played some of the grandest innings. In a Pentangular tournament match for the Hindus in 1938 he hit 241, at that time the highest score by an Indian. A year before that, he had demonstrated his dazzling footwork to Jack Ryder's Australian team in India. In the only match the tourists lost, to Moin-ud-Dowlah's XI by an innings, Amarnath scored 144 with 24 fours.

When Lindsay Hassett led the Australian Services team to India in 1945–46, Amarnath once again contributed to a home win. In the final unofficial test at Madras, India won the match and the series – thanks to Modi's 203 and Lala's 113. Lala also scored a majestic 163 for Prince's XI again Hassett's team. Tour member R.S. Whitington, later a prolific sportswriter, expressed the opinion that 'Amarnath best blended brilliance and judgment'. Not that Lala had reserved his best only against the Australians ... When Lord Tennyson's MCC team toured India in 1936–37, he hit three hundreds, including one in the Calcutta unofficial Test.

In 1936, on his first tour to England, Lala was involved in a bitter controversy. By the end of May he had scored 613 runs including centuries in each innings against Essex, and taken 32 wickets –

both highest among the tourists – when he was sent home on disciplinary grounds. An enquiry conducted by a High Court judge completely exonerated him. However, after that unpleasant incident, Amarnath was known as the 'Stormy Petrel of Indian Cricket'. His contemporary, and friend, Mushtaq Ali described him as 'quick to love and quick to fight'.

On his second tour to England in 1946, Lala shone more as a bowler. In the first Test at Lord's, he dismissed master batsmen Len Hutton, Cyril Washbrook, Wally Hammond and Denis Compton – the latter two off successive balls – as England slumped to 4 for 70; his analysis being 4 for 24. He mostly bowled in-swingers, but occasionally an out-swinger. With his odd, hopping run-up, he baffled batsmen, many of them convinced he bowled off the right foot. But this was only an illusion. In the Ranji Trophy, Lala had two incredible bowling performances: 4 wickets for 2 runs in 1938 and 4 wickets without conceding a run in 1958 – when he was 47.

Lala led India in three Test series, losing to Australia (1947–48) and the West Indies (1948–49) and defeating Pakistan in 1952–53. He had an incredibly poor record in tossing, losing four out of five tosses in Australia and then all five to John Goddard's West Indians in India.

The final Test at Bombay against Goddard's men in 1949 was the most spine-chilling game ever witnessed in India. India had to score 361 runs in 395 minutes to square the series. With the tension mounting, India was 8 for 355 and two minutes were still remaining. For some inexplicable reason, the umpire called it stumps and the match was drawn. Apart from leading India with flair, Lala had contributed a swashbuckling 39 which set the tempo. Also, he had substituted for an injured wicket-keeper in that Test and accepted five catches behind the sticks.

Vijay Merchant, who did not see eye to eye with Amarnath on many issues, considered him 'one of the most brilliant cricketers I have had the privilege to play with ... A man with tremendous initiative, imagination and the will to fight it out at all times.' Soon after his retirement from Test cricket in 1953, Lala was appointed a national selector and he served in this capacity until 1960, for the last seven years as the chairman.

Forty-two years after Lala's sensational Test debut, Surinder was selected to represent India for the first time, against Sri Lanka in an unofficial Test at Ahmedabad in 1975–76. He scored 118, a score identical to his father's. Two months later Surinder played his first official Test at Auckland against New Zealand in 1976 and hit 124. However, he performed poorly after that, both in New Zealand and the West Indies, and lost his place in the Indian team. Surprisingly, Surinder was not a natural left-hander. Some intuition told Lala that Surinder would do well as a left-hander, so the son had to switch over.

Surinder played his first Ranji Trophy match when 15, for Punjab, and scored 89. He was an outstanding member of the Indian Schoolboys' team to tour England, covering himself with glory in the final 'Test'. In a pulsating finish, India needed nine runs to win with only two balls remaining. Surinder hit two sixes to clinch the issue. In 1971, he hit an unbeaten 200 for Punjab against Madhya Pradesh in a Ranji Trophy match, adding 249 with Madan Lal. The following year, against Delhi, Surinder (202 retired hurt) and Mohinder (100 not out) added 233 unbeaten runs, hitting 37 fours and a six between them.

Much was expected from Surinder on Australian pitches in 1977–78 but the awaited confrontation with Jeff Thomson did not eventuate. Against Tasmania his face was badly smashed and he had to return home halfway through the tour. He fought his way back into the Indian side and played all three Tests in Pakistan. His highest score in the series was a chancy 60 at Lahore where he added 99 runs with Gundappa Viswanath.

Sunil Gavaskar gave us an insight into Surinder's personality in *Sportsweek's World of Cricket*: 'Surinder is still a very quiet person, involved in his own world and a difficult chap to know. A dreamer ... he is nevertheless a tough competitor. Once you break the ice with him, he is a delightful person and his mimicking his father with the pipe in his mouth is hilarious.'

Mohinder Amarnath inherited his father's toothy smile and the ability to fight. Quiet and retiring, Mohinder had little of Lala's glamour and charisma. He had a phlegmatic temperament and worked hard for his success. He played three 'Tests' against the Australian Schoolboys as a 15-year-old. As a schoolboy, he toured England in 1967 and Australia in 1967–68. In 1968–69 he led the North Zone University team to a spectacular triumph, hitting 163 in the final. In a Ranji Trophy match the following season he captured 7 for 27 and 5 for 7 for Punjab against Jammu-Kashmir. Thus it was as an all-rounder that Mohinder made his debut against Australia in the Madras Test of 1969. He scored 16 not out and had a memorable early spell in the second innings. He clean-bowled Keith Stackpole for four and Ian Chappell for five, as Australia nosedived to 6 for 24. Still, Australia won by 77 runs.

His moment of triumph came in April 1976, in the third Test against the West Indies in Port-of-Spain. India was set what then appeared an impossible task of scoring 403 runs for a win. They made it with five wickets in hand. Mohinder was one of the heroes, adding 108 runs for the second wicket with Gavaskar and 159 for the third wicket with Viswanath. In all, he stayed for almost seven hours, scoring a priceless 85 before being run out.

According to Tony Cozier: 'The real batting find of the tour for the Indians was Mohinder Amarnath who looked one of the best visiting batsmen every time he walked to the middle.'

Then, in the controversy-filled final Test at Kingston when the Indian batsmen were rattled by Michael Holding's short snorters, Mohinder showed the way with a courageous death-or-glory knock of 60 (with three sixes) out of India's second innings of 97.

He touched his peak in Australia in the summer of 1977–78 – remembered for the World Series Cricket controversy. Wrote Dicky Rutnagur in *Wisden* (1979): 'Mohinder reached an unexpectedly high stature as a batsman during the series. Batting at No. 3, he almost always arrived in difficult situations and batted with great heart.' In the pulsating Perth Test which India lost by two wickets he scored 90 and 100, batting comfortably despite a finger injury. In the second innings he added 193 runs with Gavaskar for the second wicket. At Adelaide in the final series-deciding Test, India was set a mammoth target of 493 to win. They managed 445, Mohinder top-scoring with 86 after a memorable 131-run partnership with Viswanath. It was batsmanship at its highest level, Mohinder excelling at on-side deflections, the more classical Viswanath showing his off-side stroke-play.

Mohinder totalled 445 runs at 49.44 in the series. On the tour he topped the aggregate with 731 runs at 48.73. In the match against New South Wales at the Sydney Cricket Ground he batted brilliantly to score 137, adding 128 with Viswanath. This century filled a gap in the Amarnath book of records. Father Lala Amarnath had scored a century on every ground in Australia except the SCG during his tour of 1947–48.

Mohinder had a mediocre tour of Pakistan in 1978 and was dropped after the first Test at Bombay against the West Indies. He was brought back in the final

Test at Kanpur where he scored an unbeaten 101 in India's highest-ever score of 7 for 644. He topped the Test batting, his average being 142.00.

As a batsman, Mohinder had his limitations. Bowlers could restrict his scoring by bowling to the off, for he was at his best when glancing or defecting to the leg and pushing to mid-on. He often lost his wicket when trying to hook – his weakest shot. As a medium-pacer, he swung the ball both ways. His best bowling spell was in a Duleep Trophy semi-final match at Bangalore in October 1977, when he took 6 for 34. At one stage he had taken 6 for 2, including three wickets in four balls.

Mohinder had a disappointing, injury-ridden tour of England in 1979 and suffered a hairline fracture of the skull after being hit by a Richard Hadlee bouncer in the match against Nottinghamshire. His eyesight was affected and he was not selected in the Test team for three years. It appeared to be the end of the road for the 32-year-old warhorse but he came back with a vengeance in 1982–83, first in Pakistan and then in the West Indies.

In six Tests in Pakistan against Imran Khan at his best he scored 584 at 73.00, inclusive of three centuries and three fifties. Imran commented, 'At the age of 32, he [Mohinder] had fought back after several years in the wilderness and he batted magnificently in a beaten side against us'. Skipper Gavaskar concurred. 'Mohinder has the technique to counter peak pace and is potentially our soundest batsman today [1982–83]. He has the temperament too.'

Mohinder fared equally well in the Caribbean the same season. In five Tests he amassed 598 runs, including two glorious centuries and a hard-fought 91, at an average of 66.44. He had countered and mastered the much-feared Windies all-pace attack of Holding, Joel Garner, Andy Roberts and Malcolm Marshall. He

rates his 91 in the Bridgetown Test as 'my finest ever innings for India, considering how fast the Caribbean quickies bowled and how consistently I middled the ball on a lively wicket'. By 3 May 1983 he reached 1000 Test runs in the calendar year, a feat not reached by anyone else by so early a date.

In that glorious 1982–83 season he accumulated 2355 runs at an average of 81 – a record run aggregate in first-class matches outside England. However, the next season was disastrous for Mohinder. After scoring 4 and 7 in a Test against Pakistan in India he passed through a horrible patch against the West Indians in India. He made five ducks in six Test innings, scoring 0, 0, 1, 0, 0, 0 to average a bemusing 0.16. What an anticlimax after his 598 at 66.64 against the same bowlers only a year earlier. Still, Gavaskar had confidence in him and he was picked to tour Pakistan, where he hit 36 and 101 in the Lahore Test to accentuate the glorious uncertainties of the game.

Another unforgettable moment in Mohinder's career came when the little-fancied India won the World Cup in England in 1983. Against all odds, India beat the West Indies (champions in 1975 and 1979) by 43 runs and Mohinder was adjudged Man of the Final for taking 3 for 12 and scoring 26 in a low-scoring match. He had also been Man of the Match in the semi-final against England after scoring 46 and dismissing David Gower and Mike Gatting. He was honoured as *Wisden*'s Cricketer of the Year in 1984.

In 69 Tests, Mohinder scored 4378 runs at 42.50 with 11 centuries and took 32 wickets at 55.69. In all first-class matches he made 13,849 runs at 43.68 with 31 hundreds and captured 272 wickets at 33.13. Cricket writer Raju Bharatan summed up Mohinder Amarnath as 'the perfect support player, the tireless Trojan', in *Indian Cricket 1995*.

What is the story behind his nickname 'Jimmy'? 'The nickname was given by my father. No particular reason. He calls Surinder "Tommy",' replied the quietly spoken, handsome-looking Mohinder.

Was he inspired seeing his father bat in big matches? 'I was too young when father was playing active cricket. By the time I got interested in cricket, he had retired. But he took great pains in coaching the three of us.'

Lala's youngest son, Rajinder, showed the family flair in school cricket. A right-hand batsman and a right-arm medium-pacer, he first played for Delhi School in 1970, when 13. In 1973 he scored 96 against Jammu-Kashmir and captured 8 for 28 against Punjab in the North Zone school tournament. When 16, he toured England with the Indian Schoolboys and scored 69, 70 and 39 in the unofficial 'tests'. Subsequently, he was named in the Delhi squad for the Ranji Trophy, but Test doors did not open for him.

Approaching 90, Lala Amarnath appears frail, a shadow of his previous stormy petrel image. The recipient of the prestigious C.K. Nayudu Award in 1996, he is proud of the Amarnath influence spanning six decades. In 103 Tests from 1933 to 1987 the Amarnath trio scored 5806 runs at 36.98 including 13 centuries and 31 fifties, and took 78 wickets at 41.90 and 64 catches.

The Amarnaths in Test Cricket

	Tests	Runs	Avrge	HS	100s	50s	Wkts	Avrge	Best	5w/i	Catches
Lala	24	878	24.38	118	1	4	45	32.91	5–96	2	13
Surinder	10	550	30.55	124	1	3	1	5.00	1–5	0	4
Mohinder	69	4378	42.50	138	11	24	32	55.68	4–63	0	47
Total	103	5806	36.98	138	13	31	78	41.90	5–96	2	64

CHAPTER 22

Sir Richard
and Other Hadlees

— ● —

*Walter Hadlee, his sons Barry, Dayle and Sir Richard, and Richard's wife
Karen have represented New Zealand in international cricket. Walter,
Dayle and Richard played 123 Tests between them, the sons spearheading
the Kiwi attack. Richard is the first bowler to take 400 Test wickets
and is considered one of the best all-rounders.*

IN ONE OF THE most explosive series in Test history when hardly a day passed without an umpiring controversy, the home team, New Zealand, defeated the star-studded West Indians 1–0 in early 1980. The margin of victory was a leg bye in the first Test at Dunedin which New Zealand won by one wicket.

The Kiwi win staggered the critics since only a month earlier the Windies had won the Benson & Hedges World Series Cup in Australia and then thrashed a full-strength Australian side. The man behind New Zealand's surprise victory was the tall, razor-sharp all-rounder, Richard Hadlee. In the Dunedin Test which New Zealand won with a solitary wicket to spare, he took 5 for 34 and 6 for 68 and scored 51 and 17, the second-highest score in each innings. In the visitors' second innings he became the highest wicket-taker among New Zealanders at Test level.

In the second Test, at Christchurch, he scored his maiden Test century and in the process became the first New Zealander to achieve the Test double of 1000 runs and 100 wickets. He bowled splendidly throughout the series, his 5 for 34, 3 for 58 and 4 for 75 in the first innings of the three Tests contributing to the world-champion West Indians failing to reach 230 in any of those innings.

Another memorable moment in New Zealand's 50 years of international cricket came six years earlier, on 13 March 1974. In the second Test, at Christchurch, the New Zealand mouse roared at the mighty Australians under Ian Chappell, defeating them by five wickets. With centuries in both innings, Glenn Turner was the architect of this

Sir Richard Hadlee studied batsmen's weaknesses like a surgeon examining an X-ray before an operation. (*Allsport*)

shock win. However, Dayle and Richard Hadlee contributed just as handsomely. Between them, the fast-medium pacers took 12 wickets – eight of them in the second innings. Rodney Marsh, eager to get on top, clouted a ball wide of Dayle Hadlee. How Dayle, on his follow-through, managed to cover the distance in time and had the raw courage to put his hand to that thunderbolt and catch it with amazing coolness will remain one of cricket's mysteries.

In 1973–74, when a depleted New Zealand side toured Australia, skipper Bevan Congdon looked to the Hadlee brothers for vital breakthroughs. Though nowhere near Frank Tyson, Wes Hall or Dennis Lillee in speed, the Hadlee brothers' accurate seaming accounted for 15 out of 30 Australian wickets to fall in the three-Test series. But for the rain, New Zealand should have won the Sydney Test where Richard and Dayle captured nine out of 12 Australian scalps.

On 6 January 1974, on the lively SCG strip, the brothers soon had the strong Australian batting line-up in trouble. As torrential rain undid the splendid Kiwi effort, I chatted with Dayle Hadlee about his cricket, his extraordinary family, his hopes and his assessments. 'Call it a coincidence, but it was my birthday. Ian Chappell was going well and I told myself it would be a fine birthday present if I were to dismiss him. And that very ball I got him out,' Dayle recalled with relish.

Dayle was small for a fast bowler, friendly and well aware of his limitations. Richard looked more like our idea of a spearhead – tall, keen and aggressive. They are the sons of the famous Test cricketer Walter Hadlee, later the chairman of the New Zealand Cricket Council.

Walter toured England in 1937 and in 1949 as captain. He could have represented his country in rugby too, had it not been for poor eyesight. In New Zealand he will always be remembered for his shrewd leadership in England. Under him, the team developed to the stage where it was no longer regarded as an easy conquest, but as England's equal. All four Tests on the tour were drawn, but Bert Sutcliffe and Martin Donnelly batted magnificently, and Walter Hadlee's captaincy was inspiring. He guided the younger players in the intricacies of the game and remedied a Sutcliffe weakness – the left-hander's tendency to hook behind square leg on slow pitches, resulting in the loss of his wicket. By giving Sutcliffe special net practice to cultivate the hook stroke wide of mid-on, Hadlee produced a master batsman who amassed 2627 runs on the tour and 423 runs in four Tests.

The senior Hadlee himself was no slouch with the bat. He scored 1439 runs averaging 36 on that tour. He hit two centuries and of these his unbeaten 119 against Surrey included three sixes and 11 fours. To quote from *Wisden* (1950): 'In critical situations Hadlee was at his best. Few batsmen in post-war cricket have driven a ball with Hadlee's power and precision, but when his side was well-placed, he put more value on giving practice to others than allowing himself to settle down to a big innings.' Added Don Cameron: 'Walter Hadlee used to stand tall and straight, perhaps not the prettiest stroke-maker, but surprisingly quick of movement for a tall man, and he was a superb driver of the ball.' He scored 543 runs at 30.16 in 11 Tests, hitting one century.

His finest hour, however, came when playing for Otago against the Australian side of 1946. Ray Lindwall, Bill O'Reilly and Colin McCool bowled Otago out for 168 and Australia replied with 420. In the second innings, when Otago were losing wickets rapidly, Hadlee stepped in. He was badly bruised, but stayed for two days to score 198.

Walter thrived on a challenge. In a local match, when his club was set 112 to win in half an hour, he said, 'We'll have a crack at it', and proceeded to fire an unbeaten 64 as his side reached the target in 28 minutes. Against Hampshire in 1949, New Zealand were set 109 to win in 35 minutes. With supreme confidence Hadlee accepted the challenge and, with Sutcliffe hitting an incredible 46 in 13 minutes, the Kiwis made it – with five minutes to spare. After his retirement, he was made a CBE.

Now in his eighties, Walter Hadlee has a staggering memory, a quick analytical mind and a tendency to forecast correctly the progress of a match. It was predictable that he would impart his love of the game to his children. Of his five sons, he has had a cricket success rate of 80 per cent – four of them becoming cricketers of some note. Only Christopher, the youngest, was immune to the cricket bug. Music was his love.

The tall, eldest son, Barry, started as a classical batsman and an ambidextrous spin bowler, but somehow he did not scale the heights he appeared to be capable of. He represented New Zealand B team in Australia in 1972 and played in the World Cup in England in June 1975. Against England, New Zealand fielded three Hadlee brothers – Barry, Dayle and Richard. Martin Hadlee played senior-grade cricket but did not progress further. Dayle and Richard played in 112 Tests, 10 times together.

Both were the babies of the teams touring England, Dayle in 1969 and Richard in 1973. Both admit that their father forced cricket on them but they are equally grateful to him for it. 'My father has been a great influence on me ever since I can remember,' Dayle said. 'He coached me, sometimes when I was unwilling. When I was out for a low score, I got half an hour lecture. Once I gave up cricket when I was seven or eight. There was just too much pressure. But my "retirement" lasted only a week. When father found out, I was sent back to the school net. Subsequently I made a lot of runs, but I was always a fast bowler – even then.'

Dayle's proudest moment was the taking of his first Test wicket: 'In that Test at Lord's in 1969, I caught and bowled Alan Knott – and it was a difficult catch.' This could earn the understatement-of-the-century award! So marvellous was that catch that the usually calm and articulate John Arlott ran short of adjectives and out of breath describing it on the radio. 'When I walked back to my fielding position after the over, I was warmly applauded, which was very thrilling,' recalled Dayle.

After 1969, Dayle turned into a medium-pacer. 'When bowling against the Australian B team in 1970, I had John Inverarity out, but he was given not out. I was angry and bowled faster than I was capable of. That hurt my back. Also, in 1963 I broke my leg playing soccer. A second operation was necessary and a bone graft was given from my hip. A six-inch plate was placed in my leg, with six grooves to hold the plate in place. This made my right leg two centimetres shorter though I did not know about it until 1971. Now I use special shoes, but my leg hurts a lot after a day's play.'

In a way, Dayle was responsible for Richard's rise to the top. Just before a Plunket Shield match, Dayle's toe was caught in the motor while mowing the lawn. This gave Richard the opportunity to represent Canterbury. He took a hat-trick in that match and subsequently was chosen to tour Australia with the New Zealand B team in 1972. During the 1970s two Richards – Hadlee and Collinge – became the fastest bowlers in New Zealand. Richard Hadlee had a series of injuries, including a painful shoulder which put him out of the game for most of the 1975 season. However, acupuncture helped him.

Dayle was a schoolteacher and an accomplished guitar player. He was in a group called Terrega Four which made a record, won a radio competition and a trip to Germany. 'I've toured four times in four years,' said Dayle. 'My family has been tolerant about my absence. Now it's time for me to make sacrifices. No more tours. When it comes to the crunch, my wife is my greatest supporter. Every time she calls me long distance I get a wicket!' However, Richard's wife Karen was not just a supporter but a competent cricketer herself. Once in a local women's tournament in 1973 she took all 10 wickets for 12 runs. In 1977 she was selected to represent the New Zealand women's team as a medium-pacer.

Richard performed brilliantly in the Wellington Test against India in 1976. He captured 11 for 58, including 7 for 23 in the second innings. And when New Zealand toured Pakistan and India in 1976–77, he was again their most effective bowler. He also topped the batting averages against Pakistan in the

Tests. In the final Test at Karachi, Richard made 87, then his highest Test score, and was associated in a 186-run partnership with Warren Lees. This show of defiance helped the Kiwis to save the Test.

In 1977 Richard became the spectators' favourite during the second Test against Greg Chappell's Australians at Eden Park, Auckland. He stood up to the blistering pace of Dennis Lillee, scoring 44 and a well-hit 81 (out of the team total of 175). Don Cameron wrote: 'New Zealand has never known crowd fever quite like this'. Later that year Richard was named New Zealand's Cricket Personality of the Year and received the Nugget Cup. The cricket-mad Hadlee family was there in full force during the presentation.

The last time Dayle and Richard played together in a Test was at Wellington in February 1978. In this historic match, in which New Zealand defeated England for the first time, Richard took 10 wickets, his second-innings spell of 6 for 26 causing England's sensational collapse: 64 all out. It was England's lowest score since 1948 and her lowest against all countries except Australia.

After much deliberation, the New Zealand Cricket Council gave Richard Hadlee permission to play World Series Cricket. He was probably the first cricketer to play WSC without losing his Test status.

He took his 100th wicket in only his 25th Test, during the second Test against Pakistan at Napier in 1979. The following season, in the first Test against the strong West Indies, his 27th, he became the highest wicket-taker in New Zealand's Test history, surpassing Richard Collinge's career haul of 116 wickets in 35 Tests. In the second Test of the series, his 28th, he reached his Test double. Only four all-rounders have achieved this in fewer Tests: Ian Botham in 21 Tests, India's Vinoo Mankad and Kapil Dev in

23 and 25, and Australia's 'Monty' Nobel in 27.

Respected by opponents for his controlled seaming and pace variations, Richard Hadlee worked hard for his success. He told Richie Benaud in *World Series Cricket 1978–79* magazine: 'Cricket is now very much my life. I'm totally involved and committed to it. If you want to get to the top, it means getting off your backside and working hard.'

The real Richard Hadlee – as we know and admire him – stood up in the 1980s. The promising performer of the 1970s became a supremo; not the fastest on the globe but among the brainiest. He plotted the dismissals of his opponents strategically. Not only did he watch videotapes of Dennis Lillee, the bowler he admired most, but also those of contemporary batsmen. He studied weaknesses in their technique 'in the manner of a surgeon studying X-rays before probing for the source of the problem', to quote Don Mosey from *Wisden* (1991).

Hadlee moved the ball late, either going away or coming in, and specialised in leg cutters. He called his slower ball 'dangly' (which swung in to a bewildered batsman) and rarely used the bouncer, keeping it only as a surprise weapon. Subtlety was the name of his game. He often played cat and mouse and then, without warning, turned into a cat among the pigeons. He had a ball for every occasion.

Neither a batsman-hater nor a spectacular appealer à la Lillee, Hadlee did not supply 'killer' quotes to journalists like Jeff Thomson did. He just pocketed his five-fors efficiently and ruthlessly, felt 'very happy and proud' and won for New Zealand quite a few Test matches.

That is why his unpopularity in certain sections of the crowd in Australia in the mid-1980s was difficult to understand. Some offensive chants upset

Hadlee is delighted after breaking Ian Botham's record in the Bangalore Test of 1988.
(*Allsport / Simon Brutty*)

him but he carried on regardless, reaching new milestones. He became the first cricketer to capture 400 Test wickets and his 431 scalps in 86 Tests was a record when he retired in July 1990. (Since then it has been eclipsed by Kapil Dev and Courtney Walsh). Richard's

The Hadlee family: Walter, wife Lilla, sons Dayle, Richard, Barry and Richard's wife Karen. (*World of Cricket*)

taking five wickets in a Test innings (5w/i) 36 times and 10 wickets in a Test (10w/T) nine times are both records; next best being Ian Botham's 5w/i 27 times, and Lillee and Clarrie Grimmett with 10w/T seven times each.

Richard Hadlee had many outstanding bowling achievements in his Test career from 1972 to 1990. His favourite Test was in Brisbane in November 1985. Australia was cruising at 1 for 70 when he struck crippling blows. He took the first nine wickets to fall and caught the last man, Geoff Lawson, off Vaughan Brown. Richard scored 54 out of New Zealand's total of 7 declared for 553 and captured 6 for 71 in the second innings as the Kiwis won by an innings and 41 runs. He had match figures of 15 for 123 and Australia was stunned.

Was Richard disappointed in missing out on the ultimate achievement of taking all 10 wickets in a Test innings? 'No. That was, I suppose, as near-perfect a performance one hopes to achieve and one in which the whole team shared,' he said.

He was also a useful lower-order batsman who scored 3124 runs at 27.16 in Tests, hitting two centuries, his highest being 151 not out against Sri Lanka at Colombo in 1986–87. He is among four all-rounders to achieve the Test double of 3000 runs and 300 wickets; Ian Botham, Imran Khan and Kapil Dev being the others. And only Kapil and Richard have performed the 3000 runs and 400 wickets Test double.

Richard also played county cricket for Nottinghamshire and Sheffield Shield for Tasmania. For Notts in the County Championship of 1984 he became the first to achieve the double of 1000 runs and 100 wickets since 1967, scoring 1179 runs at 51.26 and taking 117 wickets at 14.05.

In first-class cricket he scored 12,052 runs at 31.71 in 342 matches, hitting 14 hundreds (highest score 210 not out for Nottinghamshire against Middlesex at Lord's in 1984). He also captured 1490 wickets at 18.11, taking five wickets in an innings 102 times (his best being 9 for 52 vs Australia in the Brisbane Test of 1985–86).

Just before the Lord's Test against England in June 1990, the 39-year-old Kiwi received a knighthood in the Queen's Birthday Honours list. To fit the occasion, Sir Richard gave a Man of the Match performance, taking 3 for 113 and 1 for 32 and scoring 86 runs embellished with 12 fours and two sixes. Then followed his final Test at Birmingham a month later. He captured 3 for 97 and 5 for 53, dismissing Devon Malcolm for a duck with his last ball in Test cricket. He was made New Zealand's Man of the Series.

'That was no sentimental gesture: the world's leading Test wicket-taker had called it a day at the peak of his powers,' summed up *Wisden*.

The Hadlees in Test Cricket

	Tests	Runs	Avrge	HS	100s	50s	Wkts	Avrge	Best	5w/i	Catches
Walter	11	543	30.16	116	1	2	0	–	–	–	6
Dayle	26	530	14.32	56	0	1	71	33.64	4–30	–	8
Richard	86	3124	27.16	151*	2	15	431	22.29	9–52	36	39
Total	123	4197	24.69	151*	3	18	502	23.91	9–52	36	53

CHAPTER 23

The
Contrasting Rowans

——— ● ———

Few brothers were as dissimilar as Eric and Athol Rowan. Eric, a batsman, was self-assertive while Athol was an off-spinner with a sense of humour. Both served South African cricket in their own distinctive ways.

THE LEEDS TEST OF 1951 between South Africa and England was virtually a Rowan brothers' match. Opening batsman, Eric Rowan, scored 236 – until then the highest score by a South African against England – and 60 not out. The rain on the last day robbed him of the chance of becoming the first batsman to score a double-century and a century in the same Test. To South Africa's 538, England replied with 505, Len Hutton and debutant Peter May hitting hundreds. Athol Rowan, Eric's younger brother by 12 years, took 5 for 174 in a marathon spell of 68 overs. His victims included May, Denis Compton and skipper Freddie Brown.

Eric Rowan's 236 was his third Test century. The first came under dramatic circumstances. In the series against F.G. Mann's England side of 1948-49, Eric scored 7 and 16 in the first Test at

Durban, and 8 in the first innings of the next Test at Johannesburg. During this Test, the team was announced for the Cape Town Test starting the following week and Eric found that he had been dropped. Cut to the quick, he produced a valiant knock which saved his country. When South Africa was made to follow on 293 runs behind, Eric scored an unbeaten 156. He stayed at the crease for 370 minutes, adding 162 runs for the unbroken third-wicket stand with skipper Dudley Nourse.

What a predicament for the selectors! Australian selectors had a similar experience when they dropped John Benaud for the Sydney Test when the Melbourne Test was in progress against Pakistan in 1972-73. Benaud scored a spanking 142 in the second innings.

The Cape Town Test from which Eric was dropped saw Athol taking 5 for 80. It was a magnificent bowling performance on an easy-paced wicket. Eric was reinstated for the fourth Test at Johannesburg where he scored an unbeaten 86 in the second innings, adding 113 runs with Ken Viljoen. Athol also shone during England's second innings, capturing 4 for 69. In the final Test at Port Elizabeth, Eric figured in a century opening partnership and Athol took eight wickets.

It was a highly successful series for the Rowan brothers. Athol took 24 wickets – the greatest number for either side – and Eric's batting average of 53 was second only to Nourse. These two series against England were the only matches in which the Rowan brothers played together – nine Test matches.

Eric Alfred Burchell Rowan was born in Johannesburg on 20 July 1909. The name Burchell perpetuates the memory of his great-grandfather, the noted South African explorer and naturalist. Eric, a teetotaller and a non-smoker, played soccer, rugby and squash. It was at cricket, however, that he flourished. There were times when he became very defensive to save his side, but he was happiest when attacking. Quickness of feet enabled him to get into position for all the strokes, although he favoured the area behind the wicket. Cuts and glances brought him a high proportion of his runs. He was mostly a back-foot player who hooked with relish. According to John Arlott, 'He would, at times, set out to prove a point, when he could be impregnably defensive or extremely venturesome.'

He was an agile fielder in any position – despite having broken his right arm when young.

In 1935 he was selected to tour England and, batting at No. 3, he scored 40 and 44 in the Test which South Africa won. It was his country's first victory in England and the visitors also won their first series in England 1–0. In tour matches he topped the aggregate with 1948 runs and was third in the averages. His six centuries included 171 against Surrey when he shared an opening stand of 330 with Bruce Mitchell. In 1935–36, he batted at No. 3 against Vic Richardson's Australians, his highest score being 66.

It was only after World War II that Eric developed as an opening batsman. In the meantime, he was turning into a run-machine. For Transvaal, against Natal in a friendly game in 1939–40, he scored an undefeated 306. Commented Dudley Nourse in *Cricket in the Blood*, 'Rowan played many invaluable innings for his country and yet I cannot associate any innings of his with a particular shot as one so often can with a leading batsman ... A cocky, little player, E. Rowan has any amount of grit and is always ready with an answer at any period of the day. He will face the fastest bowler on the most awkward pitch with no form of body guard or protection for his hands, and never shrinks from the issue. He is brave to the point of foolhardiness. He takes a savage delight in upsetting the opposition and if he can possibly disturb a bowler or annoy him, it is meat and drink to Eric Rowan.'

After having been omitted from the South African tour to England in 1947, Eric hit back with 141 as an opener against Natal. In the series against England in 1948–49 he scored 156 not out in the second Test after knowing that he had been dropped for the next Test. It was somehow typical of him – a fighter with a cause. Against Lindsay Hassett's Australians in 1949–50 he hit 143 in the third Test at Durban and scored 404 runs in the series at an average of 44.88.

Then followed Eric's finest tour – to England in 1951. His series figures of 515 at 57.22 were better than any player from either side. In the Leeds Test he scored 236 and 60 not out and added 198 runs for the second wicket with C.B. Van Ryneveld. This stood as South Africa's best partnership for the second wicket against England until 1998. On the tour Eric once again finished at the top – as he had done in 1935. He scored 1852 runs – almost 700 more than the next best, Jack Cheetham – averaging 50.05. He also scored five centuries, including two double-hundreds.

It was on this tour that Eric showed his potential as a skipper. Owing to injury to Nourse, vice-captain Eric Rowan was given an opportunity to lead the team. To quote *Wisden* (1952): '... he proved to be quick-witted and shrewd, although hard ... Often he would move a man, not to stop a stroke, but to set the batsman wondering about the likely trap.' According to Arlott, 'His consuming interest was in captaining. Quick-witted and assertive, he directed a side with much acumen, especially in attack, thinking well for his bowlers and handling them carefully.'

Under his captaincy, Transvaal won the Currie Cup in 1950–51. That season, Cheetham set a new Currie Cup record by hitting 271 not out. Five days later Eric eclipsed it by scoring an unbeaten 277 against Griqualand West (who were dismissed for 29 runs). His 1951 tour to England, while productive of runs, was not without incident. He could have been sent back for alleged misbehaviour and he never played for South Africa after the tour. He died in 1993.

Athol Matthew Burchell Rowan was born on 7 February 1921. The taller of the brothers, and wide-shouldered, his friends remember him for his healthy appetite. Full of good humour and relaxed, he was nonetheless no stranger to drama. When a private in the Transvaal Scottish Regiment, he was captured at Tobruk but escaped. Then he joined the RAF and suffered a serious leg injury from a mortar shell. For some time afterwards Athol had his left leg in irons while playing cricket and hockey. This interrupted and eventually ended his out-

standing cricket career when he was 30.

With an individual grip, Athol bowled sharp off-breaks with a marked outward spin-swerve. He could also bowl a straight one with the same action. As a variation, he used a leg-cutter which often caught batsmen unawares. A useful lower middle-order batsman, and safe and fast at cover point, he once scored an unbeaten century against Glamorgan in 1947. On that 1947 tour he captured 102 wickets in first-class matches. In the opening game against Worcestershire he took five wickets in each innings, and in the second game against the Gentlemen of Ireland he took 7 for 32 and 4 for 14. In Tests he was less successful – 12 wickets at 56 apiece.

Throughout his postwar career, Athol had the handicap of a badly damaged left knee and bowled in considerable pain. But such was his determination that he cut his run-up to a mere shuffle, his left leg in irons.

Against F.G. Mann's English team to South Africa in 1948–49, Athol took 24 wickets – the most for either side. His 5 for 80 in the Cape Town Test so impressed his skipper, Nourse, that he wrote: 'Athol bowled magnificently ... It must rank with the great bowling performances in Test cricket because Rowan had little in the way of aid from the wicket ... It was certainly Athol Rowan's day and the critics were already claiming he was the finest off-spinner in the world. Certainly I have not played against a better off-spinner than Athol Rowan.'

Athol was the first off-spinner to rout a modern Australian team. For Transvaal against Hassett's team of 1949–50 he had a devastating spell of 9 for 19 and 6 for 49 on a turning wicket at Johannesburg. In this match he also made the second-highest score in the first innings and top-scored in the second. Unfortunately, he broke down just before the Tests started and missed the series.

In 1951, both Eric and Athol toured

England. Although Eric was the star of the tour, Athol took 18 wickets in the Tests and, according to *Wisden*, 'he was a constant menace wherever he went'. He was at his scheming best in the Trent Bridge Test where he took 5 for 68. Both brothers thus ended their Test careers after that series and on a successful note. Eric was then 42 and his Test career had spanned 17 years. However, Athol was only 30 and had played only 15 Tests in five seasons. But for his war injury, he could well have served his country for many more years.

The Rowans in Test Cricket

	Tests	Runs	Avrge	HS	100s	50s	Wkts	Avrge	Best	5w/i	Catches
Eric	26	1965	43.66	236	3	12	0	–	–	–	14
Athol	15	290	17.05	41	0	0	54	38.59	5–68	4	7
Total	41	2255	36.37	236	3	12	54	38.72	5–68	4	21

CHAPTER 24

The
Bedser Twins

———— ● ————

*The Bedser motto has been: 'Keep trying, you never know what's going
to happen'. And the Bedser twins Alec and Eric gave their best
under all conditions. They shared everything from money
to an apple and cricket fame.*

ALEC BEDSER IS REMEMBERED for his
large frame, huge hands and a big
heart, rather than for loud appeals. The
only time he appealed with anguish and
hurt was as a babe-in-arms, when his
mother fed his twin brother Eric twice in
succession, ignoring a roaring Alec! With
the twins looking identical even 82 years
later, their friends find it difficult to pick
them with certainty.

Alec grew up to become one of the
giants of the game. The first Englishman,
and second in Test cricket, to take over
200 wickets, he was an institution in
cricket from 1946 to 1955 as a bowler –
England's spearhead, its start, middle
and finish – and for almost two decades
as a national selector. Sir Donald
Bradman, who Alec dismissed in five
consecutive Test innings, once wrote: 'I
am delighted to pay my tribute to a great
bowler who probably worried me more

than any other Englishman ... His
bowling against me was always accurate,
full of life, and occasionally he produced
the medium-pacer's dream ball, the one
which cuts from the leg stump to the off
at top speed.'

Eric Bedser's success was limited to
cricket for Surrey where he did well as an
off-spinner and a capable batsman who
occasionally opened the innings.

Alec and his 10-minutes-older
brother, Eric, were born at Reading in
Surrey on 4 July 1918. Their identical
appearance enabled them to carry out
jocular deceptions on all but a few.
When, in 1948, the MCC team was
sailing to South Africa, Alec travelled
first-class while Eric, on a business trip,
was in the tourist class. A woman
passenger who was making a 'lost
weekend' of the voyage, and had been
drinking non-stop for three days, was

suddenly confronted by the Bedser twins. She uttered a shrill, terrified shriek and rushed to her cabin, convinced she was seeing double in a state of delirium tremens. A barber in Sydney did no better. When Eric went for a haircut an hour after Alec, he exclaimed, 'Gee, your hair grows fast!'

The Bedser twins explain in their autobiographical *Our Cricket Story*: 'Our absolute and complete affinity is hard to explain but is true and very real to us ... So far our lives have been so close that we two are, for all purposes, one. We share everything and have never quarrelled seriously, although either is quick to criticise a bad cricket shot or ball or golf shot by the other.'

From early boyhood, the twins devoted every spare hour to cricket, and each did much to develop the ability of the other. They were headed for a legal profession when spotted at the nets by former Surrey all-rounder Allan Peach. Soon, under Peach, the twins were spending every spare moment practising cricket, bowling from 10 a.m. to 6 p.m. on weekends. They were also inspired by the English blazer worn by Wally Hammond in a village match. 'We looked at it, and twin thoughts passed through our minds. "Could we ... perhaps one day ... ?"' they recalled. To his delight, Alec toured Australia under Hammond's captaincy 16 years later.

When 17, they decided that they would have more chance of getting into the county side together if each bowled differently from the other. It was decided that Eric should develop off-spinners and Alec stick to his fast-medium. In 1938 they became professionals for Surrey. They had two seasons in the Second XI, their first success together coming against Cornwall when Eric scored 92 not out and Alec took 4 for 32 and 7 for 21. Alec topped the bowling averages in 1938. The next year, Eric hit two centuries. In Young Players'

matches, Eric headed the batting, Alec the bowling. They were beginning to think how peaceful life was when World War II broke out.

They served in the Royal Air Force, took part in the evacuation of Dunkirk and in operations in North Africa, Italy and Austria. In 1943 each was promoted to the rank of warrant officer, which meant parting. So, rather than be separated, they decided one should decline the promotion. They tossed a coin and Eric won but Alec never addressed him as 'Sir'. The twins played wartime cricket against the Australians, the West Indies and the Dominions. In an unofficial test against the West Indies, Alec performed a hat-trick.

In 1946, first-class cricket was resumed in England and the Bedsers made their simultaneous debut for Surrey's First XI against MCC. Alec started well, with 6 for 14, after which Denis Compton came into the dressing-room and congratulated Eric! In a charity match, the great Frank Woolley, as an umpire, did no better. He failed to notice that the twins bowled three balls each in the same over and remarked, 'This young bowler has a fine change of pace'.

When Alec was picked for the first Test at Lord's against India, Eric was as pleased at his selection as he would have been with his own. And it was a sensational debut for Alec, taking 11 for 145, including 7 for 49 in the first innings. His victims included India's top four batsmen – Vijay Merchant, Lala Amarnath, Vijay Hazare and skipper Iftikhar Pataudi. It was 30 years before Alec's debut figures were bettered by another Englishman, John Lever, who took 7 for 46 in his first Test – also against India, at Delhi.

In the second Test at Old Trafford, Alec took 11 for 93 – a total of 22 for 238 in his first two Tests. During the second Test, Alec also took his 100th wicket of the season – his first in county cricket. But the euphoria of 1946 was not over.

Alec gained selection to tour Australia and was elected as one of *Wisden*'s Five Cricketers of the Year. A new star had arrived. It was the beginning of a great career for the amiable giant who was a glutton for hard work.

The excitement of touring Australia was dimmed by the knowledge that he would be parted from Eric, but to their immense joy, a football pools promoter paid Eric's fare to Australia to attend the matches as a spectator. A day after hearing this news, Eric scored his first century in first-class cricket for Surrey. In Australia, when Alec was not getting many wickets, barrackers would yell: 'You'll never get 'em out. Send for your brother.'

Statistically, Alec was not very successful in the 1946–47 Test series down under, taking 16 wickets at 54.74. Even so, Bradman was so impressed that he described Alec as one of the best fast-medium bowlers he had faced. And the Don should know. In the Adelaide Test he was bowled by a certain Alec Bedser for a duck. Bradman acknowledges the Bedser delivery as the finest ball to have taken his wicket. It was bowled on the off-stump, swung very late to hit the pitch on the leg-stump, and then came back to hit the middle and off.

This tour put a severe strain on Alec, affecting him as it had affected Maurice Tate – a similar type of bowler – on an earlier tour. In 1947, Alec performed moderately against South Africa and was dropped in the last three Tests to give him some much-needed rest. To some critics, he was already finished.

However, in 1948 he swung back in top gear against one of the strongest sides Australia has ever sent to England. Although Australian speedsters Ray Lindwall and Keith Miller stole the show, Alec Bedser carried the burden for England. The master batsmen Bradman and Arthur Morris could not tame him. Four times in a row in the Test series, and

five consecutive times in his Test career, Alec made Bradman snick a catch close to leg-side by dipping the ball in late from the off. As R.C. Robertson-Glasgow noted in *Wisden* (1953): 'Not since the triumph of Harold Larwood in Australia 16 years ago, had Bradman looked so fallible.'

While Alec was busy tormenting the Don in the Lord's Test, Eric scored 128 as an opener for Surrey against Oxford University.

In the fourth Test, at Leeds, Alec had another taste of success. Sent in as nightwatchman, he added 155 runs for the third wicket with Bill Edrich, in the process making his highest Test score of 79.

The following season, the Bedsers pooled their batting resources against the touring New Zealanders, Eric scoring 65, Alec an unbeaten 45.

Although Alec had only moderate success as a bowler in South Africa in 1948 – taking 16 wickets at 34.62 – he stole some batting limelight in the Durban Test. England, set 128 in 135 minutes in bad light, had lost 8 for 116 and needed 12 runs in five minutes to win. Off the very last ball, Alec Bedser and Cliff Gladwin ran a bye to win the Test. In the next match, against Natal District XI, Alec went in with three runs needed to win and two balls to go. He hit a single off the last ball to clinch the match.

Despite the fact Eric could never get near an English cap, he continued to do well in the English County Championship. In 1949 he scored 154 against Somerset, adding 260 runs for the opening wicket with Laurie Fishlock. In the following month he hit 163. Then came the match against Middlesex, whose batsmen crumbled to the twin menace. Eric took 7 for 99 in the first innings, Alec 8 for 42 in the second.

On his second tour of Australia in 1950–51, Alec started unimpressively but

Bedser twins Alec and Eric (or is it Eric and Alec?) flanked by
David Sincock and Brian Booth. (© *R.L. Cardwell*)

then gradually began taking wickets. Five times he claimed the wicket of Morris – three times in a row – and ended the series having taken 30 wickets at 16.06. He reached his peak form in the final Test, taking 10 for 105 in the match. Thus, he was responsible for England's first Test win over Australia since August 1938.

When South Africa toured England in 1951, and India in 1952, they saw Alec at the height of his powers although he was past 33. Although the Indians found Freddie Trueman, then 21, too fast to sight, their captain Hazare ranked Bedser as a better and more dangerous bowler.

Against Lindsay Hassett's Australians the following year, Alec reached his meridian. He captured 39 wickets in the series: 7 for 55 and 7 for 44 at Nottingham; 5 for 105 and 3 for 77 at Lord's; 5 for 115 and 2 for 14 at Manchester; 6 for 95 and 1 for 65 at Leeds. As he had taken five wickets in an innings in two

previous Tests against India, he had now achieved this feat in six consecutive Tests. Only two other bowlers had achieved such consistency in Test history, namely: Charlie Turner (1886–88) and Sydney Barnes (1912–14). After Alec took 14 wickets in the Nottingham Test, Hassett remarked, tongue-in-cheek: 'Well bowled, you great big stiff, although I would like to hit you on the head. And I would if I were tall enough!'

Left-handers Morris and Neil Harvey found Alec's leg-cutters difficult to keep down. He dismissed Morris 10 times and Harvey 12 times in 10 Tests from 1950 to 1953. Twice he dismissed Harvey in five consecutive innings, if we ignore a run-out. In 21 Tests Morris and Bedser played together Alec claimed the Australian opener 18 times. This prompted journalists to nickname Morris as 'Bedser's Bunny'. In the Manchester Test, the witty Hassett had the last laugh. When Bedser came in to bat at No. 11, Hassett gave the ball to Morris. And

Morris, in his reversed role, promptly dismissed his tormentor.

To keep up the joke, the Australian players made way for Morris to precede the team through the gate as if he were a bowling hero. In that series Alec became the second player – after Australia's Clarrie Grimmett – to top 200 wickets in Test cricket. And before the series was over he had passed Grimmett's record. Thanks to 'Big Fella' Bedser, England had regained the Ashes after 20 years.

After reaching his zenith in 1953, Alec's downfall was sudden and sad. Just before the second Test of the 1954–55 series in Sydney, skipper Len Hutton went out with him to inspect the wicket, but to everybody's surprise Alec was dropped in this Test and the rest of the series. This was the series dominated and won by express fast bowlers Frank Tyson and Brian Statham. Sir Alec played only one more Test – against South Africa in 1955 – before retiring. However, as Chairman of England's Test Selection Committee, Sir Alec Bedser remained actively involved in the game in the late 1970s and early 1980s.

In 51 Tests he captured 236 wickets averaging 24.89. He took five wickets in an innings 15 times and 10 wickets in a match five times. Against Australia, he bagged 104 wickets at 27.49.

Bedser the bowler is often compared with Maurice Tate and as Robertson-Glasgow said: 'Of the two, I would say that Tate had the more natural genius, Bedser the more invention and variety ...

Tate in his prime had the faster, and so the more suitable, pitches to bowl on [in Australia]. Bedser in Australia had attacked on slower surfaces.' The Bedser motto has been: 'Keep trying, you never know what's going to happen.' And certainly, the Bedser twins gave their best under all conditions.

A theoretical point keeps haunting me. What if Alec had switched over to off-spinning and Eric had continued his natural development as a fast-medium bowler? Would Morris then have become 'Eric's Rabbit' and Alec remained no more than a county player? Was Eric ever jealous of Alec's international reputation? In their autobiography, the Bedsers provide the answer to the second of these questions: 'We can say with perfect honesty that success by either is shared, and there is never the slightest hint of jealousy. Eric was as pleased at Alec's selection as if it had been for himself. This is no doubt due to the fact that we have always shared everything – from money to an apple.'

The Springbok Bedser Twins

When Alec and Eric Bedser were touring Border in South Africa, a pair of twins was born to a couple named Bedser. Not surprisingly, the twins were christened Alec and Eric. In 1971–72, 23-year-old Alec played first-class cricket for Border in three Currie Cup matches. He also distinguished himself in hockey, softball and soccer.

Alec Bedser in Test Cricket										
Tests	Runs	Avrge	HS	100s	50s	Wkts	Avrge	Best	5w/i	Catches
51	714	12.75	79	0	1	236	24.89	7–44	15	26

CHAPTER 25

The
Harvey Boys

———●———

Australia is proud of the Harvey brothers. All six played first-grade
cricket for Fitzroy in Melbourne. Four of them represented three States
in the Sheffield Shield. Two played for Australia and one – Neil –
is recognised as among cricket's all-time greats.

IN THE THIRD TEST at Old Trafford in 1948, Sid Barnes – that whimsical Australian opener – was hurt badly while fielding in the 'suicide' position. Unfortunate though it was, this gave the 19-year-old Neil Harvey a chance to play his first Test against England. Six months previously, Harvey had made his Test debut against India on the Adelaide Oval. And in his second Test shortly afterwards, at Melbourne, he had hit 153 heart-warming runs. However, so strong was Australia in 1948 that centurion Harvey could not get into a Test XI in England until the Barnes injury.

In the Leeds Test, England for once had the mighty Aussies on the run – having scored 496, they dismissed Arthur Morris, Lindsay Hassett and Don Bradman for 68. As Hassett and Bradman had fallen in three deliveries by Dick Pollard, newcomer Harvey had not

even finished strapping his pads when called upon. Instead of feeling overawed by the occasion, Harvey coolly walked to the middle and greeted Keith Miller at the other end with: 'Let's get stuck into them, eh?' And the left-handed rookie did just that. He drove Pollard and Alec Bedser with nonchalance. He hit some, missed some, but stayed on.

When off-spinner Jim Laker was introduced to the attack, Harvey was in trouble but Miller shielded the youngster by hitting Laker into the pavilion for a couple of sixes. Inspired, Harvey broke through with an audacious pull-drive and a daredevil sweep – both against Laker's spin. When the end seemed near, Harvey's bat became all middle. Perfectly timed shots zoomed hither and thither. Eventually, he was joined by his room-mate Sam Loxton and soon completed his memorable century.

The Harvey brothers, Ray, Mervyn and Neil, going out to field for Victoria vs NSW. (*Jack Pollard Collection*)

Harvey had become the youngest batsman playing his first Test against England to score a hundred on English soil. He was also the first Australian left-hander to score a century in his maiden Test against England. Sir Jack Hobbs was moved to write: 'I want England to win, but directly I saw Harvey's masterly yet carefree batting I wanted him to get his hundred.' From Australia, Neil received a cable from his brother Ray, on behalf of his parents, sister and five brothers: 'You beaut. Congratulations. We played every shot with you. Tremendously proud of you.'

The Harvey family is justifiably proud of its record as a producer of top-class cricketers. There were six Harvey brothers and a sister. Neil, the second-youngest, reflects: 'A young cricketer is very fortunate if he has parents like I had.' Eldest brother, Mervyn, and Neil represented Australia. Mervyn, Clarrie

(also named 'Mick' because he was born on St Patrick's day), Ray and Neil played for Victoria. Clarrie also represented Queensland and Neil, from 1958, New South Wales. All four hit centuries in first-class cricket and Ray, Neil and Clarrie once hit hundreds in the same match. Harold and the youngest brother, Brian, played first-grade cricket with Fitzroy.

Their father, Horace Harvey, played reasonably well in Newcastle in New South Wales before he moved to Melbourne where he continued playing junior cricket. Their sister – eldest in the family – scored for Dad's team.

All the Harveys were natural stroke-players, but Neil was the only left-hander. He recalls in his autobiography, *My World of Cricket*, that the Harvey household on a Saturday morning during the cricket season resembled a madhouse. At the age of 15, Neil was promoted to the First XI. That season Fitzroy's First XI's listed batting order looked rather odd as the first four names were Harvey – Mervyn and Clarrie to open, followed by Ray and Neil.

According to Neil, 'Mervyn was the best player of us all'. He was an opening batsman with solid defence and a quick eye. He was capable of tearing an attack to shreds. Ray Robinson described Mervyn as a whole-hearted hooker. A.G. Moyes called him 'a delightful stroke-maker, possibly a little unsound'. Mervyn was more comfortable against quickies than against spin. Unfortunately, war years interrupted his first-class career. His best innings was a century against New South Wales at the Melbourne Cricket Ground. The full fury of Ray Lindwall did not worry him and once he hooked a typical Lindwall bouncer into the crowd for a six.

When Sid Barnes was unavailable for the Adelaide Test against England under Wally Hammond in 1946–47, Mervyn, then 28, was selected. It was a strange coincidence that Barnes' injury in England subsequently led to Neil playing his first Test against England in 1948. In that Adelaide Test, Mervyn scored 12 and 31, and although he added 116 runs for the opening wicket with Morris this was his first and last Test.

Clarrie was also an opening batsman, but was more defensive than his brothers and less attractive to watch. Spin posed problems for him. He opened for both Victoria and Queensland and hit three centuries for the latter. Against Len Hutton's side in 1954–55 he scored 49. He later became a Test umpire.

The third brother, Ray, was considered by experts to be as good as Neil – if not better. A brilliant, aggressive batsman, Ray was a delight to watch when in full cry. Ray Robinson wrote in *Green Sprigs*: 'Ray, three years older than Neil, is such a fine batsman that I once thought he would rival Neil's achievements but the doors did not open for him'. During the 1953–54 season, he scored two centuries which showed his class. To quote Moyes from *Australian Batsmen*: 'There was no prodding or pushing but a free swing or wristy cut which made the onlookers glad that he was there. At times when batting with Neil he was not overshadowed and there are those who have always claimed that he was a better batsman.'

Neil explains in his autobiography why Ray did not reach the top: 'The better class bowlers in Shield cricket detected a weakness in his footwork, a thing which kept his scores to moderate proportions. I often thought that if this flaw in his footwork had been worked upon and rectified, Ray could easily have been a Test player.'

One of the biggest thrills for the Harvey family came in 1947 when Mervyn, Ray and Neil were selected for Victoria vs New South Wales at the SCG. Mervyn scored 45, Ray 43 and 22 not out, and Neil 61, as Victoria won by nine

wickets. The Harvey trio played several times together that season. Once, in 1953, after Clarrie had moved to Queensland, Ray, Clarrie and Neil hit hundreds in the same match – Clarrie for Queensland, Ray and Neil for Victoria.

Neil burst upon the cricket scene like a fiery comet. Soon people were talking about this exciting teenaged left-hander – the dashing stroke-player who believed the ball was meant for hitting. When Neil was 16, Ray Robinson predicted in England's *The Cricketer*: 'Neil Harvey may have too far to go to reach the Test team next season [in 1946–47] but he will get there sooner or later, sure enough.'

He got there all right – too quickly, and stayed too long, if you ask bowlers and fielders from six countries! Neil made a century in his first club match; 154 in 169 minutes in his second match for Victoria when only 18; 160 in his first game for New South Wales; 153 in his second Test; and 112 in his first Test in England. His first-class career spanned 16 years and he lost none of his brilliance or grace while batting or fielding.

Born on 8 October 1928, Neil was only 13 when he hit 101 and 141 not out in the grand final while playing for Fitzroy Third XI. 'This is a feat I have never managed since in any form of cricket, 'he recalls. He became an instant schoolboy hero. Joe Plant – himself a left-hander – coached young Neil and taught him how to go down the wicket to slow bowlers and hit the ball hard. Cricket-lovers all over the world owe a lot to him. 'Plant put more time than anybody I've ever known into helping boys become good cricketers and obviously gained a lot of satisfaction in my success over the years,' Neil told Ronald Cardwell in his book, *The Fitzroy Urchin*.

Neil played his first representative match for Victoria against Tasmania at Hobart in 1946–47 and scored 154. In his first Sheffield Shield game, against New South Wales in Sydney, he scored a duck after feeling 'as nervous as a kitten'. But in the second innings, 'Nina' (Neil's nickname) scored 49 despite the fact that Ray Lindwall gave him the full treatment. For Victoria against Hammond's England side that season, Neil scored 69 in the middle of a collapse. When he reached 50, wicket-keeper Godfrey Evans commented: 'Well played, son, we'll be seeing you in England next year.' The next season, in a match at Perth between Victoria and Western Australia, the Harvey brothers were associated in a 173-run stand, Mervyn scoring 141, Neil 94.

Barely 19, Neil made his Test debut against India in 1947–48. As Mervyn's had been the previous year, it was also at Adelaide, in the fourth Test. Also like Mervyn, Neil was not successful, but unlike Mervyn he was given a second chance and at Melbourne in the final Test of the series he hit the high spots with a stroke-filled 153. He became the youngest to score a Test century at 19 years and 121 days. In England the next year he made such an impression that Patsy Hendren remarked, 'The boy looks like another Clem Hill.'

After his memorable 112 in the Leeds Test, Neil was the toast of all England. Within two years he was the most popular cricket personality in South Africa too. When he was rested for a match against Border, the spectators protested: 'No Compton [the year before]. No Harvey. No match.' Neil had to be included! Writes Neil: 'From a personal point of view, this was the most successful of all my tours.' In 25 first-class innings there, Neil scored 1526 runs – a record for an Australian in South Africa – and hit eight centuries, setting a record for any touring batsman. In the Test series he collected 660 runs, averaging 132. He hit four centuries, 178 at Cape Town, 151 not out at Durban, 116 at Port Elizabeth and 100 at Johannesburg.

Neil's undefeated 151 in the Durban Test is the innings he cherishes most. It turned impending disaster for Australia into a glorious five-wicket win. With champion off-spinner Hugh Tayfield taking 7 for 23, Australia was shot out for 75 on a sticky pitch. Set 336 to win on a bad wicket, Australia was 4 for 95, but incredibly, they reached their target with the loss of only one more wicket in the last session. The 21-year-old had played a superbly controlled innings.

When South Africa returned the visit to Australia in 1952–53, Neil was once again in great form scoring 834 runs at 92.6 in the series, with four more hundreds. In the Adelaide Test, Australia needed quick scoring to win. Harvey raced to his 100 in 106 minutes – then the fastest Test hundred in Australia since the war – and Australia reached the target. In the final Test, at Melbourne, Neil hit his highest Test score of 205. This was the Test Australia lost despite scoring 520 runs in the first innings!

Neil has pleasant memories of his tour to England in 1953. Although Australia lost the Ashes, it was roses, roses, all the way for him. 'My form against the Counties was easily the most consistent of my career and the Test series was equally happy,' he recalls. He totalled 2040 runs on that tour, averaging 65.8, and hit 10 hundreds. Prior to the first Test he made 109, 103, 82, 137 not out, 109 and 14 in successive innings. He considers his 180 in 165 minutes against Glamorgan at Swansea to be his best: 'I don't think I have ever hit the ball better.'

However, Neil's 1956 tour to England was the least successful of his four trips. The pitches made run-getting very difficult – especially in the Manchester Test where Laker took 19 wickets. After that tour, Australia paid a flying visit to Pakistan and India. I will always cherish his 140 in the Bombay Test as among the finest innings I have seen. As he walked out to bat, there were comments about

Harvey's weakness against spin bowlers and how the leg-spinner Subash Gupte would tie him in knots. However, in the first over, Neil showed who was the master by repeatedly stepping out and driving Gupte's wrong 'uns to the fence. Neil cut, drove, pulled and glided with exquisite timing and Gupte was never the same bowler afterwards.

In 1955 Neil had another successful tour in the Caribbean. He totalled 650 runs in the series at 108.3 and hit three hundreds. In the final Test at Kingston, Australia was 2 for 7 when he entered. The next wicket did not fall until the 300 mark had been passed. Australia totalled 758 with Harvey contributing 204. He played for a little over seven hours – his longest innings – and was offered a prize of 10 shillings a run if he scored 365. But a seven-hour spell was long enough for Neil, who never tried for pointless records.

Harvey is also remembered for his shorter innings played against heavy odds. For example:

- His masterly 83 against the mystery spin of West Indian Sonny Ramadhin in the Melbourne Test of 1951–52.
- His gutsy 96 against the bowling genius of Fazal Mahmood in the Dacca Test of 1959–60.
- His top score of 69 in the Calcutta Test in 1956–57 when the flood-hit wicket had made off-spinner Ghulam Ahmed virtually unplayable.
- His heroic 92 not out against the beastly fury of Frank Tyson and Brian Statham in the Sydney Test of 1954–55. No one else could reach 17 in that innings.
- His technically perfect 73 and 53 on the 'powder-puff' surface in the Leeds Test of 1961.

According to Harvey himself, his 167 against England at Melbourne in 1958–59 was among the best of his 21 Test centuries. 'It was one of those innings every Test batsman produces at some time in his career,' he says.

Apart from his value to the side as a batsman and magnificent all-round fielder, Harvey was a team man for whom Australia came first. Once, in Lahore, he threw away his wicket so Australia could win. Realising that the Pakistani fielders were getting more opportunity to waste time with a left-hander and a right-hander batting, he deliberately let a ball hit his wicket so that two right-handers could get together.

Harvey was twice passed over for the Australian captaincy – a job he deserved – while his juniors, Ian Craig and Richie Benaud, were preferred. But Neil did not let his personal disappointment embitter his approach and he gave his fullest support to both skippers. And when Benaud's painful shoulder made him unavailable for the Lord's Test in 1961, Neil got his only chance to captain his country. And although he was leading a weakened side, and despite losing the toss, he led Australia to a meritorious win in what is referred to now as 'The Battle of the Ridge'. The heroes of this victory were Alan Davidson, Bill Lawry and newcomer, Graham McKenzie. Before the Test, a far from fit Alan Davidson told the emergency skipper: 'I'll try to pull out something special for you today'. He did just that with a deadly spell of 5 for 42, shattering England in the process.

Neil Harvey retired from cricket in 1963. He was 34 and still in form. In his final Test series – against England in 1962–63 – he hit his 21st century. And in his farewell Test he took six catches – sharing a Test record since broken by Greg Chappell and India's Yajurvendra Singh. In his final Shield game he hit his career-best score of 231 not out in 285 minutes, playing for New South Wales against South Australia. This included 120 runs between lunch and tea.

In first-class cricket, he played 306 matches, scored 21,699 runs, averaged

50.93, hit 67 hundreds (highest, 231 not out) and 94 fifties, took 30 wickets and 228 catches. He scored centuries on 35 grounds in six countries, hitting more centuries outside Australia (38) than at home (29). In Test matches, he totalled 6149 runs at 48.41, hitting 21 centuries and 24 fifties. Perhaps he has given more pleasure to cricket-lovers than any other Australian, for Victor Trumper, Hill and Bradman were not seen in action in the West Indies, India, Pakistan and New Zealand. Besides, he was a brilliant fielder in the deep.

Harvey's sparkling footwork inspired the following comments. Bob Simpson wrote in 1968: 'Harvey to me was the best technically equipped batsman for all wickets, that I have seen ... he was without doubt, the best all-round fieldsman that I have ever seen.' A.G. Moyes: 'His drive is terrific and when he hooks, the sound of the ball hitting the fence is like an explosion from Bikini'.

In 1966 Harvey was appointed a national selector, and when Bradman resigned in 1971 he was made chairman. Australia regained its cricket supremacy in the 1970s, never losing a Test series under chairman Harvey. His children, Robert, Anne and Bruce, were born when he was either touring abroad or about to tour.

The Harvey brothers, between them, played 146 Sheffield Shield matches, scoring 9264 runs at 40.28. Apart from Mervyn, the three Harveys exceeded 1500 runs each in Shield cricket, Neil dominating with 5824.

Ray Robinson paid Neil the ultimate compliment in *On Top Down Under*. 'Had Michaelangelo been a cricketer he would have batted like [Neil] Harvey, with the touch that made chips of marble fly everywhere as he pressed on with the creation of a great piece of sculpture'.

The Harveys in Test Cricket

	Tests	Runs	Avrge	HS	100s	50s	Wkts	Avrge	Best	5w/i	Catches
Merv	1	43	21.50	31	0	0	0	–	–	–	0
Neil	79	6149	48.41	205	21	24	3	40.00	1–8	–	64
Total	80	6192	48.00	205	21	24	3	40.00	1–8	–	64

CHAPTER 26

The
Cricketing Cowdreys

—— ● ——

The first cricketer to play 100 Tests, Colin Cowdrey hit a hundred in his 100th Test. His 120 catches in Test matches remained a record for almost two decades. He was a touch artist who strove for perfection. His eldest son, Chris, preferred power to perfection and played six Tests for England. Colin's younger sons, Jeremy and Graham, shone as school cricketers, Graham representing Kent for a decade. Between Colin, Chris and Graham, they played first-class cricket continuously from 1950 to 1997.

THERE WERE SHOCKED REACTIONS on the announcement of England's team to Australia in 1954–55. 'What, no Jim Laker, Tony Lock, Willie Watson? And who is this Colin Cowdrey chap?' Within months, the relatively unknown Cowdrey became a household name in the cricket world and the passage of time has done nothing to diminish his fame.

Along with Peter May, Brian Statham and Frank 'Typhoon' Tyson, Cowdrey was responsible for England retaining the Ashes that summer. Even before the tour, skipper Len Hutton had held a high opinion of the 21-year-old Colin. Regarded as an uncommunicative captain, Hutton nevertheless gave young Colin plenty of attention during the early part of the tour. Before the ship had left for Australia, Hutton had spent some time talking earnestly with Colin's

father, Ernest Arthur Cowdrey, and promised him, 'I'll look after Colin'. But before the ship reached Perth, Colin heard of his father's death. Hutton, knowing exactly how the youngster felt, kept him busy at the nets and during matches, giving him no time to feel sorry for himself.

Colin has never forgotten the debt he owed to his father, who instilled in him a love of cricket. E.A. Cowdrey coached his four-year-old son to play off-side shots on a tennis court in Ootacamund in the south of India, Colin's birthplace. Even at that age, leg-slide slogging was condemned. 'Gradually my education widened and by the time I was 12, I could play most of the shots,' he recalled in his *MCC: The Autobiography of a Cricketer*. It was his father who christened him Michael Colin Cowdrey,

Lord Colin Cowdrey and family including cricket-playing sons Chris, Jeremy and Graham.
(*Allsport Historical Collection*)

probably to get the game's most famous initials – MCC.

Colin remembers his first cricket match in England in 1940, when he was seven. In an Under-11 game for Homefield School in Surrey, he was in fine form, hitting sweetly timed fours everywhere. After a couple of hours, there were cheers on the boundary line, the boys chanting: 'Seven more for your century, Colin'. He carefully scored those seven runs, raised his bat with the panache of a youthful Denis Compton and threw away his wicket. 'I had never been happier in my life,' he recalled. Nor was he more heartbroken than when told minutes later that, on recounting, his score was 93. No wonder he had tears running down his chubby cheeks.

The same Colin Cowdrey was the star performer for Kent and England for 26 years, creating quite a few firsts, mosts and onlys. He was at his best in crises; wickets falling quickly and bowlers on headhunting sprees brought the best out of him. Despite his gentle nature, opponents could feel the steel within this sensitive man of charm and wit. He weathered the storm against four of the greatest pace duos in cricket history: Ray Lindwall and Keith Miller, Neil Adcock

and Peter Heine, Wes Hall and Charlie Griffith, Dennis Lillee and Jeff Thomson.

Colin's first Test ton came in his third Test, on the MCG in 1954–55. He became the 50th England batsman to score a century against Australia. More remarkable was the fact that he had contributed to 53.4 per cent of the England total of 191. The grandmaster had arrived. He was also a maestro at punishing spin bowling and one of his most memorable innings was his 154 against the West Indies in the Birmingham Test of 1957. With unorthodox spinner Sonny Ramadhin taking 7 for 49, England was bowled out for 186. England, facing a deficit of 288, were in a helpless position when Colin joined May. Together they put on 411 glorious runs which not only saved England but almost defeated the Windies. May remembers Colin's steadying influence throughout this stand. When England declared, the visitors were so disheartened that they lost 7 for 72 before being saved by the bell. Colin followed this 154 with 152, 55 and 68 in subsequent Tests.

He continued in the same vein when England toured the Caribbean in 1959–60, scoring 114 and 97 in the Kingston Test and 119 in Port-of-Spain against the fury of Hall, Griffith and Chester Watson. When he led England to the West Indies eight years later, in 1967–68, he recorded two more Test hundreds – once again at Kingston and Port-of-Spain. However, his best two innings in the series were scores of 70-odd. In the first Test, Griffith tried to intimidate him into submission with a barrage of short-pitched balls at lightning speed. But Colin, to quote Peter Smith, 'stood erect without flinching, meeting brute force with graceful composure and even having time to play his strokes'.

After three exciting draws, the fourth Test was heading towards a yawning

Brett Lee is ecstatic after his 5 for 47 in his Test debut.
(*Allsport / Hamish Blair*)

Jeff Crowe, a studious accumulator of runs.
(*Allsport / Adrian Murrell*)

Hanif Mohammad, the Little Master.
(*Allsport / Hulton – Getty*)

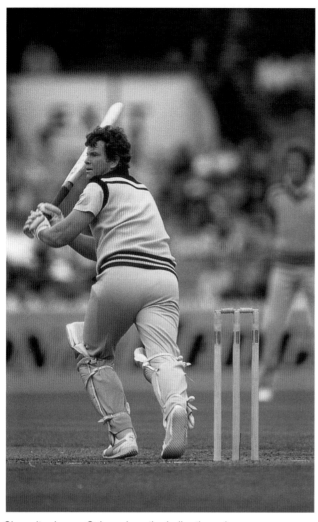

Six-smiter Lance Cairns gives the ball a thumping heave-ho. (*Allsport / Adrian Murrell*)

Martin Crowe, a magnificent driver, during his 115 against England in the 1994 Manchester Test. (*Allsport / Adrian Murrell*)

Andy (left) and Grant Flower against New Zealand.
(*Allsport / Mark Hewitt*)

Greg Chappell gloriously driving on his way to a century on the
MCG in 1979–80. (*Allsport / Adrian Murrell*)

stalemate when Garry Sobers sportingly declared, setting England 215 runs to win in 165 minutes. Thanks to a brilliant 71 by Colin, England won the match – and the series – with three minutes to spare. Captain Cowdrey was the toast of England. In the Birmingham Test of July 1968 against Australia, he celebrated his becoming the first cricketer to appear in 100 Tests by scoring a century. Two runs later he became the second batsman after Wally Hammond to score 7000 Test runs.

Now Colin's ambition – to captain England in Australia – appeared about to become a reality. Unfortunately, an Achilles tendon injury in a Sunday League match put him out for a season and he lost the captaincy to Ray Illingworth. England regained the Ashes in Australia in 1970–71 under Illingworth, but for vice-captain Cowdrey it was a frustrating tour. His form was disappointing and he was dropped for the fourth and subsequent Tests. He took the disappointment with a stiff upper lip and in 1973 became the 16th player to hit his 100th first-class century.

When Lillee and Thomson were making life miserable for English batsmen in the 1974–75 down-under series, the players' unanimous choice as a reinforcement was 42-year-old warhorse Cowdrey. Without any match practice and very little at the nets, he faced the 'Cyclone Lilian Thomson' without flinching. Although he did not score many runs, he showed his younger colleagues how to face pace without touching your toes. When he played his final Test on the MCG, grateful spectators put up a huge banner: 'MCG FANS THANK COLIN – SIX TOURS'.

Thus, his Test career started and ended in Australia. Five of his 22 Test hundreds were against Australia, three of them on the MCG. His highest score in a first-class match was against South Australia on the Adelaide Oval

in 1962–63. He amassed 307 runs in heatwave conditions, then ordered a new registration plate for his Jaguar: MCC 307.

Colin played in 114 Tests, scoring 7624 runs at 44.06, and he accepted 120 catches. Both his run aggregate and catches were Test records at that time. The two catches which delighted him the most were the ones which gave fast bowler Freddie Trueman his 299th and 300th wickets in the Manchester Test of 1964. This enabled Trueman to become the first to reach the 300-wicket milestone.

In a first-class career lasting from 1950 to 1976, Colin scored 42,719 runs (13th highest) at 42.89 and hit 107 centuries. He scored 1000 runs in a season 27 times (only W.G. Grace and Frank Woolley were ahead of him with 28 each). Apart from English seasons, Colin also recorded 1000 runs in a season in South Africa, the West Indies and Australia. He scored centuries in both innings of a match on three occasions.

These are staggering figures but they do not reveal his popular personality, his jovial nature, his glorious drives and cuts executed with superb timing and minimum effort, or his encouragement to others when in poor form. When semi-retired in 1975, Colin played for Kent against Ian Chappell's Australians and, mainly due to his masterly 151 not out, Kent defeated Australia for the first time since 1899. 'It was the best innings I have played,' he recalls.

'It was an eventful week for the Cowdrey family. My eldest boy Christopher, captain of Tonbridge, made a hundred and chose his younger brother Jeremy, 15, to play in the Tonbridge XI for the first time as a leg-break bowler; while "Mimimus", 11-year-old Graham, at Wellesley House made 48, his top score for the first XI, and my wife Penny made 18, easily her top score – for the Mothers on an adjoining pitch.'

As Colin Cowdrey bade farewell to top-class cricket in 1976, his son Chris, 18, was gradually introduced to county cricket the same season. He had played with Kent Second XI in 1972 when 15, but did not hit the headlines until 1977. He was in Sydney in 1977–78 to gain experience and played first grade for Cumberland with fair success. I had the pleasure of interviewing him.

'My father encouraged me a lot but did not push me into cricket. He coached me with tennis balls when I was four or five and then seriously when I was seven. Although he passed on helpful hints, he wanted me to develop my own style … When I was first picked for Kent's Second XI at 15, I really didn't deserve a place,' he said. 'I felt I was picked in the team because I was a Cowdrey. People expected too much from me too soon. He also encouraged me to play all games and never once brought up the subject of a professional career until I had been offered my first Kent contract in 1976.'

Richard Boddington, the captain of the English squash team, coached him until he was 13, advising him to say to himself, 'watch the ball' every time he faced a delivery. At 19, he captained a team to the Caribbean which returned home undefeated. Chris topped the tour aggregate with 485 runs at 37.30. In an exciting unofficial Test, he contributed to his team's success by scoring 49 out of 180 and 69 out of 201.

Chris played frequently for Kent in 1977 when they became joint County Champions with Middlesex. He batted in the middle order although he frequently opened in one-dayers, but with Kent packed with medium-pacers he hardly got a chance to bowl. In a Benson & Hedges one-dayer against Sussex he scored a fluent 114 which enabled Kent to win. His maiden first-class century was against Glamorgan the same season.

Chris' best and worst memories thus far came in a match against Northamptonshire. Set 260 runs to win, Kent were in trouble at 5 for 100 when Chris went in to bat. He was in fine touch and added 90 runs with Alan Knott but threw away his wicket and Kent lost. Chris kept playing for Kent for 15 years before resigning as captain in 1991. Later he played for Glamorgan. He played six Tests and captained England once in 1988. But his performance was disappointing, only 101 runs at 14.42 (highest score 38) and four wickets at 77.25.

Performances apart, his refreshing personality was one of the bright features of the game. His ability to change the tempo to achieve results, to communicate with players and the crowd, made him a captivating figure. In 1985 he became captain of Kent, and under his leadership Kent went from 16th to fourth place in a short time. Against Northamptonshire at Maidstone he took wickets off his first, fifth and sixth balls in an over. Also, he scored 1035 runs at 33.38 with two centuries, 159 being his highest.

When Chris toured India with the England team in 1984–85 he met friends of his family and saw his cricket-mad grandfather's name on the club board in Madras (now Chennai). And when he visited Bangalore, where Colin had grown up, 'I was for special, sentimental reasons, keen to play in the one-day international', he wrote in his autobiographical *Good Enough*? Unfortunately, the day before the match Richard Ellison bowled a bouncer at him at the nets, striking a painful blow on the arm. 'I was passed fit but still only made 12th man. A major disappointment.' Chris played three Tests in India without achieving much. How good was he as a cricketer? 'I don't mind if I'm not as good as my father, as long as I'm good enough,' he wrote.

He is disappointed that he did not see his father bat more when he was a child, and even more that his parents got divorced. 'My father and my mother have been through a lot. I hope they will both find happiness. They deserve it.'

Chris has a soft spot for his mother, Penny. 'Through rain or shine she'll come to watch Kent, praying I'll do well, yet philosophical about whatever the day brings. There's always tomorrow ... my mother has supported all the family with remarkable vigour; she has supported us in the best possible way, quietly and modestly, never wanting or expecting the limelight.'

Younger brother Jeremy was also talented. He played every sport well, without being outstanding at any, yet everyone expected him to shine at cricket. Wasn't he Colin's son? He was in Tonbridge School 1st XI as a leg-spinner but did not work hard to get any further. He loved playing cricket for enjoyment, not as a profession. He would play club games over the weekend – a couple of drinks, a quick 25, a few wickets. He enjoyed the camaraderie of social matches.

Then there was the youngest brother, Graham. He toured India in 1985–86 as a 21-year-old and played in Bangalore, Madras and Hyderabad in a style 'less classical than his father's but more orthodox than brother Chris's', to quote skipper Vic Marks. He impressed with a century and some accomplished fifties in the country where his father was born. A middle order batsman, Graham played for Kent from 1986 to 1997, scoring at least one century a season from 1986 to 1993 and from 1995 to 1997. In 1995 he was second in averages after Sri Lanka's Aravinda de Silva. Both Chris and Graham scored centuries in 1989 and 1990.

The Cowdrey era which had started in 1950, when the likeable Colin made his debut for Kent, ended in 1997 when Graham played his last match for the county. Colin was proud to see his sons grow in stature although they never approached his greatness. Colin was rewarded for his services to cricket with a knighthood in 1991, and became Baron Cowdrey of Tonbridge in 1997.

When reviewing *The Last Roman: A Biography of Colin Cowdrey* by Mark Peel, Frank Keating neatly summed up the gentleman cricketer in *Wisden Cricket Monthly*: 'As an administrator, he had been all cricket's congenial and faithful curator – the Pelham Warner of the second half of the century, if you like. M'Lord Cowdrey, cricket's Queen Mum.' Indeed, the jovial, rotund, Oliver Hardy-like face of Colin Cowdrey has spread goodwill and entertainment wherever he played; with decorum and a sense of humour. Will we ever see the likes of him again?

The Cowdreys in Test Cricket											
	Tests	**Runs**	**Avrge**	**HS**	**100s**	**50s**	**Wkts**	**Avrge**	**Best**	**5w/i**	**Catches**
Colin	114	7624	44.06	182	22	38	0	–	–	–	120
Chris	6	101	14.42	38	0	0	4	77.25	2–65	–	5
Total	120	7725	42.92	182	22	38	4	103.25	2–65	–	125

CHAPTER 27

The
Young Archers

———— ● ————

Ken Archer was an elegant stroke-player and a glorious cover field. Ron, his younger brother by six years, was an all-rounder in the Keith Miller mould. The brothers made their debuts for Queensland when only 18, but before they had reached 24 it was farewell to Test cricket for both.

To TALK WITH KEN Archer is like going back to the time when cricket was a fun game – an enjoyable sport. Cricket in the late 1940s and early 1950s had an amateur attitude and, although Australians always played hard, the intense and serious dedication to winning at all costs was not there. Both Ken Archer and his younger brother, Ron, contributed handsomely to Queensland and Australian cricket, but if things had been different they would have contributed even more significantly.

Blue-eyed Ken was not the Australian selectors' blue-eyed boy. He was dropped after adding 61 and 56 with Neil Harvey in his Test debut at Melbourne against England in 1950–51; 121 with skipper Lindsay Hassett in the following Test at Sydney; and 53 with Hassett in Adelaide. Two years later he was recalled to the Test side for the series against the West Indies.

In what proved to be his final Test innings he scored 47, adding 49 with Arthur Morris and 74 with Hassett, thus contributing to Australia's seven-wicket win. As a reward, he was dropped and was never picked again. The selectors apparently wanted centuries – not forties. Did he feel bitter about it? 'Never,' he replied. 'Perhaps disappointed at the time. I got a lot of enjoyment out of cricket. I'd say, in retrospect, that I played with an amateur attitude. Cricket was good to me.'

The Archer story begins with their father, Percy Archer, a furniture dealer. He played first-grade club cricket for Woolloongabba and, had it not been for the Great Depression, he would undoubtedly have represented Queensland. Ken's cousin, Jack Mattheson, also represented Queensland Colts XI and Country XI and played first-grade cricket in Brisbane.

Ken made his first-class debut for Queensland against Wally Hammond's 1946 English team. He was a university student of 18 and, even then, according to Ray Robinson, 'batted and fielded like a Test player-to-be'. However, just as former England wicket-keeper George Duckworth was exclaiming that young Ken Archer's fielding was worth the entrance money, Ken crashed into the fence and strained an ankle.

In the 1948–49 Sheffield Shield season he scored 523 graceful runs at 43.6, which earned him a place to tour South Africa the following season. Although he did not make the Test team, he fared well in other matches, scoring 826 runs and finishing fifth in the averages. 'It was a happy trip,' he recalled. A trip made happier by watching Harvey bat and field so magnificently, as Ken considers Harvey the most splendid batsman of his era, followed by Morris, Everton Weekes, Frank Worrell, Denis Compton, Peter May and Len Hutton in that order.

Previously, Ken had batted at No. 3 or 4, but in the 1950–51 season he volunteered to open the Queensland innings because of its fragile batting. It was as an opener that Ken played against Freddie Brown's MCC, making an elegant 63. Then, for an Australian XI against MCC, he scored 81 – an innings which prompted his selection in the second Test at Melbourne, as an opener. He made a promising debut with scores of 26 and 46 under difficult batting conditions and top-scored in the second innings.

Ken considers his first-innings score of 26 as one of his best innings. 'We struck a treacherous Melbourne wicket which had a lot of life and movement,' he said. 'After Arthur [Morris] left at 6, Neil and I got through till lunch. Surviving the session against intelligent bowlers like Alec [Bedser] and Trevor [Bailey] was a challenge. If either of us had been dismissed quite a few wickets would have fallen before lunch.' So difficult were the conditions that Harvey was dropped five times in that session. Ken vividly remembers playing his first ball in Test

Although treated shabbily by the selectors, Ken Archer kept smiling. (*Jim McDougal*)

cricket. Bailey was the bowler. He started to bowl, lost his rhythm and pulled back. He pulled back four times, and then bowled a full-toss!

In the next Test at Sydney, Ken made 48 and shared a partnership of 121 with Hassett after Morris had gone for nought. In the Adelaide Test, Ken made 0 and 32. Despite having been engaged in four 50-run partnerships in his five innings he was dropped in the final Test. He played two more Tests, against the West Indies in 1951–52. His final Test innings was at Sydney and he scored 49. He was only 24 then and had shown enough potential. The following season he was appointed Queensland's captain, the youngest skipper Queensland ever had. But the haste with which he was removed from the international scene was indeed sad, as his thirties and forties appeared sound and attractive.

Would he have survived longer in the Test arena had he batted at No. 3 or 4 position, which would have allowed him to bat more freely? Ken pondered and replied: 'I might have scored more at No. 3 or 4, but then I would never had made the Test side, except as an opener.'

Ray Robinson, not known for outbursts in his writings, had this to say on the selectors' hasty judgment on Ken in his book *Green Sprigs*: 'In circles where they call a bat a bat, they have a word – "murdered" – for this kind of treatment of a young player. Each season the selectors dumped him cruelly just when he was gaining the confidence to uncork his best.' Added A.G. Moyes in *Australian Batsmen*: 'Archer had apparently tried to model himself on Bill Brown and developed a liking for the deflection which Brown affected; but the pupil never managed to equal the master'.

This, according to Moyes, affected Ken Archer's batting adversely: 'Perhaps he worried himself too much ... but a player of his natural skill should have done better. In the field he was a magnificent saver of runs and made the green grass take on a brighter hue ... A good player naturally, but somehow never able to inspire confidence or a belief that he was as good as his graceful style indicated.'

In 1977, Ken was elected vice-president of the New South Wales Cricket Association and made a Member of the Order of Australia in 1980.

After the West Indians left Australia in 1952, Queensland introduced another Archer, Ron, who played alongside Ken for the last Sheffield Shield match of the season. The younger brother was only 18 but already 185 centimetres tall and bigger-boned than Ken. In his debut match, Ron took 8 for 132, including five wickets in the first innings. The big sensation of the match was Ron taking a wicket off the first bumper he let go in first-class cricket. The ball hit South Australian opener Bruce Bowley, who fell onto his stumps and was out hit-wicket. As a schoolboy, Ron had been inspired by Keith Miller using an early bumper to unsettle an opponent. Little did he imagine in those early days that within a few years critics would call him 'a Miller in the making'.

Ron represented Queensland against the touring South Africans the following season. The famous off-spinner Hugh Tayfield had taken three wickets for only two runs when Ron took matters into his own huge hands. He hit the dreaded Tayfield for a soaring six and was associated in a racy century partnership with Ernest Toovey. He caught the selectors' eyes after capturing seven West Australian wickets for 62 and then scoring a gutsy, unbeaten 86 out of his team's 140.

Like Ken, Ron also made his Test bow at Melbourne – but he failed with both bat and ball. The selectors, however, had recognised the potential of the young Queensland giant and picked him for the tour to England in 1953. In his first innings in England, vs Worcestershire, he scored 100 in 87 exciting minutes. At the age of 19 years and 188 days, Ron became the youngest Australian to score a century in his first match in England. And he bowled there as if he had been brought up on English soil. On a fast Oval pitch, he captured 11 for 56. Then, against Northamptonshire, he took 5 for 76 in the first innings.

In the final Test at The Oval, Australia lost the Ashes but still Ron Archer kept the Aussie morale up with a whirlwind 49 after Australia was five down for 61 and Jim Laker and Tony Lock looked devastating. Ron's innings included a six and seven fours. On the tour he totalled 627 runs at 36.88 and took 57 wickets at 16.75.

Against England in the home series in 1954–55, he took 13 Test wickets at 16.5 – the best average among the Australians. And in a Sheffield Shield match against New South Wales during the same season, he scored 75 not out and his brother Ken 52.

The real Ron Archer stood up prominently during the Caribbean tour of 1955. After scoring 84 in the Trinidad Test, he hammered 98 and 28 in the Barbados Test. His best was to come when he recorded his first and only Test century in the final Test at Kingston. In two Tests he shared double-century stands with Miller: 206 at Barbados and 220 at Kingston. In the Test series Ron totalled 364 runs at 60.66. He toured England again in 1956, scoring 649 runs at 30.9, with 148 against Glamorgan his highest. Among the Australians he took the most wickets – 61 at 22.18.

His most memorable hour was in the third Test at Leeds in 1956. With Miller handicapped by sore knees, Ron opened the attack with Ray Lindwall. In a magnificent spell of nine overs he captured three for three, his victims being Colin Cowdrey, Alan Oakman and Peter Richardson. After 65 minutes of play, England was 3 for 17 and in walked Cyril Washbrook on the comeback trail. An Archer delivery beat the veteran Englishman, rapping him on the pads. All 11 Australians appealed jubilantly for lbw, but the umpire disallowed it. To the Australian players this was the turning point, for Washbrook went on to make 98 and was associated in a 187-run stand with Peter May.

In the final Test at The Oval, Ron captured 5 for 53 – the only time he took five wickets in a Test innings. In one devastating burst he dismissed Denis Compton (94) and Lock (0) off successive deliveries. In the next over, Washbrook faced Ron on a hat-trick. Although the hat-trick was averted, Ron had Washbrook lbw for a duck.

At 23, Ron Archer had the cricket world at his feet. He was groomed to take Miller's place as a dynamic all-rounder and he was also tipped as Australia's future captain. However, this all changed in one tragic instant. While playing on the matting wicket in the Karachi Test in Pakistan, the mat became loose and the sprig of Ron's shoe got caught in the fibres, causing him to injure his knee badly. This mishap brought an end to his highly promising Test career.

Ron was chosen to tour South Africa in 1957–58, but after long deliberation he pulled out of the tour. To quote his team-mate Ken Mackay: 'Ron was a great team man and rather than risk being a passenger on tour, he felt he should withdraw there and then'. Ron's place was taken by Mackay, who returned home as the success of the tour. Subsequently, Ron played for Queensland as a batsman for a few more seasons before fading out.

Where does one place Ron Archer as a cricketer? He was a genuine all-rounder for not only did he bat and bowl with force and penetration, he was brilliant at first slip. He was faster than Alan Davidson, but not as quick as Lindwall and Miller. His tendency to bowl at an angle towards the stumps prevented him from being an express bowler but, according to Ray Robinson in 1955, 'No Australian bowled a better off-cutter'. Bob Simpson calls him a magnificent all-rounder, a superb fielder.

One of Ron's peculiarities was that he never looked at the scoreboard while batting. 'It brings me bad luck,' he once told Mackay. 'Three times in a row I've been skittled after looking at the board. I don't do it now.' However, he can look back on his brief Test career spanning four years with justifiable pride. Had it not been for a loose mat, Ron Archer could have become one of the greats of cricket.

	Tests	Runs	Avrge	HS	100s	50s	Wkts	Avrge	Best	5w/i	Catches
The Archers in Test Cricket											
Ken	5	234	26.00	48	0	0	0	–	–	–	0
Ron	30	713	24.58	128	1	2	48	27.45	5–53	1	20
Total	35	947	24.92	128	1	2	48	27.45	5–53	1	20

CHAPTER 28

The
Chappell Charisma

——— ● ———

*The late Victor Richardson, among Australia's most versatile sportsmen,
left behind him cricket's richest legacy – grandsons Ian, Greg and
Trevor Chappell. Ian and Greg appeared together in 43 Tests. They were
the first brothers to score a century each in the same Test and the only
ones to record centuries in both innings of a Test. Victor, Ian
and Greg all captained Australia with distinction.*

THE SYDNEY TEST OF January 1984 against Imran Khan's Pakistan was Greg Chappell's 87th and final Test. Prior to this match, he had scored 6928 runs and taken 119 catches. He needed 69 runs to get past Sir Donald Bradman's Test aggregate of 6996 and 72 runs to become the first Australian to amass 7000. He also required two catches to overtake Colin Cowdrey's Test record of 120.

Despite these landmarks in his sight, he announced on the second day that this was to be his final Test. And what a glorious swansong it turned out to be. He accepted three catches to overtake Cowdrey's record in 27 fewer Tests and played a masterly innings of 182. It just about summed up his career, as it contained a dazzling array of strokes, the most eye-catching being his inimitable on-drives. I was there, clapping his every four and slip catch as he reached the momentous

milestones: overtaking Sir Donald and reaching 7000 runs in one over.

What a finale for one of the most majestic batsmen of the century. He ended his Test career as he had begun it – with a flourishing hundred. That debut was in the Perth Test of December 1970, which he made memorable by scoring 108 of the best. He remains the only cricketer to record a hundred in his first and final Test innings.

Elder brother Ian was the proud commentator when Greg took his final bow in Sydney – along with other legends and mates Dennis Lillee and Rodney Marsh, each with 355 Test victims. The nostalgic match also marked the end of the Chappell era at Test level as Ian had played his last Test in 1979–80 and youngest brother Trevor in 1981. They are the only three brothers to represent Australia in Tests and only the fourth in the world after the Graces, Hearnes and Mohammads.

The Chappell brothers and grandfather Victor scored 13,240 runs at 45.19 in 184 Tests with 39 centuries and 58 fifties, took 67 wickets and 253 catches. Along with the Mohammads (four brothers and a son), the Richardson–Chappell complex were the most prolific families in the Test arena.

Ian and Greg played 43 Tests together, which remained a cherished record until the Waugh twins, Steve and Mark, dismantled most brotherly statistics in the late 1990s. The Chappells played many memorable Tests in tandem, but perhaps their best was the final Test of the 1972 series against England at The Oval. Australia had to win this match to square the series. After several fluctuations, they succeeded mainly through Lillee's sustained pace and centuries by Ian and Greg, as they added 201 runs for the third wicket. Two days after the centuries at The Oval their teenage brother Trevor hit a hundred for a club in Essex in England. Their cricket-loving father, Martin, was in England at the time and was in ecstasy to see his three sons scoring centuries within a week.

Ian and Greg were the first brothers to hit hundreds in the same innings of a Test. And they did it again on a larger scale in the Wellington Test of 1974 against New Zealand, as detailed elsewhere. However, it was the 1972 Test series in England that marked the turning point for Australian cricket. From then on, they started their climb to the top.

The 1972 series of Tests against England was Ian's first full season as Australia's captain – his last as skipper was also at The Oval in 1975. He made the series memorable by winning 1–0 and scoring 192. Greg was unfortunately out first ball. Trevor also made headlines the same day. In the Lancashire League he became the first Central Lancashire League player since Sir Garfield Sobers to score 1000 runs and take 100 wickets.

The 1975 Oval Test was the 30th captained by Ian, then an Australian record. By winning 15 Tests, he equalled Sir Donald Bradman's victory record. That Test was also the 100th Test for the Chappell brothers, Ian's 66th and Greg's 34th. Two months after Ian's retirement as Australia's captain, Greg became the new skipper. Just as he had made a dramatic debut in the Perth Test in 1970 with a spectacular century, Greg's bow as Australia's 35th captain, against the West Indies, was inspiring. He virtually won the Test off his own bat, with two glorious centuries and scoring the winning run. Ian played a supporting but equally important role; his vital, unbeaten 159-run stand with Greg enabled Australia to win.

In the following Test, at Perth, Australian batsmen struggled against the pace of Andy Roberts and Michael Holding. All except Ian Chappell, who hit a spirited 156. After clashes with administration, his future at this stage was in doubt, but those runs kept him in the game. Thus four centuries were scored by the Chappells in three consecutive Tests. As the series progressed, Greg showed his promise as a leader and crushed the West Indians 5–1. Potentially, there was little between the two teams, but Greg's self-confidence converted the visitors' strengths into their weaknesses.

Comparing their leadership, Greg was modest enough to say: 'I don't lose control, but in a tough position I may feel desperate, whereas Ian just seems to be able to go along. This is probably one of the reasons he has been so successful as captain.'

Ian was an inspirational leader in the Richie Benaud mould. He often lifted his team from quicksand, and with a well-chosen word (expletives not deleted) told them exactly what he thought of them. At the same time he encouraged, cajoled and used reverse psychology. He once called Lillee a 'fussy old tart' to bring the devil out of him. He remained one of the boys who put mateship above hierarchy and burnt his fingers for it. But he would rather lose a Test chasing victory than go for a drab draw. Either you loved Chappell or disliked him – there was no middle course.

Greg led by example, but lacked the charisma of Ian. His strength was batting and crowds flocked to see his classic on-drives, cover drives and square cuts. Many felt that Rod Marsh would have made a superior skipper when Ian relinquished the leadership in 1975. As a captain, Greg once committed what turned out to be perhaps the folly of the century. That was the notorious underarm incident of 1 February 1981, involving Greg, 'the ruthless executive', and Trevor, 'the reluctant executioner'.

In the third final of the Benson & Hedges World Series Cup match, New Zealand needed six runs to tie the match off the last ball. The bowler, unfortunately, was Trevor – neither a deadly quickie nor an economical run-restrainer. Out of desperation, Greg asked Trevor to bowl an underarm grubber to tail-ender Brian McKechnie. This caused a mega-furore in Australian–New Zealand relations and is still not quite defused. McKechnie blocked the grubber and threw his bat in disgust as the Kiwi captain, Geoff Howarth, ran onto the field to protest. He had mistakenly believed underarm bowling to be illegal. It was not so for one-day internationals then, but was made illegal the next week. Greg later said, 'I regret the decision, which was made in the heat of the moment.'

He claimed he was mentally exhausted and wanted to leave the field 10 overs earlier, but vice-captain Marsh insisted he should not. Marsh also pleaded with Greg not to instruct Trevor to bowl underarm, but Greg went ahead with the unwise ploy. For this aberration, Greg was chastised by just about everyone, including the Australian Cricket Board, Donald Bradman, Australian Prime Minister Malcolm Fraser and New Zealand Prime Minister Robert Muldoon who called the underarm delivery 'an act of cowardice appropriate to a team playing in yellow'. It was the biggest stir in cricket since the Bodyline series of 1932–33 and the World Series Cricket breakaway in 1977. And all this to stop a highly unlikely six by a No. 10 batsman not known for his hitting potential. Big brother Ian condemned this action by writing, 'Fair dinkum, Greg, how much pride do you sacrifice to win $35,000? Because, brother, you sacrificed a lot in front of a huge TV audience and 52,825 people.'

Not that Ian was a stranger to controversy himself. He clashed head-on with the South Australian authorities on several occasions, in 1975–76 even threatening strike action. However, he ended that season on a high note when South Australia, under his astute leadership, regained the Sheffield Shield after five seasons in the wilderness. During 1976, Greg also aroused mixed emotions in different countries after leading the International Wanderers to South Africa. On the positive side, that tour broke through some race relations barriers. Then came World Series Cricket, which split the cricket world in two in the late 1970s. Both Ian and Greg were very much for the 'revolution' and contributed wholeheartedly to it.

The Chappell world is synonymous with cricket and public relations. Their life story concerns three gifted brothers with personality plus, their dedicated parents – who spent a fortune paying off neighbours to replace the broken windowpanes – and their grandfather, the great Victor Richardson, who started it all.

Victor York Richardson played 19 times for Australia – five times as captain. All-time greats Alan Kippax, Stan McCabe and Jack Fingleton, who played under Richardson in South Africa in 1935–36, described him as the ideal captain. 'He managed to play cricket hard, yielding nothing, and to retain a host of enemy-good-wishers at the end,' wrote Fingleton. A description which fits his grandsons to some degree.

Richardson is considered one of the most versatile of Australian sportsmen. Besides dual captaincy of South Australia at cricket and football, he represented his State at baseball and partnered Cliff Harvey at tennis to win two State doubles. In 1926, when 30, he won the American Helms award for outstanding contribution to sports and for being the best Australian athlete.

R.S. Whitington, his biographer and a State player, described Richardson as 'The John Barrymore of Sport' because of his magnetic personality. Richardson captained Australia in an unofficial test against New Zealand in 1928 and then officially against South Africa in 1935–36. He was vice-captain of the Australian team touring England in 1930 and at home against Doug Jardine's team in 1932–33. He also captained a team which toured Canada and the USA in 1930. (Incidentally, Ian also led an Australian team to Canada in 1975.)

Richardson led South Australia from 1921 to 1935 – a record. He became the first South Australian to score two centuries in a Sheffield Shield match – both times during a crisis. For South Australia against the MCC in 1932–33 he made 231 in five hours, mostly against Harold Larwood's thunderbolts.

Fingleton ranks Richardson as the greatest close-in fielder he knew. He was the first player to hold five catches in a Test innings. Grandson Greg shared with India's Yajurvendra Singh a Test record of seven catches in a match – at Perth, versus England in December 1974. A year later, Ian became the fourth player to hold over 100 catches in Test cricket. According to Ray Robinson, Richardson dropped only one catch in 15 years.

He subsequently became a popular cricket commentator and was well known for his humorous stories. He had the pleasure of seeing Ian and Greg make their successful Sheffield Shield debuts when he was at the mike. But not once did he come up with unwanted advice. Recalls Greg, 'He was the sort of bloke who enjoyed playing cricket, played in his own way, and he wanted us to play our way too'.

Just before he died in October 1969, aged 75, he received the pleasant news that all three of his grandsons were selected for cricket tours abroad. Ian was to be Australia's vice-captain to tour Sri Lanka, India and South Africa; Greg made the Australian B team touring New Zealand; and Trevor was selected in the Australian Schoolboys' team to the West Indies. Ian Chappell wrote in *My World of Cricket*: 'Vic Richardson occasionally passed on a few words of advice, but generally left the coaching to Lynn Fuller, regarded as an excellent coach, and my father'.

Martin Chappell had a strong influence on the development of his sons. Martin was good at baseball and cricket and headed the district first-grade averages, as an opening batsman, when Ian was seven. His main contribution to cricket was coaching his son Ian, at two and a half years, to hold his bat straight and never, never to lift the ball. Twenty-seven years later, in 1972, Martin accompanied Ian and Greg to England. After watching Ian repeatedly getting out hooking, he cautioned his skipper-son in the dressing-room. Ian's reply is not printable!

Fast bowlers Mike Procter, Peter Pollock and John Snow exposed Ian's limitations in 1970, but gradually he got on top. In a crisis Ian always rallied, fighting fire with oxyacetylene flame. He proved his reputation as the best player of spin by scoring 138 at New Delhi and a gem of a 99 at Calcutta against India's spin wizards on slow turners. By his tenacity and confidence in his team, he converted seemingly lost Tests into incredible wins.

No wonder Ray Robinson referred to him as a cricketing Houdini!

Australian cricket owes a great deal to the Chappells for its top position from 1972 to early 1977. When Ian took over the captaincy in 1971, the future looked gloomy. But he changed all that in a short time. Many among the older generation felt that the following of cricket in Australia in the mid-1970s was the best since the 'Bradmania' of the 1930s and 1940s. His critics may call him 'Ian the Terrible' because of his no-nonsense, no-frills straight talking and his on-field clashes with Glenn Turner, Sarfraz Nawaz, Len Pascoe and a few umpires. Others preferred to look the other way every time he clutched at his abdominal pads while batting. But nobody doubted his nerveless temperament, his ability to play pace and spin bowlers on bad pitches. As an Aussie captain he was 'Ian the Conqueror', in command at all times, his team-mates ready to die for him.

In return, he has often burnt his fingers protecting the rights of his players. Richie Benaud had an equally successful reign, but he had inherited a well-knit side. Ian had to rebuild from a team thoroughly demoralised in South Africa in 1970. He not only improved Australia's record, but also gave his country a colourful image. Fingleton called the trendily dressed, golf-loving Ian 'Young Mod'. He was a rugged individualist who expected people to accept him as he was. The Ian Chappell era produced four golden years for Australian cricket, reminiscent of the Bradman days. Some of his wins were so incredible that a writer once headlined his story: 'Chappell Walks on Water Again'.

Greg Chappell became the third in the family to lead his country – a unique occurrence. Five years Ian's junior, Greg went through the same gruelling practice sessions. He shadow-batted before a mirror, ran miles to strengthen his legs and tried to catch balls as they ricocheted off walls at lightning speed. Daily practice in the backyard since early childhood was the secret behind the Chappell success story. When their father was asked what their success had cost him, he replied: 'About 150 broken windows – ours and our neighbours'. Martin surrounded the backyard pitch area with wire netting, but as he later revealed: 'Once, the ball broke through the wire netting, smashed a window and a tomato sauce bottle of a neighbour enjoying his breakfast'. Rushing to the scene of the crime, he saw red and was petrified: 'I thought it was blood!,' he remembered.

Greg Chappell treated the English pace attack of John Snow, Peter Lever and Ken Shuttleworth with similar disdain when scoring a century in his Test debut at Perth in 1970. The last 50 runs took him only 58 minutes.

County cricket with Somerset refined his stroke-play and converted him from a leg-spinner into a useful medium-pacer. His move to Queensland in 1973 led to a revival in the appeal of Sheffield Shield – making the competition more razor-sharp. To quote Australian off-spinner Ashley Mallett, 'To catch Greg Chappell in full flight is sheer ecstasy'. His 131 in the Lord's Test of 1972, his series-winning unbeaten 182 in the Sydney Test against the mighty Windies in 1976 and another series-clinching 182 on the same venue against Pakistan in his farewell appearance in 1984 were masterpieces.

Another Greg Chappell innings I treasure was his magnificent double-century against India in the Sydney Test of January 1981. Despite a severe stomach upset, he hammered 204 runs off 296 balls, smashing 27 fours. As India could total only 201 and 201, he had outscored his opponents in both innings. However, Australia depended so much on Greg that when he scored a duck in the final Test of the series, the team collapsed for 83 when set a modest target of 143.

When Greg declared his inability to tour England in 1981, there was a well-justified air of anxiety as Australia kept losing Tests after being in winning positions. 'Australia snatched defeat from the jaws of victory', was how Brian Mossop summed it up succinctly in the *Sydney Morning Herald*. Mercurial character Ian Botham was behind these magical English victories and the absence of Greg Chappell was keenly felt.

Trevor Chappell made his Test debut on this tour. In three Tests he scored 79 runs at an unimpressive average of 15.80. This was also the end of his Test career, although he continued to play for New South Wales as a batsman and occasionally for Australia in limited-overs matches as an all-rounder.

Greg came back to Test cricket and showed that he was a mortal after all. The 1981–82 season was nightmarish for him as he developed 'duck fever' on a massive scale. It was quite inexplicable, as he had started the season with a dazzling 162 (two sixes and 20 fours) for Queensland against Pakistan, followed by a brilliant 201 in the Brisbane Test against Imran Khan and Sarfraz Nawaz. But the wheels soon started falling off. In 15 consecutive innings (against Pakistan and the West Indies) he made only two fifties (highest score 61) and seven ducks, including four in a row. He was out first ball three times, twice in Test matches. Cartoonists had a field day depicting his plight and a poster on the first day of the Sydney Test in January 1982 read: 'EVERYONE GOT TURKEY FOR CHRISTMAS, OUR GREG GOT FOUR DUCKS'. A live duck was let loose when he went out to bat in a one-dayer in Melbourne and a restaurant named a duck dish 'a la Greg'.

'I'm embarrassed by my string of failures,' he told Dick Tucker in the *Daily Mirror* (Sydney). 'Maybe now that I feel this way, it will provide me with motivation to regain my usual high standard.' Critics who had heaped praise on him in the past now clamoured for his exclusion as a captain and a player. But he

Greg's ducks make a front-page story.
(*Sydney* Sun, *John Benaud*)

refused to budge. 'Standing down as captain or not playing isn't the way to rectify that,' he said. 'Walking away from the problem isn't the answer. It's not in my make-up and certainly would not help my confidence. I've just got to hang in and try to get some runs.'

The national selectors gave him the vote of confidence and he returned from the New Zealand tour in March 1982 a happier man. His stroke-filled 176 (two sixes, 23 fours) in the final Test in Christchurch, coupled with his tactics as a captain, enabled Australia to level the series.

Although a friendly person in the dressing-room, Greg appeared aloof – at times arrogant – in the middle. However, a Queensland University student who wrote a thesis on him found him warm and unaffected.

Despite their globetrotting and recording a combined aggregate of 12,455 runs at 48.27 in 162 Tests with 38 centuries, 57 fifties, 67 wickets and 227 catches, Ian and Greg Chappell found time to write quite a few cricket books and invest in an expensive restaurant in Adelaide in the late 1970s, aptly named Leg Trap. Ian is a senior telecaster with Channel 9, giving his no-frills, straight-from-the-hip comments. Greg occasionally gives expert comments on TV and on ABC radio.

The Chappells were the first pair of brothers to hit centuries together in Test cricket, and they did it on three occasions in two Tests. The first time was the cliffhanging Oval Test of 1972. Then, in the Wellington Test of March 1974, they created new records. Out of 971 runs by Australia in the two innings, the Chappell brothers contributed 646 – both Ian and Greg hitting centuries in each innings of the Test: Ian 145 and 121, Greg 247 not out and 133. By scoring 380 runs in that Test, Greg created a world record – since then eclipsed by Graham Gooch's 456 runs (333 and 123 for England vs. India at Lord's in 1990) and Mark Taylor's 426 (334 not out and 92 for Australia vs. Pakistan at Peshawar in 1998–99).

The Chappell duo also hit a hundred together in the Sydney International of 1971–72 against the Sobers-led Rest of the World XI. In 1973, against Barbados in the Caribbean, they were associated in a 300-run stand – Ian 209, Greg 142. The following week, in the second Test at Bridgetown, both scored 106 – Ian in the first innings and Greg in the second.

One can understand the trepidation of Trevor Chappell following such larger-than-life-size brothers. But rather than developing feelings of inferiority, Trevor feels that the continued success of Ian and Greg made him work harder. Trevor, the most mild-mannered of the trio, was given the same intensive coaching by his father. Like his brothers, he attended Prince Alfred College in Adelaide and in the

annual match against St Peter's College, Trevor achieved something his brothers had not. He hit a brilliant 227. In their days, Greg had scored 106 and Ian 70-odd.

Trevor was an opening bat, a medium-pace bowler and an agile fielder. His physique and mannerisms were like Ian's. Constant comparisons often got him down and in utter frustration he once said, 'I'd rather be Bill Smith, or just an ordinary person'. After his promising Shield debut in 1972, Trevor's luck deserted him and he was subsequently dropped. In 1975, in the Central Lancashire League in England, he made a rare double of 1000 runs and 100 wickets. He had several offers to play county cricket but was not interested. 'I came to Lancashire to gain experience, but will eventually return home and bid for a Test place,' he declared.

In the 1973–74 season against Victoria, Trevor (57) added 115 runs in 108 minutes with brother Ian (130) for the fourth wicket. Ian had also made an unbeaten 141 in the first innings, including 125 before lunch. Despite the Chappell aggression, South Australia lost the match outright. That was the season both Ian and Greg topped 1000 runs. With disappointing performances in Sheffield Shield matches, Trevor could not gain a regular spot for South Australia. Then he had a mediocre season with Western Australia. This provides one of cricket's little mysteries, for according the Chester Bennett, who coached the three Chappells at Prince Alfred College, Trevor at 18 was a more complete player than Ian and Greg were at that age.

Early in 1979, Trevor toured the West Indies with World Series Cricket Australians, captained and vice-captained by Ian and Greg Chappell. In the first 'Supertest' at Jamaica, the Chappells went in at Nos. 2, 3 and 4. Trevor opened the innings and was struck on the jaw by a blistering Andy Roberts bumper. He came back, however, to register the second-highest score for his side.

In the second Supertest, Windies

speedster Collis King dismissed all three Chappells. Ian and an injured Greg were out when in sight of their hundreds. Greg continued his run-getting spree in the subsequent matches and was adjudged the Man of the Series in the Caribbean, having hit three splendid centuries and an 85 run out. He totalled 620 runs in nine innings at an average of 68.89 against the most awesome pace attack.

In the inaugural year of WSC in Australia in 1977–78, Greg scored 661 runs at 60.09, with 246 not out his highest. He considers his form in the West Indies in 1979 as the most satisfying. 'Nothing I did in Test cricket ever surpassed my performances in the West Indies.'

Two seasons later – the season of compromise between the Australian Cricket Board and World Series Cricket – the Chappell brothers were back in the limelight. Staging a comeback in Test cricket, Ian became Derek Underwood's 100th Australian victim in the second innings of the Sydney Test after top-scoring with an authoritative 42 in the first. At Melbourne, in the final Test against England, he scored 75 and 26 not out as Australia won the series 3–0. It was his final Test.

His best moments were in the Sheffield Shield matches that season. He hit two centuries in the last three crucial games, against New South Wales and then against Victoria – the winners – in what was virtually a grand final, and was voted the Benson & Hedges Player of 1979–80.

Although not 100 per cent fit, Greg hit two magnificent centuries in the twin Test series: 74 and 124 against the West Indies at Brisbane and 114 and 40 not out at Melbourne against England, besides his match-winning 98 not out against the Englishmen in the Sydney Test. His captaincy – often criticised – was good enough to crush Mike Brearley's men in what turned out to be a 3–0 win. However, Australia suffered a humiliating defeat against the Windies' non-stop pace.

In the series against Pakistan, Greg hit 235 in the Faisalabad Test in March 1980, but the innings did not please him for it was on a pitch which favoured only the batsmen. He was criticised for prolonging the Australian innings up to the fourth day of the Test but this was his way of protesting against pitch preparation which favoured the host country. As Pakistan had won the first Test, they appeared smugly happy with a draw or two.

Trevor's best season was 1979–80 when he made his debut for New South Wales memorable by scoring a career-best 150 as an opener in the second innings against a West Australian attack which included Dennis Lillee. It was on his 27th birthday and his century enabled New South Wales to win the match against heavy odds. His second century of the season, 144, was against Tasmania. When batting at No. 3, he added 227 runs with the dour opener, John Dyson. But he faded away after moderate form in three Test appearances in 1981. In 1999 he was appointed as Sri Lanka's fielding coach.

When Ian was asked which of the two brothers was the better captain, he replied: 'I wouldn't like to answer that question. Ask me who is the best player and there's no doubt – Greg by a street.' Tony Greig did not agree. He wrote in 1976: '… if I were given the opportunity of dismissing one Australian batsman for nought in a Test match, I.M. (Ian) Chappell would be my automatic choice. Greg has grace and elegance – a batsman in the classic mould. But Ian has effective qualities of character and resilience that, in my estimation, make him a more formidable opponent.'

It is interesting to point out a few trivia points of their career. The first Test Greg captained was at Brisbane in 1975, the 36th Test between Australia and the West Indies. It was also the 36th Test together by the Chappell brothers, if the washed-out Melbourne Test against England in 1970–71 is included. It was the 36th time Australia was captained by one family.

Victor Richardson had led his country in five Tests and his grandsons Ian and Greg in 30 and one. At one stage on the final day of that Test the scoreboard read: Australia 2 for 164, Ian Chappell 64 not out, Greg Chappell 64 not out.

In the Sheffield Shield season of 1973–74, Ian and Greg scored the same number of runs at an identical average against Victoria. Captaining Queensland, Greg caned the Victorian attack to score 180 and 101 in Brisbane, and subsequently 115 and 53 not out on the Melbourne Cricket Ground, to total 449 runs at an average of 149.66. Against the same bowlers, Ian made 83 and 95 for South Australia on the MCG and 141 not out and 130 at Adelaide. Aggregate 449 runs, average 149.66!

The Chappells scored centuries in tandem on three separate occasions during 1979–80. Greg and Trevor started the season with hundreds – Greg a magnificent 185 for Queensland vs Victoria at Brisbane and Trevor a career-best 150 for New South Wales vs Western Australia at Sydney two days later. On 29 December 1979, Ian scored 154 for South Australia vs Western Australia and Trevor 144 for New South Wales vs Tasmania. Then on 8 March 1980, Greg recorded 235 in the Faisalabad Test against Pakistan and Ian made 112 run out in the deciding Sheffield Shield match vs Victoria.

The three Chappell brothers and grandfather Vic Richardson made fifties in their Sheffield Shield debuts, Vic an unbeaten 51, Ian 59, Greg 53 and Trevor 67.

To honour Vic Richardson, a road was named after him – the road which leads to the 'Victor Richardson Gates' at the eastern entrance of the Adelaide Oval. The charismatic Chappells, Ian and Greg, will be remembered in future, just as Grace, Ranji and Trumper are remembered today – not only for the runs they made and the matches they won, but because they added something to cricket.

Victor Richardson and the Chappells in Test Cricket											
	Tests	Runs	Avrge	HS	100s	50s	Wkts	Avrge	Best	5w/i	Catches
Victor Richardson	19	706	23.53	138	1	1	–	–	–	–	24
Ian Chappell	75	5345	42.42	196	14	26	20	65.80	2–21	–	105
Greg Chappell	87	7110	53.86	247*	24	31	47	40.70	5–61	1	122
Trevor Chappell	3	79	15.80	27	–	–	–	–	–	–	2
Total	184	13,240	45.19	247*	39	58	67	48.19	5–61	1	253

CHAPTER 29

The
Mohammad Dynasty

———— ● ————

The Mohammad brothers' domination of Pakistani cricket was unique and absolute. At least one of them played in 100 out of Pakistan's first 101 Tests over 27 years. The Mohammad brothers produced four Test cricketers and a fifth nearly made it, being 12th man in a Test. On 64 occasions, two of the brothers played together in Tests, once three of them. Then came Hanif's son, Shoaib, who added 2705 runs and seven centuries in 45 Tests to the family statistics, taking them to an awesome 13,643 runs and 36 hundreds in 218 Tests.

THE STORY OF THE Mohammad brothers of Pakistan reads like a chapter out of a schoolboy fiction. Their run flow went on undiminished for a quarter of a century: a single generation dominating one sport for three decades. It began at international level in 1952, when a five-year-old nation and an 18-year-old Hanif Mohammad made simultaneous Test debuts in Delhi. Indeed, over a period of 27 years at least one Mohammad brother played in 100 of Pakistan's first 101 Tests. In 64 Tests two Mohammad brothers were members of the team, and on one occasion three took part.

In the Karachi Test against New Zealand in 1969, Hanif, Mushtaq and Sadiq all played together, thus emulating the feat of the Grace brothers (1880) and the Hearnes (1891–92). However, in that Test, all three Mohammads batted and bowled – and that is unique. Apart from that occasion, the eldest brother, Wazir, and Hanif played together in 18 Tests; Hanif and Mushtaq in 19; Wazir and Mushtaq in one; and the youngest brother, Sadiq, and Mushtaq in 26 Tests. In her first 101 Tests, of the 83 centuries by Pakistanis, the Mohammads contributed 29 (Hanif 12, Mushtaq 10, Sadiq 5 and Wazir 2). Hanif became the first batsman from the Indian subcontinent to record a Test triple-hundred. And of the 81 century stands in that period, a Mohammad brother was involved in 49. This included two century partnerships between Hanif and Wazir.

It was a pleasure to me to discuss the careers of this amazing family with Mushtaq, the rotund, moustachioed all-rounder who has a smile as crisp as his cover drives. 'I'm grateful to my elder brothers, Hanif, Wazir and Raees, for their coaching,' he said. 'To have such well-known brothers was an inspiration.' Unfortunately, Raees was one brother who missed out – although very narrowly – on Test selection. According to Mushtaq and others, he was almost as good a batsman as Hanif as well as a useful bowler, but an injury kept him out.

Mushtaq started young. With his own natural ability and guided on the right lines, he became the youngest cricketer to play first-class cricket, the youngest to make a Test debut and the youngest to score a Test century. When only 41 days past his 13th birthday, he made 87 runs and took 5 for 28 with his leg-breaks against first-class opposition. He made his Test debut in 1959, facing the fury of Wes Hall, just four months after his 15th birthday. In 1960–61, Pakistan was on the brink of defeat against India at Delhi, but was rescued by 17-year-old 'Mush' who made a hundred including 19 fours. He was made one of *Wisden*'s Five Cricketers of the Year in 1963, five years before his more celebrated brother Hanif.

The Mohammad brothers were born in Junagadh in India, of parents who loved sports. Their father was a fair club cricketer and never missed a game when an overseas team toured India. He had a great admiration for Lindsay Hassett and advised his sons to emulate him. Unfortunately, he died young in 1948 and Keith Miller's 'Hail Mr Mohammad' was a tribute to the sports father of the century. However, it was their mother, Amir Bee, who was their source of inspiration. She was a badminton champion in India and a regional table-tennis and carrom champion. Her ambition was to see her children develop into sportsmen of renown. Riaz Ahmed Mansuri, editor of Pakistan's *The Cricketer*, calls her 'Cricket's greatest mother since Martha Grace'.

Amir Bee had seven children, six sons and a daughter. One son and the daughter died in their teens, but five sons lived to play and score centuries in first-class cricket – four at Test level. She always regretted that Raees did not represent Pakistan. As she revealed to Mansuri in an interview in *The Cricketer International:* 'At Dacca, in 1955, when India was touring Pakistan, the skipper, Mr Kardar, came one evening to Raees' room and asked him to take to bed early. "You are going to play in the Test tomorrow morning," he said. But a great disappointment awaited Raees – he was made twelfth man.'

Wazir and Raees learnt to play cricket in India and Hanif's formative education in the game was gained from practising by electric light on the concrete terrace at Junagadh. But when Hanif was 14, Mushtaq five, and Sadiq only three, the shattering upheaval of partition in 1947 put an end to the brothers' small and peaceful world. The way in which they settled down in Pakistan and enriched the game is part of cricket history.

'I am extremely grateful to my mother,' recalled Mushtaq when I interviewed him. 'She brought us all up in a sporting atmosphere and is a driving force to all of us. When we are on tours, she keeps writing encouraging letters and when I was not getting runs in the earlier part of the 1973 tour she wrote to me – virtually ordering me to go out in the middle and cane the Aussie bowlers! I did just that yesterday, and everything turned out right.'

Mush made a stroke-filled 121 in the 1973 Sydney Test, but the attack he caned was minus Dennis Lillee. And he must have received another stiff letter from Amir Bee the following month before he attacked New Zealand's bowlers by slamming 201 runs at Dunedin, and in the second innings took 5 for 49. Only one other cricketer, Denis Atkinson of the West Indies, had achieved such a Test double.

Mushtaq continued: 'When representing Pakistan Airlines in the national championship of 1969, Hanif scored 187 and I got 124. Sadiq was playing for our opponents, Karachi Blues, and when he was 96 I caught him. My mother did not talk with me for days!'

With such a demanding mum, it is not surprising that her four sons between them scored 10,938 runs in 173 Tests: Hanif with 3915, Mushtaq 3643, Sadiq 2579 and Wazir 801, at a combined average of 38.65. They hit 29 centuries and 47 fifties at Test level besides taking 80 wickets (79 by Mushtaq) and 115 catches.

Hanif was one of the most prolific among Pakistani batsmen. Known as 'Little Master', he was a 'Rock of Gibraltar', a 'Mr Concentration', an opening batsman with time to spare. In run-making, he approached Bradman proportions although he took twice the time. Hanif had all the strokes, but because of Pakistan's weak batting line-up he had to deny himself. His epic 337 in the Bridgetown Test in 1958 took him over 16 hours – by far the longest innings in Test cricket. He was associated in century stands with his first four partners: Imtiaz Ahmed, Almuddin, Saeed Ahmed and elder brother Wazir – a feat without parallel in Tests.

That Caribbean tour was a run bonanza for Hanif and Wazir, who made 628 and 440 runs in the series. Wazir was at his best in the final Test, scoring 189, which enabled Pakistan to win the Test and salvage some prestige. After his retirement, Wazir served as a national selector.

Hanif held the record for the highest score in first-class cricket. For Karachi against Bahawalpur in 1958–59 he amassed 499 and was run out when rushing for his 500th run in the final over. What a way to go! This record was eventually broken by Brian Lara, who made an unbeaten 501 for Warwickshire against Durham at Birmingham in 1994. Hanif scored a century in each innings against Ted Dexter's Englishmen in the Dacca Test in 1961–62, but to make 215

runs in the two innings (111 and 104) he took 893 minutes. This crawl was agony for the onlookers and almost killed cricket as a spectator sport.

Once again, Hanif approached a century in both innings when compiling 104 and 93 in the Melbourne Test of 1965. He started as a wicket-keeper and went on to captain Pakistan eight times. On any pitch, against any bowler, he scored consistently if not always attractively. Although an orthodox batsman, he mastered an unconventional stroke – the reverse sweep. 'Pakistan in the early mid-1950s, needed someone to focus on as an embodiment of the new nation and it was Hanif and cricket that filled the vacuum,' wrote Scyld Berry in *Wisden Cricket Monthly*.

Although alike in appearance – all four Test brothers are short and stocky – Mushtaq's game was more appealing to watch. His free-flowing drives and spectacular hooks impressed Everton Weekes when he played a charity match in Pakistan. Young Mushtaq hit a scintillating 131 off Richie Benaud, Ian Meckiff, 'Dusty' Rhodes and 'Sonny' Ramadhin. Later in the day, he asked Weekes for some tips. After complimenting him, the great West Indian advised: 'Three fours are better than two sixes'. That taught Mushtaq to keep the ball on the ground and he became a sounder batsman. Professional cricket with Northamptonshire gave his batsmanship a smoother finish, and with his leg-spinners he was recognised as an all-rounder. Besides his personal contributions, Mushtaq constantly guided younger players and generated confidence among his team-mates. This maturity led to his being appointed captain of Northamptonshire in the year of his benefit.

Subsequent to his instant rise in Test cricket and scoring two centuries as a teenager, Mushtaq did not achieve much at Test level until he was 24 – although that

Amir Bee, cricket's greatest mum since Martha Grace. (*Family album*)

Shoaib Mohammad, son of Hanif and almost as prolific. (World of Cricket)

for Mushtaq. In January he led Pakistan to a stunning and convincing win over Greg Chappell's Australians, then regarded as world champions. This was in the Sydney Test and the win enabled the underrated Pakistanis to draw the series 1-all. His batting form, however, was disappointing and the bad patch haunted him in the Caribbean. In the first three Tests his scores were 0, 6; 9, 21; 41, 19 and Pakistan was down 0–1.

The fourth Test at Port-of-Spain started on April Fool's Day and Mushtaq found himself fighting for his cricket life. Clive Lloyd, the West Indies skipper, won the toss and sent Pakistan in to bat. The score was 3 for 51 when Mushtaq came to the crease. He added 108 runs with Majid Khan, scoring 121 out of Pakistan's 341. Mushtaq then captured 5 for 28, his best figures in a Test, as the strong West Indians tumbled for 154. However, he was not finished yet, making 56 runs in the second innings after the score was 5 for 95. He then took 3 for 69 as Pakistan won comfortably to level the series with one Test remaining.

Soon after his finest hour, his involvement with World Series Cricket came to light. Mushtaq missed two Test series against England: at home in 1977–78 and in England in 1978. Pakistan's poor show in England led to a change in selection policy (and the selectors as well!) and Mushtaq was reinstated as the captain of a full-strength Pakistan side against India in 1978. Pakistan won the series 2–0 although Mushtaq found scoring difficult. His highest in the series was 78 at Karachi. He was more successful as a leg-spinner, taking 4 for 55 in the Faisalabad Test.

Mushtaq led Pakistan to a 1–0 win over New Zealand, where he took 11 wickets in the series, and a 1–all draw with Australia in 1979. During the explosive two-Test series in Australia in March 1979 he had to be at his mature best to keep incidents under control. When Australia's speed sensation, Rodney Hogg, was declared

was through no fault of his. 'From 1964 to 1967 when I turned 24, Pakistan did not play a Test series,' lamented Mushtaq. However, during that barren period he recorded eight centuries against Commonwealth teams with Test-class bowlers. The year 1977 was a dramatic one

run-out under controversial circumstances, Mushtaq sportingly called him back. He also kept inspiring quickie Sarfraz Nawaz whose 9 for 86 converted a certain defeat into a memorable win. As this was Pakistan's 100th Test, Mushtaq was doubly happy. 'We are no longer a side that gives up with added pressure,' said a beaming Mush.

In a first-class career spanning 30 years (1956–85), Mushtaq scored 31,091 runs at 42.07 for Karachi, Pakistan and Northamptonshire, hitting 72 centuries, the highest score being an unbeaten 303 for Karachi Blues in 1967–68. He was the second non-English player – after Roy Marshall of the West Indies and Hampshire – to top 30,000 first-class runs.

Mushtaq graduated from a teenage marvel to the elder statesman of Pakistan cricket to lead Pakistan to eight wins. Under him, Pakistan recorded victories over Australia and the West Indies at their strongest and won the series over traditional rivals India.

At one stage he was optimistic about his son, Munaf, following in his footsteps. 'In the 1972 season in England I was batting against Surrey, and Munaf, about seven then, got so excited that every time I ran in the middle he ran simultaneously in the pavilion. I made 120 and he ran with me every time. He was so exhausted.' But it was his other son, Sohail Mohammad, who represented Glamorgan B team in the early 1990s.

Sadiq, the youngest Mohammad brother, was a dashing left-handed opening batsman. Oddly, he was neither a left-hander nor an opener to start with. It was all his elder brothers' doing. Hanif, seeing the scope for left-handed batsmen in Pakistan, asked him to take up batting left-handed early in his career. Sadiq found it extremely difficult, but with the perseverance of a Mohammad he stuck to it. Still, he could not break into the Pakistan side which was flooded with batsmen. Selector/brother Wazir advised

Sadiq (left) and Mushtaq relaxing during the Sydney Test of 1973. *(K.M.-H.)*

him to become an opening batsman – and it was as an opener that he made his Test debut against New Zealand in 1969 when he was 24.

It was a delight to see Sadiq bat – a flamboyant batsman, flaying an attack, be it a one-day or a three-day game for Gloucestershire (where he played as a professional) or a Test for Pakistan. Sadiq was also a brilliant outfielder and a natural crowd-pleaser near the boundary line. He impressed the English critics in the final Test at Headingley in 1971 when Pakistan was set 201 runs on the final day. It was a slow turner and all the top-line batsmen had failed except Sadiq, who made a precious 91, and Pakistan lost by a mere 25 runs. 'That innings makes the hair stand on the back of my neck whenever I think about it,' he recalled.

He also showed his class to the Australians with his neat 137 against Dennis Lillee, Jeff Thomson and Max Walker in 1972–73. On that twin tour of Australia and New Zealand he totalled 1169 runs at 41.75 including two Test centuries, at Melbourne and Wellington. Mother Amir Bee considered Sadiq to be 'in the footsteps of Hanif', but according to

Sadiq scares away a streaker. (*Sadiq souvenir*)

Sadiq himself: 'I shall never catch up with Hanif and his concentration. But Mush – yes. I shall take over soon.'

Sadiq was playing club cricket for Tasmania in 1975 when recalled by Pakistan to play in the series against Clive Lloyd's West Indians. In the Karachi Test of 1975 he played a gallant and priceless knock. Despite an agonising neck injury, he scored an unbeaten 98 to save his country from certain defeat. When representing Gloucestershire he hit four centuries in a row: 108 against Somerset, 163 not out and 150 against Derbyshire, and 109 against Worcestershire in the last three matches of 1976. That year, against the touring New Zealanders in the Hyderabad Test, Sadiq and Mushtaq became the second pair of brothers – after the Chappells – to record centuries in the same innings of a Test. But unlike the Chappells, they were not associated in a century partnership.

However, a record of sorts was created in the Karachi Test of January 1978. Against England, Pakistan fielded a team without a single Mohammad brother. This broke a sequence of 89 Tests in 25 years when at least one Mohammad – often two, once three – had represented their country. Mushtaq was not allowed to play because of his WSC contract and Sadiq's form was slipping.

Sadiq fought his way back into the Pakistan team and toured England in 1978. He scored 79 in the first Test at

Birmingham and 97 in the final Test at Leeds. No other Pakistani batsman could score a fifty against the nagging English attack in the entire series. However, with the return of the WSC players, Sadiq found it difficult to retain his place. He was dropped from the tour to New Zealand and Australia in 1979, but played in the second World Cup in England that year. He also played in three Tests in India in 1979–80, but scored only 106 runs at a poor average.

In domestic cricket, the Mohammad brothers combined brilliantly. In the final of the Qaid-E-Azam Trophy in 1954–55, Hanif (109), Wazir (118) and Raees (110) hit separate hundreds against Services XI, thus emulating the feat of Neil, Clarrie and Ray Harvey. Then during an Ayub Trophy match in 1961, all five Mohammad brothers played together: Wazir and Sadiq for Karachi Blues and Raees, Hanif and Mushtaq for Karachi Whites.

The Mohammad saga did not terminate with the retirement of Sadiq in 1981. Three years later, Hanif's son, Shoaib Mohammad, arrived on the Test scene. He carried on the family's run-scoring business as he made 2705 runs at 44.34 in 45 Tests, hitting seven centuries (highest score 203 not out twice) and 13 fifties. He developed into a gritty batsman (who usually opened the innings) with a solid defence and quick reflexes. A man for all seasons, he was a useful off-spinner who broke vital partnerships, and an agile fielder.

Hanif and Nazar Mohammad, who had opened Pakistan's batting in the 1950s, proudly watched their sons, Shoaib and Mudassar Nazar, start their country's innings against New Zealand in the Karachi Test of 1984–85.

Despite unfair comparisons, Shoaib ended with a Test average superior to his celebrated father's and uncles'. Hanif and Shoaib are the only father and son to score double-centuries in the Test arena, and they each recorded it twice! Shoaib's first double hundred was against India in the Lahore Test of 1989–90. His unbeaten 203 included 19 crisp fours and he added 246 runs for the fourth wicket with Javed Miandad. The Test was a sort of 'sons' special' as India's Sanjay Manjrekar, the son of Vijay Manjrekar, also scored a double-century. Their fathers had played against each other in the 1950s and 1960s.

It was a series to remember for Shoaib as he topped the batting averages, scoring 412 at 103.00. He was again at his prolific best the next season against New Zealand. He amassed 507 runs at a phenomenal average of 169.00, hitting three centuries in three Tests, with 203 not out in Karachi his highest. In the series he scored 203 not out; 105, 42 not out; 15 and 142. As he had scored centuries in the previous two Tests against the Kiwis (163 at Wellington and 112 at Auckland in 1988–89) he had the distinction of hitting five tons in five successive Tests against New Zealand.

In the series against the West Indies in 1990–91, Shoaib added 174 runs for the fourth wicket with Salim Malik in the Karachi Test. This was a new record for the series, which was previously held by dad Hanif and uncle Wazir who had added 154 runs in the Port-of-Spain Test 33 years earlier.

Subsequently, Shoaib's form slipped and he played his final Test against Sri Lanka at Sialkot in September 1995. It was the end of the Mohammad dynasty, which had started on 16 October 1952 when Pakistan played her first-ever Test. In that match, 17-year-old Hanif had opened the innings and top-scored with 51 out of Pakistan's 150. The domination had started and mountains of runs kept coming to the Mohammads for 218 Tests in 44 summers.

The statistics are staggering. Four brothers and a son accumulated 13,643 runs, averaging almost 40 runs an innings. Between them they hit one triple, four double and 31 centuries. They were known more for their reliability than aggression or elegance but the new country born out of strife and bloodshed needed stability and identity. Through cricket, the Mohammads achieved just that.

The new millennium may produce another Mohammad of renown. Sadiq's son, Imraan, aged 23, was signed by Gloucestershire in 2000. Like Dad, he is an opening batsman who scored a double century in Pakistan in early 2000. He has represented Cambridge University from 1997, and the following year scored a century against Yorkshire at Headingley.

The Mohammads in Test Cricket											
	Tests	Runs	Avrge	HS	100s	50s	Wkts	Avrge	Best	5w/i	Catches
Wazir	20	801	27.62	189	2	3	0	–	–	–	5
Hanif	55	3915	43.98	337	12	15	1	95.00	1–1	–	40
Mushtaq	57	3643	39.17	201	10	19	79	29.22	5–28	3	42
Sadiq	41	2579	35.81	166	5	10	0	–	–	–	28
Shoaib	45	2705	44.34	203*	7	13	5	34.00	2–8	–	22
Total	218	13,643	39.66	337	36	60	85	31.61	5–28	3	137

CHAPTER 30

The
Mighty Khans

——— ● ———

The Khan family has produced five Test players including three captains,
Javed Burki, Majid Khan and Imran Khan. The Pakistan batting was
opened by the elegant touch artist Majid and her bowling by his cousin
Imran Khan, the ticking dynamo and one of the most colourful
all-rounders in the history of the game. Majid's father and uncle
also played Test matches for India.

PAKISTAN HAS PRODUCED TWO Khan families of world renown. The more celebrated is the family of squash players, led by Hashim Khan, a legend in his own lifetime. He won the British Open Squash title (then called the World Championship) seven times in a row, 1950–56. His younger brother, Azam, took over in 1957 and won it for four consecutive years. Their cousin, Roshan Khan, and nephew, Mohibullah, kept the title in the family until 1963. Later, Roshan's son, Torsan Khan, frequently hit the headlines as Pakistan's squash representative.

The cricketing Khans – unrelated to the squash emperors – have not been so dominating. All the same, they have produced five Test cricketers, three of whom captained Pakistan, and nine first-class cricketers.

Majid Khan was considered among the top 10 batsman in the world in the 1970s and was adored by the spectators for his style, effortless hitting and complete lack of histrionics in the middle. Struggling and haggling were not his game. Either he middled or got out. He was cricket's Mr Cool Dude.

His cousin, Imran Khan – younger by six years – became one of the greatest all-rounders, colourful, charismatic and dynamic.

Another of Majid's cousins, the eight-years-older Javed Burki, played 25 Tests for Pakistan in the 1960s. An Oxford Blue, Burki made his Test debut against India in 1960–61. The following season he scored two centuries in two Tests against Ted Dexter's Englishmen. In the Lahore Test, he hit 138 (one six, 17 fours) and was associated in century partnerships with Saeed Ahmed and Mushtaq Mohammad. In the next Test, at Dacca, he made his highest Test score of 140 with 18 boundaries. Burki was appointed Pakistan's captain on the 1962 tour to England. Pakistan lost the Test series 0–4, and although Burki hit three centuries on the tour, including one in the Lord's Test, he did not prove himself an inspiring leader. He continued playing Test cricket until 1969, but he was never the force he had been in the early 1960s.

I often wondered how the cousins Burki, Majid and Imran were related. Majid explained that their mothers were sisters. Baqa Jilani was his father's brother-in-law. He was a fast-medium bowler with a gigantic frame who played one Test for India, at The Oval, in 1936. However, it was from his father, Dr Jahangir Khan, that Majid inherited his love for cricket and his talent.

Jahangir Khan was a famous fast-medium bowler for Cambridge University and India in the 1930s. He played in the first-ever Test for India, at Lord's in 1932, and in the second innings took 4 for 60 in 30 overs, clean-bowling Percy Holmes, Wally Hammond and Eddie Paynter, and had Frank Woolley caught. He played three more Tests for India – all in England in 1936 – without doing anything out-standing with bat or ball. His name, however, is remembered even today because of the sparrow incident. Once, while bowling in England, the ball hit a flying sparrow and accidentally killed it. That sparrow is preserved in the Lord's museum.

When South Africa toured England in 1935, Dudley Nourse was amazed by the pace generated by Jahangir Khan after a run-up of only six yards. Nourse wrote: 'In the field, he was one of the most energetic men we met on the tour. His throw-in from any part of the field travelled with incredible speed straight into the wicket-keepers' hands ... Lithe and loose-limbed, he also kept us entertained after the day's play, with some clever conjuring tricks.'

Dr Khan migrated to Pakistan after partition and became Director of Education for the West Pakistan govern-ment and a Lecturer in History at the Punjab University. He did not coach son Majid a great deal, but clearly implanted in him a love of the game. As Majid told me during the 1977 Sydney Test: 'My father left me on my own and never interfered. I was inspired by his library of cricket books. Then there was the sporting environment in my family. Besides cricketers, there were four to five hockey internationals in my family – Feroze Khan and Niyaz Khan being celebrities of their time. They all represented India or Pakistan in Olympic hockey.'

Jahangir Khan was the national cricket selector when Majid was making a name for himself. As a lad of 15, Majid had hit an unbeaten 111 and taken 6 for 67 – his best bowling performance so far. Tactfully, Dr Khan resigned. Majid explained: 'Apart from being suspected of favouritism, he probably felt that had I failed, he would have been blamed'.

Surprisingly, it was as an opening bowler that Majid, 18, made his Test debut against Australia under Bob Simpson in 1964–65. His bouncers dismissed Bill Lawry twice and Brian Booth once in that Karachi Test. But his bowling was considered suspect by some, and when Simpson was asked his opinion he hinted that Australian umpires might call him. With his bowling action in doubt, he was dropped from the tour to Australia in 1964–65. By that time he had also developed a nasty back injury.

Soon, Majid the tearaway bowler became a specialist batsman and fought his way back to the Pakistani team. He toured England in 1967 but failed dismally in the Tests, scoring 38 runs in three matches. Yet it was on this tour that Majid matured and entertained. Against Glamorgan at Swansea, he hit an incandescent 147 in 89 minutes, which included a century before lunch. His 100 came in 61 minutes, the fastest hundred of the season. This innings included 13 sixes, five of them in one six-ball over from Roger Davis. It was a record for English cricket, and only two short of New Zealander John Reid's then world record. Suddenly, the Test flop, Majid, had become the glamour boy of cricket – the game's dashing six-symbol. Glamorgan signed him up the following year and he continued playing for them until 1976. That season he had a few disagreements with the county officials and decided to settle down in Pakistan.

When Majid joined them in 1968, Glamorgan had been at the bottom of the table for several years. In 1968, they were among the top three and were the champions the following year. Majid had played a leading role. In the last game he hit 156 on a difficult pitch, out of the team's total of 250. 'I consider this as among the two best innings of my career. The other was when I was in Punjab University. Against Karachi, we were four down for three runs when I entered and scored a double-century. Yes, those two knocks I value much more than the 13 sixes I hit at Swansea,' recalled Majid – a relaxed and clear-headed person. It was in 1969 also that he scored a century before lunch for Glamorgan against the touring West Indians. From 1968 to 1971, Majid scored more than 1800 runs each season. However, 1972 was his most prolific year. He captained both Glamorgan and Cambridge University, leading the latter to a win over Oxford University.

In all, he hit 2074 runs that glad season, the only batsman to top 2000 runs. The highlight was his 113 for Glamorgan against Warwickshire at Edgbaston. His century was recorded before lunch, the third time he had achieved it in six years. Still, his Test record was disappointing. He broke through that hoodoo in the Melbourne Test of 1972–73 when he scored 158 off Dennis Lillee, Max Walker and Jeff Thomson. What impressed the Australian critics most was how late he played a ball, yet timed it so sweetly.

Majid was made Pakistan's captain in the home series against England in 1973. Although he scored well, making 99 in the Karachi Test, the flair one associates with Majid was missing. His captaincy was defence-oriented and all three Tests were colourless draws. He had a fairly successful Sheffield Shield season with Queensland in 1973–74. But in the home series against New Zealand in 1976, Majid bounced back as a hard-hitting, fluent stroke-player. He scored a century before lunch on the first day of the Karachi Test – joining the immortals Victor Trumper, Charles Macartney and Sir Donald Bradman in this super-exclusive century-before-lunch club.

This was the fourth time Majid had hit a hundred before lunch in first-class cricket. What was his secret? 'It's just luck. There are days when everything goes your way,' he replied, making it all seem so easy.

In first-class cricket, Majid accumulated 27,444 runs at 43.01 with 73 centuries, his highest score being 241. With Shafiq Ahmed he added 389 runs for the opening wicket for Punjab vs Sind at Karachi in 1974–75, then a Pakistan record. He took over 200 wickets, including a hat-trick for Glamorgan against Oxford University at Oxford in 1969. His 335 catches established a record for a Pakistani fielder.

Wilf Wooller, the Glamorgan secretary, was quoted by M.H. Stevenson in *The Cricketer International* saying: 'A valuable trait in Majid's character is his calm approach to any problem in the middle … I've always maintained that 50% of cricket is played in the mind and Majid is one of the players who has got just the right kind of mind.' J.H. Morgan wrote in *Wisden* (1973): 'He [Majid] had such flair and authority that one could sense the changed atmosphere when he was not batting.'

Imran, like Majid, is fair in complexion, and handsome. But, against Majid's tranquillity, Imran is a ticking dynamo. His 12 wickets in the Sydney Test of

January 1977 represented one of the finest pieces of sustained swing-bowling I have seen. And, unlike lightning, he struck twice on the same spot. That was Imran's finest hour – as, indeed, it was Pakistan's.

Born on 25 November 1952, he made his first-class debut in 1969–70 and toured England in 1971, playing his first Test at 19. He stayed on in England, playing for Oxford University from 1973 to 1975 – as captain in 1974. He scored 1000 runs in the English seasons of 1975 and 1976, hitting 10 centuries. His highest score was 170, against Northamptonshire in 1974. The same year he hit two centuries in one match, 117 not out and 106 against Nottinghamshire, and when captaining a Combined Oxford–Cambridge side against the touring Indians he hit 160 and 49. He received his county cap for Worcestershire in 1976, in which year he totalled 1092 runs at 40.44, with four centuries and a highest score of 160.

However, in Australia Imran gained renown and respect as a bowler. In the Sydney Test, assisted by Sarfraz Nawaz, keen fielding and ideal swing conditions, he worried the best of Australian batsmen. Imran was soon among the Aussie bats – like a wolf among pigeons – scattering them and shattering their morale. On 14 and 16 January 1977 Imran, to some, appeared as the David who had cut the 'Go-Lillee-aths' to size. To others, he seemed as a direct descendant of the dreaded Genghis Khan!

Imran is an interesting talker. 'When I was young, I just wasn't interested in bowling fast, which was nothing unusual because no one in Pakistan was particularly interested in bowling fast. The wickets over there don't encourage fast men and the climate isn't particularly friendly. I did not start bowling seriously until I was 16 or 17. However, as there was such a shortage of quick bowlers in Pakistan, I used to get put on by my club. It was when I got into the Pakistan team that I began to realise that my team-mates

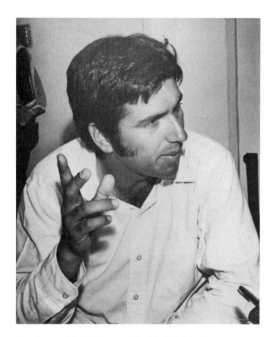

Cool man Majid Khan. (World of Cricket)

relied on my bowling more and more.'

For Oxford University and Worcestershire he was considered a batsman who could bowl medium-pace. 'Whenever I bowled a bit faster, the experienced players in my teams would tell me to cut down on pace and concentrate on line and length. Thus I arrived in Australia in 1976 a batting all-rounder. All that changed in the second innings of the second Test at Melbourne. My team-mates encouraged me to try and bowl faster, to become a bit more aggressive and I said, "Why not?" We were all looking forward to the Sydney Test which followed the next week. That was the game of my life when I actually went into it thinking of myself as a genuine fast bowler. I can't tell you how satisfying my figures were. I will never forget that match.'

When Alan Davidson presented Imran with the Man of the Match award, he said it was one of the most outstanding feats he had seen on the SCG. 'To my intense embarrassment, favourable comparisons were being made between the pace of Lillee and myself,' Imran wrote in his autobiography.

Both Majid and Imran played stellar

roles when Pakistan toured the West Indies in 1977. Majid scored 530 runs and Imran captured 25 wickets in the series. In the third Test, at Georgetown, Majid scored 167, his highest in Tests, adding 159 runs with Zaheer Abbas. In the following Test at Port-of-Spain, Majid made 92 and took 3 for 22. With useful contributions from skipper Mushtaq Mohammad (121 and 56, 5 for 28 and 3 for 69) and Imran (4 for 64), Pakistan recorded a series-levelling win. At Kingston, Jamaica, in the final Test, Imran bowled at his fastest to pick up 6 for 90 in the first innings.

Then came the World Series Cricket revolution and the Khan cousins were among the first to be signed up. Imran did not suffer in comparison with the fastest bowlers. In fact he was timed third-quickest in the world, after Jeff Thomson and Michael Holding. After Pakistan's miserable performances in England in 1978, its Cricket Board decided to include WSC players in the series against India which Pakistan won 2–0. Sixteen months later, with Majid out of form and Imran unfit, Pakistan surrendered the series 0–2.

In 1979, Pakistan toured Australasia, winning in New Zealand and drawing the series 1-all in Australia. Majid scored an unbeaten 119 in the Napier Test against New Zealand. Then, in Pakistan's 100th Test, against Australia at Melbourne in March 1979, he caned the attack to hit a majestic 108. With Zaheer he added 135 runs in 149 minutes. He hit 16 fours in that innings and 'lifted batsmanship to its highest plane', according to Ray Robinson. In the next Test, at Perth, he bagged a pair. Despite his inconsistency – either he batted brilliantly from the first ball or got out through a reckless shot – he became the fourth Pakistani to top 3000 runs in Test cricket.

A non-smoker, non-drinker and extremely fond of food, Majid is married and has a daughter. He appears aloof and disinterested but gets a gleam in his eyes when discussing his ancestors. 'My family has produced innumerable first-class cricketers,' he says. 'Eight or nine captained Aligarh University before the partition and quite a few captained the Punjab University before and after the partition. Salamuddin Khan, who toured the UK in 1911 with the All India team, was also from my family.'

Majid can laugh at his own expense. When asked whether, like all batsmen, he enjoyed bowling, he replied: 'Sure, especially once when New Zealander Rodney Redmond hit me for five fours in an over in 1973.'

The cousins Majid and Imran had disappointing tours of India in 1980, the series Pakistan lost without a fight. Majid, for once, lost his cool and form and called Indian umpiring 'biased and ridiculous'. Many thought it was the end of the road for the 33-year-old touch artist but he bounced back a month later with useful contributions against Greg Chappell's Australians in Pakistan. In the low-scoring Karachi Test he made 89 and ended the series which his country won by hitting an unbeaten 110 at Lahore. That was his eighth and last century in a Test during the course of which he added 111 runs with Imran (56), the highest partnership for the eighth wicket against Australia. He retired in 1983 and served Pakistan cricket as a selector and as Chairman of the Pakistan Cricket Board. In 1995, he severed connections with the Board, saying, 'I have been harassed, maligned and insulted in the press.'

During the 1980s, Imran emerged as a world-class all-rounder – charismatic and glamorous, a sex symbol with a playboy image. He considers the time spent with World Series Cricket in the late 1970s as decisive in making him a complete cricketer. During this series he learnt from masters of the craft; Mike Procter improving his run-up and John Snow assisting him in turning the left shoulder more towards square leg to help achieve the out-swinger.

He was at his best technically in Australia in 1981–82, when adjudged Player of the Series. Earlier he had scored his first Test hundred (against the West Indies at Lahore in 1980–81) after coming in at a crisis when Pakistan was five down for 95. During this series he became the second Pakistani after Intikhab Alam to achieve the Test double of 1000 runs and 100 wickets. This was followed by his capturing 14 for 116 against Sri Lanka at Lahore the same season – his best Test figures.

Pakistan cricket is replete with controversies and internal dissension. Javed Miandad, a magnificent batsman, did things his way as captain which did not endear him to senior players – Imran included. There was a strong protest against Miandad's leadership and he was replaced by Imran in 1982. Captaincy brought out the maturity in him without affecting his all-round excellence. He was a natural leader of men, perhaps autocratic at times – especially in selecting players he wanted. A talented but undisciplined Pakistan team needed a strong man at the helm and Imran was just that. Players were at times in awe of him but he insisted on discipline and got it.

His happiest moment came in Melbourne on 25 March 1992, when he lifted the 1992 World Cup in front of nearly 90,000 wildly cheering spectators. After the presentations he said it was 'the most fulfilling and satisfying cricket moment of my life'. He described the victory as a triumph for his young team's talent over finalist England's experience.

Imran's role in the World Cup triumph went deeper. He had virtually hand-picked the squad. After losing the key fast bowler Waqar Younis to a stress fracture before leaving Pakistan and a disastrous start when they lost four of the first five matches, he urged his players to imitate the action of a cornered tiger before they went on to five consecutive wins. Apart from his inspiring leadership, Imran had enjoyed an all-round triumph himself, making the final's highest individual score (72), adding 139 with Miandad for the third wicket and capturing the final English wicket.

He was then in his 40th year and soon hung up his pads after scoring 3807 runs at 37.69 in 88 Tests (with six centuries, 126 being his highest score) and taking 362 wickets at 22.81 (capturing five wickets in an innings 23 times and 10 wickets in a Test six times, his best effort being 8 for 58) and 28 catches.

Only four all-rounders have achieved the Test double of 3000 runs and 300 wickets and Imran is one of them. Their records are presented below. Taking into account his captaincy record, Imran could be considered the best all-rounder of the four. The sobriquet 'Lion of Pakistan' fitted him admirably.

Apart from his on-field performances, Imran will be remembered as one of the pioneers who mastered the art of reverse swing. This happens when an intended in-

	For	Tests	Runs	Wkts	*Tests for double	Tests won	Tests captained
Imran Khan	Pak.	88	3807	362	30	14	48
Ian Botham	Eng.	102	5200	383	21	0	12
Richard Hadlee	NZ	86	3124	431	28	–	–
Kapil Dev	Ind.	131	5248	434	25	4	34

* Number of Tests taken to complete the double of 1000 runs and 100 wickets.

swing delivery swings out – especially if the ball is roughened on one side. The Australian bowlers learnt this from Imran when he played Sheffield Shield for New South Wales in the mid-1980s.

Even after retirement, Imran continued to make headlines. His mother's death from cancer inspired him to set up a well-equipped hospital for cancer patients in Pakistan. He travelled around the world to collect funds for this worthy project.

On 16 May 1995, Imran, 42, married socialite Jemina Goldsmith, daughter of rich British financier Sir James Goldsmith. Jemina, 21, converted to the Islam faith and became known as Haiqa Khan after a brief wedding ceremony in Paris. The media made it into a 'royal wedding' of the decade, a playboy sportsman meeting his affluent match. Although she helped greatly in the establishment of the cancer hospital, the Pakistani press accused Imran of double standards for marrying a woman of Jewish descent soon after announcing that he had discovered Islamic values. 'It so happens that the girl who shares my ideas, visions and values is English,' he countered.

However, his aspirations to be a politician to rid Pakistan of corruption and poverty was unsuccessful; he lost heavily in the national election.

Imran, the tall Pathan with a Hollywood actor's looks, was a many-splendoured personality. He was a supreme character who put glamour into an ageing sport. He had a candid look at himself in his autobiography, *Imran* (1983): 'When I read articles in the press about "Imran, the sex symbol", I am frankly amazed. Initially, it came as a surprise, because I grew up with a complex about being ugly – fostered by my elder sister who remains astonished to this day to read comments about my alleged good looks. ... As a Moslem, I pray every night for strength to be honest in life and beg for health and happiness. I have worked hard at my cricket and the success has been doubly satisfying.'

The Khans in Test Cricket

	Tests	Runs	Avrge	HS	100s	50s	Wkts	Avrge	Best	5w/i	Catches
Jahangir (Ind.)	4	39	5.57	13	0	0	4	63.75	4–60	0	4
Baqa Jilani (Ind.)	1	16	16.00	12	0	0	0	–	–	–	0
Javed Burki (Pak.)	25	1341	30.47	140	3	4	0	–	–	–	7
Majid (Pak.)	63	3931	38.92	167	8	19	27	53.92	4–45	0	70
Imran (Pak.)	88	3807	37.69	136	6	18	362	22.81	8–58	23	28
Total	181	9134	35.96	167	17	41	393	25.56	8–58	23	109

CHAPTER 31

The
Pollock Magic

—— ● ——

The Pollock brothers – the graceful, run-hungry Graeme and the pacey,
perceptive Peter – produced champagne cricket in the 1960s.
Their reign, however, was cut short because of their country's apartheid
policy. In the 1990s emerged another Pollock, Peter's son Shaun,
who was arguably described by coach Bob Woolmer as
'one of the finest all-rounders since Garry Sobers'.

'For all sad words of tongue or pen the saddest are these: it might have been.'
— John Greenleaf Whittier

ONE OF CRICKET'S SADDEST 'might-have-beens' was provided by South Africa's marvellous cricketers of the 1960s, Graeme and Peter Pollock, Barry Richards, Mike Procter ... Their country's apartheid policy over which they had no control led to their isolation from the Test scene at a time when they were at their peak. What might have been for Graeme Pollock, for instance?

Graeme had just turned 26 when he played his last Test. He was then at the height of his powers, having scored 517 runs at 73.86 in the 1969–70 series against Australia which included a magnificent 274 in the Durban Test. He had made 2256 runs in 23 Tests at 60.97 and the sky was the limit for this graceful left-hander with

a dazzling array of strokes and a solid defence. But that was it. The end. La Finis! Due to a chain of events, South Africa was boycotted from Test cricket from 1970 to 1990 because of its hateful racist policy. Had Graeme, for instance, continued in the Test arena for 10 more years, he might have scored more runs than Allan Border and hit more centuries than Sunil Gavaskar. He had the elegance of Mark Waugh, the stubborn streak of Steve Waugh and the firepower of Vivian Richards, Sachin Tendulkar and Brian Lara.

It was a tragic case of might have been. He retired from cricket in 1974, not a bitter man, but frustrated as both he and brother Peter detested their country's apartheid policy.

When Greg Chappell's International Wanderers toured South Africa in 1976, Graeme jumped back into top gear as if the lost, lonely six years had been wiped out in a sporting time machine. Australia's strong attack of Dennis Lillee, Gary Gilmour, Max Walker and Ashley Mallett did not know what hit them in the second unofficial Test in Johannesburg. The left-hand legend stroked 124 of the best with 21 superbly timed fours. Had the previous six years not been lost, he could have established himself as one of the greatest batsmen of all time. Even his shortened Test career from 1963, when he was only 19, until 1970, has ensured that he will be remembered by posterity. He will be revered for his symphonies at Trent Bridge and Durban, Adelaide and Cape Town, Sydney and Port Elizabeth.

His brother, Peter, the elder by two and a half years, was respected as a dynamic fast bowler, an inspiring cricketer's cricketer who became a journalist and wrote with insight and sensitivity. Later in life, he discovered religion in a big way and is now a lay preacher.

For the Pollock brothers, the Trent Bridge Test of 1965 was a memorable occasion. Graeme hit 125 and 59, took a useful slips catch and trapped England's captain Mike Smith lbw at a vital stage. Peter took 10 for 87 and scored valuable runs. Graeme's century was an innings of such beauty and seemingly effortless power that it left writers and commentators short of superlatives. E.W. Swanton in the *Daily Telegraph* wrote: 'It was an innings which, in point of style and power, of ease and beauty of execution, is fit to rank with anything in the annals of the game'. Favourable comparisons were made with another great left-hander – Frank Woolley. Peter West wrote: 'I can only say that I never saw the great man (Woolley) play better than Graeme Pollock did here ... Everything is pure beauty, right out of the text book.'

South Africa were on their knees at 4 for 43 when Graeme started the onslaught. The English spearhead Tom Cartright was breathing fire, but soon it was Graeme who was on the warpath. His magnificent 125 – out of 162 added when he was in the middle – came in 139 minutes and included 21 fours. Old-timers were reminded of Australia's great Stan McCabe and his incandescent 232 in 240 minutes on the very same ground in 1938.

That innings by Graeme was Churchillian in eloquence and laid the foundation for a triumphant Springbok march to victory. And yet, to him, it seemed like just another innings and another enjoyable outing. It was South Africa's first triumph in England in 10 years. Coincidentally, the Test had started on 5 August, their mother's birthday. And as the players celebrated, Peter and Graeme remembered their cricket-loving parents and wished they could have been present.

Graeme played his first game of cricket when 18 months old – with four-year-old Peter and their mother, Edith, who had represented Durban in tennis. As he recalls in his autobiography, *Down the Wicket*, his mother instructed Graeme to hold the bat with the right hand nearest the blade. But the moment she moved away, he would revert to his left-hander's stance. 'No, no, Graeme,' she pleaded, correcting him, but the toddler stood firm. Even at 18 months he resented any interference with his natural game.

Oddly, Graeme bats left-handed but bowls, writes and plays tennis right-handed. Their father, Andrew Maclean ('Mac') Pollock, played cricket as wicket-keeper for Orange Free State and also won provincial hockey colours. He often used to tell his sons, 'Hundreds are not good enough. You have got to aim for double and even triple-centuries.' He died just a month before Graeme scored those magnificent 274 runs against Bill Lawry's Australians in February 1970 – then the highest score in Test cricket for South Africa. But the old man had the satisfaction of seeing his sons develop as world-class cricketers.

Their mother's uncle, Jock Howden, was the President of the South African Cricket Association. With such a sporting background the Pollocks naturally shone – not only in cricket, but also in rugby, hockey, athletics and tennis. Graeme was so good at tennis that he succeeded the well-known Cliff Drysdale as singles champion at the Grey School.

'As a kid,' remembers Peter, 'Graeme had an almost obsessive desire to stay at the crease, so much so, that often fisticuffs proved to be the only satisfactory method of effecting a dismissal.' When seven, Graeme made a vow: 'One day I am going to show these Aussies just what it is like to play against a Neil Harvey'. And he kept his word, as teams under Bob Simpson (1963–64 in Australia, 1966–67 in South Africa) and Lawry (1970 in South Africa) realised. When nine, Graeme hit 117 – with seven sixes and 12 fours – in a school match. In another, he took all 10 wickets as a fast bowler. In those days he was nicknamed 'Shortie', but today stands almost 190 centimetres. The Sussex international George Cox coached the Pollocks and, watching Graeme bat, said: 'Son, to hell with the coaching manual, just go out there and do what comes naturally.'

Graeme became the youngest century-maker in South African cricket when, a month prior to his 17th birthday, he hit a hundred for Eastern Province in a Currie Cup match. He showed his class at international level when he hit a spectacular 209 (three sixes, 36 fours) against Richie Benaud's Cavaliers. He was then 19 and already an exciting prospect in Springbok cricket. He was the baby of the team to tour Australia in 1963–64. His debut in the Brisbane Test was modest, but he had the pleasure of seeing brother Peter take 6 for 95. Graeme decided to play his natural game in the third Test at Sydney and hit a majestic 122. Ron Roberts called it 'the most promising Test match innings I have seen by a young player since Norman O'Neill'.

After seeing Graeme play an Australian Combined XI attack for a merciless 122 at Perth, Sir Donald Bradman told him: 'If you ever score a century like that again, I hope I'm here to see it'. Sir Donald's request was soon granted, for in the fourth Test at Adelaide Oval Graeme hit 175 glorious runs, including three sixes – two in one over from Simpson – and added 341 in 280 minutes with Eddie Barlow (201) for the third wicket. It was champagne cricket. The visitors won this Test to even the series. The following year, Graeme hit his first Test hundred in South Africa, on home ground at Port Elizabeth against England. He was still under 21. Subsequently, he topped 500 runs and had an average of 70-plus in each of the two successive home series against Australia.

In 1966–67, in the Cape Town Test, Graeme hit a priceless, gallant 209, despite a pulled muscle. For the ninth wicket, Peter helped him to add 85 runs. In the second innings, Peter made his highest Test score, 75 not out. Yet South Africa lost the Test. On 27 February 1967, his 23rd birthday, Graeme stroked 105 on his home ground and South Africa won the series 3–1.

In early 1970 when Lawry's men visited them, South Africa was at its strongest and proved their high standing at international level by crushing the Australians 4–0. In the Durban Test, Graeme broke Jackie McGlew's record of 255 not out by galloping to a majestic 274. – adding 103 in 60 heart-pounding minutes with Barry Richards and 200 for the sixth wicket with 'Tiger' Lance. Graeme played in the two Rest of the World series, against England in 1970 and against Australia in 1971–72.

After failing in the earlier internationals in England, he played a classic innings of 114 at The Oval, adding 165 runs with Garry Sobers. For once, Sobers had to play second fiddle with Graeme in his element. Australians saw a different Graeme Pollock – in glasses. Out of practice, he struggled against the pace of Dennis Lillee in Melbourne and the swing of Bob Massie in Sydney, but the South African maestro came back with vengeance in the final international at Adelaide. His 136 was an innings of contrasts. The first 101 on the second day was a masterpiece from a touch artist at his mature best, but on the following day he played an uncharacteristic knock, struggling against bowlers he had flayed the previous day.

In his 23 Tests Graeme scored 2256 runs, with seven centuries and 11 fifties, averaging 60.97 runs an innings. It is still the best among South African batsmen. Besides his batting, Graeme was an occasional right-arm spinner and his four victims in Test cricket were Ted Dexter, Jim Parks, David Brown and Mike Smith.

Peter Pollock is among the game's deep thinkers, full of suggestions, solutions and encouragement. His strong belief in what he considers cricket, matches his dynamic displays in the Test arena. His Test career lasted 10 years and in 28 Tests he took 116 wickets at 24.18. He bowled fast to fast-medium with hostility and, according to John Arlott, he had 'a genuine hatred of batsmen' on the field. His menace was digging the ball in and making it rear awkwardly. In the Tests in England in 1965 he took five wickets in three consecutive innings. His best bowling was a marvellous 7 for 51 against Kent. In that match, Graeme made 203 in 270 minutes.

The combined pace of Mike Procter and Peter Pollock put the Australian batsmen of 1970 in sad disarray. Peter finished the series with 15 wickets at 17.20. His best was 5 for 39 in the third Test in Johannesburg. However, fast bowling was not the only thing in Peter Pollock's life. Like England's John Snow, he also wrote poetry. A frank and friendly person, it was a delight interviewing him during the Rest of the World series in Australia in 1971–72.

An attack of jaundice changed Peter and, in a way, the cricket world. 'Until I was 15, I was a short, fat little fellow who used to open the batting for my school. Even now, I do not consider myself a tail-ender,' Peter told me with a smile. 'Then in 1956 I had jaundice. It kept me in bed for three months, in which time I gained six to seven inches in height. Soon after, I could bowl much faster.' So fast that he made his debut as a speedster two years later and was partly responsible for South Africa's stunning wins over England and Australia.

'Among batsmen I have bowled to, Bob Simpson comes very high on my list. Among bowlers, Neil Adcock, the South African quickie, is my hero. Graham McKenzie had also impressed me.' It was the fiery pace bowling of Adcock and Peter Heine against Australia in the Port Elizabeth Test of 1955–56 that inspired him to bowl fast, super fast. He was then a 15-year-old chubby room attendant who watched the bouncers of Heine and Adcock (53 out of 56 balls as counted by Richie Benaud) and made mental notes for the future.

The moments Peter cherished the most in his cricket career? 'My Test debut in 1961 against New Zealand: I took nine wickets, including six in the second innings. Also the Trent Bridge Test in 1965 was a very happy occasion for my family and my country. Then, of course, the stand with Garry Sobers who made those brilliant 254 in the Melbourne International in 1971–72 [Peter added 186 with the maestro, scoring 54 himself]. I enjoyed it. There can be no greater cricketer than Garry.' Unless it was younger brother, Graeme, for whom Peter has the greatest admiration.

Peter tried all he could to introduce multiracial cricket in South Africa at club level. He was one of the many Springbok cricketers who staged a walkout in 1971, to record their protest against apartheid in sport. As he wrote in the June 1971 issue of

The Cricketer (England): 'Whether the walk-off was the right thing to do and whether it will, in fact, help to save the tour to Australia and other cricket visits is basically incidental. What is more important is that it was a genuine and sincere gesture in the name of cricket and all the game stands for.' His plea for the inclusion of two non-whites in the South African team to tour Australia in 1971–72 was not considered by the government and the tour was subsequently cancelled. His suggestions were eventually taken up at a higher level.

Lack of Test incentive perhaps hastened the retirement of physical-condition-fanatic Peter at the early age of 30. As he wrote to me subsequently: 'A time comes for everyone to say goodbye. I have had an extremely good run, and I would like to get out at a stage when I am still enjoying the game. By so doing, I feel that I will always remember the game kindly and, as a writer, there will be no chips on my shoulder. I remember, as a youngster, I wanted to be one of the fastest in the world. I reckoned I achieved that in Australia in 1963. Then I wanted to be a bowler who could use his brains, varying pace and swing – and this happened in England in 1965. My next ambition was to be the most successful fast bowling wicket-taker in South African history. This happened against the Australians in early 1970.'

With the dismantling of apartheid policy, South Africa made a welcome return to international sports in early 1990. It was too late for Graeme and Peter to stage a comeback, but it seemed that the Pollock cousins, Anthony (Graeme's son) and Shaun (Peter's son), would start from where their illustrious fathers had left off.

Anthony had more pressure to perform because Graeme was still an active player and a legend. He represented Transvaal when a teenager but struggled and played with their B team until the late 1990s.

Graeme (left) and Peter Pollock, the pride of South Africa. (*The Herald and Weekly Times photographic collection*)

Shaun had to survive fewer unfavourable comparisons because Peter had retired from the scene in 1975. His progress was steady and, without consciously trying, he fitted well into his dad's shoes. In fact he has taken more wickets than his father did and at a better average (175 wickets at 20.34 against Peter's 116 at 24.18).

Was the name Pollock a big cross to bear? 'As a kid I realised that people took an interest in me because of my name,' he told Jonathan Agnew in *Wisden Cricket Monthly*. 'But I didn't feel there was any pressure on me. Dad had finished by 1975 so he was out of the limelight.' Also, Peter was very easy with him when at school, and if Shaun did not want to play cricket he never forced him to don the pads. He did not often come to watch him play, and if he did, he would stand far away behind a tree.

However, Shaun was keen on the game, and competitive. He made his Test debut at 22 against England at Centurion in November 1995. It was an impressive series for him as he topped his country's bowling averages, claiming 16 wickets at 23.56 (best being 5 for 32) and scoring 133 runs at 26.60 (highest score 36 not out). *Wisden* (1997) opined that he was the find of the series and added, 'He immediately looked the part and his cricket combined some of the best features of both his famous relatives, uncle Graeme and father Peter'.

Shaun was even more successful in the Limited-Overs Internationals that season against England and was adjudged Man of the Match in the first and third matches. At Cape Town, he top-scored with an undefeated run-a-ball 66 and grabbed 4 for 34. He went on to form a frightening opening bowling partnership with Allan Donald, just as his father had with Mike Procter. Unlike Peter and Mike who could compete only against England, Australia and New Zealand, Shaun demonstrated his swing, cut and pace all over the cricket world.

After recording his highest Test score – so far – of 92 against Sri Lanka at Cape Town in 1997–98, he played his most memorable, yet paradoxically his most disappointing, Test. This was against Australia in Adelaide in early 1998. He captured 7 for 87 (his best spell to date) and 2 for 61, scored 40 runs and was adjudged Man of the Test. So why disappointing? In the second innings, with the South Africans scenting victory, Shaun bowled a lifter to a well-set Mark Waugh. It hit the Australian on the arm and as he walked away in pain his bat brushed the stumps and dislodged a bail. After repeated replays lasting about five minutes, Waugh was declared not out by the TV umpire. To add to Shaun's agony,

Waugh was dropped the next ball by Adam Bacher. Australia saved the Test and won the series.

It was Shaun's most frustrating match despite his heroic performance. It was sweet revenge for him and his team-mates when, under his captaincy, South Africa beat Australia in the final of the Commonwealth Games held in Kuala Lumpur, Malaysia, in September 1998. Shaun took 4 for 19. He was also behind South Africa's whitewash of the once mighty West Indies, who they humbled 5–0 in the 1998–99 Test series. Shaun captured 29 scalps at 16.65, with match-winning performances at Johannesburg (5 for 54 and 4 for 49), Port Elizabeth (5 for 43 and 2 for 46) and Durban (1 for 45 and 5 for 83).

He was at his all-round best against New Zealand in 1999 when he bagged 13 wickets at 14.85 in a three-Test series and scored 112 runs without getting out. Such consistency against all countries made South Africa's English coach Bob Woolmer describe Shaun as 'one of the finest all-rounders since Garry Sobers'. This appeared going over the top as he has yet to score his first Test century (against Sobers' 26). Quite embarrassed at Woolmer's hyperbole, Shaun told Jonathan Agnew, 'Ach, the coach is always blurting his mouth off! ... I really won't know how I can be measured up until my career is over and until then I really can't be bothered with it at all.'

The shock revelation of skipper Hansie Cronje's involvement with an Indian bookmaker thrust Shaun into captaining his country in three one-dayers against Australia in April 2000. He passed this fiery assignment in flying colours by beating Steve Waugh's rampaging Aussies 2–1.

Shaun is a shining role model for aspiring young cricketers. He neither smokes nor drinks, and very rarely swears – surprising for a fast bowler. Also, he is playing a vital role in his country's developing program – unearthing potential Vivian Richardes, Curtly Ambroses and Brian Laras from the underprivileged townships and introduc-ing cricket to African children. His progress as the world's leading fast bowler is a matter of immense pride to his family. Now his dad watches him play from the stands and not from behind a tree!

The Pollocks in Test Cricket

	Tests	Runs	Avrge	HS	100s	50s	Wkts	Avrge	Best	5w/i	Catches
Graeme	23	2256	60.97	274	7	11	4	51.00	2–50	0	17
Peter	28	607	21.67	75*	0	2	116	24.18	6–38	9	9
Shaun	42	1444	29.47	92	0	8	175	20.34	7–87	10	25
Total	93	4307	37.78	274	7	21	295	22.27	7–87	19	51

CHAPTER 32

The
Kiwi Crowes

———●———

Martin Crowe was New Zealand's most prolific batsman, a jewel in the New Zealand crown and one of the classiest batsmen ever. Elder brother Jeff was a studious accumulator of runs for Auckland, South Australia and New Zealand. Both captained their country in Tests and in World Cups. Their dominating father, Dave, had played first-class cricket.

IN LATE APRIL 1981 arrived a tall, quiet 18-year-old to Lord's. He had won a scholarship as New Zealand's young player to practice with the MCC staff. He immediately impressed head coach Don Wilson, who raved, 'This is the best young batsman I've ever seen'. The youngster outshone everyone, including Wayne Phillips and Tim Zoehrer, who had won similar scholarships from Australia.

He went home at the end of the season and no one was surprised when he made his Test debut the following year. He was Martin Crowe, who developed as New Zealand's most prolific run-getter; 5444 runs in 77 Tests with 17 centuries, a highest score of 299, besides accepting 71 catches – all New Zealand records. Apart from the figures, he was his country's classiest batsman and among the best of his time. His batting style and bowling action reminded many of Greg Chappell.

Martin comes from a cricketing family. His father, Dave, played first-class matches in New Zealand and elder brother, Jeff, for Auckland, South Australia and New Zealand. Although Jeff lacked the elegance or fluency of Martin, he was a studious accumulator of runs. Martin adds that his mother, Audrey, was 'our best all-round sportsman', being a swimming and tennis champion at school. Martin was versatile too. A competent rugby player, he later enjoyed squash, tennis and golf with the rest of the family. But it was in cricket that he really excelled, becoming the youngest first-class debutant for New Zealand.

Older by four years, Jeff made his Test debut a year after Martin. Both captained New Zealand, Jeff four years before Martin. Earlier, the brothers used to play on the home lawn for hours, and being younger, Martin had to bowl and bowl.

'Come on, Dad, give us a game of cricket,' was their constant plea, remembers Dave in *The Crowe Style*.

Jeff's talent as a batsman was recognised in 1976 as an 18-year-old when he was invited to South Australia to play for West Torrens club. He stayed six seasons, quickly graduating to the South Australian Sheffield Shield side. He scored 1701 runs at 34.02 in 29 Shield matches, making five centuries (highest score 157) and eight fifties. He was unconcerned at being called a 'crow-eater' and is very grateful to Phil Ridings, then the Australian Cricket Board chairman, and his wife for their kind hospitality. 'Little did I realise that I was to be singled out for attention by the incomparable Sir Donald Bradman himself,' he wrote in *The Crowe Style*.

He made his presence felt in the 1979–80 season when adding 129 runs in 106 minutes with Ian Chappell against Western Australia in oppressive heat. His best season was 1981–82, scoring 704 runs at 50.28 in 10 matches for South Australia, hitting three centuries. His favourite foes were the New South Wales bowlers against whom he top-scored with 157 in Adelaide and an unbeaten 137 in Sydney. In an extraordinary climax to the season, the previous year's wooden-spooners, South Australia, beat Victoria to clinch the Shield – cheered on by a crowd of over 10,000 on a Monday. Victoria collapsed from 1 for 230 to 297 all out and South Australia replied with 8 for 423 (Jeff a quickfire 126). Set 161 to win in even time, South Australia just made it with Jeff remaining unbeaten.

He returned to New Zealand and made his Test debut against Sri Lanka at Christchurch in 1983. He could get only 13, but New Zealand won by an innings. Jeff and Martin played together for the first time in a Test against England at The Oval in July 1983. However, it was a double disaster as both were out for ducks in the first innings. They did little better in the second knock; Jeff 9, Martin 33.

They became the fifth set of brothers to play together for New Zealand after Dayle and Richard Hadlee (10 Tests together), Hedley and Geoff Howarth (4), Norman and John Parker (3) and John and Brendon Bracewell (1). The Crowes went on to play together in 34 Tests, which is currently fourth-best after the Waugh twins, Steve and Mark (who have played together 85 times), the Chappells (43) and the Flowers of Zimbabwe (42).

Jeff played 39 Tests scoring 1601 runs at 26.24, hitting three centuries. His maiden Test hundred was at Auckland in 1983–84, when he scored 124 and New Zealand won her first Test rubber against England. His second Test ton (112) was against the strong West Indians at Kingston in 1984–85, when he added 210 runs with Geoff Howarth in 294 minutes to establish a New Zealand second-wicket record which stood until 1991–92.

His last Test century was against Sri Lanka at Colombo in 1986–87. This was his debut as captain and the match was drawn. His unbeaten 120 was painful to watch as it took 609 minutes, reaching his 100 in 516 minutes. It remains the fourth-slowest Test hundred and the slowest by a Kiwi bat. At one stage he did not score a run for 60 yawning minutes. The next two Tests were cancelled because of political unrest and not, I might add tongue-in-cheek, due to Jeff's run-crawl.

Jeff's captaincy record was mediocre, with one loss and five draws. Captaincy appeared to affect his batting and he had a nightmarish tour of Australia in 1987–88. The Kiwis lost the Trans-Tasman Trophy they had held since its inception two years earlier, and the captain managed a measly 78 runs in three Tests at 13.00.

However, brother Martin was in top flight, stroking 396 runs at 66.00, hitting a polished 137 in the Adelaide Test. He became the first New Zealander to notch eight Test hundreds. During the final Test, in Melbourne, he became the seventh batsman, and the first after Len Hutton in

1948, to score 4000 first-class runs in a calendar year. As Jeff's fortunes plummeted, Martin's rose and rose. Apart from his silken stroke-play and faultless technique, Martin was mentally strong and ambitious, even as a child. Their father remembers Martin at eight dreaming of scoring a century in a Lord's Test.

Two of his 17 Test tons were at Lord's and that gave him immense satisfaction. He was 23 when he hit his first in 1986, to realise a cherished ambition. To add to the tension, he was 99 at lunch and could barely look at food, but he reached his goal soon after. His second Lord's century came towards the end of his career when he was 31, in 1994. His 142 included 20 fours and three sixes and he reached his 5000th Test run during this innings. It was all the more remarkable as he was then recovering from knee surgery.

In the next Test at Old Trafford, Martin scored 70 and a match-saving 115, his 17th and final Test hundred. He had fought off not only the English bowlers but also a mind-numbing influenza which slowed his reflexes and an antibiotic which made him swoon. He was also struck in the first innings by a Craig White bouncer which hit his helmet and neatly removed the silver fern badge. Despite all these misadventures, he scored 70 off 91 balls with 11 fours and a six out of his team's 151. Still, New Zealand was staring at defeat and Martin – battling a crook knee, a sore upper arm, runny eyes and blocked nose – scored a magnificent century.

His highest Test score is 299 against Sri Lanka at Wellington in 1990–91. He was devastated to miss a triple-century by a run and groaned, 'It's a bit like climbing Everest and pulling a hamstring in the last stride'. His marathon innings was far from being a selfish indulgence. Dismissed for a paltry 174, the Kiwis faced a huge deficit of 323. Martin dug himself in and batted for 610 minutes, faced 523 deliveries, slammed 29 fours and three sixes and added 467 runs with Andrew Jones (186),

which was then a record for the highest Test partnership. With only three balls remaining, Martin needed a single for a triple ton but was caught behind.

As most of his innings were gems, it is difficult to pick his best, but here are some of my favourites. His 188 in the Brisbane Test of 1985–86 was a masterpiece. In all first-class matches on that tour, Martin scored 562 at 112.40 with 242 not out as his highest. 'The younger Crowe is a class player,' wrote Ian Chappell in *Channel 9 Cricket Yearbook 1986*. 'He presents the full face of the bat in defence and has the ability to drive well on both sides of the wicket with Greg Chappell-style preference to on-side. He deals safely and surely with anything pitched short.'

Martin played a gallant innings of 137 against Australia at Christchurch in 1985–86. A bouncer from Bruce Reid hit him on the face when he was on 51, forcing him to retire. He returned with eight stitches on his massive jaw and was last out. The stitched-up Crowe had raced from 51 to 100 in only 47 balls, spanking 10 fours.

His century in the Colombo Test against Sri Lanka in December 1992 was controversial. When 39, he stood his ground after umpire I. Anandappa upheld an appeal for a catch. Martin was sure that the catch had not carried. This was before TV umpire technology, but square-leg umpire T.M. Samarasinghe, who had a clearer view, asked Anandappa to rescind his decision. Martin survived to hit a sparkling 107 in 121 balls with 10 fours and four sixes. Earlier, his 186 against the West Indies in the Georgetown Test of 1984–85 remains one of his favourites as it was hit against the intimidating pace attack of Malcolm Marshall, Joel Garner and Michael Holding.

Strongly built and curly haired, Martin played like a millionaire. He was a destroyer of bowling, especially when pitched short, and was always an entertainer. His nimble footwork enabled him to bestow maximum power to his graceful shots. But for his bad back and knee surgery, he would have scored many more runs. He retired at 33. However, his captaincy record was not outstanding: two wins, seven defeats and seven draws.

Earlier in his career he had successful seasons with Somerset. In 1984, 21-year-old Martin replaced Viv Richards as Somerset's overseas recruit. Indeed, a hard act to follow but Martin did extremely well despite a broken thumb and a salmonella infection he had contracted when in Sri Lanka. He hit four centuries in four successive Championship matches. It was a golden June for him as he smashed 719 runs at 143.80, reported *Wisden* when making him one of their Five Cricketers of the Year in 1985.

That season Martin scored 1769 runs at 53.60 and, 'I learnt more about cricket in six months with Somerset than in the previous six years', he said. He especially remembers his 70 not out and a brilliant 190 against Leicestershire when the Windies quickie Andy Roberts was bowling with fire on a green pitch. He calls it 'the gutsiest innings I played. I was against a guy in form and it was a fantastic experience in the sense that it frightened the death out of me ... It was total instinct, like fighting blow for blow.'

Just as Jeff had captained New Zealand in the 1987 World Cup in India and Pakistan, Martin led his country in the 1992 World Cup in Australasia. His 456 runs at 114.00 in 1992 took New Zealand to the brink of the final. In the opening match at Auckland, New Zealand shocked the reigning 1987 World Cup champions, Australia, beating them by 37 runs. Martin scored an unbeaten 100, his only World Cup hundred, and disoriented the Aussies by giving the new ball to off-spinner Dipak Patel. In the semi-final against Pakistan, he scored a scintillating 91 in 83 balls, enriched with seven fours and three sixes. However, after straining his hamstring during this innings he was an agonised spectator as Pakistan narrowly won and a week later lifted the World Cup.

In 21 World Cup matches he scored 880 runs at 55.00. He amassed 4704 runs at 38.55 in 143 Limited-Overs Internationals with four centuries and six scores in the nineties. In all first-class matches, he hit 71 centuries, only Glenn Turner (103 hundreds) being ahead of him among New Zealanders.

When he retired from the game in 1995–96, Martin helped invent the latest form of the game called Cricket Max. After visiting over 150 schools and talking with a pay TV station in late 1995, he designed a new format of cricket to embrace the best components of the existing formats. In 1998, Cricket Max took off and international matches were played between England and New Zealand, drawing up to 12,000 spectators.

Cricket Max is an 11-a-side match lasting three hours and can be played at night, morning before school, pre-season – you name it. There is no ambiguity about wides, as chalked lines are drawn. Also, a no-ball is penalised by making the next ball a free hit to a batsman and 'the crowd loves it', said an enthusiastic Martin.

It is somehow ironic that such a new-fangled idea should come from a cricketer as traditional as Martin Crowe. But then he is a paradoxical character, as depicted by Joseph Romanos in his unauthorised biography *Martin Crowe – Tortured Genius* (1995). According to Romanos, Martin is meticulous, organised, well-groomed and single-minded. However, when his team-mates fall short, he can be intolerant and testy. He tended to argue with his players, selectors, administrators and umpires. 'Like [John] McEnroe he does not shy away from confrontations' in his quest for perfection, adds Romanos.

'He is full of paradoxes,' to quote Romanos from his no-holds-barred biography. 'He invites the media into his home, then complains about having his privacy invaded ... His quest for perfection is especially fascinating as he plays a sport in which perfection is impossible ... In fact, he is the most fascinating New Zealand sports personality of the past 15 to 20 years.'

How do other great New Zealand cricketers view Martin Crowe? Bert Sutcliffe told Romanos that Martin stood out like a beacon among New Zealand batsmen since World War II. John Reid said in 1995: 'He is still one of the best players in the world, knee and all. He is better than the Englishmen and Aussies. There are others as talented. For instance, Mark Waugh has all the hallmarks of class.

The difference is that Crowe has better concentration and can therefore make bigger scores.' Richard Hadlee: 'Well, I never got him out. He often reminds me of that ... He's technically correct, with a good concentration level. And he has an intense desire to prove a point. You have to rate him very, very highly. He is one of the best batsmen New Zealand has produced. His record speaks for itself.'

Martin Crowe and excellence go together. Despite being controversial and not always popular with the media, Martin David Crowe, MBE, is regarded as a jewel in the New Zealand crown and a genius with the bat.

The Crowes in Test Cricket

	Tests	Runs	Avrge	HS	100s	50s	Wkts	Avrge	Best	5w/i	Catches
Jeff	39	1601	26.24	128	3	6	0	–	–	–	41
Martin	77	5444	45.36	299	17	18	14	48.28	2–25	–	71
Total	116	7045	38.92	299	20	24	14	48.93	2–25	–	112

CHAPTER 33

Cairnses
– the Six Symbols

●

Lance Cairns and son Chris have been dynamic all-rounders for New Zealand with a penchant for six-hitting. Both took over 130 Test wickets and are the only father–son combination to capture 10 wickets in a Test.

CHRIS CAIRNS RESERVED HIS best for his 43rd Test. He was 29 then and had played Test cricket for 10 years with only a few outstanding feats with bat or ball. But he had more lows than highs, suffering from injuries, a kidney operation and mood swings which had retarded his progress. This changed in a hurry in the Hamilton Test against the West Indies in December 1999. And what a pulsating, topsy-turvy Test it turned out to be! On the first day, Chris was hammered by the West Indies opening pair of Sherwin Campbell (170) and Adrian Griffith (114), who piled on 276 runs.

Medium-pacer Chris had laboured on to 0 for 62 before he took his first wicket on the second day. Inexplicably, the visitors collapsed and were shot out for 365, losing their last 10 wickets for 89 runs as Chris claimed 3 for 73. New Zealand were 6 for 258 when Chris went in to bat and was all

but run out before he had scored. The third (TV) umpire, David Quested, scanned several unsatisfactory replays and gave Chris the benefit of the doubt. Fortunately for Chris, the special side-on cameras were not filming at that time and he admitted later that he was lucky to survive. He went on to top-score with 72 which included nine fours and two sixes. When 48, he reached his 2000th Test run.

The Kiwis led by 28 runs. Demoralised, the Windies fell to pieces and were bowled out for a paltry 97. Man of the Match Chris Cairns was their nemesis, capturing 7 for 27 to finish with a rather symmetrical match figure of 10 for 100. By taking 10 wickets, he joined his dynamic dad, Lance Cairns, who had grabbed 10 for 144 (7 for 74 and 3 for 70) against England in the Leeds Test of 1983. The two form the only father–son combination to capture 10 wickets in a Test.

Two months earlier, in the Kanpur Test against India, Chris had claimed his 131st Test wicket, to get past his father's Test tally. As at April 2000, only Sir Richard Hadlee (431 wickets) is ahead of him as he shares second place with Danny Morrison (160 wickets each) among New Zealanders.

Chris was not finished with the Windies yet. In the Boxing Day Test at Wellington he captured 5 for 44 and 2 for 25 and scored 31 runs as New Zealand won the Test and the series 2–0. The New Zealanders completed the whitewash by slaughtering the Windies 5–0 in the Limited-Overs Internationals. Chris had contributed to two victories by hitting a whirlwind 75 (two fours, six sixes) and adding 136 runs with Nathan Astle in the first Limited-Overs International at Auckland and by capturing 3 for 25 in the third in Napier.

His next series was against Steve Waugh's all-conquering Australians in March–April 2000. Although the Aussies extended their Test-win sequence to 10 by beating the Kiwis 3–0, they could not curb Chris Cairns, the cavalier batsman. He belted 13 sixes in the series while making 341 runs at 56.83. He sparkled in the Wellington Test where he played two spectacular innings, 109 with 14 fours and two sixes, and 69 (six sixes and four fours), besides taking four wickets.

In the first innings, he came in to bat when his country was on her knees at 5 for 66. Boldly, adventurously he plundered 72 runs in 54 minutes with Astle and 109 in 113 minutes with Adam Parore. Reported Phil Wilkins in the *Sydney Morning Herald*, 'For almost 3$\frac{1}{2}$ hours, Australia felt the bludgeoning bat of the beefcake no. 7 batsman [Cairns]. Shane Warne's Test record was forgotten in twin puffs of smoke as Cairns sent two deliveries hurtling back overhead in four balls, the first disappearing high into the top tier of the Bob Vance Stand on the straight hit, the second over the mid-wicket fence.'

Chris was even more of a daredevil in the second innings when 75 per cent of his score came in sixes and fours. In the next Test, in Hamilton, the swashbuckling Kiwi hit 37 and 71 (including two sixes) in a bid to rescue his country. Although he disappointed as a bowler in the series, often delivering loosely and taking 10 wickets at 37.90, he was a colossus as a batsman.

This was sweet revenge for Chris Cairns as a leaked document from the Australians prior to the series had stated that he was fragile. 'A good frontrunner but lacks confidence if you get on top of him,' said the secret dossier. Perhaps this inspired him to a man-of-the-series performance in the three Tests. He not only topped the batting average among the New Zealanders, but outscored the Australians. 'Fragile, me? Forsooth!' he could have been forgiven for saying, which he did not. He let his bat do the talking.

Prior to the Wellington fireworks in 1999 and 2000, Chris' happiest Test was at Eden Park, Auckland, against Zimbabwe in January 1996. He scored his maiden Test hundred, belting nine sixes in his 120 off 86 balls. One of the sixes was lifted over the covers onto the roof of the stand. His first 50 came in 58 minutes off 49 balls, and his next 50 in 48 minutes off 37 deliveries. He had missed by only one six to equal the then Test record of 10 sixes, hit by English great Wally Hammond (also at Auckland against New Zealand in 1932–33). Subsequently, Pakistan's Wasim Akram lifted 12 sixes against Zimbabwe at Sheikhupura in 1996–97.

The tall hitting by Chris delighted his father, Lance, who was a six symbol of his time. Although primarily a medium-pacer with an 'unlovely' style, he was massively built and hammered the ball vast distances with a blacksmith's might and relish. Although he represented New Zealand in 43 Tests from 1973 to 1985, Lance is remembered for his hurricane hitting in all classes of cricket. In 1979–80, when already a Test player, he hit a century in 52 minutes off 45 balls for Otago against Wellington – the fastest ton in New Zealand. And he went berserk for Bishop Auckland in Durham, England, against Glostrap, a visiting team from Denmark. He slashed 174 runs in 64 minutes with 16 fours and 15 sixes.

Colossal strength and superb timing enabled Lance to lift sixes beyond the ropes and over the stands. Once in 1992–93 he hit English off-spinner Vic Marks and the ball cleared the roof of Lancaster Park Stand.

The most ecstatic moment in Lance's career was hitting Dennis Lillee for amazing sixes in the Benson & Hedges final on the Melbourne Cricket Ground on 13 February 1983. The Kiwis were in strife, 6 for 44 against Australia's 302 and with Lillee on the kill – cheered on lustily by a parochial crowd of 71,393. Lance was greeted by Lillee with a bouncer that hit him on the helmet. Commentating on Channel 9, Bill Lawry squeaked, 'Cairns' head must be going ding-dong, ding-dong inside that helmet'. When the ringing stopped, cavalier Cairns lifted Ken MacLeay for two sixes in the next over. Not quite satisfied, he smashed Lillee over mid-off for a big six.

'That was okay,' he recalls in his autobiography, *Give it a Heave, Lance Cairns*, 'but two balls later he [Lillee] fired another, right at my toes. I tried to jump out of the way and I sort of swung my bat one-handed. The ball just took off. I couldn't believe it. Greg Chappell was on the fine-leg boundary and he was racing in. Then all of a sudden he stood and stared at the ball. It went miles over his head. He couldn't believe it either!'

At the other end MacLeay was replaced by Rodney Hogg and Cairns lanced his first ball over his head for a six and repeated the dose two balls later. He reached his 50 in 21 balls with six sixes before being caught off a deceptively slow ball by Geoff Lawson.

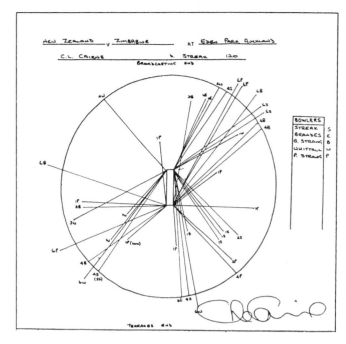

Chris Cairns' run-chart – hitting nine sixes against Zimbabwe (Courtesy *Boundary NZ*).

Six legend Lance Cairns played for Central Districts, Otago, Northern Districts, Durham and New Zealand. He was a bowling all-rounder who swung the ball late and sharp in a heavy atmosphere. He had a hopping, open-chested action reminiscent of Mike Procter although he was much slower. 'Everything I did was natural,' he recalled. 'I never thought which way I held the seam, I just ran in and bowled. It was all so uncomplicated. I was so lucky not to be coached!'

Lance was in and out of the Test teams as his bowling lacked penetration on good pitches and it took a long time to make his presence felt against strong opposition. His first success was against India in the Madras Test of 1976 when he took 5 for 55 in 33.1 overs. He went on to capture 6 for 85 against the mighty Windies in 1979–80, 5 for 87 vs Australia at Brisbane in 1980–81 and 4 for 88 in the next Test at Perth.

In many ways 1983–84 was his finest summer. In the Leeds Test against England he had the marvellous figures of 7 for 74 and 3 for 70 and New Zealand won by five wickets. In the process, he became the first New Zealander to take seven wickets in a

Test innings against England. He did it again, 7 for 143 in the Wellington Test, capturing the first six wickets to fall. It was in this Test that he took his 100th Test scalp, Allan Lamb's. 'There is no pretence about him; nothing but honest endeavour and an outstanding ability to entertain,' wrote Dick Brittenden, the doyen of New Zealand journalists.

Lance's Test career lasted 13 years, from 1973 to 1985, and he scored 928 runs at 16.28 and took 130 wickets at 32.92.

Exit Lance Cairns in 1985 and enter Chris Cairns in 1989. A similar type of cricketer, Chris has a sounder batting technique. To quote Sir Richard Hadlee from *Wisden Cricket Monthly* (January 1997): 'A match winner, probably more with the bat than the ball ... Hits hard and straight ... I think he should bat higher up than he does in one-day games where he could tear an attack apart – he's wasted coming in with only a few overs to go ... shows the potential to become a very good opening bowler or first change. A different type of player than his father, he's technically a better batsman, although he hits the ball nearly as hard! Seems to be enjoying his cricket more these days.'

Despite being close to Lance, Chris proclaims himself a self-made bowler. 'Dad never pushed me. In fact, he taught *me* nothing at all until I was about 14.' Chris made his Test debut against Australia in the Perth Test of November 1989. He was flown in as a replacement for an injured Brendon Bracewell but developed back strain and could not bowl from the second day onwards.

He appeared a threatening bowler in the Auckland Test against England in 1991–92 when he took 6 for 52 and 2 for 86. In the earlier Test at Christchurch he scored 61 with 11 fours and added 117 for the seventh wicket. His other notable Test performances were:

- 4 for 136 and 5 for 75 vs Sri Lanka at Auckland in 1990–91;

- 6 for 52 and 2 for 86 vs England at Auckland in 1991–92;
- 4 for 113 and 78 runs vs Australia at Perth in 1993–94;
- 4 for 90, 3 for 54 and 64 runs vs Australia at Brisbane in 1997–98;
- 4 for 95 and 52 runs vs Australia at Perth in 1997–98;
- 6 for 77 vs England at Lord's in 1999 and 5 for 31 and 81 runs vs England at The Oval in 1999.

His 72 and 10 for 100 against the West Indies at Hamilton in December 1999, his 109 against Australia in March 2000 and his swashbuckling 120 off 86 balls against Zimbabwe in 1995–96 have already been detailed. When in the mood, he can devastate any attack but often he went into a shell and appeared non-communicative. According to Dave Crowe in *ABC Cricket Book 1999–2000*, Chris 'is only a touch away from greatness. Injury, illness and personal tragedy have dogged his career, but he keeps coming back with sensational performances – although, not always consistently. Hits like a mule with straight sixes a specialty and can make a ball sit up on a shirt front. A world beater on his day but enigmatic and unpredictable.'

Chris' tour to Australia in 1993–94 became controversial when he withdrew unexpectedly from the team on the morning of the Hobart Test, citing a bruised heel. He then faced a play-or-go-home ultimatum from the management before the next Test in Brisbane. He played but underperformed. The personal tragedy mentioned above happened in 1994 when his 19-year-old sister, Louise, was killed in a freak train accident near Christchurch. It took Chris a long time to get over this loss.

On current form at Test and limited-overs level, Chris could be considered among five genuine all-rounders. He was made Man of the Series against England in 1999 and the readers of *Wisden Cricket*

Monthly voted him the best all-rounder of the 1999 English season. He won 186 votes, 139 more than South Africa's Lance Klusener who finished at number 3. The same poll ranked Chris as the fourth-best Player of 1999 after Andy Caddick, Steve Waugh and Klusener. As a climax, *Wisden* honoured him as one of the Five Cricketers of the Year 2000.

Chris also played county cricket for Nottinghamshire and is remembered for his blistering 114 against Gloucestershire at Trent Bridge in June 1996. He broke the dressing-room window with one of his three straight sixes and Notts won by an innings in three days. This was their first victory in their 13th championship match in 11 months. There was widespread jubilation in the Notts camp with Chris (who also had taken four wickets) as the hero.

He brushed aside the praise, saying that he had not achieved enough for his county. Instead, he gets inspired by photographs of well-known cricketers on the wall. 'These are my biggest source of motivation, those photographs on the pavilion walls, because I've achieved very little compared with many of them,' he said modestly.

One does not normally associate modesty with bulky opening bowlers and six-smiters, but with Lance 'Steptoe' and son, they do co-exist.

The Cairnses in Test Cricket

	Tests	Runs	Avrge	HS	100s	50s	Wkts	Avrge	Best	5w/i	Catches
Lance	43	928	16.28	64	0	2	130	32.92	7–74	6	30
Chris	47	2396	31.12	126	3	19	160	29.84	7–27	9	14
Total	90	3324	24.81	126	3	21	290	31.22	7–27	15	44

CHAPTER 34

Star
Waughs

——— ● ———

Rock of Gibraltar, Steve Waugh, and poetry in motion, Mark Waugh, are the only twin brothers to play Test cricket. The boys from Bankstown have participated together in 85 Tests to date, setting new milestones in practically every series. From December 1985 till October 2000, one or the other twin has played in 146 of the 147 Tests played by Australia. Each has played over 100 Tests and the run flow goes undiminished. As a leader and a mind-reader, Steve has added new concepts to an old game although he remains a traditionalist. Their uncle, Dion Bourne (now retired), and younger brothers, Dean and Danny, are talented cricketers. Parents Bev and Rodger have been their guiding lights.

JOY COMETH IN THE morning. It came three times in the very early mornings in June 1999 for patriotic Australians watching the final stages of the World Cup in England on television. The two matches against South Africa which enabled them to enter the semi-final and the final were among the most heart-pounding, hair-raising thrillers I have ever witnessed. New captain Steve Waugh, with a lot to prove to come out of Mark Taylor's shadow, and Mark Waugh – all elegance when batting or gobbling up acrobatic slip catches – were two of the heroes to beat a strong South African line-up. Australia, under Steve, out-smarted the opponents, psyching them into mental paralysis at the end.

Compared to these spine-chillers, the final against Pakistan was an anti-climax, but the superhuman catches by Mark Waugh and Ricky Ponting are images impossible to wipe from one's memory bank. The victory kept true-blue Aussie cricket fans awake all night, and they must have agreed with Lord Byron's sentiment: 'On with the dance! Let joy be unconfined / No sleep till morn, when youth and pleasure meet / To chase the glowing hours with flying feet.'

The two Australia vs South Africa cliffhangers were classics in the Brisbane tied-Test mould. South Africa's opener, Herschelle Gibbs, was both the hero and the villain of the first encounter at Headingley, Leeds, on 13 June. He scored

Shane (left) and Brett Lee having a brotherly chat during the CUB final against Pakistan on the SCG in January 2000. (*Allsport / Jack Atley*)

Chappelli, the happy hooker. (*Allsport / Don Morley*)

Danny Waugh, the youngest of the famous brotherhood. (*K.M.-H.*)

Emotionally charged, Chris Cairns claims another wicket during the 1999 Oval Test.
(*Allsport / Adrian Murrell*)

Adam (left) and Ben Hollioake made simultaneous Test debuts vs Australia in 1997.
(*Allsport / Clive Mason*)

Terrific together. Neil Harvey with Alan Davidson and Richie Benaud. (*J. Fairfax*)

Brett Lee shows off his baggy green cap before his sensational debut against India. (*Allsport / Hamish Blair*)

"HE WAS A SUPERB CRAFTSMAN, AND A MATCH PROFESSIONAL" JOHN ARLOTT

J.T.Hearne

J.T. Hearne performed four hat-tricks in first-class cricket.
(*Courtesy, Percy Samara-Wickrama of Australian Cricket Society*)

101 of his team's total of 7 for 271. Australia lost 3 for 48 when Steve Waugh came in. He was in superb touch and reached his 50 in 47 balls, his backfoot drives fairly burning the Headingley grass. When 56, he offered a straightforward catch to Gibbs at mid-wicket. In excitement he 'caught' it and immediately threw it up before controlling it and the umpire ruled not out.

'Ice Man' Steve allegedly mumbled something about Gibbs dropping the World Cup. This turned out to be accurate and the catch-that-wasn't proved morale-shattering for the Proteas. Give one chance, one whiff, to Steve when he has that glint in his eyes and the opponents are finished. He added 126 runs with Ponting and remained unbeaten with 120 when Australia reached the target with five wickets and two balls to spare. There was joy unconfined on the Australian balcony. They had started their World Cup '99 campaign shakily in May, losing to New Zealand and Pakistan. But this victory took them to the semi-final and mentally they were at their toughest.

It was like an action replay in the semi-final, with the same combatants at each other's throats four days later. It was 'High Noon' at Edgbaston, Birmingham, the shining silver guns ready in the skippers' holsters. Steve played mind games, stressing the fragility of the Proteas under pressure; Hansie Cronje reminding him of his country's gold medal in the Commonwealth Games at Kuala Lumpur the year before.

Shaun Pollock and Allan Donald fired the first salvos and Australia was dismissed for 213 (Michael Bevan 65, Steve 65). What followed was heart-stopping stuff as the match fluctuated bewilderingly. South Africa recovered from 4 for 61 when Jacques Kallis and Jonty Rhodes added 84 runs. The 45th over signalled the start of madness. Kallis was dropped in the deep, Shaun Pollock hit a six and a four, then Shane Warne had Kallis caught by Steve.

Just as the Proteas looked sunk, in walked Lance 'Zulu' Klusener, the Man of the World Cup '99. He counterattacked and brought his country close to victory. Steve remained icy cool and confident. Damien Fleming bowled the final over and the scores were level with four balls to go and the last pair at the wicket. Klusener was on strike and only one was needed in four balls. Surely they couldn't lose now. There was a near run-out during the third ball, panic and pandemonium, but Steve kept his cool. The next ball was a fuller delivery, Klusener hit it and ran. Last man Donald remained rooted to the crease watching the ball; both he and Klusener were at the bowler's end. Mark Waugh's backhand flick went to Fleming who rolled the ball to wicket-keeper Adam Gilchrist. Waking up, Donald dropped his bat and ran, but it was too late and he was easily run out. It was musical comedy stuff for the Aussies, but a tragic opera without songs for the South Africans.

Although the game resulted in a tie, the Australians entered the final because they had finished higher on the Super Six table. There was confusion, agonising heartbreak and sheer ecstasy, all-night celebration and tear-filled eyes. 'The best cricket game I've ever played,' said Steve.

Anything after this real-life drama would be an anticlimax and the final against Pakistan at Lord's was just that. Australia won by eight wickets with 29.5 overs in hand. What a night for Steve Waugh and his merry band of men! He and squad member, the tall Tom Moody, also recalled Australia's surprise World Cup win in Calcutta in 1987. But nothing could equal those two matches against South Africa in June 1999.

Before the '99 victory, Steve's captaincy had been under the microscope; un-favourable comparisons were made with Taylor's leadership. Steve had made his Test captaincy debut in the West Indies, and although he won two Tests the critics came down heavily on him for his two losses – one by just a wicket, thanks to

Brian Lara's magnificent one-man show. However, those cliffhanger victories over South Africa won over the doubters.

Since then, Australia has lost only one Test (to Sri Lanka in Kandy when Steve and Jason Gillespie had an on-field collision and ended up in a hospital) and five one-dayers. More importantly, they have won 10 Tests in a row, victories over Zimbabwe and 3–0 clean sweeps over Pakistan, India and New Zealand in 1999–2000. This 10-win sequence is a record for Australia and only one short of the world record by the West Indies in the 1980s. Steve Waugh is his own man and no longer in Taylor's shadow ('we are different individuals'). Now he is compared favourably with attacking Australian captains Warwick Armstrong, Don Bradman, Richie Benaud, Ian Chappell and Mark Taylor. The secret behind Steve's success as captain is that he puts enormous faith in his players. Justin Langer says he owes his recent success to Steve, who believed in his ability.

Under Taylor, Australia had problems chasing small targets (e.g., against South Africa on the SCG in 1993–94, against England at The Oval in 1997 and on the MCG in 1998–99), or suffered a loss after a Test series was won – the so-called 'dead series syndrome'. Steve has seen to it that such complacency does not creep in. Australia's top batsmen still collapse (viz., 4 for 54 vs Pakistan at Perth; 4 for 52 vs India at Adelaide; 4 for 51 and 5 for 29 vs New Zealand at Wellington and Hamilton in 1999–2000) but they do not get perturbed. Someone comes along – usually Steve himself – and not only saves the sinking ship but converts it into a luxury ocean liner.

Steve has scored 22 Test centuries and nine scores in the nineties (one world record he does not cherish). He is the only cricketer to play an innings of 150 against all Test-playing nations. In 128 Tests he has scored 8373 runs at 50.44, taken 89 wickets and 92 catches. Most of his runs have come during crises and it is difficult to pinpoint an innings as his greatest. Personally, I would go for his twin hundreds in the Manchester Test of 1997.

Australia was one down in the series and Taylor shocked friends and foes by electing to bat on a green pitch. The score was 3 for 42 when in walked Steve, twirling his bat and doing some sit-ups, touching the lucky red rag in his pocket. At first he fumbled, played and missed but survived, and despite a painful injury to his right hand he scored 108. It was his 13th Test century and was watched by wife Lynette, one-year-old daughter Rosalie, mother Bev and Lynette's family.

The second innings was a TV replay of the first. Arrives Steve, bat twirling, red rag at the ready, with the Aussies 3 down for 39, and scores 116 despite crippling pain. To quote Greg Baum from the *Sydney Morning Herald*, 'Few batsmen in the world could have made Waugh's first innings century and he alone could have made another in the second innings, with his right hand so badly bruised from the battery of the first match that he was still wearing a bandage on it the day after the match. It was the ultimate "Waugh wound".'

In all, he had batted for 10 hours and hit 24 fours practically one-handed. An English columnist suggested that ball bearings, and not blood, flowed through his defiant frame. AAP correspondent Doug Conway added in my *The Waugh Twins*: 'The more pressure you put on Steve Waugh the more he concentrates and bats all day. He becomes so totally engrossed in the mental struggles of cricket that there is no room for anything else ... It is as if his batting becomes a cocoon from the cares and woes of the world outside.'

I was fortunate enough to see the 100th Tests played by both Steve and Mark Waugh, both on the SCG, Steve's against South Africa in January 1998 and Mark's against India in January 2000. Steve made

85 in his 100th Test but Mark celebrated his brother's big day by scoring a round 100. In Mark's 100th Test he made 32 and Steve 57, but as Australia won by an innings they did not have a second chance to hit a ton. In the in-between Sydney Test, against England in January 1999, Mark scored 121 and added 190 runs with Steve who made 96, his ninth score in the nervous nineties – an unenviable Test record. Mark also took his 100th catch in this Test.

Born four minutes before Mark on 2 June 1965, Steve played Sheffield Shield a year before Mark and Test cricket five years before him. Parents Bev and Rodger, both excellent tennis players, married at 18 and had the twins a year later. Both boys had exceptional hand–eye–ball skills when toddlers. 'They were barely two but seldom dropped a catch,' remembers Rodger. 'I couldn't believe it.' And there was cricket on Bev's side. Her brother, Dion Bourne, played first-grade with Bankstown for 21 years, captaining it later with distinction. He scored 8243 runs at 28.03 and was a selector for New South Wales. He could see talent in the twins when they were 12. 'They were obviously first-grade cricketers,' he told me. 'I was keen for Lennie Pascoe [former fast bowler for Australia] to meet the 12-year-olds and help them. He agreed but returned saying, "Look, they can teach me more than I can teach them".'

The only time Mark was ahead of Steve was when he played first-grade cricket a year before. Mark made his presence felt by scoring 98 as an opening batsman in 1981–82, when 16. Mark has been nicknamed 'Junior' and 'Afghan' (the forgotten Waugh). Steve has been nicknamed 'Drobe' (from wardrobe) and 'Tugga' (tug-of-Waugh).

It took Steve four years to score his first Test century. He had made his debut in the Boxing Day Test of 1985 against India on the MCG and scored his first Test ton, 177 not out, at Headingley, Leeds in 1989. This was his 27th Test. He followed this with 152 not out in his next Test at Lord's and finished the series on a high: 506 runs at 126.50. The British press gave him the full treatment with punny headlines: 'Declaration of Waugh', 'Post-Waugh Depression for England', and 'The New Don Bradman'.

A no-frills realist, Steve only smiled when compared to Sir Donald. 'That's bull,' he said. Just as well that he is a realist. Sixteen months and 10 Tests later he was unceremoniously dropped from the Australian team. And who should replace him in the Adelaide Test of January 1991? His twin brother Mark, not an 'Afghan' any more. There were mixed reactions in the family, Bev not knowing whether to dance with joy for Mark's well-deserved call-up or shed tears for Steve's cruel dumping.

Mark's Test debut was sensational. Against 27 Tests taken by Steve to hit his first ton, Mark reached one in his first. He scored 138 of the best after waiting in the wings as Steve played 42 Tests. Raved John Thickeness in *Wisden* (1992): 'He produced an innings which a batsman of any generation would have been overjoyed to play any time in his career, let alone in a first Test appearance and in a situation which verged on crisis'. A few months later, Mark scored 139 not out with three sixes and 11 fours in the St John's Test in the West Indies against a frightening pace attack of Curtly Ambrose, Malcolm Marshall, Patrick Patterson and Courtney Walsh.

As Mark was scaling the heights, Steve refused to sit back and bask in his past glory or his twin's recent star status. He went back to basics, eliminated all risky strokes, scored mountains of runs at first-grade and Sheffield Shield level and reappeared on the Test scene in the Port-of-Spain Test in Trinidad, four months after his premature exit.

This Test is unique as it is the first time twin brothers had played together in a

Test. Since that Test in Trinidad, the Waugh twins have played 85 Tests together. Next best among brothers are Ian and Greg Chappell (43) and Zimbabwe's Andy and Grant Flower (42 so far). From December 1985 to October 1999, one Waugh brother or the other has been included in 146 of the 147 Tests Australia have played. The Perth Test of February 1992 against India has been the only Waugh-less Test since 1986.

Most of the time, the twins have shone in different matches, but twice they combined brilliantly. The first time was in a Sheffield Shield (now Pura Cup) match against Western Australia on the WACA ground in Perth on 20 and 21 December 1990. They produced the highest partnership in Australian first-class history. Both recorded unbeaten double-hundreds (a unique feat for brothers at first-class level) and they added 464 runs – a world record for the fifth wicket. Both played chancelessly and majestically, exhibiting glorious strokes against a Test-class attack including Terry Alderman and Bruce Reid. 'The best bowling attack in Australia was reduced to a gibbering rabble, because of the pair's inexhaustible batting talents,' reported Greg Growden in the *Sydney Morning Herald*.

Mark's unbeaten 229 came off 343 deliveries and included 35 fours and a spectacular six off Ken MacLeay which cleared 15 rows of seats in the pavilion. Steve's 216 not out came off 339 balls as he belted 24 fours. Rodney Marsh ranks this Waugh batting extravaganza the greatest he has witnessed on the ground.

It was a great year for Mark as he amassed 3079 runs at 81.02 for Essex and New South Wales in 1990 to become the 10th Australian to total over 3000 runs in a calendar year. The selectors could ignore him no longer and he made his sensational Test debut the following month – as already described.

The second time the twins combined prodigiously was in the Kingston Test in the Caribbean in 1995. It was a partnership to cherish, the partnership that destroyed the wall of superiority of the Windies. For 15 years and 29 Test series, they were the undisputed kings of cricket. They had a galaxy of great batsmen and a quartet of intimidating speedsters who not only defeated their opponents but pulverised them. However, 3 May 1995 saw a changing of the guard at Sabina Park, Kingston. After losing their last eight Test series to the Windies since 1978, Australia suddenly staked their claim as world champions by defeating them by an innings and regaining the Frank Worrell Trophy 2–1. The Waugh twins were the heroes behind this remarkable turnaround.

In reply to the opponents' total of 265, Australia totalled 531, thanks to an incandescent stand of 231 runs by the awesome twosome. On 30 April, Mark knuckled down to score 116 runs and Steve was unbeaten on 110, playing with an air of invincibility. Big, fiery Ambrose, with whom Steve had had an on-field altercation in the previous Test, bowled only 11 overs that day and his pace partner, Winston Benjamin, sat weeping during the drinks break. Steve continued relentlessly the next day and was unremovable until he hit his only Test double hundred.

Robert Craddock wrote in *Wisden* (1996): 'He [Steve] was the last out, batting for close on 10 hours and 425 balls, more than 150 short-pitched, and had 17 fours, one six and six aching bruises at the end of his greatest innings'. Trailing by 266 runs, the Windies were bowled out for 213 and lost the Test, the series and their world-beating image by one gigantic knockout punch. It was the pinnacle in the lives of Steve and Mark Waugh. In the series, Steve totalled 429 runs at a Bradmanesque average of 107.25 and Mark 240 at 40. No other Australian could average 30. Steve was adjudged undisputed Player of the Series.

Further triumphs awaited the twins in South Africa in 1997, where Steve added 385 winning runs with Greg Blewett in the Johannesburg Test, which Australia won by an innings. Not to be sidelined, Mark etched out a masterly 116 in the next Test at Port Elizabeth which enabled Australia to win the series. Following this, the Waugh twins were ranked as the two best batsmen in the world by the Coopers & Lybrand rating system. Steve had been ranked number one since his Kingston masterpiece in 1995 and Mark leapfrogged over Brian Lara and England's Alec Stewart after his heroic century at Port Elizabeth.

At 32, Steve was appointed as Australia's vice-captain and as captain of Australia in Limited-Overs Internationals. In early 1999 he took over as Australia's skipper in both forms. He was 33 then and has led Australia with authority and success. Australia's World Cup '99 victory and 10 Test wins in a row (sequence still unbroken) have been already chronicled. He stressed the mental aspect of the game ('Cricket is 95 per cent mental,' he maintains). Under him, everyone in a baggy green cap performs above his ability.

Steve has wisely changed gears since he first started his career. 'In 1985, Steve Waugh was Australia's batting Porsche ... a young thrasher,' wrote Robert Craddock in Sydney's *Daily Telegraph*. 'Now he is a trusty Bentley who might not break speed records but invariably goes the long journey.' Steve concurs. 'If I played the same way I did when I was 20, I wouldn't be playing now. I was flashy and good to watch, but like so many other players who have batted for Australia, would have been out of the team.' Mike Coward wrote in *The Australian*: 'The most complete person in the Australian first-class game, [Steve] Waugh has had a prolonged effect on countless Test, Sheffield Shield, grade, schoolboy, parkland and backyard cricketers. And like Border before him, he is a hero not only to kids but to many of the men who play alongside him under the baggy green cap he considers so sacred.'

Mark tries to be tougher in his approach without divorcing his wristy and risky flicks and glances. He is among the most fluent stroke-players in the world, along with Stan McCabe, Denis Compton, Neil Harvey, Greg Chappell, Mohammad Azharuddin, Martin Crowe and Sachin Tendulkar. The year 1998 saw the emergence of a new Mark Waugh. He proved that he can now bat all day without loss of concentration or a rush of blood. He showed Border-like doggedness against the South Africans on the kill in Adelaide in February and against confident Indians in Bangalore, to rescue Australia from the brink of disaster in March. Despite his inconsistent form of late, Mark has scored 6593 runs at 41.73 with 17 centuries in 103 Tests. He has also taken 50 wickets and 132 catches. He needs only 26 catches to surpass his namesake Mark Taylor's Test record of 157 catches.

Apart from his superlative record as a batsman and captain, Steve is a man of compassion. When he toured India in early 1998 he visited the children of leprosy sufferers at Udayan Resurrection Home, 35 kilometres north of Calcutta. The plight of the children and how they took to him galvanised him to devote considerable time and energy to raise funds for a building block to accommodate female children of leprosy victims. In a short time he raised US$33,000 and in recognition of his efforts he was appointed patron of the girls' wing at the Udayan Home.

The spotlight is focused so intensely on Steve and Mark that the younger brothers Dean and Danny have become the real 'Afghans'. Dean, 31, is a delightful striker of the ball who has spasmodically represented both New South Wales and, of late, South Australia. He blazed 1019 runs at 56.61 for Bankstown in 1995–96, including a blockbuster knock of 210 against Mosman on the North Sydney Oval. This prompted his inclusion in the New South Wales team against Allan Border-led Queensland in the Sheffield Shield on the SCG. Going in at No. 5, Dean scored 19 and 3 and caught Border. As this was Border's final innings on the SCG, Dean remembers this catch with pride. It was also his last Sheffield Shield appearance.

In the first-grade final the following month he captained Bankstown, and among the players under him were Steve, Mark and Danny Waugh. 'Pity we lost, but it was a moment to cherish; all four brothers in the same team in a grand final,' he recalled. He opened and made 22 and a top score of 59, Steve 23 and 14, Mark 3 and 13, Danny 4 and 23.

The youngest, Danny, now 23, is not overawed by his elder brothers' reputations. Unlike them, he is blond, a left-hander, a spinner, and he smiles a lot. He was selected for New South Wales Under-16s and has played first-grade for Bankstown and Sydney University. As a left-arm orthodox spinner he has taken a few five-wicket hauls, and as a batsman hit a few centuries. 'Steve and Mark give me occasional tips but I try to iron out my faults myself.' His role model was Border, but his favourite cricketer is Vivian Richards. Danny and Steve have a special bond and they enjoy each other's company.

For all the brothers, their guiding light has been their parents – especially mum Bev, who somehow managed to watch all four sons playing on different venues every Saturday. 'The boys are talented but that's just a gift. It's how you use talents you have is the thing to be proud of,' says Bev, a squash champion who teaches handicapped children to swim and never to give up. 'To see your children – whatever their age – perform, be it ballet, music or sport, you want them to achieve their best. And when they do, it is one of the greatest thrills in life.'

The Waughs in Test Cricket

	Tests	Runs	Avrge	HS	100s	50s	Wkts	Avrge	Best	5w/i	Catches
Steve	128	8373	50.44	200	22	42	89	36.03	5–28	3	92
Mark	103	6593	41.73	153*	17	38	50	39.22	5–40	1	132
Total	231	14,966	46.19	200	39	80	139	37.18	5–28	4	224

The Waughs in Limited-Overs Internationals

	Tests	Runs	Avrge	HS	100s	50s	Wkts	Avrge	Best	5w/i	Catches
Steve	295	6705	31.78	120*	2	40	191	34.87	4–33	0	103
Mark	217	7517	38.35	130	14	47	83	33.55	5–24	1	90
Total	512	14,222	34.94	130	16	87	274	34.47	5–24	1	193

CHAPTER 35

Flower
Power

———— ● ————

The Flower brothers, Andy and Grant, have been synonymous with
Zimbabwe cricket. Andy has, so far, appeared in all Tests played by
Zimbabwe since its baptism in 1992–93, and Grant has missed only one.
In their country's first Test victory they scored centuries in the same
innings. Occasionally, they have opened Zimbabwe's batting
in Limited-Overs Internationals.

IT WAS A MAGICAL moment for the youngest Test-playing nation. They had played 10 Tests that far in three years without winning one. Then came the Test in Harare against a strong Pakistan line-up in early 1995. The Test began on a farcical note. Pakistan 'won' the toss but as match referee Jackie Hendricks of the West Indies did not hear the call, he requested a re-spin. Andy Flower, Zimbabwe's captain, wicket-keeper and two-years-older brother of Grant Flower, won the re-toss and elected to bat. They were soon in trouble, losing 2 for 9, then 3 for 42 when Andy (aged 26) joined brother Grant.

They remained unbeaten until the end of the day, adding 247 runs in Zimbabwe's 3 for 289. Grant, who had opened the innings, was steadfast on 88 and Andy, the lucky captain, batted as if there was no tomorrow and was unbeaten on 142. They had resisted some testing overs from

Wasim Akram, whose seven overs after lunch were maidens. The following day, the brothers added 22 more runs before Andy was caught for a chanceless 156. Their partnership of 269 was not only a record for Zimbabwe (since then broken by Andy Flower and Murray Goodwin in March 1998), but also a fraternal record, overtaking Ian and Greg Chappell's record partnership between brothers of 264 runs (vs New Zealand at Wellington in 1973–74). It still stands, despite strong challenge from the Waugh twins, Steve and Mark. (See the table at the end of this chapter for a list of centuries by brothers in the same Test innings.)

Andy was the dominant partner, reaching his second Test century in 210 minutes. However, Pakistan's joy of seeing his back was short-lived because a stand as enormous and morale-sapping developed between Grant and Guy

Whittall. They added 233 for the unbroken fifth wicket, Grant 201 not out and Whittall 113 not out. It was maiden Test hundreds for each. This was too much for the Pakistani bowlers. Only a week before, these two had added 215 for the second wicket for the President's XI (Grant 137, Whittall 104).

Back to the Harare Test. Grant was dropped at 24 and 98 and took 343 balls to reach his hundred but then accelerated to convert it to a double-century in another 177 deliveries. He had batted for 11 hours and hit only 10 fours in a marathon display of discipline and concentration. Andy declared at 4 for 544 as Pakistan's captain, Salim Malik, sorely regretted match referee Hendricks' poor hearing on the previous morning. The visitors replied with 322 and 159 as Zimbabweans celebrated their first Test triumph and that too by a huge margin of an innings and 64 runs. Asbestos man Grant was on the field on all five days. Apart from contributing 357 runs, the Flower brothers took five catches, Grant holding two blinders in the gully to dismiss well-set batsmen Ijaz Ahmed (65) and Inzamam-ul-Haq (71). The brothers were adjudged joint Men of the Match.

Three years earlier, they were also made joint Men of the Match. In the Delhi Test against India in March 1993, Grant (96) and Andy (115) had added 192 runs for the fourth wicket. Andy had scored Zimbabwe's first overseas century and Grant was poised to follow. However, a solitary lapse in concentration on Andy's part was sufficient to kill the momentum. He was stumped and Grant soon followed four short of his ton and Zimbabwe collapsed from 3 for 275 to 321 all out. They lost by an innings despite Andy's defiant 62 not out in the second innings. Cricket is indeed a leveller. In the Rawalpindi Test against Pakistan in December 1993, Grant scored 0 and 0, Andy 12 and 0; three ducks in the family in one Test.

A match to remember for Grant was in the Lonrho Logan Cup in November 1996.

His team, Mashonaland, declared at 4 for 503 against Matabeleland. He remained unbeaten with 243, adding 231 for the first wicket with Stuart Carlisle (96) and 233 for the second with A.C. Walker (104). This was reminiscent of the 1995 Harare Test against Pakistan. Brother Andy was 4 not out at the declaration as the Flower brothers amassed 247 runs without being dismissed.

The inaugural Test against England was remarkable and ended in bitter controversy. Played at Bulawayo in December 1996, it ended in a draw despite both teams making an identical total of 610. With Andy scoring his third Test century (112) and Grant 43, Zimbabwe totalled 376. England led by 30 runs and on the final day were set 205 runs to win from 37 overs. That is when the drama began and 'a gently smouldering match burst into full flame on the last afternoon', to quote *Wisden* (1998). England batsmen were frustrated by Zimbabwe's alleged negative bowling. The match seesawed and in the end England needed five runs to win from the last three balls but could only manage four. As all the wickets had not fallen, the match was not a tie but a draw. The English team was incensed as the umpires did not call 'wide' when Heath Streak bowled off-line in the final pulsating over. In an outburst of temper, England's manager David Lloyd said, 'we flipping murdered them'. Streak himself admitted later that he was lucky not to have been called.

Born on 28 April 1968, Andy Flower is a left-hand middle-order batsman who keeps wicket on occasions. He has opened the batting with Grant in some Limited-Overs Internationals. Although he is more adventurous with the bat than Grant, he is not as spectacular as team-mate Alistair Campbell. Both Andy and Grant are capable of playing defiant innings with total concentration for hours and know the discipline involved in heavy scoring at Test level.

Andy hit five successive fifties in

Limited-Overs Internationals against Kenya in 1998, but so far has made only one limited-overs century. That was his unbeaten 115 in the 1992 World Cup against Sri Lanka in New Plymouth. With Andy Waller, he added 145 dazzling runs in the last 13 overs as Zimbabwe totalled 4 for 312 at 6.24 runs an over, but still lost. Another match to remember for Andy was his unbeaten 139 off 149 balls (23 fours and a six) against Queensland at Maryborough in December 1994. On this short tour to Australia, Andy was the captain but did not keep wicket. Normally a sound wicket-keeper, he is not brilliant and experts believe his batting will improve if he is relieved of his wicket-keeping duties.

Grant William Flower, born on 20 December 1970, is a determined right-hand batsman, slow left-hand bowler and a brilliant close-in fielder. He plays long innings and is among the most stylish batsmen in Zimbabwe. His cover drives are a treat to watch. He reserves his best for Tests in Harare. His unbeaten 201 against Pakistan and his two double-century stands have already been detailed. His finest series to date was against New Zealand in 1998. In the first Test at Harare in February he became the first Zimbabwean to record centuries in both innings; 104 and 151. Cricket is a strange game. This Test could well have been among his worst. Before he had scored, he was caught off a no-ball and went on to make history, reaching his second century of the Test with a six. Set 403 runs to win, Zimbabwe was lucky to draw the match, being 9 for 311 at the close. Grant was made Man of the Match.

This Test is referred to as a 'Happy Family' reunion. For the first time in Test history, three sets of brothers played for the same side. They were Andy and Grant Flower, Paul and Bryan Strang and John and Gavin Rennie. Also, the 12th man for Zimbabwe was Andy Whittal, the cousin of Guy, who was in the team. To add to the family touch, the New Zealand team included Chris Cairns (son of Lance) and

he took 5 for 50. In the second Test at Bulawayo, Grant scored 83 and 49 and was voted as the Player of the Series.

Not that Flower power blossomed only at home. Earlier, against Pakistan in the first Test in Sheikhupura, Grant scored 110 and 46, full of stylish cover drives. In the first innings he added 131 runs with Paul Strang for the seventh wicket.

Zimbabwe lost an acrimonious Test series in Sri Lanka in 1997–98. The second Test in Colombo was fairly explosive. Andy scored an unbeaten 105 in the second innings. Set 326 runs to win, Sri Lanka reached the target with five wickets in hand but the visitors were very unhappy with decisions given in favour of home batsmen. Zimbabwe's coach, David Houghton, was reported as saying, 'I feel the umpires raped us'.

The Test against Pakistan at Bulawayo in March 1998 was a Flower brothers match, as Grant scored 156 in the first innings (adding 77 runs for the fourth wicket with Andy) and Andy hit an unbeaten 100 in the second. Andy added 277 for the unbroken fifth wicket with Murray Goodwin (166 not out). This broke the 269-run partnership record between the Flower brothers in the 1995 Harare Test.

One landmark was established and one lost during Zimbabwe's Test against India in Harare in October 1998. Zimbabwe won, their second victory in 31 Tests, and Andy became the first Zimbabwean to reach 2000 runs. Before this Test, Grant was the leading scorer with 1991 runs, but he had to miss this Test after breaking a finger in a club match. This ruined the brothers, unbroken sequence of playing together in all of Zimbabwe's Tests. At the time of writing, Andy has played all 43 Tests for his country and Grant 42. Only the Waugh twins, Steve and Mark, and the Chappell brothers are ahead of them in dual representations.

Then followed the World Cup 1999 in England, and Zimbabwe recorded some shock wins. In a thriller, they defeated

India by three runs after Zimbabwe totalled 252, mainly through Grant's 45 and Andy's unbeaten 68. Grant also took a marvellous catch at cover to dismiss India's in-form batsman Rahul Dravid and was adjudged Man of the Match. Zimbabwe went on to defeat the mighty South Africans and entered Super Six.

Andy dominated the series against Sri Lanka at home in late 1999. He scored 86 and 15 not out in the first Test at Bulawayo; 74 (when coming in at 3 down for 0 after Nuwan Zoysa had completed a hat-trick) and 129 in the second Test at Harare; and 14 and 70 not out in the final Test, also in Harare. Thus he had totalled 388 runs at 97.00 in the three drawn Tests. Grant's performance was disappointing but aroused interest among triviologists as his last three innings were 13, 13 and 13.

In the Port-of-Spain Test of March 2000 against the West Indies, Andy scored 113 not out, his seventh Test hundred. This helped Zimbabwe to a 49-run first-innings lead. However, when set an easy target of 99 they collapsed for a pitiful 63, succumbing to the ageing and recharged Windies pace factory. Grant was the only one to enter double figures, scoring 26 valiant runs when wickets shattered all around him.

Between the two, Andy and Grant Flower have scored 5129 runs at 36.90, hit 12 centuries and 25 fifties, accepted 136 catches and effected five stumpings. By hitting centuries in the same Test twice and appearing together in 42 Tests out of a possible 43, they have placed themselves in the same category as the Mohammads, the Chappells, the Pollocks and the Waughs. No higher compliment is possible.

The Flowers in Test Cricket

	Tests	Runs	Avrge	HS	100s	50s	Wkts	Avrge	Best	5w/i	Catches/ stumpings
Andy	43	2842	44.41	156	7	17	0	–	–	–	109/5
Grant	42	2287	30.49	201*	5	8	6	93.33	1–4	–	27
Total	85	5129	36.90	201*	12	25	6	93.33	1–4	–	136/5

Centuries by brothers in the same Test Innings

Brothers (score)	Partnership	Wkt	For/against	Venue	Season
Grant (201*) & Andy (156) Flower	269	4th	Zim. v. Pak.	Harare	1994–95
Ian (145) & Greg (247*) Chappell	264	3rd	Aus. v. NZ	Wellington	1973–74
Mark (126) & Steve (200) Waugh	231	4th	Aus. v. WI	Kingston	1994–95
Ian (118) & Greg (113) Chappell	201	3rd	Aus. v. Eng.	The Oval	1972–73
Sadiq (103*) & Mushtaq (101) Mohammad	–	–	Pak. v. NZ	Hyderabad	1976–77
Ian (121) & Greg (133) Chappell	86	3rd	Aus. v. NZ	Wellington	1973–74

CHAPTER 36

The
Pacey Lees

———— ● ————

The Aussie media proclaimed Brett Lee's Test debut as Lee-thal.
The Lee brothers, Shane and Brett, joined the Waugh twins in the
one-day internationals in the new millennium and jointly contributed to
Australia's near invincibility. As Brett revs up to become the first bowler
to beat the 100 mph (about 160 km/h) speed barrier, Shane does not like to
bask in his younger brother's glory. An attacking batsman, he became the
second batsman after Steve Waugh to hit the Mercantile Mutual sign in
1998. And there is a third brother, Grant, who gave up cricket for music.

THERE ARE NOT MANY bowlers who can make spectators tremble by just watching them perform 100 metres away. The Windies super-quickies, Wes Hall and Roy Gilchrist, made me duck and weave at that distance in Brabourne Stadium, Bombay, in the late 1950s. So did Jeff Thomson, John Snow (not express but demonic) and Curtly Ambrose in the 1970s and 1980s, and a young blond New South Wales bowler during a Sheffield Shield match on the Sydney Cricket Ground in 1997.

He was Brett Lee, and was he fast! He bored holes in the wicket-keeper's gloves – or so it seemed – and sent shivers down my spine. Therefore, I was not surprised when he was picked in the 1999 Boxing Day Test against India. Conservatives felt

there was no need to include a new paceman when Glenn McGrath, Damien Fleming and Michael Kasprowicz had sent capable Pakistani batsmen packing in Perth, but Brett oozed confidence. He had just broken West Australian player Jo Angel's forearm and impressed all who saw his lightning speed in Perth in a Pura Cup match and when playing for the Prime Minister's XI against India in Canberra. 'I'm ready,' he said prior to his Test selection. 'At the start of the year the plan was just to establish myself with the Blues [NSW team], but with the way things have gone and with the way I've matured, I feel I have the confidence to handle a call-up if I get one.'

In 16 first-class matches that far, he had captured 71 wickets at 22.07, a superior average to those of Dennis Lillee and Jeff Thomson before their Test debuts. However, statistics only partly measured up his potential. There was the speed factor, the fright factor – especially with most Indian batsmen's dislike for short, rib-cage bouncers. Both the Waugh brothers lauded Brett's pace like fire in Perth. Steve labelled him as the fastest he had witnessed that summer, the 'Rawalpindi Express' Shoaib Akhtar included. 'He [Brett] has got genuine pace, there is no disputing that,' he added. Mark Waugh at first slip concurred, his fingers sore from trying to stop nicks off Brett streaking to the fence. 'The fastest guy I had faced before was West Indian Ian Bishop,' said West Australian quickie Jo Angel, whose forearm Brett had broken a week before the Melbourne Test. 'But I'd say Brett is as quick as, if not quicker than, Bishop ever was.'

'He's lightning,' Bob Simpson said. 'If the selectors deem him ready, then the fact he is inexperienced shouldn't come into consideration.' NSW coach, Steve Small, summed it up neatly: 'He knows where he wants to be, where he's going and, from what I've seen, he deserves a chance.'

It was a Christmas of expectation and anxiety for the Lee family. A month earlier, Brett was included in the squad for the final Test against Pakistan but only carried drinks. Would he play in the Melbourne Test? Wrote elder brother, Shane, a member of the Australian teams for the World Cups in 1996 and 1999, in the *Sun-Herald*, 'My little brother Brett is probably the most ferocious fast bowler in the country but he has been in hell to get there. Today when he makes his debut in the Australian cricket team against India in Melbourne, I will be in the stand watching, the proudest big brother in the country. Back in Wollongong Mum and Dad – and no doubt a horde of friends – will watch from home.'

And what a sensational debut it turned out to be! Brett batted before he bowled and was more nervous being padded up than when handed the ball. Going in at No. 10, he scored 27 and added 59 runs with Fleming for the ninth wicket. Then coming as a first-change bowler, he took a wicket in his first over, another wicket soon after and three wickets in four balls in his 14th over. It was a spectacular start, a real-life Boy's Own Adventure.

The Test belonged to the 'Master' (Indian captain Sachin Tendulkar who hit a magnificent century) and the 'Blaster' (Brett Lee who captured 5 for 47 in 18 terrifying overs). He became the first Australian to take five wickets in his first Test innings since Simon Cook in 1997–98 against New Zealand. This is how Brett destroyed the Indian batting. He clean-bowled opening batsman Sadagopan Ramesh off his fourth delivery, making him the first Australian to grab a wicket in his opening over since leg-spinner Tony Mann did so in Brisbane against India in 1977–78. Then he had classy bat Rahul Dravid caught behind. In his 14th over he bowled Mannava Prasad and had Ajit Agarkan lbw off successive balls. Two balls later he had Javagal Srinath caught in the slip, thus missing the coveted hat-trick on debut, but had India on the run from 5 for 167 to 8 for 169.

Brett excited spectators with the incisiveness of his approach, resembling a fire-spitting dragon as he shattered wickets and came perilously close to the as yet uncharted 100 mph (159.1 km/h) milestone. His fastest in this Test was 154.1 km/h, just 0.4 behind Shoaib Akhtar's vociferous velocity. In the second innings, Brett took two wickets and crushed Ramesh's thumb with a lifter that aborted the Indian's tour. Brett had proved that he was as good as the hype surrounding him and that he was a star in the making.

'I'm still waiting to wake up, I reckon,' said the exultant debutant. 'I think I might be dreaming this. This is an experience I'll never forget. It's a very proud feeling. I'm honoured and very happy.' His parents,

Bob and Helen, watched their son's dream debut on TV. 'Brett is no one-Test wonder,' said Bob Lee. 'He is going to be playing Test cricket for a long time and we will have plenty of other chances to watch him in action. For starters, the next Test in Sydney.' On the Tendulkar–Lee contest for excellence, Peter Roebuck eulogised in the *Sydney Morning Herald*, 'It was a glorious confrontation between old and new, mighty and promising, an expression of the great gifts of the game, the brilliance of batsmanship, the excitement of pace and the powers needed to reach the gods'.

'It was not so much a Test match as a joyride back to those hell-raising years of the mid-1970s when Jeff Thomson and Dennis Lillee ruled the world,' reminisced Robert Craddock in the *Daily Telegraph* (Sydney). 'Blond bomber Brett Lee became the comet that surged through the gloom which had descended on the Boxing Day Test at the MCG ... Brett is modest, handsome and dripping with star quality.'

Heeding Lillee's advice, 'Australian selection marks the beginning of the hard work, not its completion', Brett carried on in the Sydney Test from where he had left off in Melbourne, capturing 4 for 39 and 2 for 67. Although contributing richly to Australia's easy wins over India in Tests and one-day internationals, Brett has not become a brat. He was full of praise for Tendulkar, whose wicket he has not claimed in a Test match. 'Tendulkar's bat looks so heavy. It's so long and thick and he's got so much time. He waves it around like it's a toothpick ... He's just a class batsman. It's a great experience bowling to him.'

Lillee, who passed on a few tips to Brett, believes that the boy from Wollongong is the one to watch. 'Brett has a very good wrist action,' opines the doyen of fast bowlers. 'He gets a lot more out of his bowling by coming down hard with the wrist. Doing that, and following through, can add an extra two or three kilometres.' In one-day internationals in

the 1999–2000 season, Brett twice recorded a speed of 154.8 km/h to eclipse Shoaib Akhtar's previous series record.

Meanwhile, what about his brother, Shane? Three years older than Brett, he has been in and out of Australian one-day teams without cementing his position. A batting all-rounder, he provided spectators with a real treat in the pre-Christmas Sheffield Shield match at the Adelaide Oval in 1997 when he blitzed the South Australian attack on the way to his 10th first-class century, a sparkling 183 not out from 206 balls – scoring his last 129 runs between lunch and tea. It was a big weekend for the Lee household, with Brett turning out for Australia A against South Africa.

Shane's Adelaide fireworks turned my mind to the time, almost exactly two years earlier, when he slaughtered the West Indies attack at the same ground in a World Series match to help Australia score a memorable victory. His other impressive innings in 1997–98 was an unbeaten 99 from 79 balls in the Mercantile Mutual Cup match between New South Wales and Western Australia at Perth. Inefficient scoreboard operators were blamed for him not reaching his century, notes Allan Miller in *Allan's Australian Cricket Annual, 1998*.

Luck, however, was on Shane's side the next season. The bold, hard-hitting stroke-player hit the 'bullseye' at Manuka Oval, Canberra, on 31 October 1998, when his straight drive connected with sponsor Mercantile Mutual's sign to win a cool $90,000 for the NSW team. He won a free end-of-season trip to Hawaii. Then in January 1999, when Damien Fleming succumbed to shoulder trouble, Shane was pulled out of a trial match at Canberra and flown to Hobart to play in a World Series match.

The recall ended his three-year stint in the international wilderness, after his participation in the 1995–96 international series and then in the 1996 World Cup. At home he took a career-best 5 for 33 in the last preliminary match against Sri Lanka, but a knee injury and lack of form saw him on the sidelines for the last eight matches, including the final of the World Cup. It was a case of déjà vu for him when he was selected in the squad for the 1999 World Cup in England but did not play in the final. 'My goal was to be part of a World Cup winning team,' Shane recalls. 'I was part of the squad [in 1999] but it's never quite the same [when not playing in the final].'

His second ambition, to play Test cricket, remains unfulfilled. He came close before the final Test at The Oval in August 1997. He was playing in the Lancashire League when he got an SOS call from the touring Australians to replace the injured Jason Gillespie and Paul Reiffel who returned home for the birth of his child. Unfortunately for Shane, Shaun Young of Tasmania and Gloucestershire was preferred. As Young contributed only 0 and 4 not out, did not take a wicket and Australia lost by 19 runs, Shane could be forgiven for feeling disappointed.

Although delighted at Brett's meteoric rise, Shane must have felt sorry for himself, but a pep talk from Michael Bevan inspired him. Acting NSW captain Bevan said, 'Everyone has been waiting for Shane Lee to show his true colours and be the all-rounder Australia has been looking for'. A senior NSW official told Dean Ritchie of the *Daily Telegraph* (Sydney), 'Shane Lee is dedicated but not super dedicated. He enjoys the good life but he certainly has the ability to go higher'.

Stirred up, the real Shane Lee stood up in a Mercantile Mutual match against Queensland in October 1999, when he hit 112 off 97 balls and captured 3 for 35. During a Sheffield Shield match, also against Queensland, he scored 32 and 98 and captured 4 for 87. This was to no avail as New South Wales lost, as they did all matches in the forgettable 1999–2000

season. Team-mate Brad McNamara said, 'Shane has a good work ethic and I know he is concentrating on his bowling which has let him down on occasions. I think bowling is the missing piece in Shane Lee's jigsaw.'

With a more positive attitude and improved performance, Shane joined Brett in the Carlton United Brewery World Series internationals against India and Pakistan in January 2000, which Australia won easily. Little had they dreamt as children playing backyard cricket that they would simultaneously represent Australia one day. The Lees – Shane, Brett and youngest brother Grant – come from Wollongong where their father Bob works for BHP. Bob was not a sports-lover, but his wife Helen was an athlete. At first he discouraged his sons from playing cricket as it was 'too boring', but later on he installed a paved pitch in the backyard which, according to Shane, played like the WACA ground in Perth. Shane, being the eldest, mostly batted; Brett mostly bowled and Grant mostly fielded.

Shane and Brett played for Oak Flats Club, Brett beginning with the Under-14s at nine. In the first over of his first match he captured six wickets – all bowled. But in the backyard he struggled as Shane averaged 50 with a top score of 362. Brett took his revenge. In an Australia A against Australia exhibition match at the Adelaide Oval in 1997–98, Brett dismissed Shane cheaply and repeated the dose in a New South Wales trial match.

The third brother, Grant, was also a promising cricketer and was selected in the NSW Under-17 team but retired at 19. He studied economics at university and taught piano. 'He's really into music,' Shane said. 'He plays everything. He's a freak.' All three brothers have an aptitude in music, studied classical music and play the piano. Shane and Brett perform together with three other New South Wales cricketers in a band called Six and Out. Both feel that cricket is not their entire life and there should be other diversions. Brett has a job selling suits in Centrepoint, Sydney, and wants to hold onto it despite his hectic cricket career. 'It takes my mind off cricket,' he says.

The brothers are close but don't want to live in each other's pockets. They sometimes fight and criticise each other's weaknesses but will not allow anyone else to speak one bad word against the other. Shane spoke out openly against those who hinted that Brett's bowling action was suspect. 'That is absolute rubbish, and is probably just an attempt to throw him off his game,' he wrote in the *Sun-Herald*. 'It hasn't, and he is more determined than ever to prove these knockers wrong.'

When at the Cricket Academy, 'Bing' Lee (Brett's nickname) impressed former Test cricketer and head coach Rod Marsh so much that he said the youngster looked capable of taking 200 Test wickets. 'I really enjoy seeing the stumps fly,' Marsh said. 'It's just great to see the ball skid through the batsmen.'

'Inevitably, Brett Lee suffered stress fractures which meant it took him years to become this [1999–2000] season's overnight sensation,' wrote Greg Baum in the *Sydney Morning Herald*. Part of the season he spent in a brace 'from my neck to my bum' 24 hours a day for nine weeks. But he persevered and is where he always wanted to be, an Aussie spearhead.

After his stunning start against India, Brett continued to make headlines in New Zealand. He affected early breakthroughs in Test matches but created a stir during a tour match against Northern Districts. He was warned by New Zealand umpire Dave Quested for attempting to injure No. 11 batsman Bruce Martin. 'A normal no-ball is an inch or an inch and a half over the crease and you can't prove it intentional,' said Quested. 'But he went two and a half feet over the crease and it seemed an intention to injure the striker.' Brett settled down and took 18 wickets at 17.50 in the Test series which Australia won 3–0, capturing 5 for 77 and 3 for 46 in the final Test at Hamilton.

Brett breathes in as he runs in to bowl and breathes out as he delivers a thunderbolt. In the beginning of his career, he took only two deliveries seriously: the bumper and the yorker. Even now he says he is not going to bother unduly about out-swingers or off-cutters, he stated before his Test debut. In April 2000 he was named NSW Player of the Year with 10 points, one ahead of Bevan and two ahead of brother Shane.

According to Ian Chappell, 'Brett Lee has more than just pace as he showed in both the Test and limited overs arena. He can swing the new ball away from the right-handers, and he had the old ball diving in at either the base of the stumps or perilously close to the batsmen's toes. Despite immediate and continuous success, Brett remained level-headed and regularly flashed a big smile, showing he was a fast bowler who enjoyed his role rather than performed it.'

Brett Lee in Test Cricket								
Tests	Runs	Avrge	HS	Wkts	Avrge	Best	5w/i	Catches
5	47	15.67	27	31	16.10	5–47	2	1

CHAPTER 37

Other
Families

———— ● ————

*The hardest part about selecting a World XI is that you cannot please
everyone – not even yourself. Then you select a second XI and a third XI
and you still leave gaping holes. Writing a book on cricket families is
equally frustrating. Although as many as 34 families have been featured,
spanning over 150 years and eight countries, quite a few are still missing.
This chapter attempts to mini-profile some of these important omissions.*

The Hills

Seven Hill brothers played first-class
cricket for South Australia at the turn of
the previous century. They were Percival,
Ronald James, Arthur, the famous Clem,
Henry John, Leslie Roy and Stanley.
Clem was the only left-hander among
them and the only one to play Test
cricket. Apart from Clem, Leslie was the
only brother to score a century for South
Australia: 123 vs New South Wales at
Sydney in 1910–11.

Clem was the most distinguished
among all Australian left-handed
batsmen. In first-class matches, he scored
17,216 runs at 43.47, hitting 45 centuries. In
49 Tests, he made 3412 runs at 39.21 with
seven centuries and five scores in the
nineties. In front of his adoring home
crowd in Adelaide, he made 98 and 97
runs, following his 99 in the last innings of
the previous Test at Melbourne. It was a
classic 'nervous nineties' syndrome for
him.

His father, H.J. Hill, was the first player
to score a century on Adelaide Oval (102
not out for North Adelaide vs the visiting
Kent CC) in January 1878.

The Lillywhites

Two generations of Lillywhites produced
five first-class cricketers including the
youngest, James jnr, who led England in
the inaugural Test match of March 1877
in Melbourne.

His uncle, William Lillywhite, was one
of the game's earliest characters and was
nicknamed 'the non-pareil'. He took 179
wickets in 24 matches for Sussex in 1844,
when past 50. He had three sons,
Frederick, John and James snr, who played
for Sussex.

England's first captain, James jnr was William's nephew. In his first appearance at Lord's in June 1862, for Sussex vs MCC, he took 5 for 28 and 9 for 29. He represented Sussex in all their matches from 1862 to 1881 and captured 1210 wickets at 15.23 apiece. His finest spell was for Souths vs Norths at Canterbury in 1872 when he took all 10 wickets.

He toured the USA and Canada in 1868 and Australia six times, first in 1873–74. Under him, England lost the inaugural Test at Melbourne but he retaliated by winning the second Test, also at Melbourne, to level the series. His contribution in the second Test was 2 for 36 and 4 for 70.

The Townsends

The Townsend family is unique as they provided four successive generations of first-class cricketers – producing six first-class cricketers between 1870 and 1965. Frank Townsend represented Gloucestershire from 1870 to 1891. His three sons, Charles, Miles and Frank jnr, also played for Gloucestershire. Charles played two Tests for England against Australia in 1899, and his son David three against the West Indies in 1934–35. David's son, John, represented Oxford University in 1964 and 1965.

Charles was an all-rounder and made his debut for Gloucestershire when 16. Two years later, he took 124 wickets at 12.73 in only 12 championship matches. However, at Test level neither Charles nor David could attain success.

The Palwankars

Before the advent of Test cricket in India, four brothers from an 'untouchable' Hindu family broke the caste barrier to dominate the first-class scene. Refused admission to Hindu clubs because of their low caste, they rose to shake-hand terms with princes and viceroys because of their cricketing ability.

They were the Palwankar brothers: Baloo, a penetrating left-arm spinner; Shivram, a stylish bat; Vithal, a doggedly defensive batsman and an agile fielder; and Ganpat, an attacking stroke-player. A fifth brother, Krishna, showed all-round talent but died when only 16.

Baloo and Shivram toured England in 1911 with an all-India team. Baloo took 75 wickets on that tour and impressed the great Wilfred Rhodes with his accuracy and prolific spin. Shivram topped the batting averages. His best innings was an unbeaten 113 against Somerset.

Vithal captained the Hindus regularly and did not tolerate nonsense from even the Maharajahs. Ganpat attacked the best of European and Muslim bowlers with gusto.

The Hardstaffs

Joe Hardstaff and his son, Joe jnr, represented Nottinghamshire and England with success. Joe snr played five Tests in Australia in 1907–08 and scored 311 runs at 31.10, impressing critics with his 61 and 72 in the Adelaide Test.

Joe jnr made his county debut as a teenager and played his first Test against South Africa at Leeds. He scored 94 against India in the Manchester Test of 1936 and followed it with centuries against New Zealand at Lord's and The Oval in 1937. A year later, on the same ground against England, he scored an unbeaten 169 and added 215 for the sixth with Len Hutton (364).

Then came World War II, but in the first postwar Test in England he continued from where he had left off six years earlier, scoring a magnificent 205 not out in the Lord's Test of June 1946. When he came in, England was in strife at 3 for 61 and was soon 4 for 70. He went on to outscore 11 men from India, who had totalled only 200.

In 23 Tests, young Joe scored 1636 runs at 46.74, hitting four centuries and 10 fifties. 'There have been few more handsome batsmen in recent years than young Joe Hardstaff,' summed up John Arlott.

The van der Bijls

Three generations of van der Bijls produced four first-class cricketers who played in the Currie Cup in South Africa. One of them, Pietre, played in the Test arena, and two others came close.

Vintcent van der Bijl and his brother Voltelin were all-rounders, while Vintcent's son, Pietre (who scored 460 runs at 51.11 in five Tests, with one century), was a patient opening batsman and his son, Vintcent jnr, was a fast bowler.

Vintcent snr represented Western Province, who won the Currie Cup in their first attempt in 1892. He toured England in 1904. Brother Voltelin also played for Western Province and was selected to tour England in 1894 but business commitments forced him to withdraw. He did not get a second chance.

World War II interrupted the Test career of Pietre after his highly successful home series against England in 1938–39. His proudest moment came in the final time-less Test at Durban in March 1939 when he scored 125 and 97. Had he scored three more runs in the second innings he would have become the first South African to amass a century in each innings of a Test.

Pietre, however, had the pleasure of seeing his son, Vintcent jnr (known as 'Big Vince' because of his 202-centimetre height and heavy build) graduate from school cricket to the Currie Cup and be selected for the tour to Australia in 1971–72. Unfortunately for him, the tour was cancelled because of his country's apartheid policy. Vince was a prolific wicket-taker who broke many records in the Currie Cup. He later played for Middlesex and *Wisden* honoured him as one of its Five Cricketers of the Year in 1981. When representing South Africa against Graham Gooch's 'Rebel' England XI in an unofficial test in March 1982, he

had devastating spells of 5 for 25 and 5 for 81. This makes one wonder how far Vince jnr, the 'Gentle Giant', would have gone had it not been for his country's exclusion for two decades.

The Grants

From a Cambridge Blue to a West Indies captain to a missionary in South Africa. This is the fascinating story of George Copeland ('Jackie') Grant's life. His younger brother, Rolph S. Grant, was also a Cambridge Blue and a Windies skipper. Jackie captained the West Indies to Australia in 1930–31, and to England in 1933. Rolph led the West Indies to England in 1939.

The brothers played together in all four Tests against England in 1934–35, the series the West Indies won 2–1 under Jackie's leadership. In the final Test in Jamaica, in which the home team triumphed by an innings and 161 runs, both the rival captains, Jackie Grant and R.E.S. Wyatt, had to retire with injuries. This was Jackie's last Test and it was made memorable by George Headley's unbeaten 270. Rolph scored his highest score of 77 in this Test.

Jackie captained his country in all 12 Tests that he played in. In his Test debut at the Adelaide Oval in December 1930 he scored 53 and 71 without being dismissed, becoming the first player to score an unbeaten fifty in each innings of a Test match. After losing the first four Tests in the series, the West Indians turned the tables on the Australians in the final Test at Sydney. Winning the toss, the visitors declared at 6 for 350, F.R. Martin scoring 123, Headley 105 and Jackie 62. The mighty Aussies with Woodfull, Ponsford, Bradman, Kippax and McCabe were dismissed for 224, a deficit of 126. Jackie showed courage in closing the Windies innings once again at 5 for 124, himself scoring 27 not out. On a sticky wicket, Australia were shot out for 220 and lost by 30 runs.

Rolph Grant was also a popular captain. In the Manchester Test of 1939 he opened the batting on a difficult pitch and attacked to make 47 out of 56 scored when he was at the wicket. He hit Tom Goddard for three sixes and four fours before holing out in the deep.

Jackie retired from cricket at 27 and with his wife moved to South Africa where he became a teacher and a missionary for hundreds of children for some 30 years. He was a champion of human rights and an opponent of apartheid. Unfortunately, both Jackie and his wife were expelled from South Africa in 1977. The following year he died at the age of 71.

The Nayudus

C.K. Nayudu was India's first Test captain and a six-hitter of towering proportions. He hit 11 sixes in one day, 1 December 1926, in Bombay against an MCC attack of Maurice Tate, George Geary and J. Mercer, reaching his 100 in 65 minutes. Indian commentator Berry Sarbadhikari described this innings as 'full of daring shots which terrified the fieldsmen, dazzled everybody's eyesight, broke all rules of batting, science and logic and stirred the crowd to wonder and delight'.

C.K. played seven Tests for India. In the Calcutta Test of 1933–34 against England, he was joined by his 19-years-younger brother, C.S. Nayudu. C.S. played 11 Tests as a leg-spinner and googly bowler. His Test record was ordinary, but he held an unenviable record at first-class level. For Holkar against Bombay in 1944–45, he delivered the greatest number of balls by a bowler in a match, 917. He took 11 for 428 (6 for 153 and 5 for 275), becoming the first bowler to concede over 400 runs in a match.

C.K.'s sons, Bobji and Prakash, and grandson, V.K. Nayudu, played first-class cricket. His daughter, Chandra Nayudu, became the first woman cricket

C.K. Nayudu, India's first captain and a tall hitter. (*Chandra Nayudu*)

commentator in the world when she broadcast the MCC vs Bombay match at Indore in February 1977. Earlier, she had captained Madhya Prades for the National Women's competition in the 1970s.

The Mankads

Vinoo Mankad, India's right-handed opening batsman and left-arm spinner, is recognised as among the all-time great all-rounders. In his heyday, 1946 to 1956, only Keith Miller was ranked higher. Mankad completed his double of 1000 runs and 100 wickets in only 23 Tests, which stood as a record until Ian Botham broke it three decades later. In 44 Tests, Mankad scored 2109 runs at 31.47 (with five centuries, highest score 231) and took 162 wickets at 32.32 (best being 8–52). He was behind India's first Test victory, capturing 8 for 55 and 4 for 53 against England in the Madras (now Chennai) Test of 1951–52.

Australians remember him for his centuries in the two Melbourne Tests against Ray Lindwall and Miller in 1947–48. Jack Fingleton described him as 'the best bowler of his type since Hedley Verity'. On that tour was coined the phrase 'to be Mankaded' when he ran out Bill Brown (after warning him) in the act of delivering the ball.

When 38, Vinoo Mankad scored two Test double centuries against New Zealand: 223 in Bombay (now Mumbai) and 231 in Madras in 1955–56. In the Madras Test he was associated in an opening partnership of 413 runs with Pankaj Roy, which still stands as a record. Mankad will be remembered for his magnificent performance in the Lord's Test – now recognised as the Mankad Test – of 1952. He scored 72 and 184 against Alec Bedser and Fred Trueman, bowled 97 overs and took five wickets in the first innings. On his bowling John Arlott wrote, 'Clearly the best of his type in post-war cricket and possibly as good as any in any period'.

Vinoo Mankad had three sons – Ashok, Atul and Rahul – all of whom played first-class cricket. Ashok, the eldest, scored 991 runs at 25.41, highest score 97, in 22 Tests from 1969 to 1978.

The Manjrekars

Vijay Manjrekar was a batsman in the classical mould, whose cover drives and square cuts were a delight to watch. From 1952 to 1965 he scored 3208 runs at 39.12 in 55 Tests, hitting seven centuries. He was a man of contrasts and of fluctuating moods. In the Leeds Test of 1952 he scored 133 runs (adding 222 runs with his captain, Vijay Hazare) against Alec Bedser, Fred Trueman and Jim Laker. However, in the second innings he was dismissed for a duck as India plummeted to a disastrous start of 4 down for 0.

Vijay Manjrekar's highest score was also against England: 189 not out in the Delhi Test of 1961–62. He faced fast bowlers with courage and was a master on a bad or turning pitch. Later he became over-defensive and his fielding suffered. His was a sad exit from the Test arena. He was dropped after scoring an unbeaten 102 against New Zealand at Madras in 1965. He died when only 52.

Vijay had the satisfaction, however, of seeing his son Sanjay develop into a promising cricketer. He advised Sanjay, 'If you score 30, you should not get out till you are 100'. Sanjay soon developed into one of India's great batsmen, not suffering in comparison when batting with maestro Sachin Tendulkar. Sanjay scored 2043 runs at 37.14 in 37 Tests. He hit four hundreds and his highest score was 218 against Pakistan at Lahore in 1989–90. He retired in the mid-season of 1997–98 to take up commentary work on a commercial television channel.

The Ranatungas

Three Ranatunga brothers represented Sri Lanka at Test level. Arjuna was in many ways 'Mr Sri Lanka', playing in his country's inaugural Test in 1981–82 and then almost non-stop till 2000. Short and stocky, he moved round the field in the 1990s like a Napoleon, 'a monarch of all he surveyed'.

Under his astute leadership, Sri Lanka won the 1996 World Cup against all odds. It gave him the ultimate satisfaction of beating his arch enemy, Australia, in the final at Lahore, himself scoring an unbeaten 47. The no-balling of off-spinner Muttiah Muralitharan by Australian umpires in 1995–96 and 1998–99 had angered Arjuna Ranatunga and during a one-dayer against England in Adelaide on 23 January 1999 he almost staged a walkout when umpire Ross Emerson no-balled Muralitharan for chucking.

In 87 Tests he scored 4774 runs at 35.10 with four centuries and 34 fifties, took 16 wickets and 41 catches. In 269 Limited-Overs Internationals, he scored 7454 runs at 35.84 with four centuries and 49 fifties, took 79 wickets and 63 catches. However, he will be remembered as a demonstrative leader.

Elder brother Dammika played two Tests in 1989–90 (both times with Arjuna) and younger brother Sanjeeva nine Tests (eight times with Arjuna) from 1994–95 to 1996–97.

The Hollioakes

Adam Hollioake and his six-years-younger brother, Ben, arrived on the international cricket scene in 1997 with a bang, but have not been able to maintain the momentum. Both were born in Melbourne but moved to England as children and grew up in England's cricket system.

The Limited-Overs Internationals against Australia in 1997 were memorable for their contribution. Adam hit the winning run in all three matches at Leeds, The Oval and Lord's. In the first international he scored an unbeaten 66 in a crisis and finished the match with a pulled six off Jason Gillespie. He was made Man of the Match for each of the first two internationals and was voted Player of the Series.

In the final match, at Lord's, Adam was joined by Ben, 19, who made his debut memorable by spanking 63 runs in 45 balls, with 10 fours, and a six off Shane Warne. Glenn McGrath was also punished severely by the teenage marvel. He had become England's youngest Test cap in 50 years.

Both the Hollioakes made simultaneous Test debuts in the fifth Test at Trent Bridge, Nottingham. They became the first pair of brothers to appear in the same England team for 40 years. The earlier instance was provided by Peter and Dick Richardson, who had played together against the West Indies in 1957, also at Trent Bridge. That 1997 Test provided a rare brotherly interlude. When Steve Waugh joined Mark Waugh at the batting crease, Adam and Ben were bowling in tandem. More remarkable was the fact that all four were born in Australia.

After their limited-overs triumphs of 1997, the Hollioake brothers were the toast of England and both received sponsored Mercedes cars. Adam was also appointed England's captain in Limited-Overs Internationals. Both brothers were selected to tour Australia in 1998–99 but their form slipped and they did not play in a Test. To add insult to injury, they had to return their Mercedes to the sponsor.

Like Adam, Ben has an engaging smile, but there are noticeable differences. Ben is less rugged and has not got Adam's distinctive Aussie accent. 'We're both aggressive characters on the field but Adam is more so off the field than me,' he told Jonathan Agnew in *Wisden Cricket Monthly*.

There was cricket in the family. Their grandfather, Rex Hollioake, played for Victoria Country against MCC in 1955 and had Len Hutton dropped off his second ball before dismissing Tom Graveny. Hutton later said Rex was the fastest bowler he had faced on that tour outside Tests.

Adam and Ben were coached by their father, John, an engineer by profession. John and his wife, Daria, have divided loyalties when Australia plays England, but for Adam and Ben there is only one country, England.

One can go on and on about other families, the canvas is too vast to be confined within the covers of a book. The search is endless. For errors of omission let Oliver Goldsmith come to my rescue: 'A book may be amusing with numerous errors or it may be very dull without a single absurdity'.

CHAPTER 38

Family XIs
and Celebrated In-Laws

———————●———————

A FASCINATING ASPECT OF CRICKET has been the fielding of cricketing XIs by several families. The Edrich family XI of Norfolk in the 1940s has been well documented, but the concept of family XIs was inherited from the 19th century.

The first instance of 11 brothers playing together in a team was reported in 1845. According to Robert Brooke, the former editor of *The Cricket Statistician* (UK), a team of 'Eleven Gentlemen of Letheringsett and Hold' played 11 brothers Colman at Letheringsett, near Norwich, on 6 August 1845. They were genuine brothers and, according to Ralph Barker, they belonged to the Colman's mustard family. The family won this encounter by seven wickets, but two days later when they took on a Norwich side they were beaten by five wickets. In 1846 they sought their revenge and had the better of a two-innings match against

11 resident members of the Norwich club.

In the mid-19th century there were several other family teams. At Godalming, Surrey, in 1850, 12 members of one family, Caesar, played against Gents of Godalming and lost. The Caesar XI was made up of sons of three brothers. In 1862, the Paynes, the sons of two brothers, played and beat the local team at East Grinstead. Three years later, R. Brotherhood and his 10 aptly named sons played Shaw House at Chippenham and beat them by an innings. The following July, the Brotherhood brothers, again led by their father, had the better of a draw against the full Chippenham team.

To quote Brooke from *World of Cricket* (Australia): 'One can in fact go on and on. In the latter part of the 1800s, the Lucases, the Lytteltons, the Walmsleys, the Garnetts, the Graces and the Robinsons all had family teams. The Graces and the

Robinsons actually met each other in 1891, the Graces winning by 37 runs. Even the Graces perhaps could not field so strong a team as the Hearnes though. In the 1880s, calling on cousins but all having the same name, they several times fielded teams with nine or 10 first-class and several Test players.'

It appears the first family team in Australia were the Leaks from South Australia. In 1893–94 the Leak family defeated a side from Basket Range (which was also dominated by family members) in Basket Range by 55 runs. The Leak XI scored 103 and dismissed the Basket Range team (inclusive of nine blood relatives) for 48.

The Harraways of New Zealand perhaps provided the second example of a family XI down-under. Herbert Harraway and his 10 sons played against the Pollards Opera Co. team at Carisbrook, Dunedin, on 29 November 1898. The match attracted a large crowd. The Harraways won by 59 runs. The opening bowler was George Harraway, who took 6 for 20. The opposition was dismissed for 65. The Harraways replied with 142, the opening pair hurrying to 61 runs before being separated four runs short of a 10-wicket victory.

More recently the Miles XI, playing in the Country Week Cricket Carnival in Brisbane in December 1983, nonplussed the scorers. All the players were from the Bidgood family. Grazier Gordon Bidgood from Miles, a small town 370 kilometres west of Brisbane, captained the team which included his five sons David, Ken, Neil, Bruce and John. Then there was Gordon's brother, Reg, and his three sons Mervyn, John and Brian, with cousin Victor completing the 11. Victor's son, Larry, and his brother Larry were the 12th and 13th men.

Australia has produced at least two important family XIs. They have been fielded by the related Clifton-Davidson family in Gosford, 70 kilometres north of Sydney, and the Richardsons of Tasmania.

The Edrich Family XI beat Norfolk XI in 1947. Bill Edrich, left front, is padded up.
(*Courtesy*, Eastern Daily Express)

The Clifton-Davidson joint XI comprised mainly first-grade cricketers and Alan Davidson, the great Australian all-rounder. One of the finest left-hand swing bowlers, an attacking batsman and a superlative slip fielder, Davidson scored 1328 runs and took 186 wickets and 42 catches in 44 Tests. He captured five wickets in a Test innings 14 times (best being 7 for 93 against India at Kanpur in 1959–60) and 10 wickets in a Test twice. He was the hero of the first-ever tied Test, against the West Indies at Brisbane in December 1960. He scored 44 and 80 and took 5 for 135 and 6 for 87, becoming the first player to complete the match double of 100 runs and 10 wickets in a Test. There was cricket on both his mother's (née Clifton) and father's sides, hence the double-barrelled name for the XI.

The Richardsons of Tasmania also fielded a strong family XI, including Les Richardson and his nine sons who played first-grade for the Tasmania Cricket Association. They played as a family team in the 1920s and 1930s.

The family XIs mentioned above are only the tips of the iceberg, so to speak. No

The Clifton–Davidson Family XI. Alan Davidson is in the back row, extreme right. (*Alan Davidson*)

effort has been made to give an exhaustive list, which is beyond the scope of this book. Another aspect of cricketing families has been the celebrated in-laws.

The names Lal Johnson, Virginia May and Kim Hilditch may mean little to an average cricket follower. They form, however, a fascinating chain of heredity. Both their fathers and husbands had played Test cricket, with one of them captaining his country. Virginia May is unique in that her father Harold Gilligan, uncle Arthur Gilligan and husband Peter May had captained England.

Lal Johnson's father, Roy Park, played one Test in 1920–21 against England on the Melbourne Cricket Ground. So brief was his Test career – batting at No. 3, he made a duck in his only Test innings – that his wife missed it completely. When he came in to bat, she battled her nervousness by bending to pick up her knitting. Before she surfaced, there was a roar – Roy was bowled first ball. Their daughter, Lal, did better. She married off-spinner Ian Johnson, who played 45 Tests, 17 times as Australia's captain.

Bob Simpson's daughter, Kim, joined this select group in March 1981 when she married Andrew Hilditch. Simmo had

captained Australia 39 times, but the nearest Hilditch came to leading his country was as Kim Hughes' deputy in 1979. Interestingly, both Kim Hilditch's father and husband opened Australia's batting. Although not exactly cricket-mad, Kim enjoys a match when 'Dad or Andrew is batting'.

Petite Kavita Viswanath is another cricketing novelty. Her maternal uncle, Madhav Mantri (India's wicket-keeper of the 1950s), brother Sunil Gavaskar and husband Gundappa Viswanath have played Test cricket – the last two as captains. Between the three, they scored 16,269 runs at 46.48, hit 48 centuries, 80 fifties, took 179 catches and stumped one in 220 Tests. They won nine out of 49 Tests they captained.

Another such example was provided by Nellie Donnan – herself a good cricketer. Both her brother, Syd Gregory, and husband, Henry Donnan, played for Australia.

On 18 June 1981 Mrs Jeanne Chappell became the only person whose father, the late Vic Richardson, and sons Ian, Greg and Trevor played Test cricket; three of them leading Australia with success. Between the four, they played 184 Tests, scoring 13,240 runs at 45.19, hit 39 centuries, 58 fifties and took 67 wickets and 253 catches. They won 40 out of 83 Tests they captained. How were the Chappells as boys? Jeanne Chappell said, 'Ian was very, very good as a child. Greg was the opposite, adventurous all the time. Trevor was just average.'

Some of the famous brothers-in-law to play Test cricket are as follows: Syd Gregory and Henry Donnan who played four times together for Australia; Joseph L. Cox and Lindsay R. Tuckett for South Africa; John H.B. Waite and Peter L. van der Merwe (seven times together for South Africa); England's Percy Chapman and New Zealand's Thomas C. Lowry (both captained their country); Sunil Gavaskar

The Harraway Family XI. (World of Cricket)

and Gundappa Viswanath (84 times together, both captaining India); Sarfraz Nawaz and Younis Ahmed (twice together for Pakistan); Majid Khan and Javed Burki (seven times together for Pakistan; they were also cousins).

The legendary Victor Trumper married James J. Kelly's sister-in-law. Trumper and Kelly played together for Australia 28 times.

CHAPTER 39

Heritage —
Help or Hindrance ?

———————●———————

DOES IT HELP TO have cricket in one's family? Or would a talented youngster rather start on his own to avoid excessive pushing and unfavourable comparisons? And, after becoming famous, would he like his sons to follow in his footsteps? My interviews with members of the families involved in this book and their quotes from their autobiographies/biographies have provided interesting and differing viewpoints.

In an interview shortly before he died in 1973, the immortal Jack Gregory told David Frith in *The Cricketer* (UK): 'Plum Warner gave me my chance, you know. It was the name that did it. He found out I was Syd's cousin.' Frith asked: 'Are you sure it wasn't because of your performance?' Jack Gregory: 'No, I went from my artillery outfit in France and when Warner heard there was a Gregory in the AIF team, he started the ball rolling for me. I was a batsman then.'

Ian Maddocks, the Victorian wicket-keeper who almost made the Australian team in 1978–79 and is the son of Len

Maddocks, the Australian keeper of the 1950s, said, 'Being the son of a former Test keeper means everyone watches you a bit closer, if only to see how you compare. If you are good enough, then the men who count really take interest in you.'

Mushtaq Mohammad, the former Pakistan captain, is grateful to his elder brothers Wazir and Hanif for their guidance and coaching. 'To have such well-known brothers was an inspiration,' he told me on his way to a polished century in the Sydney Test of 1973. But it does not help to have brothers at their peak at the same time. Mushtaq felt that after choosing Hanif and Wazir in the squad to tour India in 1952–53 the selectors were reluctant to include another brother, Raees.

'Raees was a batsman as good as Hanif and a better leg-spinner than I am,' Mushtaq said. But the closest Raees got to a Test spot was as 12th man in the Dacca Test in 1954–55. The hypothetical question is: if there was no Hanif or Wazir on the cricket scene, would Raees have become a regular player for Pakistan?

Even the youngest of the Mohammad quintet, Sadiq, had to make major changes in his batting fundamentals to make the Pakistan team. He was a right-handed middle-order batsman at a time when Pakistan had many of that type. So brothers Wazir and Hanif asked Sadiq to be a left-handed opener. Sadiq became just that and made the Test side – eventually pushing ageing Hanif out of the side.

Wisden wrote on the Grace brothers: 'But for the accident that his own brother proved greater than himself, E.M. Grace would have lived in cricket history as perhaps the most remarkable player the game has produced'.

Did Vic Richardson influence his grandchildren Ian, Greg and Trevor Chappell? Wrote Ian in *Chappelli*: 'I have never consciously set out to model myself on anyone as a cricketer or as a person but I think it's safe to assume that some of Vic Richardson's attitudes and thoughts have had a great effect on me. Although he never said much to me about cricket, there was always a spirit of quiet en-couragement from Vic. Often I'd come home from playing in a game and Mum would ask me if I had seen Vic there. I never did see him because he would park his car behind a tree somewhere and watch from there ... Occasionally, if I made a good score in a school match, he would ring up and say "Congratulations, you played well". But before I could say anything, the telephone had gone dead.'

Constant comparisons with his illustrious brothers sometimes got Trevor Chappell down. Although proud of his cricket heritage and an admirer of Ian and Greg, he once said, 'I'd rather be Bill Smith or just an ordinary person'.

This echoes what John Benaud went through in the 1970s. Ever since John can remember, he has been 'Richie's young brother', often without a name. Unfavourable comparisons – often well-meant – were hurtful to John, a powerful cricketer in his own right. Always, he had to fight for recognition, to gain his own identity. All the same, John is proud of his family name: 'I'm very grateful to my father [Lou] for all the time he put in with me as a youngster. He deserves to have sired two sons who played Test cricket for Australia.'

Mansur Ali (Pataudi jnr) wrote in *Tiger's Tale*: 'My father's name and fame have followed me throughout life and following father's footsteps can sometimes be a drag. Since the [eye] incident ... I have had to compensate with my ambition to become a truly great batsman. I have concentrated instead at trying to make myself a useful one and a better fielder than my father was.'

Few fathers have planned for their sons' cricketing career as Iftikhar (Pataudi snr) had done for Mansur. Although he died when Mansur was 11, he had arranged for his son's coaching in England at the hands of the best-known cricket professionals.

The Hadlee brothers, Dayle and Richard, admit that their father, Walter, forced cricket on them but they are grateful all the same. As Dayle said: 'My father has been a great influence on me ever since I can remember. He coached me, sometimes when I was unwilling. When I was out for a low score, I got half an hour lecture. Once I gave up cricket when I was six or seven. There was just too much pressure. But my "retirement" lasted only a week. When father found out I was sent back to the school net.'

Ashok Mankad was taught by his father, the great Vinoo. 'I owe a lot to my father. His coaching methods were original and practical. Under his guidance at least four of his pupils became Test cricketers, Eknath Sokar, Kulkarni, Ghulam Parkar and myself. The schoolboys under him – and I was one of them – were made to play 20 matches in 20 days against strong opposition. It was tough and we learnt fast.'

One of cricket's most touching stories

concerns Fred Tate dropping a vital catch which resulted in England losing a Test by three runs in 1902. On his way home, the inconsolable Fred reportedly told his team-mate Len Braund: 'I've got a little kid at home who'll make it up for me'. After 22 years 'the little kid at home' grew up to be the big Maurice Tate who took four wickets for 12 runs in his Test debut, to help skittle out South Africa for 30 runs at Edgbaston. Bill Ponsford considered Maurice the greatest bowler he faced.

Wrote Maurice: 'I want to put it on record that I was never coached in bowling. It came to me naturally and must have been inherited from my father ... My baby milk was diluted with cricket. I was weaned on it and it was served after every meal.'

Dr Jahangir Khan was a national selector when his son, Majid Khan, was fast approaching Test status. To avoid embarrassment, he resigned from the high post. Majid explained: 'Apart from being suspected of favouritism, he probably felt that had I failed, he would have been blamed.' Did his father coach him when he was a schoolboy? Was he inspired by his father's eminence? 'My father left me on my own and never interfered,' Majid said. 'I was inspired by his library of cricket books.'

The Indian commentator and former captain, Maharajah of Vizianagram ('Vizzy' for short), commented in a light-hearted fashion: 'When the elder brother is on the selection committee, the younger brother is in the Test team'. He was referring to the inclusion of spinner C.S. Nayudu in the Indian team when elder brother C.K. Nayudu was the national selector. An unfair assessment, even though tongue-in-cheek, for C.S. was a useful all-rounder – an agile fielder, potentially a very good leg-spinner and a superb runner between wickets, although his Test record was poor.

Similarly, the great Australian all-rounder George Giffen was accused of using undue influence to ensure the inclusion of his not very talented younger brother, Walter, in the team to tour England in 1893. The following lines appeared in that year's issue of Sydney's *Bulletin*:

What boots it, if before attack
Of English foes, our fellows falter?
I am the great Australian crack,
And love my little brother Walter.
If I should take the trip and 'tin'
And leave him, I'd deserve a halter:
And I'll be hanged if I join in
If they pass over little Walter. – ANON

Walter Giffen did go to England that season but did not play in any of the Tests, although George made up for it by taking 16 wickets in three innings, including 7 for 128 in the second Test.

Colin Cowdrey is thankful to his cricket-crazy father who taught him how to hold a straight bat when he was four. 'Gradually my education widened and by the time I was 12, I could play most of the shots,' Colin recalls in his autobiography *MCC: The Autobiography of a Cricketer*.

What was Colin's influence on his cricket-playing son, Chris? 'My father encouraged me a lot but did not push me into cricket,' Chris revealed during a personal interview. 'He coached me with tennis balls when I was four or five and then seriously when I was seven. Although he passed on helpful hints he wanted me to develop my own style ... When I was first picked for Kent's Second XI at 15, I really didn't deserve a place. I felt I was picked in the team because I was a Cowdrey. People expected too much from me too soon.' In his book *Good Enough?*, he wrote, 'I don't mind if I'm not as good as my father, as long as I'm good enough'.

John Edrich joined the junior staff of Surrey rather than Middlesex to avoid comparisons with cousin Bill. As he elaborated in *Runs in the Family*: 'If I was going to make the grade in county cricket and eventually to international honours, I wanted to make it on my own ability. I did not want accusations that the Edrich name had opened doors on my behalf ... I have never once turned to Bill for advice in sorting out my cricketing problems. And there have been many.'

Baloo Gupte, the younger brother of India's eminent leg-spinner Subash Gupte, and a leg-spinner himself, is even more emphatic on his ability. 'Once Subash offered to stand down so that I can get a chance in the Test side but I refused. My greatest achievement was when I replaced Subash in the Test team because of my performance. Don't misunderstand me. I place Subash along with Richie Benaud as the best spinners in the world.'

Richard Hutton, the tall, handsome son of Sir Len Hutton, feels that he was always conscious of being the son of a famous father in his school and university days. All the same he was extremely anxious to make a good impression. 'Such an attitude of mind was very beneficial to me because as a schoolboy I played not only for my love of the game of cricket but also from a great desire to be as good a player as I possibly could be,' he wrote in the March 1967 issue of *The Cricketer* (UK). When he first played for Yorkshire, Fred Trueman told him, 'If you're a quarter of the player your father was, you'll do for us'. This pleased young Richard enormously as he was accepted as a cricketer in his own right. However, when a spectator said, 'Tha'll niver be as good as thi' faither' as he returned to the pavilion after being dismissed for a low score, he had to use all his self-control to prevent him from striking that spectator on the face with his bat.

To be introduced to people as 'the son of Sir Leonard Hutton' and not by his own name was another thing Richard found most tedious. But there were compensations. When in Calcutta with E.W. Swanton's team in 1964, Richard was approached by a little boy who asked whether he was Len Hutton's son, and when he replied in the affirmative the little boy said, 'I love him. We all love him.'

'I was amazed,' wrote Richard, 'but I have never forgotten that little conversation ... I have no doubts that I shall never be as good as my father. I am not sure that I really want to be – I have set him on a pedestal in my own mind and I do not want to knock him off it.'

Mark O'Neill, the son of Norm O'Neill, also finds lack of identity as his major problem. 'The main thing is that you are always Norman O'Neill's son and never just plain Mark O'Neill,' he told Ian Brayshaw, the former West Australian player in an interview in *Cricketer* (Australia). 'People seem to expect so much more from you if you have a famous father ... and there are the eternal comparisons which make things so much harder,' thus echoing the sentiment of John Edrich, Richard Hutton, John Benaud and Trevor Chappell.

'Dave' Nourse did not push his son Dudley and the son grew up to eclipse most of his records. But it was not easy. Dudley wrote in *Cricket in the Blood*: 'Strangely enough, he [Dave] never in any way – as far as I can remember – encouraged me in my games ... I saw little of my father in the impressionable years. He was often away from home ... travelling around with sporting teams. Never, for instance, did my father even show me how to hold a bat. It is no sinecure being the son of a famous sportsman. Somehow, even subconsciously, one becomes aware of the hopes and aspirations of parents at a tender age. Will the traditions be carried on? ... When folks begin to look for signs of future prowess in early youth as one's father is carrying all before him and his name is a household word, one finds it a bit of a strain.' Strain notwithstanding, Dudley grew up to outshine Dave, just as Ernest Tyldesley equalled his legendary elder brother Johnny's first-class records.

Shaun Pollock recalls that when his famous father Peter Pollock came to watch him play in junior cricket he would hide behind a tree so as not to make him nervous. Also, because Peter had retired over a decade before Shaun arrived on the scene, fewer unfavourable comparisons were made between them. His cousin Anthony, however, was under greater pressure because his dad, the legendary Graeme Pollock, was still an active cricketer when the junior represented Transvaal. Shaun said, 'I didn't feel there was any pressure on me as Dad was out of the limelight.' Also, Peter did not force his son to take up cricket.

Dean Headley concedes that he will always be remembered as the great George Headley's grandson. He is extremely proud because his is the only family to provide three direct generations of Test cricketers. However, his dad, Ron, who played two Tests for the West Indies, talks about cricket all the time and it drives Dean mad. 'That's where we differ because I need to switch off from the game but he just loves it,' Dean says. Also, as George and Ron were batsmen and Dean is a bowler, there is little chance of unfavourable comparisons.

What about Dean and Danny Waugh, the younger brothers of Steve and Mark? A delightful hitter of the ball, Dean is his own man and does not copy either of his illustrious brothers. Danny is not overawed by his elder brothers' reputation and is not sure whether it is a help or hindrance to be the kid brother of the current Australian captain (Steve) and the elegant entertainer (Mark). 'All I know is that it's a thrill to watch them on the field. Earlier on I used to feel nervous every time they went out to bat – even on TV. Not so now.'

'It was very hard for Danny to get into the first-grade with his elder brothers so successful,' said Rodger Waugh, their father. 'If he had another surname, he would probably have played earlier and more regularly in first-grade.'

Is it helpful or a hindrance to have a legend at your dining table or a VIP driving you to school? Mostly it appears to be neither. Often, talent is in the genes, although not proven scientifically. But the fact remains that a father or an elder brother has almost always tried to help – actively, coercively or by setting an example as a role model. Exulting on his protégé Denis Compton's rapid advance in cricket, Patsy Hendren had said, 'It's a proud day when a pupil becomes a master'. For a father or an elder brother to see his son or kid brother erase his landmarks would be an equally momentous sensation.

CHAPTER 40

Family
Snippets

——— ● ———

Australiana

- Australia has produced only one father and son combination at Test level: Ned Gregory (1876–77) and Syd (Test span 1890–1912). However, there have been instances of Test cricketers whose sons played Sheffield Shield matches. They are, in chronological order:

- On the other end of the scale, four

Father (for Australia)		Son(s)	State
Ned	and	Charles Gregory [also Syd (for NSW & Australia)]	NSW
Tom	and	Tim and Tom jnr Horan	Vic.
Hugh	and	Jack Massie	NSW
'Alfie'	and	Harwood Jarvis	SA
Victor	and	Victor jnr Trumper	NSW
Bill	and	Bill jnr Howell	NSW
Ted	and	Ted jnr a'Beckett	Vic.
Bill	and	David Johnston	SA
Len	and	Ian Maddocks	Vic.
Ken	and	Rob Meuleman	WA
Les	and	Allan Favell	SA
Norman	and	Mark O'Neill	WA/NSW
Jeff	and	Ashley Hammond	SA
Rod	and	Daniel Marsh	SA/Tas

Test cricketers are the sons of Sheffield Shield players. Test great Graham McKenzie's father Eric, and uncle Doug McKenzie, played for Western Australia. The current Test opener Greg Blewett's father, Bob Blewett, played for South Australia. Dirk Wellham's uncle, Wally, represented New South Wales and his father Charlie, brother Greg and cousin Dale enjoyed success in Sydney's first-grade for Western Suburbs.

- Leg-spinner Stuart MacGill (59 wickets in 12 Tests) is a third generation first-class cricketer. His father Terry and grandfather Charlie represented Western Australia. Stuart moved from Perth to Sydney in 1995–96 after receiving limited opportunities from his native State.

- Current Test cricketer Justin Langer's uncle, Rob Langer, represented Western Australia in the Sheffield Shield. Outside the Test arena, Ian Brayshaw and son Jamie represented Western Australia, and Sam Trimble and son Glenn played for Queensland. Claude Rock and his son, Harry, both scored centuries in their first-class debuts; Claude for Tasmania (vs Victoria at East Melbourne in 1888–89) and Harry for New South Wales (vs South Australia at Sydney in 1924–25).

- The Raysons from Victoria provided the first instance of three successive generations of one family playing first-class cricket in Australia. Bill Rayson appeared in six matches in the early 1920s, his son Max three times in the late 1930s and his grandson Roger played in the 1960s.

- Brothers Francis and William Martin, of the 19th century, produced three generations of 10 first-grade cricketers, five of whom played first-class matches for Tasmania and Queensland. Both of Francis' sons,

Gordon F. (1885–1910) and Geoffrey played for Tasmania. Geoffrey's son, Geoffrey B. ('Paddy', 1927– ?), represented Tasmania. William's son, Charles W.B. (1885–1951) and Charles' son, William B. (1926– ?), also played first-class cricket for Tasmania.

- In the 1930s, the Balmain cricket team in Sydney included five Hird brothers – Syd, Jack, Bill, Harry and Lew. All-rounder Syd was the best-known, having scored two centuries in 11 first-class matches. For New South Wales against the visiting South Africans on the SCG in December 1931 he scored 101. After capturing 6 for 135 against Doug Jardine's Englishmen in 1932–33, he was made 12th man in the first Test of the Bodyline series. According to Ray Robinson, Syd Hird scored a century on every Australian ground he played on. Five years with Ramsbottom in the Lancashire League in England brought him 4136 runs and 389 wickets. Brothers Jack and Bill Hird played first-grade for Balmain, Harry was a schoolboy cricketer of note, and Lew captained NSW Schoolboys.

- An unusual landmark passed unnoticed during the Wellington Test of March–April 2000 between Australia and New Zealand. In this Test, Steve and Mark Waugh played their 85th Test together. Among relatives, the record was previously held by India's great batsmen Sunil Gavaskar and brother-in-law Gundappa Viswanath. (Viswanath married Gavaskar's sister in 1978.)

Kin Coincidences

- On 27 July 1989, brothers Robin and Chris Smith scored centuries in separate matches; Robin hit 143 in the fourth Test against Australia at Manchester, while Chris scored 107 for Hampshire vs Gloucestershire at Portsmouth. Both were born in

Durban, South Africa, and both played Test cricket for England but not together.

- In the English summer of 1978, bespectacled David Steele (who played eight Tests for England in the 1970s) scored 1182 runs for Northamptonshire in all first-class matches at an average of 38.12. By a coincidence, his brother John also totalled 1182 runs that season for Leicestershire at an identical average.
- James Langridge and brother John made their separate debuts for Sussex when 18. James' son, Richard, also played his first game for Sussex at 18.
- South Africa produced five Tancred brothers of whom three, Bernard, Louis and Vincent, played Test cricket. The eldest, Bernard, was regarded by some contemporaries as the first of the great batsmen produced by his country. He seemed to have a partiality for the number 29. He averaged 29 with the bat in the two Tests he played and his highest score was 29. In his Test debut, against England at Port Elizabeth in 1889, he top-scored in both innings, scoring – you guessed it – 29 and 29.
- The Northern Districts team to play Australia at Hamilton in March 2000 included James and Hamish Marshal. They were identical twins who scored 200 runs between them in that match. Earlier, at the Northern Districts Under-18 tournament in Hamilton, New Zealand, on 11 December 1995, Hamish Marshal scored 111 for Northland vs Thomas Valley. He shared a second-wicket stand of 111 with twin brother James, then added 111 runs for the third wicket with Jamie Burgess.
- The Studd brothers, Kynaston, Charles and George, captained Cambridge University in consecutive years: 1982, 1983 and 1984.
- Sir Learie Constantine is recognised

as among the most dynamic all-rounders in cricket history. However, very little is known about his father, Lebrun, who was a member of the first West Indian side to England in 1900. Lebrun scored the first century by a West Indian in England, against MCC at Lord's. The visitors faced an innings defeat when Lebrun (113) and W.J. Burton added 162 runs for the ninth wicket in an hour. Sir Pelham Warner described Lebrun's innings as 'a dashing and faultless display'.

- In the final of the Pentangular Tournament – a first-class match – in Bombay (now Mumbai) in 1943–44, Test batsman Vijay Hazare and his younger brother, Vivek, added 300 runs for the sixth wicket. Yet their team, The Rest, lost to the Hindus by an innings. More remarkable was the fact that to Vijay's 309, Vivek contributed only 21. Vijay, who later captained India, is remembered in Australia for hitting two centuries (116 and 145) in the Adelaide Test of January 1948 against an attack comprising Ray Lindwall, Keith Miller, Colin McCool, Ian Johnson and Ernie Toshack. Despite Hazare's heroics, India lost by an innings. Vijay Hazare holds a world record. For Baroda v. Holkar at Baroda in 1946–47, he and Gul Mahmood added 577 runs, the highest partnership for any wicket in first-class cricket.
- In the 1965–66 Ranji Trophy final against Bombay, Rajasthan's Hanumant Singh – an elegant Test batsman – scored 109 and 213 not out. His brother, Suryaveer Singh, made 79 and 132. They added 176 and 213 runs for the third wicket in the two innings, but their team lost.
- Vinet Gupte and Surinder Sharma from India umpired the third Limited-Overs International between India and New Zealand at Delhi on 18 November 1999. They are the sons of

former Test umpires M.Y. Gupte and Harprasad Sharma.

Wicket Women

- The famous Gregory family contributed greatly to the beginning of women's cricket in Sydney from 1886 to 1910. Nellie and Lily Gregory had contested many backyard cricket battles with their famous brothers, Syd and Charles. They were the daughters of 'Ned' Gregory, who had played in the inaugural Test in Melbourne in March 1877. In one of the earliest women's cricket matches played on the Association Cricket Ground, Sydney, in 1886, Nellie captained the Siroccos team which also included sister Alice. Their opponents, the Fernleas, were captained by another sister, Lily. Here is how the three sisters dominated the 12-a-side game:

  Siroccos: 86 (Nellie 35, Alice 27, Lily 6 for 14) and
  6 declared for 65 (Nellie 47 not out)

  Fernleas: 63 (Nellie 8 for 37, Alice 3 for 17) and
  53 (Nellie 6 for 12, Alice 5 for 18).

Thus, the Siroccos won by 35 runs. Nellie scored 82 runs for once out from a total of 151 (54 percent off her bat) and took an incredible 14 wickets at 3.50. Surely, a superwoman-of-the-year performance.

Nellie married Test player Harry Donnan, went on to captain New South Wales and in 1927 became the first President of the NSW Women's Cricket Association. When New South Wales met Victoria in the first match of the 1910 series, it included the three Gregory sisters and two of their nieces (Miss Varley and Miss Donnan). Five members from one family in a State team must be a record. By 1910, the Gregory dynasty could boast that over 20 had represented New South Wales in cricket, football, sailing and athletics.

- Steve and Mark Waugh are the only twin brothers to play together at Test level, from 1991 till now. However, in women's cricket at least two pairs of twins have represented their country. Jamaica fielded identical twin sisters, Molly and Polly Coombs, in the inaugural Test series against England in 1970. They confused the English girls with their incredible likeness which made captain Rachael Heyhoe Flint comment, '... it was more difficult to spot the difference between them than the Bedser twins'. (Incidentally, Eric Bedser did not play Test cricket.) Subsequently, in the Headingley Test against England in July 1984, New Zealand included twin sisters Elizabeth and Rosemary Signal. They were not successful, making only nine runs between them in four innings and bowling nine wicket-less overs.

- Australian medium-fast bowler Terry Alderman (170 wickets in 41 Tests) has a four-years-younger sister, Denise. She opened Australia's batting in the World Cup of 1981–82, scoring 117 and 77. At 19, she made her debut for Western Australia against Queensland in 1979 memorable by scoring an unbeaten 105. She later married international umpire Ross Emerson. Emerson is remembered for no-balling the Sri Lanka off-spinner Muttiah Muralitharan for chucking in one-day internationals in 1995–96 and 1998–99.

- Roger and Ruth Prideaux were the first husband-and-wife combination to play cricket at an international level. Roger played three Tests for England in the 1960s, top-scoring with 64 in his debut against Australia at Headingley, Leeds, in 1968. Ruth Westbrook first represented England as a wicket-keeper in the 1957–58 series in Australia. In her final Test in

1963, also against Australia, she took one catch and stumped three, thus contributing to England's victory.

- Sir Richard Hadlee and Karen Hadlee provided another Test-playing cricket couple. Karen represented New Zealand in the 1970s. Her finest performance was in a minor match in 1973 when she captured all 10 wickets for 12 runs. Even the great Richard has not been able to match her figures.

- Both the mother and sister of former Somerset captain and eminent cricket writer Peter Roebuck played cricket for Oxford University. His younger brother, Paul, represented Cambridge University and Gloucestershire.

- Tom Lowry, New Zealand's first Test captain, had two sisters who married cricket captains; England's Percy Chapman and Reg Bettington of New South Wales and Oxford University.

Minor Masterpieces

- The Mundin family had two hat-tricks to celebrate on 16 May 1987. After 24 years of club cricket for South Lakeland club Ibis, in Kendal (UK) without performing a hat-trick, Brian took two in successive League matches, on 25 April and 16 May 1987. The first was for Kendal vs Conistron in Fourth Division when he captured 5 for 25 and the second was for Ibis A vs Galgate A. His second hat-trick coincided with son Phillip's first, on the same day. For Kirkbie Kendal vs neighbouring Dallam in an Under-15 match, Phillip claimed 5 for 3.

- Ron W. Hedley and father R.J. Hedley performed hat-tricks for East Preston Cricket Club against Collingwood Sports Club at Kingsbury Ground, Melbourne, in the Jika Competition in December 1981. In the first innings, on 12 December, Ron took a hat-trick with the fourth, fifth and sixth deliveries of his ninth over. A little later, R.J. took the last two wickets to dismiss the opponents for 132 (Ron 5 for 42 in 13 overs, R.J. 2 for 4 in 3.2 overs). East Preston declared at 9 for 250, father and son scoring 18 runs each, both clean-bowled by D. Inguanzo. Then off the first ball in the second innings, R.J. grabbed a wicket with his first ball to give him a hat-trick, the catch being taken by Ron.

- In the Haig National Cricket Championship, England, in 1975, a father was associated in century partnerships with his two sons in different matches. Ernie Lamb, of Castle Eden in Durban, scored 52 runs in the first round and added 145 runs for the first wicket with his son, Barry, who made 89. In the third round, to show that he was not partial to one son, he made 71 and added 127 for the second wicket with his other son, Geoffrey.

- The Flynn family of Canberra has possibly set an opening wicket record between père et fils. In ACT cricket's fourth-grade competition in 1979, Pat Flynn of Western Creek hit a chanceless 115 against East Canberra, adding 208 runs for the opening wicket with son Greg who made an unbeaten 102. Their team won on the basis of a first-innings lead.

- Mark Page of Showling Rambler's Cricket Club dismissed three Trant brothers, Tim, Simon and Patrick, in three balls – all three bowled by balls which hit the off-stump.

- Bill Mossop of Penrith's third XI performed an unusual hat-trick against Gamblesby Village side in the Eden Valley League in England. He clean-bowled Norman Little and his nephews, Ian and David, in three consecutive balls.

- What can be more confusing than Lillee c. Willey b. Dilley 19 in the Perth Test of 1979–80? It would be H.W. Lee

c. F.S. Lee b. J.W. Lee 82. The three Lees were brothers. It happened in a first-class match between Middlesex and Somerset at Lord's in June 1933, as recorded in *Wisden* (1934).

- On 14 January 1995 the Castle Hill Church of Christ team played Holy Trinity, Baulkham Hills, at Kellyville in the NSW Churches C grade competition. In three balls, Daniel Tompkins of Holy Trinity dismissed Geoff Hall (age 42), his son, 18, and his father, 67; a rare hat-trick to get three generations of one family. 'The family that prays together, gets out together,' commented George Richards in Column 8 of the *Sydney Morning Herald*.

- Norm Welsh, the captain of Essendon Baptist C grade team, performed a hat-trick with a difference against St Aidans XI in 1964–65. All three batsmen were caught behind the stumps by Norm's 57-year-old father, Norm snr.

- Triplets Graham, David and Robert Mowbray played together for Lindfield vs Gordon in the Gordon DJCA D grade competition in Sydney. In March 1962, Graham and David took eight wickets for no runs in consecutive overs. Off-spinner Graham captured 6 for 0 including a hat-trick;

five of his victims were bowled. Then David joined in the fun, taking wickets with his first two balls as Lindfield nose-dived from 0 for 20 to 8 for 20.

- A record 376-run partnership between brothers Rury and Scot Field propelled South Africa to a 10-wicket victory over Pakistan in the final of the first World Cricket Cup for the Blind held in Delhi, India, in 1998. Sent in to bat, Pakistan made 5 for 372 in their 40 overs. Thanks to the Field brothers, South Africa reached the target in 37.1 overs without losing a wicket. Scot scored 159 not out, his sixth century of the competition, and skipper Rury was unbeaten with 193. In the semi-final against India they had put on 336 for the opening wicket.

- In the final of the Berrima District Cricket Competition between Bowral and Moss Vale at Moss Vale, NSW, in May 1926, 17-year-old Don Bradman (300) and uncle, George Whatman (227), were associated in a second-wicket stand of 374. George Whatman was the captain of the Bowral XI who sent Bradman in to open and batted himself at No. 3. Bowral won the match by an innings after five Saturdays. Don's elder brother, Vic, scored one run in the match and his other uncle, Dick Whatman, did not bat due to a broken toe.

Statistics at Test Level
(as at 1 July 2000)[+]

───── ● ─────

Great-grandfather and Great-grandson

W.H. Cooper (Aus., 2 Tests, 1881–82 to 1884–85)

A.P. Sheahan (Aus., 31 Tests, 1967–68 to 1973–74)

Grandather, Father and Son

G.A. Headley (WI, 22 Tests, 1929–30 to 1953–54)

R.G.A. Headley (WI, 2 Tests, 1973)

D.W. Headley (Eng., 15 Tests, 1997 till now)

Grandfather and Grandsons

V.Y. Richardson (Aus., 19 Tests, 1924–25 to 1935–36)

I.M. Chappell (Aus., 75 Tests, 1964–65 to 1979–80)

G.S. Chappell (Aus., 87 Tests, 1970–71 to 1983–84)

T.M. Chappell (Aus., 3 Tests, 1981)

Grand-uncle, Nephew and Grand-nephew

K.S. Ranjitsinhji (Eng., 15 Tests, 1896 to 1902)

K.S. Duleepsinhji (Eng., 12 Tests, 1929 to 1931)

K.S. Indrajitsinhji (Ind., 4 Tests, 1964–65 to 1969–70)

Father, Brother, Son and Nephew

E.J. Gregory (Aus., 1 Test, 1876–77)

E.J.'s brother D.W. Gregory (Aus., 3 Tests, 1876–77
  to 1878–79)

E.J.'s son E.S. Gregory (Aus., 58 Tests, 1890 to 1912)

E.J.'s nephew J.M. Gregory (Aus., 24 Tests, 1920–21
  to 1928–29)

Father and Son

Australia

E.J. Gregory (1 Test, 1876–77) and E.S. Gregory
  (58 Tests, 1890–1912)

England

C.L. Townsend (2 Tests, 1899) and D.C.H. Townsend
  (3 Tests, 1934–35)

F.W. Tate (1 Test, 1902) and M.W. Tate (39 Tests,
  1924 to 1935)

J. Hardstaff (5 Tests, 1907–08) and J. Hardstaff jnr
  (23 Tests, 1935 to 1948)

F.T. Mann (5 Tests, 1922–23) and F.G. Mann
  (7 Tests, 1948–49 to 1949)

J.H. Parks (1 Test, 1937) and J.M. Parks (46 Tests,
  1954 to 1967–68)

L. Hutton (79 Tests, 1937 to 1954–55) and R.A. Hutton
  (5 Tests, 1971)

M.C. Cowdrey (114 Tests, 1954–55 to 1974–75) and C.S.
  Cowdrey (6 Tests, 1984–85 to 1988)

M.J. Stewart (8 Tests, 1962 to 1963–64) and A.J. Stewart
  (99 Tests, 1989–90 till now)

A.R. Butcher (1 Test, 1979) and M.A. Butcher (27 Tests,
  1997 till now)

South Africa

F. Hearne (4 Tests, 1891–92 to 1895–96) and G.A.L.
  Hearne (3 Tests, 1922–23 to 1924) (*F. Hearne also
  played 2 Tests for England in 1888–89*)

A.W. Nourse (45 Tests, 1902–03 to 1924) and A.D.
  Nourse (34 Tests, 1935 to 1951)

L.R. Tuckett (1 Test, 1913–14) and L. Tuckett (9 Tests,
  1947 to 1948–49)

J.D. Lindsay (3 Tests, 1947) and D.T. Lindsay (19 Tests,
  1963–64 to 1969–70)

P.M. Pollock (28 Tests, 1961–62 to 1969–70) and S.M.
  Pollock (42 Tests, 1995–96 till now)

West Indies

O.C. Scott (8 Tests, 1928 to 1930–31) and A.P.H. Scott
  (1 Test, 1952–53)

New Zealand

H.G. Vivian (7 Tests, 1931 to 1937) and G.E. Vivian
  (5 Tests, 1964–65 to 1971–72)

W.A. Hadlee (11 Tests, 1937 to 1950–51) and D.R.
  Hadlee (26 Tests, 1969 to 1977–78) and R.J. Hadlee
  (86 Tests, 1972–73 to 1990)

W.M. Anderson (1 Test, 1945–46) and R.W. Anderson
  (9 Tests, 1976–77 to 1978)

P.G.Z. Harris (9 Tests, 1955–56 to 1964–65) and C.Z.
  Harris (19 Tests, 1993–94 till now)

W.P. Bradburn (2 Tests, 1963–64) and G.E. Bradburn
  (4 Tests, 1990–91)

B.L. Cairns (43 Tests, 1973–74 to 1985–86) and
  C.L. Cairns (47 Tests, 1989–90 till now)

India

L. Amarnath (24 Tests, 1933–34 to 1952–53) and M.
  Amarnath (69 Tests, 1969–70 to 1987–88) and S.
  Amarnath (10 Tests, 1975–76 to 1978–79)

Nawab of Pataudi snr (Iftikhar Ali Khan) (3 Tests, 1946)
  and Nawab of Pataudi jnr (Mansur Ali Khan)
  (46 Tests, 1961–62 to 1974–75) (*Nawab of Pataudi*

───────────

[+] *The washed-out Melbourne Test between Australia and England in 1970–71, where not a ball was bowled, is not
considered as a Test in this publication.*

snr also played 3 Tests for England, 1932–33 to
1934)

V. Mankad (44 Tests, 1946 to 1958–59) and A.V. Mankad
(22 Tests, 1969–70 to 1977–78)

Pankaj Roy (43 Tests, 1951–52 to 1960–61) and Pranob
Roy (2 Tests, 1981–82)

V.L. Manjrekar (55 Tests, 1951–52 to 1964–65) and S.V.
Manjrekar (37 Tests, 1987–88 to 1996–97)

D.K. Gaekwad (11 Tests, 1952 to 1960–61) and A.D.
Gaekwad (40 Tests, 1974–75 to 1984–85)

H.S. Kanitkar (2 Tests, 1974–75) and H.H. Kanitkar
(2 Tests, 1999–2000 till now)

India and Pakistan

M. Jahangir Khan (4 Tests for Ind., 1932 to 1936) and
Majid Khan (63 Tests for Pak., 1964–65 to 1982–83)
(*Majid Khan's cousins Javed Burki and Imran Khan
also played for Pakistan*)

S. Wazir Ali (7 Tests for Ind., 1932 to 1936) and Khalid
Wazir (2 Tests for Pak., 1954)

Pakistan

Hanif Mohammad (55 Tests, 1952–53 to 1969–70) and
Shoaib Mohammad (45 Tests, 1983–84 to 1995–96)

Nazar Mohammad (5 Tests, 1952–53) and Mudassar
Nazar (76 Tests, 1976–77 to 1988–89)

Brothers in the Same Test Team

Australia

E.J. and D.W. Gregory:	1 Test, 1876–77
C. and A.C. Bannerman:	1 Test, 1878–79
G. and W.F. Giffen:	2 Tests, 1891–92
G.H.S. and A.E. Trott:	3 Tests, 1894–95
I.M. and G.S. Chappell:	43 Tests, 1970–71 to 1979–80
S.R. and M.E. Waugh**:	85 Tests, 1990–91 till now(*The only instance of twins appearing together*)

England

E.M., W.G. and G.F. Grace:	1 Test, 1880
C.T. and G.B. Studd:	4 Tests, 1882–83
A. and G.G. Hearne:	1 Test, 1891–92 (*Their brother F. Hearne played in this Test for South Africa*)
D.W. and P.E. Richardson:	1 Test, 1957
A.J. and B.C. Hollioake**:	1 Test, 1997 till now

South Africa

S.J. and S.D. Snooke:	1 Test, 1907
D. and H.W. Taylor:	2 Tests, 1913–14
R.H.M. and P.A.M. Hands:	1 Test, 1913–14
E.A.B. and A.M.B. Rowan:	9 Tests, 1948–49 to 1951
P.M. and R.G. Pollock:	23 Tests, 1963–64 to 1969–70
A.J. and D.B. Pithey:	5 Tests, 1963–64
P.N. and G. Kirsten:	7 Tests, 1993–94 to 1994 (*Half-brothers*)

West Indies

G.C. and R.C. Grant:	4 Tests, 1934–35
J.B. and V.H. Stollmeyer:	1 Test, 1939
D. St. E. and E. St. E. Atkinson:	1 Test, 1957–58

New Zealand

D.R. and R.J. Hadlee:	10 Tests, 1973 to 1977–78
H.J. and G.P. Howarth:	4 Tests, 1974–75 to 1976–77
J.M. and N.M. Parker:	3 Tests, 1976–77
B.P. and J.G. Bracewell:	1 Test, 1980–81
J.J. and M.D. Crowe:	34 Tests, 1983 to 1989–90

India

S. Wazir Ali and S. Nazir Ali:	2	Tests, 1932 to 1933–34
L. Ramji and Amar Singh:	1	Test, 1933–34
C.K. and C.S. Nayudu:	4	Tests, 1933–34 to 1936
A.G. Kripal Singh and A.G. Milkha Singh:	1	Test, 1961–62
S. and M. Amarnath:	8	Tests, 1975–76 to 1978–79

Pakistan

Wazir and Hanif Mohammad:	18	Tests, 1952–53 to 1959–60
Wazir and Mushtaq Mohammad:	1	Test, 1958–59
Hanif and Mushtaq Mohammad:	19	Tests, 1960–61 to 1969–70
Hanif, Mushtaq and Sadiq Mohammad:	1	Test, 1969–70
Mushtaq and Sadiq Mohammad:	26	Tests, 1969–70 to 1978–79

(Wazir, Hanif, Mushtaq and Sadiq are brothers)

Wasim and Ramiz Raja:	2	Tests, 1983–84
Moin and Nadeem Khan:	1	Test, 1998–99

Sri Lanka

S. and M.D. Wettimuny:	2	Tests, 1982–83
A. and D. Ranatunga:	2	Tests, 1989–90
A. and S. Ranatunga:	8	Tests, 1994–95 to 1996–97

(A., D. and S. Ranatunga are brothers)

Zimbabwe

A. and G.W. Flower**:	42	Tests, 1992–93 till now
J.A. and G.J. Rennie:	1	Test, 1997–98
P.A. and B.C. Strang:	12	Tests, 1994–95 to 1997–98

(The three sets of brothers played in the same Test, vs New Zealand at Harare in 1997–98)

** = current cricketers

Brothers in Test Cricket (who did not play together in the same Test)

Australia

J.W. and H. Trumble, R.W. and C.E. McLeod, M.R. and R. N. Harvey, R. and J. Benaud, K.A. and R.G. Archer

England

C.E.M. and E.R. Wilson, J. and G. Gunn, J.T. and E. Tyldesley, A.E.R. and A.H.H. Gilligan, A.W. and I.A. Greig, C.L. and R.A. Smith

South Africa

A.B., V.M. and L.J. Tancred, W.H. and A.R. Richards, G.L. and L.E. Tapscott, H.F. and W.W. Wade

West Indies

W.H. and E.L. St. Hill, C.M. and R.J. Christiani, J.H. and F.J. Cameron, R.E. and N.E. Marshall, B.A. and C.A. Davis

India

S.P. and B.P. Gupte, M.L. and A.L. Apte

Pakistan

Waqar Hassan and Pervez Sajjad, Saeed and Younis Ahmed, Azmat and Shafqat Rana

Most Brothers to Play in Tests

4 (Wazir, Hanif, Mushtaq and Sadiq Mohammad of Pakistan)

Most Family Members to Play in Tests

6 (Brothers George G., Frank and Alec Hearne, their cousin John T. Hearne and his cousin John W. Hearne for England, Frank and Frank's son G.A.L. Hearne for South Africa)

5 (Brothers Edward and Dave Gregory; Edward's son Syd, nephew Jack and Syd's brother-in-law Harry Donnan)

5 (Four Mohammad brothers, plus Hanif's son, Shoaib Mohammad)

5 (M. Jahangir Khan, brother-in-law Baqa Jilani, son Majid Khan and nephews Javed Burki and Imran Khan. The first two played for India, the last three for Pakistan)

Most Tests in a Family

231 (Steve and Mark Waugh of Australia**)

218 (The Mohammads of Pakistan)

184 (Vic Richardson and grandsons Ian, Greg and Trevor Chappell of Australia)

181 (The Khans of Pakistan)

Most Test Runs in a Family

14,966 (The Waughs)**
13,643 (The Mohammads)
13,240 (Richardson–Chappells)

Most Test Centuries in a Family

39 (The Waughs)**
39 (Richardson–Chappells)
36 (The Mohammads)

Most Test Wickets in a Family

502 (Walter Hadlee and sons Dayle and Richard
   of New Zealand)
393 (The Khans)
295 (Graeme, Peter and Shaun** Pollock of
   South Africa)

290 (Lance and Chris** Cairns of New Zealand)
   (*Lance and Chris Cairns are the only father
   and son to take 10 wickets in a Test*)

Most Test Catches in a Family

253 (Richardson–Chappells)
224 (The Waughs)**
**= Current cricketers
Note: Non-blood relations Madhav Mantri
(4 Tests), his nephew Sunil Gavaskar (125 Tests)
and Gavaskar's brother-in-law Gundappa
Viswanath (91 Tests) of India scored 16,269 runs
in 220 Tests, hit 48 centuries, took 179 catches
and made one stumping.

Test Centuries by Father and Son

Father	Country	100s	Son	Country	100s
A.W. Nourse	SAf.	1	A.D. Nourse	SAf.	9
Nawab of Pataudi snr	Eng.	1	Nawab of Pataudi jnr	Ind.	6
L. Amarnath	Ind.	1	S. Amarnath	Ind.	1
			M. Amarnath	Ind.	11
W.A. Hadlee	NZ	1	R.J. Hadlee	NZ	2
Hanif Mohammad	Pak.	12	Shoaib Mohammad	Pak.	7
Nazar Mohammad	Pak.	1	Mudassar Nazar	Pak.	10
Vijay Manjrekar	Ind.	7	Sanjay Manjrekar	Ind.	4

Note:
- Hanif and Shoaib Mohammad are the only
  father and son to score Test double-centuries
- Both L. Amarnath and elder son S. Amarnath
  scored centuries in their Test debuts
- Victor Richardson and grandsons Ian and
  Greg have all scored Test centuries (Victor
  one, Ian 14 and Greg 24)

Centuries by Brothers in the Same Test Innings

I.M. (118) and G.S. (113) Chappell, Aus. vs Eng.,
   The Oval, 1972–73
I.M. (145) and G.S. (247*) Chappell, Aus. vs NZ,
   Wellington, 1973–74
I.M. (121) and G.S. (133) Chappell, Aus. vs NZ,
   Wellington, 1973–74
Sadiq (103*) and Mushtaq (101) Mohammad,
   Pak. vs NZ, Hyderabad, 1976–77

G.W. (201*) and A. (156) Flower, Zim. vs Pak.,
   Harare, 1994–95
M.E. (126) and S.R. (200) Waugh, Aus. vs WI,
   Kingston, 1994–95

Century Partnerships Between Brothers

I.M. *and* G.S. *Chappell (Aus.)*
264 v. NZ, Wellington, 1973–74
201 v. Eng., The Oval, 1972
159# v. WI, Brisbane, 1975–76
129 v. WI, Bridgetown, 1972–73
121 v. WI, Georgetown, 1972–73
100 v. Eng., Brisbane, 1974–75

M.E. and S.R. Waugh (Aus.)
231 v. WI, Kingston, 1994–95
190 v. Eng., Sydney, 1998–99
153 v. Eng., Birmingham, 1993
153 v. NZ, Perth, 1997–98
116 v. S.Af., Sydney, 1997–98
112 v. WI, Kingston, 1998–99

M.D. and J.J. Crowe (NZ)
156 v. WI, Christchurch, 1986–87
114 v. Pak., Wellington, 1988–89

G.W. and A. Flower (Zim.)
269 v. Pak., Harare, 1994–95
192 v. Ind., Delhi, 1992–93

Hanif and Wazir Mohammad (Pak.)
154 v. WI, port of Spain, 1957–58
121 v. WI, Bridgetown, 1957–58

(# = unbroken partnership)

Bibliography

———— ● ————

Altham, H.S., and Swanton, E.W., *History of Cricket*, George Allen & Unwin, UK, 1947

Arlott, John, *Rothman's Jubilee History of Cricket* 1890-1965 Arthur Barker Ltd., UK, 1965

Barker, Ralph, *The Cricketing Family Edrich*, Pelham Books, UK, 1976

Bedser, Alec and Eric, *Our Cricket Story*, Evans Brothers, UK, 1950

Benaud, John, *Matter of Choice*, Swan Publishing, Aus., 1997

Benaud, Richie, *Willow Patterns*, Hodder & Stoughton, UK, 1969

Benaud, Richie, *On Reflection*, Willow Books (Collins), Aus., 1984

Benaud, Richie, *Anything but an Autobiography*, Hodder & Stoughton, Aus., 1998

Bettesworth, W.A., *The Walkers of Southgate*, Methuen, UK, 1900

Brodribb, Gerald, *Maurice Tate: A Biography*, London Magazine Edition, UK, 1976

Browning, Mark, *Richie Benaud: Cricketer, Captain, Guru*, Kangaroo Press, Aus., 1996

Browning, Mark, *World Cup Cricket 1975–1999*, Kangaroo Press / Simon & Schuster, Aus., 1999

Cairns, Lance, *Give It a Heave, Lance Cairns*, Moa Publications Ltd, NZ, 1984

Cardwell, Ronald, *The Fitzroy Urchin*, The Cricket Publishing Co., Aus., 1999

Cashman, Richard, and Weaver, Amanda, *Wicket Women*, New South Wales University Press, Aus., 1991

Chappell, Ian, *My World of Cricket*, Jack Pollard P/L, Aus., 1973

Chappell, Ian, *Chappelli*, Hutchinson, Aus., 1976

Compton, Denis, and Edrich, Bill, *Cricket and All That*, Pelham Books, UK, 1978

Cowdrey, Chris and Smith, Jonathan, *Good Enough?*, Pelham Books, UK, 1986

Cowdrey, Colin, *MCC: The Autobiography of a Cricketer*, Hodder & Stoughton, UK, 1976

Crowe, Dave and Audrey, *The Crowe Style: Martin and Jeff's World of Cricket*, Moa Publications Ltd, NZ, 1987

Dawson, Marc, *Cricket Extras 1 & 2*, Kangaroo Press, Aus., 1993, 1994

Edrich, Bill, *Cricket Heritage*, Stanley Paul, UK, 1948

Edrich, John, *Runs in the Family*, Stanley Paul & Co., UK, 1969

Flint, Rachael Heyhoe and Rheinberg, Netta, *Fair Play*, Angus & Robertson, UK, 1976

Frindall, Bill, *The Wisden Book of Test Cricket 1876–77 to 1977–78*, Macdonald & Jane's, UK, 1979

Frindall, Bill, *The Wisden Book of Test Cricket Vol. II 1977 to 1994*, Headline Book Publishing, UK, 1995

Frindall, Bill, *The Wisden Book of Cricket Records*, Macdonald Queen Anne Press, UK, 1986

Frith, David, *The Golden Age of Cricket 1890–1914*, Angus & Robertson, UK, 1978

Golesworthy, Maurice, *The Encyclopaedia of Cricket*, Robert Hale & Co., UK, 1972

Hadlee, Richard, and Brittenden, Dick, *Hadlee*, A.H. & A.W. Reed, New Zealand, 1980

Imran Khan (with Murphy, Patrick), *Imran – The Autobiography of Imran Khan*, Pelham Books, UK, 1983

Lyttelton, R.H., Ford, W.J., Fry, C.B. and Giffen, G. *Giants of the Game*, EP Publishing, UK, 1973

Meher-Homji, Kersi, *Cricket's Great Families*, Garry Sparke & Associates, Aus., 1980

Meher-Homji, Kersi, *1000 Tests*, Strata Publications, Aus., 1984

Meher-Homji, Kersi, *The Waugh Twins*, Kangaroo Press / Simon & Schuster, Aus., 1998

Melford, Michael (editor), *Fresh Pick of the Cricketer*, Hutchinson, UK, 1969

Morrah, Patrick, *The Golden Age of Cricket*, Eyre & Spottiswood, UK, 1967

Moyes, A.G., *Australian Batsmen*, Angus & Robertson, Aus. and George G. Harrap, UK, 1954

Moyes, A.G., *Australian Cricket: A History*, Angus & Robertson, Aus., 1959

Moyes, A.G., *A Century of Cricketers*, Angus & Robertson, Aus., 1950

Mukherjee, Sujit, *The Romance of Indian Cricket*, Hind Pocket Books, Ind., 1968

Nourse, Dudley, *Cricket in the Blood*, Hodder & Stoughton, UK, 1949

Odendaal, Andre, *God's Forgotten Cricketers*, South African Cricketer, 1976

Pataudi, Nawab of, jnr, *Tiger's Tale*, Stanley Paul, UK, 1970

Peel, Mark, *The Last Roman: A Biography of Colin Cowdrey*, Andre Deutsch, UK, 1999

Pollard, Jack, *Australian Cricket: The Game and the Players*, Hodder & Stoughton with ABC, Aus., 1982

Pollock, Graeme, *Down the Wicket*, Pelham Books, UK, 1968

Raiji, Vasant, *Ranji: A Centenary Album*, Seven Stars Publication, India, 1972

Richardson, Victor, *The Vic Richardson Story*, Rigby Ltd, Aus, 1967

Robinson, Ray, *Green Sprigs*, Collins, UK, 1955

Robinson, Ray, *On Top Down Under: Australia's Cricket Captains*, Cassell Australia, 1975

Romanos, Joseph, *Martin Crowe: Tortured Genius* Hodder Moa Becket, NZ, 1995

Ross, Alan, *Ranji*, Pavilion Books Ltd, UK, 1986

Tate, Maurice, *My Cricketing Reminiscence*, Stanley Paul, UK, 1934

Webber, Ray, *First Class Cricket in Australia* Vol. I & II Ray Webber, Aus., 1991, 1997

White, Noel and Headley, George, *George 'Atlas' Headley*, Institute of Jamaica, 1974

Many editions of *Wisden Cricketers' Almanack*, John Wisden & Co, UK

Many editions of *Indian Cricket*, Kasturi & Sons Ltd., Ind.

Magazines / Periodicals / Dailies

ABC Cricket Book (Aus.)

Allan's Australian Cricket Annual (Aus.)

The Australian

Australian Cricket

Boundary New Zealand

Channel 9 Wide World of Sports Cricket Yearbook (Aus.)

Cricketer (Aus.)

The Cricket Statistician (UK)

The Cricketer International (UK)

Daily Telegraph (Aus.)

Daily Telegraph (UK)

The Indian Down Under (Aus.)

Inside Edge (Aus.)

Sadiq Mohammad Benefit Year Souvenir 1981–82

Sportsweek (Ind.)

Sydney Morning Herald

Wisden Cricket Monthly (UK)

The World of Cricket (Aus.)

Index

———— ● ————

Please note: for most Pakistani and some Indian and South African names,
the author has followed the indexing style of *Wisden Cricketers' Almanack*